8/13

ILLINOIS CENTRAL COLLEGE

W9-BCG-286

WITHDRAWN

Killing McVeigh

The Death Penalty and the Myth of Closure

Jody Lyneé Madeira

I.C.C. LIBRARY

NEW YORK UNIVERSITY PRESS
New York and London

KF
224
.M37
M33
2012

NEW YORK UNIVERSITY PRESS
New York and London
www.nyupress.org

© 2012 by New York University
All rights reserved

References to Internet websites (URLs) were accurate at the time of writing.
Neither the author nor New York University Press is responsible for URLs that
may have expired or changed since the manuscript was prepared.

Library of Congress Cataloging-in-Publication Data
Madeira, Jody Lyneé.
Killing McVeigh : the death penalty and the myth of closure / Jody Lyneé Madeira.
p. cm.
Includes bibliographical references and index.
ISBN 978-0-8147-9610-8 (cl : alk. paper) -- ISBN 978-0-8147-2454-5 (ebook) -- ISBN 978-0-
8147-2455-2 (ebook)
1. McVeigh, Timothy--Trials, litigation, etc. 2. McVeigh, Timothy--Imprisonment. 3.
Domestic terrorism--United States--Psychological aspects. 4. Domestic terrorism--Social
aspects--United States. 5. Capital punishment--United States--Psychological aspects. 6.
Victims of terrorism--Psychology--United States. 7. Victims of terrorism--Rehabilitation-
-United States. 8. Oklahoma City Federal Building Bombing, Oklahoma City, Okla.,
1995--Psychological aspects. I. Title.
KF224.M37M33 2012
364.660973--dc23
2011052256

New York University Press books are printed on acid-free paper, and their binding materials
are chosen for strength and durability. We strive to use environmentally responsible suppli-
ers and materials to the greatest extent possible in publishing our books.

Manufactured in the United States of America
10 9 8 7 6 5 4 3 2 1

Contents

5/13 B&T 39.00

The Alfred P. Murrah Federal Building was opened in April 1977. Image courtesy of the Oklahoma City National Memorial and Museum Archives.

The north facade of the Alfred P. Murrah Federal Building following the Oklahoma City bombing, April 19, 1995. Image courtesy of the Oklahoma City National Memorial and Museum Archives.

An aerial view of the Murrah Building ruins. The YMCA building in the lower left was also badly damaged in the bombing. Across the parking lot from the Murrah Building stands the Journal Record Building, now home to the Oklahoma City National Memorial and Museum. Image courtesy of the Oklahoma City National Memorial and Museum Archives.

Acknowledgments

Even a book about the myth of closure must eventually reach its culmination, a termination point at which it becomes possible to express my profound gratitude to the many individuals who have devoted so much time, energy, talent, and enthusiasm to this project.

First and foremost, I am deeply appreciative and respectful of those victims' family members and survivors who generously opened their lives, homes, and hearts to me. *The Myth of Closure* would have remained a myth without them. I hope this book is worthy of their contributions. Each had a unique influence upon this project, an impact that forever changed my research and my life in unexpected ways. In gratitude, I have taken the liberty of listing their names or aliases (marked by *) in long form.

Janet Beck	Survivor
Jamie Blansett*	Survivor
Robin Brown	Family member of Robert Westberry
Ron "Tony" Brown	Family member of Robert Westberry
Peggy Broxterman	Family member of Paul Broxterman
Ernestine Hill Clark	Survivor
Cameron Crawford*	Family member
Diane Dooley	Survivor
Tom Hall	Survivor
Vicki Hamm	Survivor
Dr. Paul Heath	Survivor
Dot Hill	Survivor
Jordan Holt*	Family member
Paul Howell	Family member of Karah Shepherd
Germaine Johnston	Survivor
Doris Jones	Family member of Carrie Ann Lenz
Marsha Kight	Family member of Frankie Merrell
Diane Leonard	Family member of Donald Ray Leonard

Stan Mayer	Survivor
Faith Moore	Family member of Paul Douglas Ice
Beverly Rankin	Survivor
Angela Richerson	Family member of Norma Jean Johnson
Taylor Rickel	Survivor
Priscilla Salyers	Survivor
Morgan Scott	Survivor
Jessie Sternburg*	Family member
Edmund Tarver	Survivor
Susan Urbach	Survivor
Ray Washburn	Survivor
Bud Welch	Family member of Julie Marie Welch
Lane Wharton*	Survivor
Richard Williams	Survivor
Charlie Younger	Survivor

This project would have been altogether impossible without the unflagging assistance and guidance of many in Oklahoma City, in particular Pam Bell, Dr. Betty Pfefferbaum and her tireless and capable staff, Joanne Riley, Helen Stiefmiller, Jane Thomas, Kari Watkins, numerous memorial volunteers, and so many others at the Oklahoma City National Memorial and Museum and Museum Archives. It has been a true pleasure to meet, work with, and learn from these unselfish individuals who are dedicated to transforming and shepherding the legacy of the Oklahoma City bombing. I thank Dr. Paul Heath for believing in this project and for contacting members of the Oklahoma City Murrah Building Survivors Association to jump-start the interviewing process. I am also indebted to Phil Bacharach and Terri Watkins for giving me access to their correspondence with Timothy McVeigh and for taking the time to explain their relationships with and perceptions of him.

In addition, I am sincerely grateful to Lou Michel for granting me an interview and permission to access the American Terrorist Collection at the Friedsam Memorial Library at St. Bonaventure University in New York. I spent two days steeped in the evocative and invaluable materials that Michel and his colleague Dan Herbeck have accumulated and generously donated, and also benefited from the invaluable assistance of archivist Dennis Frank.

Over the years, many scholars and colleagues have profoundly influenced this project through their thoughtful research, timely advice, and invaluable friendship, including Jim Acker, Susan Bandes, Elizabeth Beck, Bill Bowers,

Michelle Brown, Randy Coyne, Carissa Byrne Hessick, Joseph Hoffmann, Klaus Krippendorff, Charlie Lanier, Mona Lynch, Terry Maroney, Carolyn Marvin, Marla Sandys, Austin Sarat, Kim Lane Scheppele, Simon Stern, and Tim Waters. I am particularly indebted to my outstanding professor, mentor, and dissertation adviser, Barbie Zelizer, at the Annenberg School for Communication, University of Pennsylvania, who has provided important guidance from this project's inception. I also owe much to my respected colleague Ed Linenthal for his important book *The Unfinished Bombing: Oklahoma City in American Memory*, which has proven deeply meaningful to so many; for caring so deeply about this project; and for reading and commenting on early manuscript drafts. Many thanks as well to Elizabeth Beck, Michelle Brown, Heather Nicholson, Tanya Kaanta, and Rachel Gugliemo for reading the manuscript and providing invaluable thoughts and suggestions.

I am proud to serve on the faculty of the Indiana University Maurer School of Law in Bloomington, Indiana, and wish to acknowledge several at the law school who have played important roles in this project over the past few years. Dean Lauren Robel, Assistant Executive Dean Hannah Buxbaum, and my colleagues have provided constant material and emotional support; faculty secretary Sarah Benson has contributed expert office support and transcription; and research assistants Megan Mullett and Barbara (Bashia) Andraka have gone above and beyond the call of duty. Finally, I am indebted to the Annenberg School for Communication at the University of Pennsylvania for providing financial support for this project during my graduate studies, and to Indiana University for its financial support in the form of a grant-in-aid.

I have also been blessed with outstanding support from NYU Press, especially from my exceptional editor, Debbie Gershenowitz, through her friendship, enthusiasm, and uncanny ability to separate the wheat from the chaff, and from her able assistant, Gabrielle Begue, who is always willing and able to answer all sorts of questions. I would also like to thank Laura Helper-Ferris of the Helper-Ferris Editorial Agency for her wonderful assistance on early drafts of this manuscript.

Last, but certainly not least, I am grateful beyond words to my family, who have lived with this project for a decade. I owe so much to Matt Madeira, my husband and partner in life and love, loss and laughter, who has patiently served as my sounding board and editor for untold numbers of article and manuscript drafts. My five children—Alex, Jacen, Ty, Chloe, and Cody— have made me laugh when I most wanted to cry and continue to teach me about the true depths of parental love and about what really matters in life. I thank my mother, Patricia Burkett, for her encouragement and for her continual willingness to step into the breach, and my in-laws Ron and Carolyn Madeira, for their constant support and advice on this project. Finally, I wish to acknowledge my father, Lieutenant Colonel Lawrence Burkett, whose fierce paternal love and untimely death first planted the seeds of this project.

The Oklahoma City Bombing

A Time Line

1988	Timothy McVeigh, Terry Nichols, and Michael Fortier become friends while attending U.S. Army basic training at Fort Benning, Georgia.
1990	McVeigh participates in Operations Desert Shield and Desert Storm and earns a Bronze Star.
May 1991	Michael Fortier receives an honorable discharge and returns to Kingman, Arizona. He later marries Lori Fortier.
December 31, 1991	McVeigh leaves the army and returns to Lockport, New York, where he lives with his father, Bill McVeigh.
August 21, 1992	Agents of the Federal Bureau of Investigation (FBI) and Bureau of Alcohol, Tobacco and Firearms (ATF) lay siege to white separatist and Aryan Nations sympathizer Randy Weaver's cabin near Ruby Ridge, Idaho. After nine days, Weaver surrenders after an FBI sniper accidentally shoots and kills his wife.
February 28, 1993	ATF agents attempt to execute a search warrant at the Branch Davidian sect's compound in Waco, Texas. An intense gun battle ensues, prompting FBI agents to initiate a 51-day siege.
March 30, 1993	Toting antigovernment literature, McVeigh travels to Waco to show support for the Branch Davidians. Less than a month later, on April 19, the siege ends when the FBI makes a second assault on the

compound, triggering a fire that kills more than 75 people, including at least 20 children.

September 13, 1994	McVeigh begins to plot to blow up the Alfred P. Murrah Federal Building in Oklahoma City, Oklahoma. By the end of 1994, McVeigh and Nichols have amassed materials to construct the bomb.
October 8, 1994	McVeigh demonstrates how to construct the truck bomb in the Fortiers' kitchen in Kingman, Arizona.
April 18, 1995	McVeigh and Nichols meet at Geary Lake, Kansas, to mix the components for the bomb in barrels, which they place in a rented Ryder truck. When finished, Nichols drives home to Herrington, Kansas. McVeigh departs for Oklahoma and spends the night in the truck.
April 19, 1995	McVeigh detonates a truck bomb in front of the Alfred P. Murrah Federal Building at 9:02 a.m. on the anniversaries of the assaults on Ruby Ridge and Waco, killing 168 people, including 19 children, and injuring hundreds of others. A little more than an hour later, McVeigh is stopped for driving a vehicle without a license plate near Perry, Oklahoma; arrested on four misdemeanor charges, including unlawfully carrying a weapon, he is imprisoned in the Noble County Jail.
April 20, 1995	Sketches are released for two suspects, christened John Doe No. 1 and John Doe No. 2. A motel manager in Junction City, Kansas, identifies John Doe No. 1 as Timothy McVeigh. McVeigh gave an address in Decker, Michigan, on the hotel registration card; upon investigation, the FBI learns that Terry Nichols, a friend of McVeigh's, had lived there.
April 21, 1995	After hearing news reports mentioning his name in conjunction with the bombing, Terry Nichols surrenders in Herrington, Kansas, and is

taken into custody as a material witness. Shortly before being released from the Noble County Jail, McVeigh is identified as a bombing suspect and charged in the bombing. In a televised "perp walk," McVeigh is escorted out of the jail and taken to a federal prison in El Reno, Oklahoma.

May 10, 1995	Terry Nichols is charged in the bombing.
May 23, 1995	The remains of the Murrah Building are imploded and three last bodies are recovered.
August 8, 1995	Michael Fortier and his wife, Lori, cooperating with federal authorities, testify before a federal grand jury. On August 11, the federal grand jury indicts McVeigh and Nichols on murder and conspiracy charges. Attorney General Janet Reno later authorizes prosecutors to seek the death penalty against the two men. The grand jury indicts Fortier for four crimes. Fortier pleads guilty to helping McVeigh to move and sell stolen guns, failing to warn of the bombing plot, and deceiving FBI agents after the bombing.
February 20, 1996	After attorneys for McVeigh and Nichols argue that Oklahoma media coverage of the bombing has "demonized" the defendants and prejudiced potential jurors, U.S. District Judge Robert Matsch moves their trials to Denver, Colorado, and rules that the trials will not be broadcast back to Oklahoma City. Angry family members and survivors organize and lobby Congress for help.
April 24, 1996	President Bill Clinton signs the Antiterrorism and Effective Death Penalty Act of 1996 (AEDPA), truncating the death penalty appeals process and requiring federal courts to permit a closed-circuit trial broadcast if the trial was moved more than 350 miles from its original location.
June 26, 1996	Judge Matsch determines that bombing victims who could testify during McVeigh's sentencing

must choose between testifying and attending the trial. Victims' families and survivors, unsuccessful in legal appeals, again petition Congress for help.

July 15, 1996 — Judge Matsch upholds the closed-circuit broadcast mandate in the AEDPA to be constitutional and later orders the broadcast to be housed in the Federal Aviation Administration Center, a large government auditorium in Oklahoma City.

March 19, 1997 — President Bill Clinton signs the Victim Rights Clarification Act of 1997, allowing victims who are potential impact witnesses to attend the trial.

March 31, 1997 — Jury selection begins in Timothy McVeigh's federal murder and conspiracy trial. Opening statements begin on April 24, 1997.

June 2, 1997 — The jury finds Timothy McVeigh guilty on all 11 counts, including conspiracy to use a weapon of mass destruction, use of a weapon of mass destruction, destruction by explosive, and 8 counts of first-degree murder for the deaths of eight federal employees. Witnesses for the prosecution include numerous family members and survivors who testify as to the bombing's impact upon their lives.

June 13, 1997 — The jury decides that McVeigh should die by lethal injection.

August 14, 1997 — McVeigh is formally sentenced to death.

September 18, 1997 — Jury selection begins in Terry Nichols's federal trial. Opening statements begin on November 2, 1997.

December 23, 1997 — The jury finds Nichols guilty of conspiracy to use a weapon of mass destruction and eight counts of involuntary manslaughter in the deaths of eight federal employees, but not guilty of destruction by explosive. In January 1998, after the jury deadlocks following two days' deliberation, Judge Matsch dismisses the jury, removing the possibility of a death sentence.

May 27, 1998	Fortier is sentenced to 12 years' imprisonment and fined $200,000 for not warning authorities about the bombing plot as part of a plea bargain that secured his testimony against McVeigh and Nichols. His wife, Lori, remains free.
June 4, 1998	Judge Matsch sentences Nichols to life in prison without parole.
March 29, 1999	Nichols is charged with murder in Oklahoma District Court.
June 11, 1999	McVeigh is moved to death row at the Federal Correctional Institute in Terre Haute, Indiana.
April 19, 2000	President Bill Clinton dedicates the Oklahoma City National Memorial on the fifth anniversary of the bombing.
December 13, 2000	McVeigh files an affidavit requesting that his appeals be ended and that an execution date be set within 120 days. Finding McVeigh mentally competent, Judge Matsch grants his request.
January 11, 2001	The Federal Bureau of Prisons sets May 16, 2001, as McVeigh's execution date.
February 19, 2001	President George W. Bush and First Lady Laura Bush dedicate the Oklahoma City Memorial Museum.
April 12, 2001	Attorney General John Ashcroft authorizes a closed-circuit broadcast of McVeigh's execution in Oklahoma City and expands the number of live witnesses from eight to ten.
May 11, 2001	The FBI reveals that it mistakenly withheld thousands of documents that it should have turned over to McVeigh's defense lawyers. Attorney General Ashcroft postpones McVeigh's execution

	until June 11, 2001. McVeigh initially requests a stay of execution, which is denied.
June 11, 2001	McVeigh is pronounced dead at 7:14 a.m., executed by lethal injection at the Federal Correctional Institute in Terre Haute, Indiana. Ten family members and survivors chosen by lottery witness the execution live in Terre Haute, and 232 family members and survivors witness via closed-circuit broadcast back in Oklahoma City.
March 1, 2004	Jury selection begins in Nichols's state trial, with District Court Judge Steven Taylor of Oklahoma presiding. Nichols is charged with 161 counts of murder. The trial begins on March 22, 2004.
May 26, 2004	A jury convicts Nichols on all 161 counts of murder.
August 9, 2004	Nichols is sentenced to 161 consecutive life terms and is transferred to ADX, a supermax prison in Florence, Colorado.
January 20, 2006	Michael Fortier is released from federal prison after serving 10 years of his 12-year sentence.
April 6, 2010	Governor Brad Henry of Oklahoma signs into law legislation directing the State Board of Education to adopt a core curriculum in Oklahoma history, including information about the bombing and the role it has played in the history of Oklahoma and the United States.

Preface

This book is about difficult stories—narratives of emotionally grueling, intellectually challenging, and physically trying experiences—that are demanding for both tellers and receivers. It is also about "closure," but not as this term is used by the media, where it is often overhyped but ill-defined and manifestly unrealistic, particularly with regard to victims of traumatic events. As an Oklahoma City bombing survivor once explained to me, if you close the door forever on a past event, then you lose the ability to see what is on the other side. This, then, is my focus: What is closure? Does it exist? If so, where and for whom? If not, why?

An impoverished—but popular—usage of closure prevents us from truly engaging with these difficult stories and empathizing with those who tell them and live in them. In common parlance, this term has acquired unfortunate, inaccurate, and crude meanings: the possibility of imposing term limits on grief, of categorically resolving incoherent and fragmented tragedies. Contemporary usages of closure trivialize this dynamic concept, portraying as static what is supple, conclusive what is contingent. These characterizations are too crude to help us effectively engage with how people evolve, create, and revise transformative narratives in the wake of traumatic events. They pose offensively unsophisticated answers to questions that are profound, personal, and deeply troubling. Among this book's many purposes is to offer an extended critique and deepening of this term that has become so cheapened by its use in contemporary popular culture, allowing us to not only glimpse but also understand a crucial human element in the aftermath of catastrophe that an overly simplistic—indeed, mindless—use of the term obscures. In order to do that, I turn to the experiences of victims' family members and survivors of the Oklahoma City bombing.

Although I did not know it at the time, the seeds of this book were planted on February 2, 1984, when I was seven years old. For the past few years, we had lived in a home just off the American army base in Göppingen, Germany. That afternoon was ordinary; my father, a lieutenant colonel in the

U.S. Army and the commander of the 299th Support Battalion, was at work, and my mother was home with me. The doorbell rang; I heard my mother open the door, and her voice in conversation with two men. Afterward, my mother came into the kitchen, nervous and agitated. I don't remember her face so much as the anxiety that radiated from her. She asked me to come into the living room because she had something important to tell me.

Two officers in formal uniform awaited us in the living room. When I try to picture them, I recall a juxtaposition of discordant details: the drab olive green of their army dress uniforms spliced by black stripes on the legs and augmented by gold braid somewhere on the breast, and the brown vinyl covering the bench of my mother's Kimball electric organ. Perhaps we were sitting on the bench, perhaps the officers were, I can't remember; the plasticity of my recollection has made these figures as pliable as paper dolls, and now they seem to belong wherever I place them. But whatever their arrangement, it was there in the living room, with its windows overlooking the backyard and my swing set, that I learned that my father was dead, killed in a car accident. I'm not sure if I cried at that point; I remember trying not to. I must have been in shock. I hugged my mother and told her that it would be all right. I immediately recalled a time seemingly not too long before, when I had sat on my parents' bed talking to my father and watching him poking about the bedroom, performing some task or other. He was wearing a red Ohio State T-shirt. I don't know how or why, but I suddenly *knew* in that moment that one day my father, and indeed both of my parents, would die, and I would be left alone. That realization terrified me. It was eerie that I had had that random thought, just like that, and I couldn't help but feel that by recognizing my father's mortality, I had somehow made it possible for him to die.

My father was actually killed on the morning of Thursday, February 2, 1984. That Thursday morning, he and a fellow officer were driving from Göppingen to Böblingen on the Autobahn, behind the wheel of a brand-new Audi sedan that he had picked up from the dealership only eight days before. He was near the Bad Boll exit when, seeing a traffic jam in front of him, he slowed and came to a stop. Shortly thereafter, a cargo truck came over the hill behind him and plowed into his car, pushing him into another cargo truck in front of him. He was killed instantly. I remember the day when, as a 12-year-old with a burning need to know, I finally succeeded in locating my mother's archive of materials about the accident—the newspaper articles, the autopsy results—in boxes on the floor of the guest room closet. In these materials, I found a newspaper photograph of the scene. There, in black-and-white, was a head-on view of the crash—it was as if some hand had lifted up the truck cab and set it down my father's car; only the hood protruded from beneath the truck's grill. The roof of the car was peeled up and crumpled where the windshield should have been, with the rest of the car sandwiched beneath. A policeman had his arm out as if to direct traffic, and I vaguely recall that there were cones or other debris scattered about. I recall looking at that image and thinking to myself, "Somewhere in there is my father."

The accident precipitated a frenzy of packing and moving preparations; notwithstanding our loss, we had to vacate the house to make room for the incoming officer who would take my father's place. I recall the windowless van—again a drab, olive green—that came to take us to the airport early in the bitter morning darkness. Our first days and weeks back in the United States are now a blur of discordant details. I remember staying with family friends whom I had never met; their children had a stuffed rocking horse that I adored. I remember my father's funeral at Arlington—the caisson pulled by a string of horses, the ceremony with its "Taps" farewell, the sharp staccato of the rifle salute, the shining silver bullet of a casket onto which I tossed a soft, wilting rose. I recall so many emotions, all so visceral and raw. That disturbing awareness that my father's body would soon descend into the dark hole that yawned beneath his coffin, severing any remaining physical connection between us. Guilt over my inability to cry, and finally, after the hot tears came, confusion over whether I should try *not to* cry because I felt I had to support my mother. Unease at meeting so many relatives whom I didn't remember. I was a different person after that day, preoccupied with my angry childish logic, seething with naive yet robust indignation at the military—for I thought that if my father had never joined, he would not have gotten killed—and at the truck driver who had killed him. A decade-long wrongful death lawsuit kept my father unburied in a sense, his accident unresolved. The lawsuit's end brought a form of peace, but little justice.

Over the years, my own emotional turmoil resolved somewhat. As my anger diminished, I began to realize that stoking such bitter emotions for so long required a great deal of energy—energy that was better spent elsewhere. My anger would not bring my father back. And so I moved forward; I continued to miss my father terribly, but the pain I felt now was from his loss, and not so much from anger at how he had died.

The Oklahoma City bombing occurred in the spring of my sophomore year in college. On the morning of April 19, 1995, I was occupied with some activity in my dorm room when the telephone rang; it was my mother, telling me that I had to turn on the television, that something horrible had happened in Oklahoma City. I joined millions of others around the country who tuned in to those scenes of horror at the Alfred P. Murrah Federal Building, following developments in the hours, days, then weeks, months, and years after the bombing. I felt a sense of kinship with Timothy McVeigh's victims: my father's death was incomparable to the experience of surviving the bombing or having a loved one murdered that day, but I too had lived through a loss mediated by the law.

The story of my father's death is inextricably connected with this project. Before and during my interviews with family members and survivors, I recounted this narrative to explain how I became interested in this particular subject matter, and to provide reassurance that I genuinely wanted to hear about their thoughts, feelings, and experiences and was not seeking to support a particular ideological agenda.

My comfort in telling my story—and my participants' comfort with hearing it—are no doubt related to contemporary cultural norms governing when, where, and with whom we share personal information. Many scholars—sociologists, psychologists, philosophers, media and communication researchers, to name a few—have noted that contemporary popular culture simultaneously encourages public confession and catharsis, self-introspection, self-improvement, and self-fulfillment. But not all the stories that we want to share can be happy ones. Bad things happen, and we want, indeed need, to talk about them. Perhaps our fascination with tragic narratives is just part of our therapeutic ethos; telling one's story is conventionally thought to be part of the process of working through difficult issues, a major step on the road to self-fulfillment. Sad or tragic tales have great value on both cultural and personal levels.

This brings me to closure. Sad stories prompt many to talk of "closure" as a panacea, a tempting but often elusive finality to tribulation. Societal institutions have coined and popularized the term, cultivating our closure desires and expectations. "This too shall pass," we tell ourselves, as we long for difficult events to be over, forgotten, buried.

In common parlance, a myth is a fabrication or half-truth; closure in its colloquial sense is certainly more fiction than fact. But properly understood, it could and should acquire more significant mythic dimensions, as a powerful narrative sacred to a community that is both constitutive of and reflective of communal identities. Closure as I have come to see it is a phenomenon that is entirely unlike the rudimentary concept currently bandied about in popular culture. It is *so* radically different that we must gut the concept in its entirety in order to redefine it, keeping only the semantic framework that points us to certain contexts in which we can appropriately apply the term.

To enter into the lived experience of closure is to step into a parallel universe where everything is jumbled and turned upside down, and nothing means what it should. It can be compared to tumbling down the rabbit hole in Louis Carroll's *Alice in Wonderland*, into a terrifyingly strange world where few if any norms apply, strange phantasms appear and disappear, and the jabberwocky prowls about. Others unaffected pass by the rabbit hole but rarely recognize it for what it is. They see what, in closure terms, is just an average, ordinary hole—a state of recovery in which the humdrum routines of life are eventually restored and finality achieved, not an extraordinarily harrowing, strange, and nightmarish realm that one must traverse sans compass or GPS, creating both map and path as one goes. Victims' family members and survivors of the Oklahoma City bombing had to negotiate their surreal losses at the same time that they moved through the motions of daily life.

This volume represents my attempt to take readers on an expedition through the lived experience of closure, into the creation of tension-filled narratives of identity and community, some of which are redemptive, others of which, unfortunately, are not. It is an effort to capture to the extent possible the profoundly robust nature of the closure inquiry; why, how, and where individuals seek it; how it is mediated by social institutions.

When this term stands before us, naked and stripped of its monstrosity, what do we see? First, closure is most affirmatively *not* what contemporary culture says it is—absolute finality, in the sense of such colloquial phrases as "over and done with," "dealt with," "put behind one's self," "let bygones be bygones," "forgive and forget." Closure is not a state of being, a quality, or even a realization. If closure exists at all, it must be as a process, a recursive series of adjustments that a self makes in response to external, often institutional, developments. It involves struggles between self and other, embodiment and disembodiment, agency and passivity, speech and silence. This view of closure as a strategic, sense-making process suggests that it not only cannot but *should not* be exorcised from contemporary culture.

This book examines closure through the lenses of communicative behavior and collected memory[1]—individual and institutional processes of memorialization, reconstruction, and sense-making. I posit that what is meant by closure is actually "memory work"—an interactive process by which individual family members and survivors construct meaningful narratives of the bombing, its impact on their lives, and how they have dealt with, adjusted to, or healed from this event. In the aftermath of an event such as the Oklahoma City bombing—a "culturally traumatic" incident that unsettles a community's most fundamental social and cultural norms—individual memory work intersects with institutional processes at several points. Such harrowing events are exhaustively (and exhaustingly) covered in the news and entertainment media, and suspected perpetrators will likely stand trial, becoming subject to verdict and punishment. The stories created and publicized by mass media institutions and the verdicts and sentences evolved through judicial institutions are both key to memory work, essential mnemonic developments. Memory work most often consists of *narrative* sense-making, whereby we learn how to tell the stories of the events through which we live. Enunciating these events gives us power over them and distance from them—exactly the results we hope to gain by our struggles to work through crises. By reenvisioning closure as processes of memory work—a search for the perspective and self-identity integral to forming autobiographical and collected memory—we see that the pursuit of closure is a predictable and natural response to suffering and culturally traumatic events, a search for moral worth within institutions that help us to form reconstructive narratives and, ultimately, within ourselves as narrators.

Conceptualizing closure as memory work reveals glimpses of the world beyond the rabbit hole, displaying the signs that demarcated the journey's beginning for bombing victims, including the smoking ruins of a building where people once conversed, accomplished errands, earned paychecks, made friends, annoyed colleagues, ate snacks, and attended meetings, where children played, where life was *lived*. From this perspective, closure becomes an immeasurably broader term that comports with individual and cultural instincts to work through trauma and "become" survivors, to endure not only the traumatic event but also the trauma of reconstruction. The term still retains communicative value because it is so common in many different discourses—law, policy, social science, media, everyday conversation. Here, closure is reconceptualized as a narrative journey, a sense-making pilgrimage; we cannot help but seek to narrate and to search for end points. As narrative subjects, we are also narrative agents, and while we lack control over plot developments, we remain in complete control of how we respond.

At some point in our constant procession through response and readjustment, we come to a state of awareness that can conclude an event in our lives. This point marks our awareness of an ongoing stasis and is an ending of sorts, even if it is not a "happy" one, even if sorrow, anger, trauma persist. From this perspective, one's ability to state that there is no closure is itself a closure.

Other endings are of course possible, in which the suffering, though present, is not so visceral, raw, or painful to handle; for instance, one might be able to relegate it to a "chapter" in one's life. Whatever the endings, closure does not foreclose awareness but instead opens it—to suffering, to acceptance, to reconstruction, but always to the story of what was, is, and might be.

In this volume I will refrain from using the term to refer to any such therapeutic feeling—relief, satisfaction, catharsis, freedom—out of respect for the community of family members and survivors that I interviewed. For these individuals, closure is anathema, something akin to *Bilderverbot*—the unspeakability of absolute finality. I would not force a term that is currently viewed with such contempt upon members of a population who have willingly imparted their own testimonies to me in trust.

It will take time for our dominant cultural understandings of closure to evolve; I hope that this book is the first step on that journey. If we do not dig deeper into our understandings of this concept, then closure will ultimately become a casualty of our confessional culture, a lexical corpse that is glibly resurrected and forced to dance to the tune of players in popular culture but that will forever remain dead to the very communities for which it was created. Perhaps that is part of the problem, that it was created *for* and not *with* or *by* victims. I believe that closure as memory work is much closer to what my participants meant when they described their reconstructive processes.

When I began to track down existing empirical research on how witnessing an execution might affect victims' family members, I was shocked that, despite the many claims that family members did or did not receive "closure" from executions, the entire body of published research consisted of two scholarly articles.[2] Neither article had actually based its conclusions on the experiences of murder victims' family members; instead, the authors' data sets had been obtained from two different samples: undergraduate students and journalists who had witnessed the execution of California prisoner Robert Alton Harris. Yet, both articles somehow concluded that witnessing executions was psychologically traumatic for murder victims' family members and thus unadvisable. I was simultaneously thrilled and terrified that my research project would be the first to address such an important question from the perspective of murder victims' family members.

I first began to interview victims' family members and survivors of the Oklahoma City bombing in 2004. I conducted all but three of these initial interviews face-to-face, in locations where participants felt most comfortable—often their homes. These interviews ranged from two to six hours in length. My participants patiently sat with me, answering the many difficult questions that I asked them. Our interviews seemed more like conversations. I was invited into participants' lives through their stories, and I in turn invited them into mine.

Over the seven years that I have been engaged in this research, the focus of the initial project has undergone fundamental changes. The experience of conducting extended face-to-face interviews with victims' family members and survivors has turned the project inside out, privileging my participants' voices instead of the perpetrators.' The project's focus on how executions affected 33 family members and survivors has expanded into an inquiry into how institutions mediate loss, incorporating news coverage, McVeigh's trial and execution, and proceedings against Terry Nichols and Michael Fortier. Time has wrought many changes; inevitably recollections have grown fuzzier, and some details have faded—alterations that some wish to celebrate, and others fight to overcome. But time has only magnified my gratitude toward all my participants and sharpened my sense of responsibility to them, strengthening my determination to share the insights they imparted—and entrusted—to me as accurately and fairly as I can. In short, I want—indeed, need—to give them my best work in turn.

As a researcher and author, I do not purport to critique the normative value or propriety of family members' and survivors' emotions, reactions, and activities as healthy or unhealthy or as desirable or objectionable. Instead, I envision my role more as a curator, entrusted with the privilege of collecting, processing, representing, and displaying these social actors and social expressions, reflecting on their significance without passing judgment. Even if I had stood in these individuals' shoes, each victim's subjective reality becomes socially and politically significant, especially when family members work passionately to transform their own experience into an influential social force. Attempting to understand the emotional dynamics of the twinned states of victimhood and survivorship is an altogether different task from assessing how they should be managed on an institutional or professional basis. Instead, I present these perspectives on their own terms, as expressive realities that simply "are," as passionately held beliefs that we as individuals can and must acknowledge, respect, and accommodate, and that institutions such as the news media and criminal justice system must grapple with. This is the story, always complex and at times contradictory, of how we as Americans, individually and institutionally, analyze, negotiate, assimilate, patronize, oblige, fetishize, exploit, avoid, diagnose, and admire these individuals.

At the time of this writing, it has now been more than 27 years since my father's death. Recent years have brought so many joys and successes in my life—marriage, graduations, a dream job, the birth of triplet boys, a daughter, and a son—that not only reignite the pain of his loss but cause it to flare up in new ways. The years since the bombing have also wrought many changes in the lives of the family members and survivors who were generous enough to sit down with me and guide me through how the bombing and its perpetrators had impacted their lives. People have divorced, had surgery, remarried, had children, moved to other states, switched occupations. So many of them have focused on the positive changes wrought at such terrible cost—fresh appreciation for life, gratitude for new friendships, awareness of what is at stake every day, determination to live fully, dedication to becoming "better" mothers, fathers, husbands, wives, siblings, and children. These positive developments do not justify the bombing; instead, they are celebrated because they happened in spite of it. Their closure journey, like mine, is ongoing. But their stories, like footprints, give us myriad ways of understanding this terrible crossing. For that, we owe them much.

Blood Relations

McVeigh is introduced to the world as a suspect in the Oklahoma City bombing during his "perp walk" in Perry, Oklahoma, on April 21, 1995. Image reprinted with permission from the Associated Press.

First Steps: The Arrest of Timothy McVeigh

The FBI, knowing their suspect was in custody at a small county courthouse in Oklahoma, proceeded to orchestrate what is now commonly referred to as the "perp walk" in which a criminal suspect is led away from confinement in shackles by law enforcement personnel for the media and all to see. The FBI was not disappointed. Mr. McVeigh was detained in the courthouse while the world media gathered and his walkout was timed for the evening network news broadcast. With the nation, and indeed much of the civilized world watching, Timothy McVeigh, wearing a bright orange prison jumpsuit and no protective vest, shackled at the wrists and ankles, and wearing a military style haircut and a "thousand yard" stare, was paraded before a mob of angry citizens, many of whom shouted repeatedly, "baby killer, baby killer" at him. This was how the Petitioner was transferred to federal custody.

—From petition for writ of mandamus
of petitioner-defendant Timothy James McVeigh
and brief in support, March 25, 1997

"A Rude Awakening"

The Origins of the Victim-Offender Relationship

This is the famous perp walk—the perpetrator walk. If somebody hadn't facilitated that walk, Tim McVeigh would be a much different character visually, and emotionally I think in people's lives.

Peter Jennings, on *Larry King Live*, CNN, May 15, 2001[1]

Well, I think the thing that stands out most for me is when they arrested him and he was being taken from the courthouse I think in Perry, when they were transporting him . . . but they would show that clip of him being led out of the courthouse in Perry, Oklahoma, over and over and over and you got this chance to watch his demeanor. Just, I mean, so much inundated with that one image of him stoically walking out. . . and that's when you thought of him, that's the impression you had of him was that stoic soldier demeanor and no hint of any real humanity I guess . . . we were all inundated with that image of him. And so it was kind of hard later to get that image out of your head.

Diane Dooley, survivor

First Impressions of McVeigh, April 21, 1995

On April 21, 1995, Timothy McVeigh and his law enforcement escort emerged from the dim confines of the Noble County Courthouse into the bright sunshine of a beautiful day in Perry, Oklahoma. A little more than six years later, he was executed in the early morning hours of June 12, 2001. But between these bookend dates, the worlds of Oklahoma City bombing victims' families and survivors shifted dramatically. McVeigh morphed from a spare and mysterious young man to a very visible perpetrator who collaborated with biographers to ensure that he left little doubt as to why—at least in his mind—he had orchestrated a plot to bomb the Alfred P. Murrah Federal Building in the heart of Oklahoma City. Victims' family members and survivors felt as if they were lashed to McVeigh (and, to a lesser extent, coconspirators Terry Nichols and Michael Fortier) for the duration of this terrible ride and beyond, and McVeigh, in his turn, perceived that he was inextricably entangled with them. Yoked together, the victims' families and survivors on one side of the crossbar and the bombers on the other, the two groups were driven forward in a torturous tandem through a gauntlet of media attention and criminal justice proceedings.

While this complicated set of relationships began on the morning of the bombing, it crystallized on April 21, 1995, when family members and survivors caught their first glimpse ever of McVeigh during the bombing suspect's perp walk. As he emerged into the sunlight of that spring morning, McVeigh was not so much led by his surrounding officers as he moved with them, pushing slowly through the throngs that had gathered to see the Oklahoma City bombing suspect. McVeigh was outfitted in a fluorescent orange jumpsuit but wore no bulletproof vest. The privilege of escorting the shackled but defiant McVeigh had been granted to a dozen FBI agents as a reward for their roles in capturing him. Immortalized by news cameras, these images of McVeigh's arrest were broadcast continuously in the following days, months, and years, becoming iconic representations of the boyish yet hardened man who had murdered 168 people, injured over 800 more, and threatened or terrorized countless others.

As penal rituals, "perp walks" allow law enforcement officials to showcase the faces of those who ostensibly deserve to be publicly shamed for their alleged crimes. Law enforcement officials and suspects participating in perp walks are expected to follow certain behavioral norms. Although paraded individuals are merely suspects, it is easy to believe them guilty. It is anticipated that the parties involved—excluding jeering crowds—will conduct themselves more or less soberly, with suspects appearing suitably chastened.

But sometimes perp walks serve not as public shaming rituals but as opportunities for private vengeance or brazen suspect behavior. Take presidential assassin Lee Harvey Oswald, who was fatally shot by Jack Ruby as he was being walked to the county jail through the basement corridors of Dallas's city hall. Or consider pop star Michael Jackson's unorthodox behavior after his arraignment for multiple child molestation charges on January 17, 2004; after pleading not guilty to the charges, Jackson departed the courtroom and, cheered on by thousands of adoring fans, clambered on top of his SUV and danced and waved to supporters. Perp walks that somehow go awry trivialize crimes and their victims, turn law enforcement and criminal justice processes into spectacles, and push the importance of legal accountability into the shadows. McVeigh's perp walk failed as a shaming ritual in that he scarcely appeared to be humbled, scared, nervous, or even concerned for his ultimate fate. His defiant gaze merely heightened the horror and trauma of the act of which he stood accused and made him a toxic presence in family members' and survivors' lives.

Picturing Perpetrators

After you get through the shock . . . what lingers are the images of the perpetrators, and not of the corpses.[2]

Viewing perp walk footage begs an important question: How do we regard photographs of perpetrators, from those on television to images on display in memorial spaces? On whom should our gaze linger—those who committed a heinous act, or those victimized by it?

In encountering visual footage of traumatic events, viewers struggle with how to regard (or disregard) perpetrators' pictures, particularly in memorial spaces commemorating victims. Looking at perpetrators' likenesses may feel like a breach of moral propriety; it somehow seems more correct to look beyond them, devoting our attention primarily to representations of victims and perhaps rescuers. Hand in hand with a natural reticence to look at perpetrators comes the uncomfortable awareness that we should know *more*, not *less*, about the perpetrators, however much one wishes to ignore and exile them from consideration. We learn the names of murder victims in order to protest the anonymity of their heinous deaths and to reclaim their humanity from bystanders' and perpetrators' malice, indifference, or detachment. When we learn about the personalities and life histories of the perpetrators, it is often because we hope to identify the origins of their antisocial acts, both to understand them and to prevent such actions in the future.

Pictures of the Murrah building site taken shortly after the bombing explicitly document the traumatic event. But can one say the same of McVeigh's perp walk footage? It is immediately apparent that the perp walk images focus upon a perpetrator and not victims, survivors, or rescue workers—on a villain, not on the helpless or heroic caught up in the maelstrom of the bombing and its aftermath. Rather than the devastation wrought by the perpetrator's acts, perp walk images portray the perpetrator's inhumanity; their counterparts to broken landscapes and dying victims are an offender's interior ruin and impaired morality. Yet, in their connotative dimensions, perpetrator images imply victims' presence, if only as the individuals who have given the perpetrator his identity.

Perp walk footage situates criminal suspects as moral subjects by positioning them as agents. The perpetrator is assigned primary responsibility for the nefarious deed. Law enforcement personnel surrounding the perpetrator appear to be in control, can claim credit for capture and maintaining custody, and are ever alert to possibilities of escape and threats of harm. These forms of agency are different than those depicted within images of the traumatic event for which he is accused. The passive victim and heroic rescue worker initially exhibit only a responsive agency, in reaction to the perpetrator's crimes; they are not actors but individuals acted upon.[3] Such images also confer moral agency upon viewers, who scrutinize the perpetrator and make inferences as to his character, motivations, and state of mind—judgments integral to the experience of understanding and coping with the traumatic event.

For Oklahoma City bombing survivors and victims' family members, the interpretive act of engaging with McVeigh's perp walk image may have helped to alter their status as victims with respect to the bombing and that of McVeigh as perpetrator. Empowered with interpretive authority, victims became not only survivors but accusers seeking justice, forcing McVeigh into the more reactive position of defender. Interpreting and adjudicating McVeigh's emotions were as much acts of accusation as of suffering.[4]

McVeigh's perp walk images allowed viewers to simultaneously determine his physical attributes and gauge his personality and his attitude toward the bombing and toward victims. These pictures appeared to offer a genuine window into his soul—or lack thereof—and so their authenticity both provided a personal impression and "the experience of a personal encounter."[5] Viewers interrogated McVeigh, rendering his body the site where traumatic history materialized. His presence not only implied a host of other absences but also constituted a traumatic spark, igniting anger, indignation, and memories of the bombing, loved ones murdered and selves changed forever.

Those intimately affected by a crime—and members of the general public—have long relied upon images of perpetrators to answer the (sometimes unanswerable) question "Why?" and to make inferences regarding offenders' motivations and mental and emotional states. It is as if the perpetrator's appearance itself could reveal culpability. Thus, it is especially upsetting when particularly notorious offenders appear handsome or nonthreatening. Serial killer Ted Bundy was known for his good looks, in contrast with Charles Manson, who appeared a bit more crazed and "helter-skelter."

Perpetrators, their personalities, and their motives will always be key components of how we understand traumatic events. Negotiating representations of perpetrators through vehicles such as perp walk footage is an important part of this process. Until his trial, McVeigh's perp walk photos offered family members and survivors the first and often the best opportunity to scrutinize the face of the Oklahoma City bombing suspect, and then make inferences about McVeigh's character. Susan Urbach, the director of the Oklahoma City Small Business Council, was in the doorway of her office in the Journal Record Building across the street from the Murrah Building when the bomb detonated; she suffered extensive injuries and spent more than four hours in surgery. She noted, "The visual impression also is important because even if it's on the mass media, you get an idea of how does that person—how do they look, how do they move, . . . what's their body language? And how does that all fit?" "That image from the jail was an extremely powerful image," she added.

Looking back upon these perp walk images from our distant contemporary vantage point, McVeigh appears cold, unemotional, and defiant. The law enforcement personnel that crowd the image's border set off McVeigh's aloof manner: he appears to be alone despite the bodies pressed closely in on one another. To survivors and family members, McVeigh's apparent unconcern magnified his victims' invisibility, inflicting additional injury on those who remained.

These perp walk images force a series of confrontations between the viewer and McVeigh. The first confrontation comes when viewers seek to understand him by drawing inferences from these photographic representations. McVeigh's apparent defiance necessitates a second, more thorough confrontation—a need to demand accountability from him, to ensure that he takes responsibility not only for his role in the bombing but also for its human costs. But while McVeigh appears confrontational, his gaze is directed past the media cameras, denying the viewer the satisfaction of a face-to-face encounter. Justice for the victims is nowhere to be found; arrest alone cannot force accountability, and McVeigh walks tall, apparently unburdened by shame. The image's violence comes from an awareness not only of what McVeigh has done but also of who he is—an American and, shockingly, a decorated veteran, among those trusted to defend, not attack, his fellow citizens. McVeigh appears young yet hardened. His everyday, boyish appearance is negated by his stoicism and his narrow, closed countenance. His physical features are not monstrous; it is his gaze that sets him apart.

One of the most haunting qualities of McVeigh's perp walk image was its endless repetition. It was ubiquitous, as was the more recent 9/11 footage of the commercial airliners' impact with the World Trade Center's Twin Towers and the buildings' subsequent collapse. Television coverage compulsively repeats certain images as it struggles with how to tell the story of an event.[6] The continuous recirculation of McVeigh's perp walk footage ensured that McVeigh was a key focus in narrating the Oklahoma City bombing story line. And the import of this footage changed according to the context and medium in which it appeared; in the words of Barbie Zelizer, these images "assert[ed] themselves" in fresh ways, evolving new meanings beyond "reasoned information relay" such as "community building, recovering from trauma and grief, arousing empathy and indignation, concretizing complex events, . . . facilitating catharsis, [and] enabling analysis and comparisons."[7]

These images helped to establish involuntary ties between McVeigh and family members and survivors that some experienced for years (often until his execution), and that others always will feel. They strengthened bonds of solidarity between family members and survivors; even if these individuals would always remain strangers to one another, they were united in their common pursuit of accountability for this man at the center of the law enforcement escort. Finally, it linked those family members and survivors to other Americans—individuals who had no other connection to the bombing than tuning in to news coverage of the event, but who nonetheless became important sources of emotional and financial support. Thus, the perp walk images created a sense that Americans, hand in hand with family members and survivors, were united in a common cause against those responsible for the bombing, beginning with McVeigh.

Putting a Face to the Deed: Family Members and Survivors React to McVeigh

For those intimately affected by the blast, McVeigh's perp walk embodied the bombing; his demeanor elicited a visceral impact. Many participants candidly acknowledged that media images influenced their impressions of McVeigh. Survivor Charlie Younger worked for the Oklahoma Department of Transportation and had entered the Murrah Building to attend a meeting on the morning of April 19, 1995; he was on the southeast corner of the building on the fourth floor when the bomb went off. "You develop opinions prior to the trial based on just what you read and see in the media," he explained, "and I saw [McVeigh] in the media when they arrested him up at Perry and some of his reactions to the crowd and stuff, he was a stone cold person then . . . that was very influential." Survivor Richard Williams, who worked for the General Services Administration (GSA) as the assistant manager of the Murrah Building, was in his office on the first floor at the time of the bombing and required immediate surgery for his injuries. Williams related, "Always etched in our minds will be that picture of him coming out of the courthouse in Perry." These images could elicit anger and hatred; for Younger, "the visual pictures of the bombing and . . . of him, that tends to intensify your hatred, and your anger and your perception of someone, no doubt." The power of these images came in part from their repetition. Bud Welch's daughter, Julie Marie Welch, a Spanish interpreter for the Social Security Administration in the Murrah Building, was murdered in the bombing; Bud has since become an internationally known anti–death penalty advocate. He acknowledged, "I guess that influenced me a lot because I think we all saw it a thousand times."

And what did family members make of this spare young man who was in custody, suspected of carrying out the Oklahoma City bombing? His identity—a young, white American male, a decorated veteran—appalled participants. As Younger noted, "You kept hoping it was somebody, some fanatic from overseas. You didn't dream it was . . . a U.S. soldier. So that was a rude awakening for this country and me for sure." Several participants acknowledged their shock. Ernestine Hill Clark, a librarian for the Metropolitan Library System, was in a meeting on the third floor of the library one block south from the Murrah Building when the bomb exploded; blown across a room and into the hall, she sustained only minor physical wounds but had nightmares and psychological problems requiring treatment for several years. Clark remembered "the shock of seeing him coming out of that jail, that still baby-faced kid coming out of that jail," and could not forget his "sharp nose" and "that look on his face of him trying to be hardened." For survivor Janet Beck, a Social Security Administration claims representative who was on the first floor of the Murrah Building when the bomb detonated, "it was . . . a shock to see that he was just, looked like the normal kid next door and not a monster."

Most important, images of McVeigh's "perp walk" gave participants insight into McVeigh's personality. Family member Cameron Crawford, whose sibling was murdered in the bombing, thought from the beginning that McVeigh appeared guilty because of "a look in his eyes": "You're looking for a face to pin this on and that look of defiance in his face just screamed it to me. I mean, you're looking for a target to hate and I know, innocent until proven guilty, but that picture, it—gosh, he looked like a guilty man to me, the first day." Survivor Vicki Hamm worked in the U.S. Army Recruiting Office on the fourth floor of the Murrah Building and was two blocks away at a doctor's office when the bomb went off. She characterized McVeigh's manner as "haunting":

> He seemed to be leading the group instead of being escorted. . . . you could tell McVeigh was the one in charge. That's the way it seemed to me. . . . And his demeanor, that look on his face, the way he stood. . . . Yeah, I can remember. He seemed like a strong person, a person that would be capable of performing such a heinous act.

Scrutinizing McVeigh's countenance for clues to his motivation and mental state, participants were horrified by what they saw. Family member Faith Moore was the former wife of Paul Douglas Ice and the mother of his two daughters; Paul was a senior special agent in the U.S. Customs Service office in the Murrah Building who was murdered in the bombing. Searching for answers in McVeigh's expression, Moore only found new enigmas: "His face was blank. No emotion, no nothing. That was really puzzling to me." Richard Williams remembered his initial impression of McVeigh quite clearly: that he had "no remorse, no feeling, maybe not understanding the enormity of what he had done, but very proud of it to a degree."

The Importance of First Impressions: The Roots of the Victim-Offender Relationship

Who McVeigh was, or, more accurately, who he appeared to be, was a key element in family members' and survivors' attempts to understand, cope with, contextualize, and move forward after the bombing. This "memory work" depends heavily on creating, enunciating, and exchanging coherent narratives—stories about the bombing and its aftermath. In the wake of homicide, family members and survivors become involuntarily and intimately linked to the offender through the offense, so that they must "live with" the offender to a greater or lesser extent until death—either the offender's or their own. As Janice Smith, a family member whose brother was murdered in the bombing, stated in a media interview after McVeigh's execution on June 11, 2001, "It's over. We don't have to continue with him anymore."[8]

The obligations of this involuntary bond are contradictory; on the one hand, the offender has murdered at least one family member, yet on the other the offender is often the only possible source of information about the offense and the victim's last moments. This connection is also most often mediated; through news coverage, other forms of media, and trial proceedings, victims become very familiar with the offender's biography, relatives, and associates. Victims and offenders may hear one another's statements through press conferences, media interviews, trial testimony, books or websites, or other forms of public communication. Less often, victims and offenders may communicate more directly, by exchanging letters, meeting face-to-face in mediation programs, or through other communicative interchanges that deepen and contextualize the victim-offender relationship.

Most participants felt as if they were targets of McVeigh's behavior and public statements, that he intended to further wound them. Survivor Priscilla Salyers worked for the U.S. Customs Service and was at her desk on the fifth floor of the Murrah Building when the bomb went off; she was buried in debris, pinned beneath her desk and a concrete column for four hours. After being rescued, she was hospitalized for broken ribs, a punctured lung, and a serious cut on her leg. As she explained, "Every time he turned around, he was doing something to jab at us and it was just very painful." Richard Williams acknowledged, "I have always felt like that if McVeigh and Nichols for example had access to the family members, survivors, through the media, through books, . . . [he] would always just keep digging at us, sticking that knife [in] and twisting." Family member Paul Howell's daughter, Karan Shepherd, was a loan officer in the Federal Employees Credit Union on the third floor of the Murrah Building who was murdered in the bombing. Howell contrasted McVeigh's malicious intent to Nichols's:

McVeigh, even though he knew that he was getting the death sentence, he was defiant all the way up to the point where it actually happened, okay? He would speak out to the media. . . . And everything that he did was doing nothing but hurting the family members here in Oklahoma. . . . Nichols is a little different because since he's been tried and convicted, you don't hear about him. . . . I can live with him being in prison for the rest of his life, for the simple reason that he is not defiant and he's not going out and getting on the news and so forth and trying to hurt the family members.

These remarks create the impression that participants felt they were involved in a dialogue with McVeigh. Unprompted by the wording of interview questions, participants variously noted that McVeigh had "jab[bed] at" or "hurt" victims, that he had "access to the family members [and] survivors" and would "tell the families" various hurtful things. It was as if participants were not only vulnerable to McVeigh but privy to what he meant by a callous remark or gesture. Several participants, for instance, claimed to "know" that McVeigh would not have sincerely meant any apology that he may have given at his execution.

Such interactions do not fit our usual conception of interpersonal communication, involving simultaneous dialogue between two people.[9] Family members and survivors never communicated with McVeigh directly, except perhaps by establishing eye contact; outside of legal proceedings, all "interactions" with McVeigh occurred through mass media broadcasts. Within the courtroom, testifying witnesses engaged in exchanges with examining attorneys, not with McVeigh himself. Several established eye contact with McVeigh, always with memorable consequences. Although it elicited undeniable responses from participants, this distanced interaction is not encapsulated by ordinary understandings of interpersonal communication.[10] How, then, can we explain this perceived intimacy and account for participants' perceptions that McVeigh was speaking *to them*?

In 1956, while seeking to explain television viewers' perceived relationship to television personalities, media researchers Donald Horton and Richard Wohl coined the term "para-social" interaction, to denote "the illusion of a face-to-face relationship with the performer" to which audience members respond as they would to friends.[11] Entirely one-sided and performer-controlled, this relationship evolves when members are insinuated into "the program's action and internal social relationships," and thereby transformed into "a group which observes and participates in the show by turns."[12] Despite the lack of communicative give-and-take, the television personality is eventually integrated into an audience member's social circle.

However artless this relationship may appear, it is also strategic and constant. Producers formulate the persona's character specifically to enhance audience members' loyalty to certain characters.[13] Subsequent research suggests that audience members actually perceive this relationship as "real."[14] Para-social relationships continue to pervade media usage today.

Research has focused almost exclusively on positive para-social relationships with likeable, trustworthy television personalities. But relationships with para-social "friends" also implicate the potential for negative relationships with para-social "enemies." Whereas the positive para-social persona is an "in-group" member, a desirable associate, the para-social enemy is an outsider, a deviant Other who engenders persistent dislike and animosity. Victims are as encouraged to be loyal to their hatred of criminal personas as audience members are encouraged to admire their media personas. The concept of negative para-social relations also necessitates broadening the concepts of "media" and "media producer" from the mass media to a broader social environment, where other institutional actors assume strategic mediating roles—including criminal justice officials who orchestrate the arrest and trial of criminal offenders from the perp walk to incarceration or execution.

Like para-social relationships, the connections that family members and survivors felt with McVeigh were engendered by news media and facilitated the illusion of intimacy. This victim-offender relationship, however, was very different from para-social ties. Family members and survivors felt their ties to McVeigh in a much more profound sense than one would experience a para-social connection to a favorite actor or athlete. It was as if bombing victims had become entangled with an infamously terrifying character such as Jason Voorhees from *Friday the 13th* or Freddy Krueger from *Nightmare on Elm Street*, except that these creatures were denizens of the real world, not a script and movie set. McVeigh became a very real and very nightmarish part of their lives the moment he detonated the bomb in Oklahoma City. His heinous crime affected the highly vulnerable and already wounded population of bombing victims in a more personal, painful, and visceral sense than mere para-social ties ever could.

The intimacy of this negative relation was particularly ironic in light of McVeigh's detached demeanor, as well as the impersonal nature of his crimes. According to numerous media interviews and statements he made to reporters and his biographers Lou Michel and Dan Herbeck, McVeigh saw himself as standing in opposition to the U.S. government, in particular the government agencies involved in the incidents at Waco and Ruby Ridge. He explained that he chose to bomb the Murrah Federal Building because he thought it would make a spectacular media target, not out of personal animosity toward anyone who worked in the building or anything housed there. Yet, the bombing immediately became intensely personal through media coverage. Almost immediately after his perp walk, news media outlets began to disseminate extreme close-ups of McVeigh derived from that footage, such as the May 1, 1995, cover of *Time*, as well as other images such as the iconic picture of Baylee Almon, the one-year-old baby girl who was cradled in the arms of Oklahoma City firefighter Chris Fields as she died. The impersonality of the bombing was an incomprehensible affront to family members and survivors, who could not see it in such dispassionate terms.

Media texts accompanying these images also highlighted McVeigh's gaze, which became crucial in constructing him as a para-social enemy. Early media stories described "hard eyes unlit by the faintest flicker of emotion," the look of a man whose "name didn't mean much then but the image did," the stare of "a poker-faced killer in a crew-cut."[15] Such impressions resurfaced continually, including on the morning of his execution; as one journalist put it, "In his last moments, his face was as blank as it was that April day six years ago when America first saw him escorted out of an Oklahoma jail."[16]

These media constructions of McVeigh were repeatedly incorporated into subsequent coverage over the months and years following the bombing until they snowballed to produce a coherent image of McVeigh as a para-social enemy. It is not surprising that the heavy media focus on the "perp walk" images influenced the early impressions of family members and survivors; first impressions are formed rapidly,[17] even from brief glimpses, and the constancy of physical appearance and behaviors is important for generating future expectations. The moment when family members and survivors were "introduced" to McVeigh via the perp walk was when the overwhelming majority formed initial impressions of McVeigh as a person and as a perpetrator.

McVeigh as a Thorn in Memory's Side

This perceived para-social relationship with McVeigh cast a pall upon family members' and survivors' efforts to reconstruct their lives, so that McVeigh's conduct—hindering many bombing victims' recoveries by "manipulating" them through the media—persisted until his execution in June 2001. McVeigh and his toxic presence were an unfortunate part of most victims' postbombing realities. Participants could not help but incorporate this para-social relationship as part of their memory work, and they did so in ways that delayed or at the very least unsettled their healing.

But whereas the formation of other relationships that emerged out of the bombing, such as those between members of community and advocacy organizations, were voluntary and free from institutional constraints, the victim-offender relationship was involuntary and entirely mediated by institutions. It was facilitated by the news media and by the criminal justice system, which controlled "exposure" to McVeigh and created forums such as the trial and execution where family members and survivors could assess his behaviors.

The criminal justice system also influenced the victim-offender relationship in a variety of other ways, ranging from how expeditiously the trial was held, to how it was to be viewed (e.g., whether it was broadcast to other venues), whether family members and survivors were allowed to attend, what verdict was handed down, and when and how the criminal sentence was carried out.

Identifying and explicating the victim-offender relationship illustrates why existing perspectives on victims' psychological and emotional states are incomplete and cannot incorporate the full range of their experiences. Going through so-called grieving stages, attending or testifying in legal proceedings, or even analyzing media representations of family members cannot provide a full account of how victims begin to come to terms with a loved one's murder. Significantly, each of these approaches positions the victim as a passive self, a body that travels through grief stages, a body that attends the trial and perhaps witnesses the execution, a body that can be represented by others. This creates the impression that victims are both defined by and confined by these models and their behavioral codes. An alternate approach is to examine the phenomenon of homicide survivorship as an involuntary relationship between the victim's family and the offender that exists even when neither party knew the other prior to the murderous act, and that like any other relationship is communicative, structured through speech and silence. Thus, acknowledging the victim-offender relationship is the first step in fully appreciating family members' lived experience in the aftermath of murder.

This relationship is only rarely tacitly acknowledged (and never explicitly defined) in criminological, sociological, and legal scholarship. It is a concept whose logic is the combined logic of several facts—publicity about the offender and the murder, families' and survivors' need to know "why" and "how" the crime occurred, and the perverse necessity for the offender to help to answer those questions. How could victims' families help but feel they know an offender through the plethora of intimate details that emerge through contemporary media coverage? Coverage of Jeffrey Dahmer's murders, for instance, extended to intimate details of his personal life: "the type of beer he drank, his cigarette preference, the types of potato chips he ate, and the brand of baking soda he used in his refrigerator."[18] This relationship may also encompass offenders' families; offenders, their relatives, and even their communities may be roped together into a category of otherness, set apart by disgust and hatred, with offenders' family members taking the brunt of the intensely negative publicity.[19] As we have seen, participants felt their relationship with McVeigh began during his perp walk; Vicki Hamm began to feel McVeigh's presence "as soon as they escorted him from the courthouse in Perry, Oklahoma," and for Charlie Younger it commenced "the day I seen him on the TV when he was led out of that prison up in . . . Perry. The minute you put a face with an act, as great as a thing he did, it had to have been that moment."

Through the perp walk and other institutionally mediated images of McVeigh, bombing victims' impressions of him as a man and, in some cases, as a monster contextualized his mannerisms and statements. Theirs was a relationship characterized by perceptions of iniquity, inequity, and inequality, in which family members and survivors very much wanted to hear why and how McVeigh carried out the bombing, and yearned in many cases to speak with him in person.

In addition, this involuntary relationship between McVeigh and family members and survivors profoundly influenced their painful, labor-intensive attempts at reconstruction—memory work—because it challenged their processes of identity formation. Many described McVeigh's continued existence as a barrier to reconstruction. Because McVeigh occupied one camp in the involuntary and adversarial relationship between family member/survivor and offender, he was linked to them and so became and remained a part *of* the collective, instead of being cast outside it. Family members and survivors found his inclusion traumatizing because it delayed or diminished their control; at any time a message could issue from McVeigh and aggravate wounds just starting to heal. Thus, the collective memory of homicide—including the collective memory of the Oklahoma City bombing—was shaped not only by the events of the murder but also by the intensity and duration of the involuntary relationship between the bombers and their victims.

Focusing attention on such victim-offender relationships recognizes that victims and survivors define as well as become defined by the experiences of survivorship. It implies an exchange and recognizes that processes of sensemaking are cyclical and not linear. Victims change and alter conceptions of grieving in the course of healing; they are active participants in the trial with the potential to change its practices and potentials. Focusing on the victim-offender relationship also effectively organizes how participants made sense of the chaos of postbombing social relations. It explains why the vast majority of participants, regardless of their political views on the death penalty, felt relief after McVeigh's execution, the event that terminated the involuntary relationship that had begun six years earlier.

2

"He Broke into My Life"

Experiencing the Victim-Offender Relationship

McVeigh's perp walk identified him as the principal suspect in the Oklahoma City bombing and also inserted him as an intensely unwelcome, even toxic, intrusion into survivors' and family members' lives. Most felt that McVeigh had not only disrupted their lives but also desecrated their physical and emotional integrity. This acute sense of violation was so strong that a few family members and survivors analogized it to rape. Experiencing McVeigh as a toxic intrusion entailed feelings of helplessness and passivity, rooted in the perception that McVeigh was at least temporarily in the driver's seat. Recovering one's identity and restoring one's dignity meant ejecting McVeigh and reasserting self-control.

"Such a Cold Emptiness": Exploring McVeigh's Toxic Presence

McVeigh was literally an *"offender,"* a perpetrator who not only had deeply wounded thousands of people through his crimes but also continued to insult and upset them even after he was tried, convicted, and condemned. The bombing might have been the first injury that he inflicted upon family members and survivors, but it was certainly not the last. The cumulative impact of these additional wounds ranged from merely annoying to debilitating.

Crimes themselves are always actual injuries; at a minimum, they violate societal norms and values and trespass upon victims' integrity and dignity. But the victim's experience of the criminal injury often extends beyond the criminal act. One might say that an offender's presence in a victim's life consists of both a *criminal impact* and a *personal impact*. Both are required for a victim to perceive that an offender has intruded into her life. Victims of certain crimes that usually force a heinous intimacy with the offender, such as murder or rape, may be more likely to perceive that an offender is a

| 19

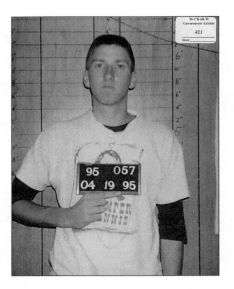

McVeigh's police mug shot, taken after his arrest on misdemeanor charges shortly after fleeing the scene of the Oklahoma City bombing. Image courtesy of the Oklahoma City National Memorial and Museum Archives.

toxic presence, and experience this intrusion more intensely, than victims of other offenses that do not entail such familiarity, such as neighborhood vandalism. Depending on the circumstances, however, victims of these latter types of offenses can certainly experience an offender's intrusive presence as well.

Examining a perpetrator's *criminal* impact emphasizes the crime and its surrounding circumstances as well as the victim's lived experience of the criminal event, and focuses on the offender only to the extent of his behavior while committing the crime. In contrast, an offender's *personal* impact is determined by his behavior after the crime has been committed. Here, the primary focus is on the offender himself, not on the facts of the crime or his demeanor during its commission. The offender's personal impact, therefore, starts but does not end with his criminal act. For a crime victim to experience a perpetrator's personal impact, the victim not only must have experienced a criminal impact (such as being frightened or inconvenienced by the offense, suffering pain, betrayal, and trust, or property loss), but also must have had the opportunity to view, hear, or learn about the offender following the crime. Depending on his demeanor, an offender's personal impact can have a positive or negative influence upon the victim: Is he remorseful or defiant? Polite or rude? Chastened or threatening? If the offender's notoriety merits media coverage, the character and tone of these media representations are also integral components of his personal impact.

All participants who were aware of McVeigh's toxic presence experienced both a criminal impact and a personal impact. For some, the personal impact was more a function of McVeigh's intense media visibility; for others, it was also related to his stoic and defiant public persona that heightened many participants' desire to silence him or hold him accountable through execution. Significantly, some participants may not even have experienced the toxic presences of McVeigh, Nichols, and Fortier as distinct, particularly at first. Family member Diane Leonard, whose husband, Donald Ray Leonard, was a Secret Service agent who worked in the Murrah Building at the time he was murdered in the bombing, recalled that "all those emotions were so intense that . . . I didn't separate them out from one person to another."

Because McVeigh came into participants' lives in his role as the suspected Oklahoma City bomber, it is not surprising that family members and survivors described his unwelcome presence as stemming from that involvement. Thus, McVeigh as an offender was inextricably intertwined with the bombing as a traumatic event, rendering references to "McVeigh's presence" synonymous with "McVeigh's impact." "Gosh, it's hard to separate him from the whole event," Cameron Crawford remarked. "The whole thing was a big mess. I mean, if you took him out of the equation, we wouldn't have had the big mess." This also meant that for many if not most participants, McVeigh's presence will always be felt.

Participants also described McVeigh's involvement in more personal terms. His truck bomb did not merely destroy a building; it annihilated lives and damaged bodies. He was not only the Oklahoma City bomber; he had also murdered loved ones and attempted to murder survivors. McVeigh was a living reminder of the bombing and participants' own personal losses long after the debris of the Murrah Building was cleared away. Accordingly, many participants regarded him as a stain upon the reconstructive memorial fabric that they were trying to weave. Doris Jones's daughter, Carrie Ann Lenz, was a contract employee assigned to the U.S. Drug Enforcement Administration in the Murrah Building when she was murdered in the bombing together with her unborn son, Michael James Lenz. Jones related:

> Because he came into my life, my whole life changed. . . . I lost my daughter, my grandson, my in-law, you know, my friend. You know, I lost so much because he came into my life. . . . I think it was an intrusion because my life was just tripping right along just fine. . . . You think of an intrusion like someone breaking into your house and basically, that's what he did, he broke into my life.

The ravaged landscape around the Murrah Building was also an undeniable aspect of McVeigh's presence. Susan Urbach explained:

> The intrusion was that . . . my whole life revolved around about a four- to six-block area around that Federal Building area. So I didn't have an office, I didn't have a credit union, I didn't have a Y, I didn't have my church, I didn't have a library, didn't have a post office, didn't have the restaurants that I dealt with . . . cause it wasn't there. . . . I knew immediately from that point, it will not be the same. Ever.

McVeigh's high media visibility exacerbated his presence; one would have had to live in a bubble to escape the onslaught of bombing coverage. Survivor Diane Dooley was a Veterans Affairs case manager who worked on the fifth floor of the Murrah Building; she was traveling to a meeting in the Federal Credit Union and was in the stairwell on the third floor when the bomb went off. Dooley sustained a crushed hand, an arm broken in 12 places, and an injured foot and underwent years of physical therapy. She recalled that McVeigh's intrusion seemed "never-ending" because "you couldn't turn on the TV, you couldn't turn on the radio for lots of time after the bombing and it was just, yes, it was harder to get back to normal." Participants who relied upon the news media for information about the bombing soon found that they had to directly confront and negotiate McVeigh's media presence. As Vicki Hamm commented, "Well, he was unwelcome, but on the other hand, this is something that happened. . . . I wanted to know everything about it that I could and that involved reading about him, hearing about him. It just involved being absorbed in him." These processes "just kind of put him in a place I didn't think he needed to be in my life," Hamm continued. "He used to really have a lot of power over my thoughts." Finally, other disruptive experiences besides media coverage, such as enhanced workplace security routines and endless parades of doctors' appointments, could also renew a sense of McVeigh's intrusive presence.

For several participants, McVeigh's presence was not merely unwelcome; it was something stronger: a permanent and involuntary tie to McVeigh. These participants often felt unwillingly joined not only to McVeigh but also to the bombing. For instance, Faith Moore stated that "just because of the bombing . . . our lives will always be tied to him," and Diane Leonard affirmed that "absolutely we were involuntarily bound by the crime he committed." Critically injured survivor Stan Mayer was on the third floor of the

Journal Record Building overlooking the Federal Plaza adjacent to the Murrah Building and saw the Ryder truck park. The blast tore Mayer's clothes to shreds and riddled him with shrapnel; he sustained severe cuts and burns from truck parts, and his jugular was severed by a piece of falling ceiling. As a result of his bombing-related injuries, Mayer has endured more than 50 surgeries. He explained that his connection with McVeigh stemmed from the "consequences of what he did" and the fact that "he knew it was going to kill children, he knew it was going to kill a lot of people and injure a lot of people." "I'd really like to not give him credit," stated Mayer, "but unfortunately I was never very far, especially in the first year, I was never very far from my absolute hatred of him."

Participants anticipated that such ties, like McVeigh's unwelcome presence, would last forever. "You don't ever forget what happened to the people that you knew in there and . . . I dealt with those people every day," said survivor Ray Washburn, who was working behind the counter of the snack bar on the fourth floor of the Murrah Building when the bomb detonated. He continued, "Some I knew, some I didn't really know, but McVeigh, he just, he more or less took over, took their lives. . . . I don't think he's completely out. I still have thoughts about the bombing."

McVeigh was a toxic or intrusive presence at different points in time for participants. While some perceived his presence immediately or when they could put a face to the offense after McVeigh was arrested, others experienced it only after months or a year had passed. Peggy Broxterman's son, Paul Broxterman, worked for the Department of Housing and Urban Development in the Murrah Building and was murdered in the bombing; Peggy was chosen as a live witness to McVeigh's execution. She felt McVeigh's intrusion "the minute my son was killed" and knew immediately "that whoever did it was going to die. Even if I had to do it."

Most participants became aware of McVeigh's presence after he was identified as the one who lit the truck bomb fuse. For family member Doris Jones, the intrusion began "when they captured him and we knew that he was the one, because right at the very first, I was not like a vigilante . . . I didn't want someone if it wasn't [the right suspect]." McVeigh's presence increased when participants saw him in person or on television; to see McVeigh was to engage with him, to make inferences and judgments about his character and motivations. Many participants linked their awareness of McVeigh's presence to his highly visible perp walk; legal proceedings could also trigger McVeigh's toxic presence. When his trial started, Paul Howell became more conscious of McVeigh's presence "because at that point I spent a lot of time trying to watch him, pay attention to what he was doing, how his reactions were in the courthouse."

Finally, some participants only experienced McVeigh as an unwelcome presence months or a year after the bombing. Cameron Crawford devoted the first months to taking care of his parents and concentrating on his job before joining with other family members and survivors to reform the death penalty appeals process; for him, McVeigh's presence began when "it was months later and I'm finally coming home by myself in my own home, it's quiet, and I think that was probably where it kind of started to evolve." Injured survivors Diane Dooley and Richard Williams both noted that intense recovery efforts delayed their awareness of McVeigh's noxious presence for approximately one year. "Because I was going through surgeries and doing physical therapy, I wasn't focused on that particular part of it," Dooley recalled. "I would say probably about a year after the bombing when I was physically kind of over the hump with my physical therapy. And then you sort of start dealing with the emotional [aspect]." At that point, her awareness of McVeigh's presence was strong: "When it starts your emotions kind of fall and start, and then you go, oh my gosh, I can't get away. . . . There was always some awareness that McVeigh was there and how are we going to deal with him."

The experience of McVeigh's presence was unique for two survivors who described personal encounters with McVeigh before his perp walk. Survivor Dr. Paul Heath, a counseling psychologist in the Veterans Affairs office in the Murrah Building who was on the fifth floor of the Murrah Building when the bomb exploded, explained that he had spoken with McVeigh the Thursday before the bombing, when McVeigh came in to "look for work." Heath sensed McVeigh's presence "the second that my brain finally put it together that they had arrested the same guy that I had talked with on Thursday." Survivor Germaine Johnston worked for the Department of Housing and Urban Development and was at her desk on the seventh floor of the Murrah Building when the bomb went off. Johnston described how she spoke with McVeigh moments after the bombing. Covered with debris, her clothing soaked from sprinklers, she was making her way to her husband's workplace after escaping the Murrah Building when she made eye contact with a tall, brown-haired young man standing with his companion in an alley by an old yellow car. The man asked Johnston what happened; upon learning of the explosion, he inquired "A lot of people killed?" After learning that McVeigh was the prime suspect, Johnston was haunted by her experience. "I was afraid, because I did not believe that he had done it alone and I was afraid to get involved and I was afraid to testify because my first thought was they know who I am and they know how to find me." McVeigh became a presence in Johnston's life for the "first few weeks and months. While the experience was so new."

Personal Impressions of McVeigh

> But Tim—well, if you don't consider what happened in Oklahoma, Tim is a good person. He would stop—he would stop and help somebody that's broken down on the side of the road. I just didn't think Tim had it in him.
> —Testimony of Michael Fortier, May 12, 1997

Unlike Michael Fortier, who knew McVeigh for years before the bombing, family members and survivors were introduced to him after and through the murderous bombing that made him infamous. How did participants perceive Timothy McVeigh? What about him was memorable, even shocking?

Several participants described McVeigh as cold or remorseless. After locking eyes with McVeigh while testifying at his trial, Diane Leonard experienced "such a cold, emptiness that I felt from him . . . it was the most cold feeling I've ever felt in my life." Susan Urbach was sure that McVeigh lacked remorse: "It's been very evident from the moment he was arrested, he wasn't sorry." Many observed that it was hard to know exactly what McVeigh was thinking; according to Faith Moore, he was "a very strange person. . . . He just kept himself really shut off and shut down." Richard Williams doubted that it was possible to truly know McVeigh:

> I think some people probably felt that, because they could read and watch TV and form their own opinions, . . . they knew him, but I don't think . . . any of us knew him well. . . . I felt like I tried to learn enough about him to know who he was, . . . why he did the things that he did, but I never felt like I got to know him. . . . when you get to know people sometimes you kind of understand how they think . . . yet, the more unsure I was.

Others believed him to be an ideologically committed individual who considered the bombing the proper response to Waco and Ruby Ridge and who took pride in his deadly creation. "He thought what he was doing was the right thing to do," recounted Germaine Johnston, "he thought that it was a means to an end, it was worth working for. He thought he was going to start a revolution."

Participants differed in assessing McVeigh's mental state, with several explicitly or implicitly stating that McVeigh must have been mentally unstable to carry out the bombing. Ray Washburn termed McVeigh a "mixed-up man," and Bud Welch believed that he had post-traumatic stress disorder (PTSD). McVeigh's veteran status was also deeply troubling for many. In attacking the very people he had fought to protect, McVeigh committed the soldier's gravest sin. "Working for the Department of Veterans Affairs, I see veterans, and that was the hardest thing for me to reconcile was that he was a veteran," Diane Dooley noted. "Somehow he lost that vision of protecting our country and he attacked." McVeigh's military career also disturbed survivor Dot Hill, who worked for the General Services Administration on the first floor of the Murrah Building but was on break in the center of the building and not at her desk at the time of the bombing. Hill, whose father was a soldier, commented: "My whole life growing up, soldiers were protectors and defenders of this country and of me and my family and someone who is willing to die for this country, not kill people in this country because of their own personal issues."

"He's Here": The Emotional Consequences of McVeigh's Toxic Presence

The physical and emotional impact of McVeigh's presence mirrored that of the bombing. Reactions among participants varied but frequently included feelings of violation, devastation, sadness, despair, deadness, a loss of control, being lost, a need to hold McVeigh accountable, being overwhelmed or consumed, nausea or sickness, and anger.

McVeigh's toxic presence left many feeling violated or further victimized. Peggy Broxterman compared this to a strong, physical, devastating penetration: "Violated, raped, shot, killed. The whole thing." Faith Moore felt robbed: "I remember one time when our house was broken into and how violated I felt by that. And it was that same feeling. . . . something being taken from you . . . you can't ever get it back." Survivor Diane Dooley too felt "further victimized": "Not only did he do what he did, but he becomes such a part of your life because people make him part of your life. And so I think further victimizing you and sort of making it harder to move on because you can't get around him. He's here."

Participants also reported extreme emotional reactions, such as anomie and depression. Critically injured survivor Stan Mayer experienced "severe depression where I couldn't do anything but just cry constantly" and remembered a profound loss of self and loss of control due to "severe traumatic brain injury":

When your skull is cracked open and your brain is swollen, severely swollen, and you have to relearn how to walk and your sense of balance, . . . your personality is radically different. Everything is different. So it's just a complete comprehensive change and you don't know who you are. . . . I didn't know if I could use my legs or my arms. I didn't know what I could or could not do. I was having constant surgeries. So my life was gone, and control of my life was completely gone. And that was a direct consequence of what he did.

Another common effect of McVeigh's toxic presence was that it was all-consuming or, in Susan Urbach's words, "simply overwhelming." Vicki Hamm described being "trapped" in a life dominated by McVeigh and the consequences of his actions:

It was all-consuming. . . . I was being consumed by it, but yet I didn't want to turn away. . . . I was saturated with the bombing at work and dealing with the victims, and the survivors, their surgeries, and everything that happened at the end later and the deaths of some of them . . . and then I'd come home and . . . [although my husband could not watch anymore] I just had to. So I'd go in another room and I would watch anything that was on about that.

Participants also responded to McVeigh's toxic presence in their lives with anger. For some, this anger was not all-consuming but experienced with other emotions such as despair or deadness. Cameron Crawford described this emotional hybrid as "a lot more deep despair than anger, although there was anger in there. But I think it was more stopping to see the incredible loss." Others did recall experiencing overwhelming anger but consciously chose to divert emotional energy toward more healing and productive projects. Diane Leonard initially felt "very, very angry"; after she began to work on reforming death penalty appeals, however, she realized that "anger takes so much energy and I needed the energy, what little I had, to work on the legislation, . . . that's when I think the anger started diminishing because I needed that energy elsewhere." Richard Williams was initially "very angry" but then found his anger "began to wane after a period of time and priorities changed, . . . even though you kept up with it every day, it was a part of your life every day." For Williams, it was important that "it did not determine or dictate your daily life," because "if you let that happen then . . . he beat you, he won."

"Putting McVeigh in His Place": Combatting McVeigh's Toxic Presence

Combating and ultimately marginalizing McVeigh's presence required that participants resolve their feelings toward him. "You want to keep moving forward and it's like he's been planted right there in your face and you can't get around him and so . . . you eventually have to say, 'Okay, I have to come to some resolution with him,'" emphasized Diane Dooley, "I've got to work this into forgiveness or some sort of peace with what he did to me." Self-maintenance—monitoring, bolstering, and safeguarding one's emotional, mental, and physical health—was crucial to resolution processes.

Relying upon support from close friends and family was a key part of coping with McVeigh's toxic presence. Susan Urbach described the importance of her networks, which included "family, friends and church": "If your life is a web, a wovenness of different people, different groups, different interests, activities, and so on, if something happens to cut cords to some of that, you don't fall through. . . . I had a bunch of cords broken and damaged, but I had many people . . . to fall back on." For critically injured survivors, relying on others was an inescapable part of life after the bombing; Stan Mayer observed that "I physically had to—in order to survive, I had to be having surgery and physical therapy and I had a lot of help from a lot of people." Unfortunately, many of the institutional support networks were not as effective as they should have been. Mayer recalled that "the first six months or so, I was on my own in terms of trying to get help and . . . coordinate the surgeries and everything like that. . . . I had home health care. . . . I didn't have anyone who was . . . trying to manage everything. I wish I had."

It was common for participants to discuss thoughts, feelings, and experiences with one or more individuals, often other victims' family members or survivors. But talking with the wrong people could be a painful and disruptive experience. Ernestine Hill Clark was very careful with whom she discussed her experiences: "I learned really early on that first year not to discuss it with anybody except survivors and family members. . . . Not my family, but [my] memorial family." Diane Dooley, who formed her own support network of survivors, explained: "As time went on, there was still people that were so stuck in it and so I had to form my own little group of, there were three of us that I could call if I was having a bad day. They were all survivors, . . . [and] we could be truthful with each other and frank about things that were appearing in the media."

Ties to spiritual organizations, whether new, renewed, or continued, were also sources of support and comfort. For Diane Dooley, a return to spiritual roots and the discovery of newfound spiritual support networks were of great assistance: "I started going to a different church that had been damaged in the bombing. . . . as they rebuilt, I was a new member in the church and . . . I sort of felt like I was healing along with them. . . . my focus became getting that spiritual part of my life back, and putting McVeigh in his place." Prayer also comforted family member Robin Brown, whose father, Robert Westberry, the Special Agent in charge at the Department of Defense and Investigative Services in the Murrah Building, was near retirement when he was murdered in the bombing. She stressed the importance of "a lot of prayer because there's no other way that we would have got through this without praying."

Sometimes the best listener was a therapist or counselor. "I used to believe that counseling is a waste of time," recalled Ray Washburn. But Washburn soon found that his counselor was tremendously supportive: "She helped me get McVeigh more or less out of my mind as she could. She talked to me. She let me sit there and talk all I wanted. And she listened. You've got to find somebody that will listen to you. . . . And the counselor told me the best thing to do is talk it out."

"Family, Faith, and Friends": Compartmentalizing McVeigh's Toxic Presence

Erecting emotional and mental barriers to separate one's self from McVeigh and his actions was also critical. One effective method was to compartmentalize McVeigh, "repackaging" him and his conduct so as to waste less emotional energy and space. The first step toward compartmentalizing McVeigh was learning to concentrate on "the bigger picture"—broadening one's focus beyond the bombing and its perpetrators. "It's easy to put McVeigh and Nichols where they belong when you've got a bigger picture," Diane Dooley stated. "[Getting that spiritual part of my life back] was like a wake-up call. . . . there's a bigger reason and a bigger purpose and then you can sort of start figuring out, okay, I hated that it happened to me, but what good can I have come out of it?" Dooley regarded McVeigh as an object to take out and "play with" every once in a while, but was always careful to put him back where he belonged—"not front and center in my existence."

It was also possible to establish physical barriers between one's self and McVeigh by "tuning out" media coverage that was more upsetting than informative. Richard Williams saw his relationship with the media as a matter of choice; not only did he have the "choice to read newspapers, read magazines, watch television," but he could also elect to grant media interviews. But sometimes participants felt that attaining distance from the bombing as an event was not in their best interests. At such times, the best way to proceed was not to "tune out" media coverage but to "tune in," consuming information in an attempt to understand the bombing. Vicki Hamm found that "tuning in," not compartmentalizing, actually helped her to manage McVeigh's presence: "I was trying to understand it, and it's something that can never be understood. But I didn't know that at the time, and I thought learning as much as I could about it would help me find some sense of peace."

Another way to erect boundaries between one's self and McVeigh and the bombing was to redirect energy to other activities or projects. Faith Moore tried "not to dwell on it" and "tried to spend more time in Bible study . . . to help me deal with all that I was feeling." Other participants erected boundaries by taking advantage of volunteer opportunities created by the bombing. Seeking for some productive way to help, Dr. Paul Heath was "asked to take on the responsibility of speaking for the Veterans Administration" and recalled that he was "more active and more productive [then] than any period in my life that first three months after the bombing." Doris Jones was involved with both the Oklahoma City National Memorial and efforts to reform death penalty appeals. Participants who joined such groups not only accomplished formidable reconstructive tasks but also met other family members and survivors who provided invaluable support. As Jones explained:

> I got involved with [the memorial] initially because I wanted Carrie's baby counted. . . . And it took me to being with other people who were in my same shoes. . . . I found people that had worked with Carrie and knew Carrie, and you know, that was what I put all my effort in[to] for a long time. . . . Anytime there was any kind of a committee, I wanted to be on it, I just got totally wrapped up in that. And I was able to talk to people about Carrie and wanted people to know who she was.

Diane Leonard also found that working to reform death penalty appeals processes fostered a renewed sense of control: "When your life is changed without any input from you, you have no control. . . . I needed to find a way to start pulling some of that control of my life back into my hands. I needed to know there was something I could do. I just couldn't sit around and do nothing."

It was optimal for participants to draw support from a variety of sources to counter McVeigh's presence, denying him the additional victories of further victimization and control over their emotions, thoughts, and lives. McVeigh's perceived control over thoughts and emotions was precisely what made his toxic presence so invidious and inequitable. Janet Beck explained, "I don't feel like one person should have that kind of control over other people's lives." Richard Williams dealt with McVeigh and his actions by focusing on "the three F's, the family, faith, and friends, the work, all those kind of things became primary, not secondary to McVeigh and the bombing. Even though it all involved it in some way." Williams greatly appreciated each of these outlets because each "could help me think about something that was more important than focusing on him and what he had done and how he had affected us. To me that was important to not, again to not let him, not let that be a part of what he accomplished."

"Always Secondary": Nichols's Unwelcome Presence

Given the correlation between an offender's presence and his criminal activity, it would have been peculiar for McVeigh to be a toxic presence while Nichols and Fortier were not. These perpetrators were also presences, but in ways qualitatively different from McVeigh. Most participants felt that Nichols was a toxic presence, albeit less invasive. In many ways, Nichols seemed to be McVeigh's foil. Participants characterized him as diminutive; Peggy Broxterman termed him a "sniveling, shivering low-life" and a "follower" who "didn't do much thinking" but was "just told what to do and did it." "He was just a sad little man," said Dot Hill, "he was just a tool." Doris Jones termed him "kind of a wimpy guy" and "a coward. . . . He didn't want to do the act, but he certainly supported it."

Participants often described Nichols by contrasting him with McVeigh. "The impression I got from Nichols was not . . . the same as McVeigh in terms of who he was, what he was about, how strong he was, how determined he was, how unremorseful he was," explained Richard Williams. "He was different." Peggy Broxterman said that Nichols, unlike McVeigh, was a "loser": "McVeigh was disappointed so many different times, but he had more potential because he had some brains. But Terry was just a nothing." "I don't think that he had McVeigh's motivation or mental capacity," asserted Stan Mayer. "I'm not trying to give credit to McVeigh for anything, but I just think that he [Nichols] was just a lower intellect, . . . disgusting in a somewhat different way. Because he just went along with things. You know, he was manipulated by McVeigh." Nichols was also generally regarded as less committed to the conspiracy than McVeigh. Diane Dooley noted that his demeanor was very different, "more passive and not quite the stoic soldier kind of attitude like McVeigh had." Doris Jones affirmed that Nichols "wasn't as bold and piercing because he wouldn't look at you, where McVeigh did." Germaine Johnston thought of Nichols as "more level-headed," and Susan Urbach noted that "Nichols was more in . . . the mainstream and then got weird. In that he was married." Richard Williams characterized Nichols as "almost scared," adding, "I felt like he . . . got caught, he didn't want to get caught and he didn't know what to do when he got caught." Nor did Nichols appear to seek the limelight as McVeigh did. "He wasn't the outspoken type, he wasn't on TV, radio, wasn't in magazines all the dang time," recalled Paul Howell. Ray Washburn opined, "I don't think that Nichols wanted the attention like McVeigh did, although he was involved. I think he just happened to be there and just got caught."

Participants disagreed on the significance of Nichols's role in the bombing. Some believed that McVeigh, as the one who "lit the fuse," was more culpable. "McVeigh is the only one that we know for sure that actually came down here with the truck and blew the truck up. And so, he [Nichols] was not as important in my eyes," Paul Howell explained. Ray Washburn thought that "McVeigh was an influence on these others." Others believed Nichols to be just as culpable as McVeigh, or even that he manipulated McVeigh. "[Nichols] was the person more culpable in this whole deal," emphasized Charlie Younger:

> He is the one that bought the fertilizer, he's the one that stole the guns . . . and got Fortier to sell them to raise the funds. He's the one that knew how to mix the bomb [and] . . . went out there with McVeigh to mix the bomb. He brought him to Oklahoma to stash his getaway car. . . . He was in every piece of it but one minor one and that's renting the Ryder truck. . . . it couldn't have happened without him. . . . He . . . probably was the smarter one. And McVeigh was just angry and wanted to get back at the government because of Waco.

Survivor Tom Hall, who worked for the GSA on the first floor of the Murrah Building, was severely injured in the blast; his hand was crushed, his jugular vein was severed, and he suffered from a closed head injury, lacerations from glass, and electrocution. Hall was off work for 19 months and endured many surgeries and extensive physical therapy. He felt that Nichols manipulated McVeigh, explaining: "He was older and I kind of thought of him as more of a mentor or more influential on McVeigh," who "was just the gullible, younger person easily influenced by his elders, you know, especially in that military follow-your-orders state of mind. . . . They pumped him up, go do this, go do this, damn government you know, . . . and he was gullible enough to do it." Participants also noted that Nichols, unlike McVeigh, had been raised in a family with strong antigovernment beliefs. Janet Beck found it disturbing that Nichols's ideology was "more of a lifelong thing" and believed that his family "still believed in his cause . . . was a lot more upsetting than just him personally." She took the Nichols family's ideology personally: "I felt [it was] more like an invasion of my ideals, my thoughts, that it was against my employer . . . he was basically saying that everything I had done as far as the career was worthless."

In contrast to McVeigh, participants differed as to whether and to what extent Nichols was an intrusive presence. While some participants sensed Nichol's presence, others were aware of it but believed it to be less intense than McVeigh's. Still other participants experienced Nichols's presence only at certain times, and a few never felt it at all.

Most felt that Nichols was an intrusive presence. Doris Jones emphasized that Nichols "absolutely was" a presence, since he "certainly came into my life" and was "very unwelcome." Stan Mayer linked Nichols's presence to the fact that he had had a "catastrophic impact" on Mayer's life. For Dr. Paul Heath, Nichols's presence was similar to McVeigh's: "It's really hard to separate, for me, those two." Like McVeigh's, Nichols's presence was aggravated by certain factors such as media coverage or the fact that Nichols was still alive. Diane Leonard emphasized that: "I still have little intrusions, like I got an e-mail recently [about] a news article where he had complained about his—diet, you know, it's unreal the effect that has on you. . . . It has a huge effect on me." Like others, Peggy Broxterman connected Nichols's presence to his life sentence: "He was [a presence], uh-huh. Just by being alive. Still is just because he's alive."

A handful of participants felt Nichols's presence only at certain times. Survivor Germaine Johnston, for instance, "never thought about" Nichols "except right around the times when I had to go testify [at his trial], and, you know, then it was just because I didn't want to go be involved and there would be quite a bit more media coverage." And a few never experienced it at all; Ernestine Hill Clark speculated that "it might have been just utter exhaustion from having gone through so much with McVeigh": "At a point you reach overload.... I was the rawest at the time that the stuff was going on with McVeigh and I was continuing to work really hard on putting the puzzle pieces together, trying to heal." By the time that Nichols was in the limelight, Clark recalled, "I was starting to do some healing."

"A 25-Cent Coin": Fortier's Unwelcome Presence

On the morning of April 19, 1995, Michael Fortier, at home in Kingman, Arizona, was the suspect farthest away in terms of geography and commitment to the conspiracy. Nonetheless, Fortier still knew of McVeigh's plans and did not report them to authorities. Participants felt Michael Fortier and his wife were toxic presences, albeit not as strong as McVeigh and Nichols. Doris Jones explained that Fortier was "not an afterthought, but he was just kind of back there, I just didn't get that involved with that one." "It didn't make me quite as sick seeing him as it did Nichols," recalled Stan Mayer. Fortier also engendered less negative reactions from participants than McVeigh or Nichols. Tom Hall stated that, at his sentencing, Fortier "wasn't as stone-cold as McVeigh" and thought he "maybe...had a little bit of remorse," but acknowledged that he was "probably wanting to be agreeable and everything...if he's a nice guy and everything, you know, sentencing might go better." Nonetheless, Hall still characterized Fortier as a "coward" for not reporting the conspiracy to authorities. Diane Dooley felt her anger toward Fortier melt when he apologized at his sentencing hearing: "It's just another step towards, okay, he's human just like the rest of us and never truly believed he was going to do it and . . . I got a sense that he did truly feel some remorse."

Unlike McVeigh and Nichols, Fortier likely participated in the conspiracy for reasons other than (or in addition to) antigovernment sentiment; many participants believed that his youth and vices partially explained his involvement. His drug use may have weakened him, making him a tool for McVeigh and Nichols to manipulate, and desperation for drug money could provide another motive for joining the conspiracy besides antigovernment sentiment. "He was dealing dope and stuff like that, and I thought, well that's how they got him in it real easy," opined Charlie Younger. Nonetheless, these factors did not answer the question on most participants' minds, namely, why

Fortier did not report the bombing. Dooley explained that Fortier "was the target of my anger for a long time," since "it was easier to be mad at Fortier than it was to be mad at McVeigh. Because, you know, you could just say, well you should have warned everybody." Janet Beck took this as a sign of Fortier's extreme indifference, even arrogance, to others' needs: "He kind of felt like he was better than us, that it was all just a big joke to him and that . . . it's almost like nobody was as important as he was to have wasted his time, to take his time up to try to do anything to stop it."

As the conspirator who was ostensibly least involved and least ideologically committed, one might expect Fortier to have the weakest presence. Participants differed in their assessments of Fortier's presence, with its strength directly correlated to what degree participants felt he was involved in the bombing. Surprisingly, what constituted "involvement" varied from participant to participant. Whereas Charlie Younger emphasized that Fortier "never was directly involved with the bombing at all. It was all more money and guns," Richard Williams espoused a broader view, intimating that "direct involvement" entailed knowledge of the conspiracy. A few believed that Fortier's presence had a major impact on their lives because of the ease with which he could have reported the bombing plans to law enforcement, potentially thwarting the entire plot. Dr. Paul Heath emphasized that it was a "tremendous intrusion" because Fortier "could have reported it and didn't. . . . A 25-cent coin could have prevented all of this." Dot Hill felt more of a presence from Fortier than she did from Nichols: "He [Fortier] evoked the second strongest emotion of anger . . . [b]ecause he had absolutely 100 percent knowledge and did nothing." But, for most, Fortier's presence cast a weaker shadow because of his diminished involvement. Diane Dooley felt Fortier's presence "even less than Nichols's because he's not the one that drove the truck and parked it and lit it and—he's further removed from the actual going through with it." "It was different in the sense that he played a secondary role in the crime," explained Charlie Younger. "I just didn't feel like he was as responsible as the other two."

Participants also credited other factors, including Fortier's low media profile, for this weakened presence. Stan Mayer said simply, "I just hadn't thought a lot about him, I don't hear a lot about him, and [he] hadn't really been in my mind." It was almost as if an offender's media visibility triggered his presence. "I didn't feel that on him like I did the others. . . . I guess just because there wasn't as much coverage on him," noted Tom Hall. "They would kind of use him as fodder when I guess there wasn't a story to be had on the other two."

Paul Howell attributed Fortier's diminished presence both to the lack of media coverage and to his cooperation with law enforcement:

> We knew when he was arrested within a short period of time that he was going to testify against both of them and there was really not that much information, TV, radio, newspapers, or anything on Fortier. . . . So I just kind of dropped him out of my mind and I think everybody else did too. . . . He resurfaced at the trial and it was just a very short period of time. Most generally he wasn't on the stand more than a couple hours. So, you don't really get a good impression on who he was. . . . I don't think he ever was [a presence] for the simple reason that I knew that he was testifying against McVeigh and Nichols. And so he wasn't a threat to us in any way.

Lori Fortier also evoked much ire among participants, who were angered that she did not receive any sentence at all. One family member in particular was indignant that she got off so easily, with so much of her life intact:

> She dealt crystal meth and she didn't spend one day in jail. And her presence in the courtroom just, that was probably one of the, that was one of my most difficult days, of here is a mother, she could have picked up the phone and everything would have been changed, and she walks off scot-free. She was a very unwelcome presence in my life. I tried to have her children taken away.

When Absence Makes the Heart Grow Fonder

The strength and physical, psychological, and emotional effects of the Oklahoma City bombers' toxic presences on participants were dependent upon several related factors. An offender's degree of involvement in the bombing plot was a crucial influence upon that offender's intrusive presence. The more involved the offender, the more responsibility fell upon his shoulders, the stronger his presence, and the more profound its impact. But there was another dimension to an offender's involvement—ease of disaffiliation or disentanglement. If an offender could have easily reported the plot but chose not to act, then this greatly amplified an otherwise weak presence. An offender's personality was also a key ingredient in his toxic presence, with a defiant, remorseless personality intensifying the presence, and a tentative, cowardly, cooperative, or remorseful demeanor diminishing it. Finally, an offender's media visibility also affected the power of his toxic presence, with heightened visibility rendering a presence more potent. Significantly, McVeigh's presence was regarded as the most poisonous and pervasive; he had lit the fuse, claimed to have masterminded the plot, appeared taciturn and remorseless, and was extraordinarily visible in the news media. In contrast, Nichols's and Fortier's very different degrees of involvement, personalities, and visibilities meant that their presences were less powerful.

Once family members and survivors were confronted with these various presences, they faced a series of choices. One could continue to live with these specters or confront them in an attempt at exorcism. Both options were not only uncomfortable but intensely painful, as well as impermanent. Time continues to revisit culturally traumatic events in cyclical fashion, with personal and external calendars tracking and commemorating birthdays and anniversaries of murderous events and murdered individuals. Offenders' presences, then, were unquiet ghosts that could be purged for a brief spell before seeping back through the cracks in a victim's permeable and perpetually vulnerable consciousness.

3

Opening Up "Closure"

Redefining a Controversial Term

Because they disturbed, inflamed, and frustrated family members and survivors, the Oklahoma City bombers' toxic presences commenced and compelled a quest for "closure." The application of this term in the Oklahoma City context raised a host of other issues, in particular the controversial assertion that McVeigh's execution would provide closure by soothing victims' troubled souls.

When the news broke in April 2001 that U.S. Attorney General John Ashcroft would allow family members and survivors in Oklahoma City to view McVeigh's impending execution via closed-circuit television, the question of whether the execution would provide closure was on everyone's mind. Media outlets exchanged headline volleys in a confusing war of words, with some headlines proclaiming that victims would "seek catharsis"[1] and "closure"[2] and that the execution would "bring closure,"[3] and others retorting that it would give McVeigh "a platform for hate,"[4] that "seeing McVeigh die may have a cost,"[5] and that his death would enable victims to "get closure but not comfort."[6] Victims' family members and survivors scarcely mentioned the term in media interviews, instead reporting they felt "satisfaction," that they no longer had to "serve [their] own sentence," and that, in the books of their lives, they had come to the "last page" of the bombing volume.[7]

It is essential to examine how those most intimately affected by the search for meaning—victims' family members and survivors—define closure and attempt to achieve it. Participants' remarks reveal that the pursuit of closure is actually "memory work," an interactive process by which individual family members and survivors construct meaningful narratives of the bombing and its impact upon their lives, and how they have moved on, dealt with, adjusted to, or healed from this culturally traumatic event. Closure is a process, not a destination, a recursive series of adjustments that involves both intrapersonal and interpersonal communicative aspects. This view of closure as a strategic, sense-making process suggests that much of what is commonly thought about closure is misplaced or inaccurate.

Closure and the Cultural Status of the Crime Victim

Ubiquitous in contemporary discourse, the term "closure" is laden with social, political, and cultural capital. Of particular interest is the extent to which closure is identified with capital punishment, the idea that victims' families require a death sentence or execution to heal. But closure has not always been tied to this context; before 1989, the term was never mentioned by the media in conjunction with the death penalty, and in that year, the terms were used together only once.[8] Beginning in 1993, however, the frequency with which closure was identified with the death penalty grew exponentially to 500 times in 2001, when an ABC News/Washington Post poll found that 60 percent of respondents strongly or moderately agreed with the statement that the death penalty was fair because it gave closure to murder victims' family members.[9]

Closure's cultural appeal is undoubtedly magnified when it is coupled with the cultural figure of the crime victim that for some time has maintained a tenacious hold on the American public imagination. The current interest in victims and their pursuit of closure is a fairly recent development, rooted in and responsive to the pronounced focus on criminal defendants and their constitutional rights that marked the Warren Court era, from 1953 to 1969.[10] America's embrace of crime victims has also been greatly enhanced by the victims' rights movement, which has extolled the "swift and severe punishment" of perpetrators as "the best remedy for the causes and effects of victimization."[11] From this perspective, crime is a transaction in which the perpetrator must pay what he owes to society *and* to the victim by serving his criminal sentence. With the victim as its moral anchor, the prosecution's pursuit of the perpetrator is based upon his infringement upon individual victims' autonomy and dignity.[12]

In 1991, the U.S. Supreme Court ruled in *Payne v. Tennessee*[13] that murder victims' family members could deliver victim impact testimony at sentencing. Since then, closure has become an especially popular topic in criminal law, and new participative opportunities have been extended to victims' families, symbolizing a legal shift in focus to more therapeutic ends.[14]

Emphasizing that the victim need not be a "faceless stranger,"[15] the Supreme Court majority remarked that murder "transforms a living person with hopes, dreams, and fears into a corpse, thereby taking away all that is special and unique about the person. The Constitution does not preclude a State from deciding to give some of that back."[16] Justice Scalia, concurring, opined that it was absurd that "a crime's unanticipated consequences must be deemed 'irrelevant' to the sentence," and that the court's former holdings "conflict[ed] with a public sense of justice keen enough that it has found voice in a nationwide 'victims' rights' movement."[17] Contemporary courts perceive closure as many things: a procedural goal, with victims' families having interests in finality; an entitlement for victims' families, with relatives, like defendants, deserving a timely trial and punishment; and a therapeutic aspiration, preventing victims from being overlooked and ensuring inclusion of their perspectives.[18]

In the decades since *Payne*, asserted closure needs have come to overlap with criminal proceedings, encompassing family members' desires to memorialize and vindicate the victim by attaining a guilty verdict and appropriate punishment. Capital trials, culminating in death sentences, impose a unique accountability that in turn confirms a victim's intrinsic worth and human dignity and demonstrates the tragedy of her loss. Many victims' relatives believe that invoking the victim's name in capital proceedings is not merely a tribute to the victim but is compelled by the horrific nature of the crime. Victim impact statements are purportedly therapeutic and empowering.[19] The cultural recognition of victims' emotional recovery as a moral imperative gives weight to victims' claims that space must be made for them and their stories in the courtroom. To these ends, the criminal justice process has rhetorically embraced closure, rendering it an independent justification for the death penalty, victim impact testimony, and increasingly limited procedural protections for condemned defendants.[20]

Finally, representations of the criminal justice system in contemporary popular culture provide further evidence that victims, their emotionality, and their therapeutic needs are properly part of the "justice" process. Courtroom dramas captivate audiences with (melo)dramatic yet seemingly realistic portrayals of empowered fictional victims, sowing the seeds for a cultural connection between courtrooms, therapy, and victims. Television trials may produce what legal scholar Richard Sherwin terms "hyper-catharsis," "a spectacle that masks rather than reveals unconscious impulses and the fantasies they produce" and "exploits images—of victims and aggressors alike—for the sake of their emotional payoff."[21] Back in the real world, victims' family members interviewed in the news media often claim to experience closure from trials and executions, providing "affirmative proof" that such events are in fact cathartic and promote healing and provide closure.[22]

It is easy to see why closure has retained such popular appeal. It reflects the notion that legal processes have social consequences beyond adjudication, which can offer victims and their families finality, catharsis, peace, relief, satisfaction, and a sense of justice. But its use is deeply contested. Most bombing victims despised the term, deeming it a fictional state, a mere media buzzword. When pushed specifically to define closure, family members and survivors often noted it was synonymous with therapeutic concepts such as "healing" or "coping" and also spoke of specific activities that contributed to healing. The term spawns heated debates about victims' proper role in legal proceedings and punishment, with some commentators asserting that these events are therapeutic for victims, providing powerful opportunities for vindication, catharsis, censure, and healing, and others arguing that such considerations have no place in criminal law, which is ill-suited to effectuate them in light of criminal defendants' constitutional rights.[23] As a final straw, closure's semantics render it difficult to empirically grasp.[24]

It is simplistic to regard closure merely as an individual's attempts to heal, or as a solely therapeutic concept. Such definitions do not even begin to address the difficult private, social, and even political struggles that family members and survivors encountered in the bombing's wake. Rather, closure must reflect family members' and survivors' need to confront, grapple with, wrest control from, and ultimately overcome perpetrators who suddenly become significant and terrible figures in their lives through their involvement in the bombing. It must embody the extreme effort of learning to tell the story of the bombing, and its immediate and long-term consequences. It must convey the challenge of learning to live with new, gaping, painful holes in one's life. Finally, it must articulate the arduous labor of pulling together a new self-identity, the yearning to move from victim to survivor.

"There Is No Closure": Family Members' and Survivors' Reflections

How did family members and survivors themselves regard closure and describe the coping process? Participants described at least two definitions of closure, finality and coping. In mass media and popular culture, closure refers to a sense of absolute finality, or "getting over it," which interviewees asserted does not exist. Closure can also denote coping with, comprehending, or contextualizing murder; participants believed that this form of closure was possible to attain, and many acknowledged experiencing it.

The pop-culture conception of closure as absolute finality has poisoned most family members' and survivors' opinion of the term; the overwhelming majority of victims emphasized that this closure stereotype never occurs. Charlie Younger remarked, "I think things get better and get worse, but as long as a person's alive and they have the state of mind that they can remember things, there's never closure." Survivor Edmund Tarver, who lived outside Oklahoma, had flown in to attend a business meeting in the offices of the Federal Highway Administration and was on the Murrah Building's fourth floor at the time of the blast. Tarver termed closure a "dirty word that should be stricken from grief dictionaries." Susan Urbach characterized it as "a word often used by people who probably haven't had anything big to go through," and Bud Welch dubbed closure a "media word" and a "buzz term."

The mass media, however, were not the only parties at fault; bombing victims also blamed others' expectations that time would heal emotional wounds sooner rather than later. Charlie Younger connected a dislike of closure to others' expectation that "people should get over it" within a certain period of time.[25] Stan Mayer was disturbed by others' anticipations that things soon would be "fine."[26] Sometimes participants' frustration with closure paralleled their dislike of therapeutic language, such as assurances that certain behaviors were "normal." Priscilla Salyers noted, "I hate it [closure], I hate it, everybody hates it. As much as we hate the word normal. . . . New normal is okay, but you know, when you were going through all the grief and the depression and you can't focus and you don't know where you left your car, oh, that's normal. Well, if this is normal, I don't wanna be normal."

Such unrealistic expectations of closure could be damaging. "A lot of people think they're going to get it, and they don't then and they're upset," survivor Taylor Rickel observed. Bud Welch also asserted that closure had become an improper justification for the death penalty:

> I can see now the horrible lies that are told to . . . victims' family members by prosecutors that are otherwise good people, . . . educated people, . . . about how that they need to get the death penalty for this guy so that they can have some type of closure and like if we bring you his dead body, you are going to feel much better about the loss of your son or daughter.

Others, however, regarded closure as a synonym for justice. Robin Brown explained, "When you see people on TV going, we just want closure, I think what they really want, I think they want justice. I don't think it's closure."

Participants were adamant, therefore, that closure could never occur because what was lost could never be regained. Edmund Tarver opted to define closure as the comfort of life before loss: "How can I terminate or end the pain that goes along with how you miss that person. . . . somehow to get over that pain and you know have that comfort that I knew before, but I know that's not ever going to come." Many observed that closure would only come with death. Family member Angela Richerson's mother, Norma Jean Johnson, was an executive secretary with the Defense Investigative Services on the third floor of the Murrah Building who was murdered in the bombing. She stressed, "I hate the word closure. . . . there won't be closure till I am dead."

With no possibility for closure this side of the grave, participants had to adjust to the knowledge that their identities were fundamentally changed, and that they would have to live with the event. "It's a part of you just like every good thing [that] happened. . . . It never goes away," explained Diane Leonard. Doris Jones described the inability to ignore memories of the bombing through a particularly apt analogy: "There is no closure. It's like a chain or a bracelet or a ring, it's all one. And when you take a piece out of it . . . that piece is gone. So it'll never be complete. . . . So there is no such thing as closure, but you can come to terms with it."

Participants would often qualify a statement that there was no closure with the observation that they had learned to "deal with it." Dr. Paul Heath noted, "I don't think there is such a thing as closure. There is such a thing as coming to live with the experience, the traumatic experience, in your own unique way." Survivor Lane Wharton explicitly rejected a definition of closure as absolute finality in favor of a more workable explanation as coping: "To me closure is just coming to grips I guess in my own mind with what has happened and being able to cope with what happened." Vicki Hamm believed that people often used closure to refer to inner peace: "I think what they mean is they found a peacefulness about living with what happened to them. And I found that."

Coping behaviors included comprehending the event and placing it in context beside other life events. Germaine Johnston opined, "I think that closure means you come to a point where you understand it, and it seems like it's more or less a certain point. A closure point." Family member Jordan Holt asserted that closure meant placing the bombing into context along with relatives' birthdays and other goings-on: "I decided consciously that the rest of my life wasn't gonna be defined by the bombing, if I wrote an autobiography it would be in there, but it would be perhaps a chapter, and I might refer to it throughout the rest of the book from time to time, but it wouldn't be my defining moment." Holt's observation reflects a very common theme of compartmentalization, echoed by Ernestine Hill Clark:

> You close off certain sections of your life and maybe in a way it is like a set of encyclopedias that's "x" number of volumes long and you finish this one book and you shut that one book, but it's not that easy. You're going on to other chapters and they're all interwoven together and sometimes you slip back to the beginning of the first one again for a little while then come over to the fifth.

Participants' ability to compartmentalize the bombing was likely to be triggered by external goings-on such as legal proceedings, with individuals prioritizing different moments. For Diane Dooley, McVeigh's guilty verdict marked a personal "end" to proceedings: "I remember sobbing when they read the guilty verdict, just because it was just such a sense of 'okay, it's done.' For me it was done. . . . I don't want to say closure, but I got a huge, I mean I moved very fast-forward." Priscilla Salyers noted that McVeigh's death formed the conclusion of her bombing chapter: "Once he was executed, that chapter was over. I could go on with something else in my life." Vicki Hamm found that the opening of the Oklahoma City Bombing National Memorial aroused similar feelings:

> I've often told the story the way I felt when the memorial opened that day, on April 19, 2000. And when I walked down the steps I could feel . . . something being lifted from me. And I felt lighter and I felt relief. . . . I could describe it as I had been wearing an overcoat for five years and had all these feelings of depression, anger, sadness, guilt, despair. All these things I'd been carrying for five years. And now I had a place to hang that overcoat and leave those feelings there. I didn't need to carry them with me anymore.

Time, measured in years, seemed to be the biggest aid in coping, contextualizing, and compartmentalizing the bombing. Edmund Tarver observed: "If healing is a good word, it's just the passage of time dulls the pain that you felt." Other life accomplishments could also be reconstructive. Tom Hall noted that "you get to a point, I guess where you're satisfied with the way you feel, I guess, whether it's get remarried or . . . maybe had another kid, or you get to a point, I think, where hopefully you felt like you put it at rest." Upon establishing a temporal and emotional distance from the bombing, participants sometimes pointed to positive changes and specific reasons to remember what had occurred. Lane Wharton remarked, "It was bad and it was horrible and I don't ever want to forget it. . . . I want to remember . . . because it was an important part of my life. It was something that made me what I am but I'd like to move on from it too."

Notably absent from these remarks is reflection on what popular culture asserts should be the "lived experience" of closure—the act of holding a suspect accountable that ostensibly motivates victims' families to attend trials, give victim impact testimony, and witness executions. With the exception of a few interviewees who discussed McVeigh's execution as a moment of closure, not one defined closure explicitly as coping or healing through testimony or execution witnessing. Instead, at other points in the interview, participants spoke of a duty or responsibility to testify, and of a personal "need" to see that justice was done connected to a desire to see McVeigh held accountable for his actions. This does not indicate that participation in legal proceedings was not tied to closure, but instead demonstrates that legal proceedings in and of themselves did not define the boundaries of the closure process. Legal proceedings both created new duties—a duty to self or a beloved victim to attend legal proceedings or witness McVeigh's execution—and provided a venue in which those duties could be satisfied. Interviewees also felt a desire to participate somehow in the process of seeking to hold McVeigh accountable. For participants, closure most often necessitated some involvement in legal proceedings through testifying in open court, attending trials, or attending McVeigh's execution.

Closure, Cultural Trauma, and the Journey from Victim to Survivor

The quest for closure must be precipitated by an extraordinarily harrowing event such as the Oklahoma City bombing, one that resounds in such disturbing ways that it is what communication studies scholar Barbie Zelizer terms a "hot moment"—"a moment through which a society or culture assesses its significance . . . by air[ing], challeng[ing], and negotiat[ing] their own standards of action."[27] Indeed, these occurrences are "culturally traumatic" for the communities in which they occur. This use of "trauma" piggybacks upon psychological and psychoanalytic definitions of the term, describing an incident that so profoundly shocks and distresses a community that it inflicts lasting injuries to its social and cultural relations. For individuals, trauma elicits an experience of emotional anguish akin to a physical wound.[28] According to cultural sociologist Jeffrey Alexander, cultural trauma is explicitly trauma of *culture* and so resonates in a collective's values, norms, expectations, roles, mores, morals, myths, and definitions.[29] It is these cultural lesions that heal the slowest.[30]

Culturally traumatic events are often violent incidents in which some communal residents are killed and others suffer severe mental and physical injuries. Recognizing an event as culturally traumatic is a communal first step toward addressing a profoundly painful event by pinpointing the event's cause and assigning moral responsibility for it.[31] In this way, collectives—special groups of people who choose to join together on the basis of some shared experience, understanding, or identity—formulate and reaffirm communal bonds of camaraderie that allow them to acknowledge and even partake in others' pain and suffering.[32]

An event becomes recognized as culturally traumatic through a claims-making process in which a certain group claims to have suffered an injury and requests "emotional, institutional, and symbolic" recompense.[33] Individuals must convey what happened that was allegedly traumatic, whom the allegedly traumatic event affected, the relation of the trauma victim to the wider community, and who was responsible for the trauma.[34] Family members and survivors, particularly those who joined advocacy groups, participated in this claims-making process in the months and years after the Oklahoma City bombing and soon learned that trauma claims-making was extensively mediated by institutions, including the news media and criminal justice system.

After a claims-making process legitimizes an event such as the Oklahoma City bombing as culturally traumatic, new narratives establish what that event has come to mean to a community in terms of its identity and legacy. The event is thereby incorporated into a community's life history and is no longer seen as a liminal incident out of time and out of place; its moral and historical meaning(s) become fixed in monuments and museums, where they can be accessed and shared by future generations.[35] Finally, those intimately involved with the event are accorded "victim" or "survivor" status, with its myriad material and cultural implications.

But trauma itself is not only something that happens to a collective but also a contemporary cultural phenomenon. As an umbrella term encompassing diverse mental, emotional, and physical experiences, trauma enjoys a pervasive presence in popular culture,[36] suffused with semantic tension between clinical and nonclinical usages and between the personal and vicarious experience of pain. Our fascination with cultural trauma has expanded expressive and emotive norms and boundaries; the private has become public, and it has become acceptable to comfortably talk about an ever-diverse array of formerly confidential events and experiences.[37] With a cultural emphasis on trauma have come a therapeutic ethos and a discourse of recovery that emphasizes the need to "recover" from trauma by reducing it to a coherent narrative. Traumatized individuals are advised to confront and work through their trauma in order to shape memories into narratives and share these narratives with others.[38] This therapeutic cultural climate positions emotional well-being as a right of all Americans.

At the heart of both the trauma maelstrom and therapeutic discourse are victims—those who live through traumatic experiences, as well as "those who suffer with them, or through them, or for them, if only by reading about trauma."[39] Victims' suffering may merit clinical diagnoses, including post-traumatic stress disorder and homicide trauma syndrome, composed of grief, bereavement, fear, rage, horror, desire for revenge, and depression. Such labels are attached to victims so that they might benefit from therapeutic processes and "recover," eventually transcending victimization and emerging as survivors.

Trauma discourse reveals the profound cultural tensions between who we expect victims to be, and who we expect them to become. Victims who are powerless to prevent or overcome their victimization do not comport with American ideals of self-sufficiency, dedication, and circumspect appraisal.[40] The ideal of the "true" victim reflects an emotionally and psychologically resilient person who refuses to stew in the experience of victimhood.[41] Victims who stay victims are criticized for being trapped in the past or maintaining glum and cynical outlooks; those who overcome their victimization are "forward-looking, energetic, functional, and optimistic."[42] The term "survivor" is imbued with hope and confers respectability upon victims by highlighting their ability to successfully cope with the traumatic event, celebrating emotional (and moral) progress.[43] If emotional well-being is perceived to be an entitlement, emotional recovery is culturally constructed as a moral imperative.

One of the paths to survivorhood—the return to well-being—is through storytelling, and victims' accounts are often regarded not only as therapy but as testimony, a public form of narrative to which one can only respond in kind and which to some degree precludes argument and analysis.[44] Testimonies may be deemed sacred and therefore unassailable; there is a sense that such personal pain speaks for itself and that one should not retraumatize victims by scrutinizing or probing their claims.[45] Indeed, some have criticized victim narratives out of concern that they may silence other voices that deserve to be heard, and because they might not be open to debate or negotiation.[46]

Reassessing Closure

In the context of the Oklahoma City bombing, closure is highly personal and far more complicated than overcoming grief and seeking vengeance, and it reveals a great deal about how expectations about what closure is and how it functions should be modified. First, it is essential to regard closure as a cluster concept that includes coping behaviors, not as a state of consummate finality. Second, closure is a phenomenon that exists in both the internal self and the external world. All too often, others situate closure in either the inward-directed context of grief recovery or the outward-directed milieu of seeking vengeance. While closure is primarily an "internal" experience, it is dependent upon institutions and events in the outside world. Developments in the external world—from preliminary events such as the arrest of a suspect or the search for and discovery of a body to later goings-on such as a verdict or execution—prompt the formation of both immediate and long-term internal reactions that range from affective responses to strategic plans. Reactions can be triggered several times a year on "anniversary" dates such as victims' birthdays, holidays, and the dates of legal proceedings. Optimally, victims' families grow more adept at managing their status and its implications over time, rendering closure a process at which victims' families must continually work.

Third, closure is not restricted to grief maintenance or vengeance-seeking behaviors. Instead, it is a balancing act that demands that victims' families simultaneously manage a multitude of concerns such as remembering the victim, representing the victim, channeling emotion into effective outlets, following legal proceedings, insisting on recognition, and moderating outward displays of anger and other emotions. Should any of these spinning plates fall to the ground, the whole act may collapse.

Finally, and most important, the process of closure is communicative. It is in actuality not concerned with effecting a "closing" but instead with creating an "opening"—a broadening of awareness, an expanded engagement with the external environment, a readiness to reencounter life. A communicative theory of closure acknowledges the interplay of the interpersonal and the intrapersonal, the interior of the self and the exterior of the other and the outside world. The search for closure is dependent upon communicative abilities and potencies. Victims' families seek to engage with others, to both speak and be spoken to. We recognize this communicative tendency when we speak of giving victims a "voice" through victim impact testimony.

But it is not enough to note closure's communicative dimensions; we need to push beyond closure's pragmatic qualities and focus more on why certain behaviors contribute to closure and why others do not. How can we account for individuals' choices about how to cope with a culturally traumatic event such as the Oklahoma City bombing, and for the collective impact of these choices? How can we effectively assess the closure effects of diverse behaviors such as joining and attending advocacy groups, media consumption, and participation in legal proceedings?

I contend that such closure behaviors are examples of individual and collective memory work, and that closure is a *memorial* process. Memory work is the process of working through and narrating experiences—in this context, culturally traumatic events.[47] Because it allows individuals to map out and structure traumatic events to better orient themselves after crises, memory work is central to individual and collective identity. If trauma threatens the loss of the self, then memory work enables self-restoration; trauma and closure are two ends of a journey. As such, it is always interpretive and constructive, and concerned with contextualizing—reaching closure on—past events. Memory offers a form and content for addressing the Oklahoma City bombing; it both structures and explains the evolving understandings of the bombing and its perpetrators formed by individuals and groups. Compelled by the nature of trauma itself, which can destroy individual and collective perceptions of normality, memory work is central to processes of recovery or "working through" trauma, potentially necessitating rituals of sense-making, accountability, and restitution such as trials and truth commissions.

Through memory work, individuals gain the distance from a life event that is necessary to understand it, stabilize it, contextualize it, and place it in causal relationships to other life occurrences—to position themselves in relation to that event. Memory work is collective in the sense that individuals share many life events, and collaborative interpretations of these events may evolve as individuals gather and share memories and interpretations; individual perceptions are in turn reshaped by these communal exchanges. Groups may therefore perform memory work by constructing areas of common knowledge that create social bonds between members.

In the Oklahoma City context, forms of remembering were at times individual and at times collective. As participants joined community and advocacy groups early on, collective processes of sense-making were key to narrative reconstruction; as group goals were accomplished and group meetings became less and less frequent or ceased altogether, processes of memory became more and more intrapersonal instead of interpersonal. Now, family members and survivors can foresee the time when the remembering process will transfer to institutional and archival actors and not to individuals; as family members and survivors age and pass on, the Oklahoma City National Memorial will absorb and preserve both their memorial narratives and the artifacts of this memory work.

In analyzing closure in the wake of the Oklahoma City bombing, I document the creation of a specific culture of interpretation and rehabilitation *against a larger national cultural backdrop* that, in the words of Jeffrey Alexander, prompts American citizens to feel "compelled to honor those . . . who have been murdered for an unjust cause."[48] Memories of traumatic events represent an interpretive culture that did not emerge because it "had" to but because it was constructed by its participants and the cumulative effects of their beliefs and actions over time. The national and regional reaction to the Oklahoma City bombing—a spontaneous "hugging" of victims' families and survivors through an outpouring of emotional, financial, and physical support—was not compulsory, but rather the product of a very specific cultural attitude toward innocent crime victims. As Alexander has emphasized, "We do not mourn mass murder unless we have already identified with the victims, and this only happens once in a while, when the symbols are aligned in the right way."[49]

Closure as a Reflexive, Internal Process and as External Intervention

In rebuilding lives and selves, victims' family members have spent much of their lives since the bombing contemplating it and its consequences and taking action. This illustrates how closure is composed of two types of behaviors: reflexivity and intervention. Closure as reflexivity denotes reflective, or thoughtful, behavior; it takes place in an individual's internal psyche, where memory intersects with emotional or imaginative experience.[50] In contrast, closure as intervention consists of external, physical action.

Understanding closure as reflexive behavior necessitates appreciating the interdependent relationship between emotion and memory work. Emotions set our reconstructive agendas and saturate culturally traumatic events.[51] Through memory work, we weather the painful realities of emotions accompanying grief and loss. Memory work is our negotiated response to these feelings, how we wrench *lived* meaning from horrifying experiences. Certain emotions may trigger, challenge, or bolster memory work; sadness is likely to facilitate social bonds through sympathetic or empathetic connections, motivating one to explore the meaning of loss and strategies or processes of adjustment. Fear focuses attention on perceived threats and can trigger self-protective efforts. Anger or injustice can marshal emotional energy into accomplishing key goals. As a communicative lubricant, emotion fosters social sharing; those who experience emotions after a crisis need to share and discuss their feelings with others before they can work through emotional experiences, identify how these events have changed their lives, and enunciate their long-term consequences.[52]

Most important, emotions fulfill a key evaluative function in memory work. Effective memory work necessitates processes of creative judgment—assessing, evaluating, balancing, concluding, stabilizing, and fixing events. Emotions help us to make sense of events and the people and institutions that they affect. We must appraise emotional states, needs, goals, and proprieties before positioning ourselves, others, and institutions as moral subjects, determining whether we—or they—have breached rules governing displays of feeling type and intensity, and with what consequences. Institutions recognize and value emotion in different ways; some are more open to emotion, even fostering highly dramatic exhibitions, while others encourage more reserved affective displays. Emotion enables us to evaluate how various institutions can facilitate memory work and plan accordingly. Just as emotion plays crucial roles in accomplishing memory work, memory work enables the effective expression of emotion—a key component of moral character. We judge another's moral character partially on the basis of his or her expressed emotions and realize that others judge us in this same manner; that is why we comport with sociocultural norms governing emotional display.[53]

Memory work helps victims learn to contextualize and organize emotion by using narrative tools to structure and ultimately tell the story of the murder. The debate over the proper place of victims in criminal proceedings is in actuality a debate over which narratives belong where, implicating two concepts that Peter Brooks has termed "narrative relevance (is the trauma of the surviving family members of a murder victim relevant to the guilt of the defendant?) and narrative closure (are the sequels to murder, in the sufferings of the survivors, part of the murder story?)."[54] Forming a narrative of an event fixes it in a certain form, stabilizing it with definite interpretive consequences.[55] For our purposes, narrative is a form of sense-making that imposes structural constraints upon a series of traumatic events, confirming that a life is progressing and changing and explaining these changes.[56] Narrative order provides coherence in the form of causality, protagonist agency, and continuity, by enunciating connections between sequenced events.[57] This narrative continuity is as important for our interpersonal relations as it is for our intrapersonal relations; introducing ourselves to others entails explaining something of our history, how we got to the present moment in our lives, how we spend our time, and with whom we interact.[58]

The struggle to narrate a traumatic event such as a murder is a struggle to pull together the self that has survived.[59] It helps to establish an appropriate "focal distance" from a tragic experience; if one is too close to the event, it becomes emotionally overwhelming, but if one is too far away, crucial details may be blurred.[60] It facilitates the process of fitting a tragic event into a familiar experiential framework or constructing a new framework. Thus, narrative is as much a tool of self-comprehension as it is of interpersonal understanding.[61] Finally, narrative is a form of communication in which we are all fluent; we engage in meaning-making by forming inferences from others' stories, and in turn telling stories about ourselves.[62] By learning how to narrate the murder, victims exercise narrative agency and thus regain a needed sense of control.[63] In forming a narrative of a tragic event, we whittle away until we have arrived at the experiential story that most ably represents our recollection and recovery process, including salient emotional textures. Emotional "rules of engagement" frame and structure the narratives that we construct through memory work, ensuring that these narratives, as cultural products, will be meaningful to others. Through narrative, we give voice to some emotions and emotive persons and silence others, and include some and exclude others, and emotion assists in these boundary-setting and boundary-maintenance activities.

As memory work, closure is a process of rebuilding, categorizing, and compartmentalizing—all of which are narrative tasks. Yet, closure is more frequently (and mistakenly) associated with grieving than with storytelling.[64] There is no doubt that victims' families grieve for murdered loved ones. However, grieving does not encapsulate the full range of emotional responses that family members experience following a murder. Grieving encompasses relatives' sadness or mourning, but they may also suffer many other emotional and psychological aftershocks, including trauma, simplified moral schemas, a desperate need for information, anger, alienation, and helplessness. These responses are intertwined with grieving behavior, and ameliorating them might assist in the mourning process. But just because these responses overlap with grieving does not mean they are synonymous with such behaviors.

Therefore, focusing on closure as reflexive or thoughtful behavior requires broadening one's analytical focus from grieving to narrativity.

Moreover, relying upon grieving terminology actually has pernicious effects. Regarding victims' families through the lens of grief may set them apart as unhealed and therefore emotionally diseased or even mentally disordered. This in turn prompts coddling reactions, reinforcing family members' powerlessness and further alienating them.[65] But healing requires precisely the opposite of coddling—empowerment through participative opportunities in which family members can fulfill perceived responsibilities to deceased victims, exercise agency, and participate in accountability. Effecting change for victims' families necessitates avoiding measures that inadvertently keep them powerless. In addition, summarizing the emotional state of victims' family members under the category of "grieving" inappropriately widens the perceived gap between these individuals and criminal adjudication. It is much harder to fathom a court playing a role in grief recovery—a task for grief counselors—than it is to envision it restoring some elements of control to victims by affording them some participative opportunities in the criminal justice process. Therefore, redefining closure necessitates broadening the focus on victim behavior from grieving to coping.

Closure as reflexivity allows victims to regain control by working through and creating a narrative of a murder's aftermath, which may well aid them in adjusting to their new status and its implications. However, such narratives can only effect change in the external world if they are shared with others. Intervention behaviors such as victim impact testimony demand the institutional presence of victims' family members—their physical availability for media interviews and attendance and participation in legal proceedings. Victims intervene to accomplish closure goals through their appearances in the media and in legal forums such as courtrooms and execution chambers. Media coverage and legal proceedings help to create a common cultural ground, reinforcing common understandings of loss as well as common narratives and common coping norms and strategies. However, individuals can make use of and participate in institutions in a variety of ways. Following the Oklahoma City bombing, some family members and survivors viewed media coverage as helpful, others did not; some believed a death sentence for McVeigh, Nichols, and even Fortier was proper, others did not. They also enjoyed differing levels of personal involvement with institutional processes—attending trials, testifying, watching news, giving interviews. Thus, an understanding of closure as intervention necessitates a more detailed assessment of how institutions affect individuals and their memory work.

Institutional Sites of Closure: The Media and the Criminal Justice System

Just as individuals are themselves embedded in numerous social institutions such as families, churches, and workplaces, narrative reconstruction and memory work are enmeshed in relationships with two external social and cultural institutions: the media and the criminal justice system. A victim's family member may turn to the mass media for details of and communal reactions to a crime and its perpetrator(s), and must rely upon the criminal justice system to hold the offender(s) legally accountable and impose punishment. Memory work is therefore linked to publication and adjudication and is influenced by media coverage and trial verdicts, marking the convergence of private and public domains. Crucially, neither institution was created with the needs of victims in mind, and so victims have been forced to adapt to and negotiate through institutional cultures and practices that seem strange, unsettling, and perhaps ill-suited to the pursuit of closure.

By granting media interviews, victims' family members and survivors can give brief or extended narrative commentary on sundry topics such as crime details; the murder's physical, emotional, social, and financial impacts; the perpetrator's actions; and legal developments. Alternatively, they can use media appearances as opportunities to advocate for change, including opportunities for increased victim involvement. As a forum for memory work, the media are much more receptive to emotionality than the courtroom, where judges are likely to quash emotional displays in the name of objective and impartial justice. Accordingly, victims are more likely to be able to share narratives and thus engage in memory work on something approaching "their terms."

But the media also impose their own strictures that victims might not find so therapeutic. The general structure of news stories—introduction, rising action, crisis, falling action, and conclusion—determines to a large extent how events will be represented. Although an event may disrupt or challenge social cohesion and social order, a story about that event will conclude by discrediting one perspective in order to restore social balance.[66] Broadcast news also may prove problematic as a therapeutic site; television, a "time-bound" medium that is heavily dependent on schedules, often finds it difficult to adapt to unscheduled events, resulting in repetition of a few newsworthy images juxtaposed with shallow analysis, providing excellent coverage of visual suffering but only superficial coverage of its contexts.[67] Because extended interviews are the exception rather than the norm, victims' families must become adept at packaging narratives into brief yet powerful segments suitable for sound bites. Yet, while media interviews allow family members to reach much larger audiences more quickly than courtrooms, and permit them to convey remarks free of legal restrictions on testimony, reliance on the media as a memory site accomplishes goals that are very different from legal closure opportunities. Sharing narratives through the media can foster a renewed sense of control and facilitate public respect, empathy, and education, but the media cannot hold the perpetrator accountable as can the criminal justice system.

By pursuing closure through the criminal justice system, the institution charged with constructing the "official" narrative of a crime and enforcing penal measures, family members stand to garner others' recognition and respect, gain a foothold in the accountability process, and ultimately deepen their trust in the legal system.[68] Here, family members' physical or narrative courtroom presence is observed by the jury, an audience more powerful and perhaps more seminal to victims' memory work than the general public. The courtroom offers unparalleled opportunities for closure. During legal proceedings, family members are closer than ever to the machinery of justice and to the perpetrator.

"Seeing justice done"—observing how verdicts, sentences, and legal opinions as cultural products are created—was essential to the vast majority of family members' and survivors' memory work. Attending legal proceedings allows family members to gather critical information and impressions firsthand, unfiltered through intermediaries. It allows them to scrutinize jurors' and defendants' expressions and other behaviors. By delivering victim impact testimony in sentencing, family members can impart reflexive narratives to jurors and defendants, confronting the accused and demonstrating self-control and perspective, thereby distancing themselves from perceived powerlessness, silence, and incapacity. But many have cautioned that satisfying victims' emotional needs may conflict with defendants' constitutional rights, and that courts must always prioritize the latter. In addition, legal proceedings are focused on legally relevant evidence, which is not necessarily the same information that family members seek to answer that haunting question "why."

With a clearer understanding of how victims use the media and the criminal justice system to engage in closure as intervention and effect change, we can assess how these institutions have in turn adapted to victims and their emotional needs. In analyzing the reconstructive roles of the media and the criminal justice system, we must look at whether these institutions have come to see themselves as sites for or sponsors of memory work, how they treat victims, and how they have developed institutional norms concerning the propriety of emotion—how, when, by whom, and why emotions are used in each forum, such as to inform or to indict.

In many respects, the media and the criminal justice system are similar institutions. Both are reflexive forums and require emotional investment from bystanders and participants; mass media coverage incorporates victims' emotional reactions to a murder and subsequent developments, and prosecutors must attempt to reconstruct or prove the defendant's state of mind. Both also produce cultural products that confer finality—verdicts and reputations. In both, professionals engage in dialogue with laypersons in the course of producing these cultural products; lawyers must persuade juries of a suspect's guilt in a courtroom open to spectators, and journalists interview those intimately affected by the crime and incorporate their remarks into media coverage. Each institution has its own set of norms, vocabularies, values, priorities, and participatory roles. Both define roles and adjudicate responsibility, marking who belongs and who does not, who can speak and who may not, who is an actor and who is acted upon. Both enhance the authority of dominant social groups. Both seek to hold perpetrators accountable through either informally holding them responsible for victims' distress or adjudicating their guilt or innocence. Finally, both institutions play narrative roles; they must create and repeatedly enunciate plausible narratives of an event in order to derive verdicts and stories that in turn inform and construct others' narratives. As institutional narrators, both the media and the criminal justice system embody testimonial culture, retelling ordinary citizens' stories of betrayal, loss, and recovery, emphasizing individual pain and resilience and not social and political forces and factors.

But there are key differences in how each institution handles emotion, treats victims, and attempts to satisfy victims' emotional needs. The media make use of emotion in both its raw and refined forms; because emotion can determine newsworthiness, media sources may seek to preserve emotionality or to amplify it. Emotion can help to inform media consumers about subjects' inner states at a certain powerful moment. The media can show emotional progress, facilitating comparisons between an interviewee's inner state at time A with his inner state at time B. Most important, the media construct newsmakers as subjects; in this role, it helped to render McVeigh visible, fostering and perpetuating his toxic presence in family members' and survivors' lives.

In contrast, the criminal justice system seeks to use "refined" emotion and is somewhat reluctant or unable to deal with raw emotion. While the media tend to embrace catharsis and play an active and conscious role in constructing historical records, courts generally eschew emotion and often regard emotion as antithetical to moral judgment. Most legal practices and regulations stipulate that raw emotion distracts from the business of justice, detracting from law's objectivity and impartiality. Accordingly, they often mandate that emotion should be controlled, detached, and considered, if at all, only alongside factual details of a contested event. If the media helped to make McVeigh a social presence, the criminal justice system helped to render him a social absence.

Victims are generally portrayed as passive individuals by both the media and the criminal justice system. Victims have to fight to be characterized as actors instead of acted upon, enduring cycles of enforced passivity and earned agency. When victims advocate, they are not only attempting to assert agency but struggling to earn recognition for their emotions and emotional needs and to broaden institutional conceptions of emotionality and emotional propriety. Because victimhood and the need for catharsis have been embraced by popular culture, victims generally need to fight these battles in the courtroom more frequently than in the popular press. However, in both forums, victims may need to assert their emotional authority and priority as well as their views on emotional propriety—their belief that they have the right to participate in the institutional and social resolution of culturally traumatic events, to insert themselves into collected memory formation.

This may be more difficult than it sounds; victims' asserted needs may violate media norms. Images that are most newsworthy under broadcast norms may also be the most hurtful to victims' families. Attorneys and reporters may breach professional norms to give victims advance notice of arguments, evidence, or upcoming media stories so that they can be aware of current developments and make informed judgments about whether to attend proceedings, read newspapers, or watch broadcasts. Victims' advocacy usually has the effect of making institutions more efficacious, explicit, and democratic sites of memory work, more amenable to reconstructive storytelling by laypersons.

Victims' hardest battles have been fought in the criminal courtroom. Prosecutors, defense attorneys, and judges have all opposed victims' attempts to insert themselves into proceedings. It is not uncommon for legal professionals to attempt to marginalize victims or render them passive by assigning them inescapably emotional roles or portraying their therapeutic needs as individual processes unconnected to the business of criminal law. Victims have responded, however, by asserting that a judicial focus on facts, evidence, and truth is incomplete without incorporating facts of suffering, loss, and violence that are inherently emotional. These efforts have been met with limited success; victims, their alleged emotionality, and their memory work have not been made as welcome in some courtrooms as in others. Legal forums that are less willing to integrate victims in legal proceedings can retard reconstruction and inflict further wounds by adding insulting exclusion to injury.

But victims have learned that they are far from powerless when faced with unfavorable judicial practices. Forced by judicial rulings that would have greatly diminished their opportunities for memory work, Oklahoma City family members and survivors fought to make the Denver courtroom a more conducive site for reconstruction, succeeding in their struggles to have the trials of McVeigh and Nichols and ultimately McVeigh's execution broadcast back to Oklahoma City via closed-circuit feed, and winning the right to both attend the trial and deliver victim impact testimony at sentencing.

As a result, victims have helped to transform courts into new types of discursive spaces, dissolving traditional forms of legal authority and evidence, rendering justice more democratic, successfully asserting the importance of making private pain public, and connecting these efforts to individual rights to bodily autonomy, emotional well-being, and personal safety. Significantly, these concepts all have moral dimensions. But while the judicial climate has become more amenable to memory work, its capacity to effectively recognize and validate victims' emotions and emotional processes is still retarded by ineffective understandings of emotion and memory. Thus, judicial norms have not yet evolved into those of a truly therapeutic space, even though law's role in popular culture and legal professionals' rhetoric have often embraced therapeutic goals.

The issue of victim participation begs the question of whether and to what extent family members expect that attending legal proceedings will fulfill memory work. Victims' family members do not indiscriminately expect every person or institution to assist them in attaining closure. This is not to say that cultural media do not exaggerate the forms and extent of closure that can be derived from legal proceedings, perhaps prompting some family members to develop unrealistic expectations. However, victims' family members realize that a trial or execution is not a counseling session; instead, they regard proceedings as an opportunity to effectuate important goals that can be accomplished nowhere else,[69] as well as a place to find certain building blocks of closure: information, the opportunity to scrutinize defendants' behaviors, and accountability. They use the courtroom as a site of memory not so much to overcome grief but to gain understanding and some measure of control that is lost upon victimization and again when they are marginalized in legal proceedings.[70]

Crucially, the ways in which the legal system can assist victims' families in their pursuit of closure are finite: allowing them to attend the trial, to view the defendant's behavior, to deliver victim impact testimony or postsentence allocution, to meet with the offender in mediation, and to witness an execution. A theory of closure as memory work acknowledges the unique benefits inherent in legal proceedings, refocuses the closure inquiry on its attainment instead of its semantics, and recognizes that media and legal institutions not only are sites of memory work but also produce cultural products such as stories and verdicts that are integral to such processes.[71] It is impossible, then, to cut closure entirely out of capital legal proceedings; if the current judicial reliance on closure is any indication, courts would already be very reluctant to do so.

As sites of memory work, the news media and the criminal justice system create cultural products—media coverage and convictions. Both institutions deploy emotionality as a promotional strategy or tool: the media to get ratings, and courts to get convictions. Thus, emotion, like a potent spice, is a key ingredient of these institutional artifacts. Individuals facilitate memory work through accessing these cultural products and the processes by which they are created. Yet, emotion may undermine as well as enhance the cultural authority of media coverage and criminal convictions. Too much emotionality spoils these institutional inventions, producing sensationalized media coverage that loses credibility and convictions based on passion or prejudice that lack integrity. So damaged, they are less able to support or sustain effective memory work. The inclusion of emotion must therefore be proportionate and balanced in order to safeguard credibility. It must be added in the right quantity, at the right times, in the right places, by the right people.

Effecting New Openings for Closure

Overcoming the myth of closure necessitates tearing down some of the most powerful contemporary myths about why and how victims seek closure, decoupling closure from grief and vengeance, exploring closure's links to restoration of control and accountability, and explicating how the criminal justice system and mass media structure how and where victims' families can speak and what input they will have upon institutional results and memory work. A more informed understanding should lead to the conclusion that both parties have much to gain from family members' participation in institutional memory work. Although institutions have not ceded the floor entirely to victims, they are recognizing, exploring, and even celebrating their subjectivity by recognizing others' subjectivities. For better or for worse, victims' families and their therapeutic expectations are now part of the cultural expectations surrounding the death penalty, as well as the mass media and criminal justice institutions that mediate our experiences of capital punishment. The privileging of victims' voices necessitates that institutions and their audiences must continually grapple with the propriety of when and how these voices should speak, since the question of "if" these voices may speak is, at least as of now, resolved.

Given the nature of victims' families' losses, closure will continue to be an important issue in mass media and criminal proceedings; as such, it must be carefully and thoroughly understood and cautiously pursued. Reconceptualizing closure as memory work reflects that victims' families are actually rather astute and selective in appraising forums for their closure potential—for instance, relying on legal proceedings to facilitate information and accountability, believing that closure is suspended until legal proceedings are over, or that closure is contingent upon a certain outcome such as a guilty verdict. Thus, the process of closure does not mandate that institutions such as the criminal justice system and mass media "heal" victims, but that victims can heal themselves, if only institutions can provide them with footholds to do so.

II

Traumas and Trials

4

"We Come Here to Remember"

Joining Advocacy Groups

> We come here to remember those who were killed, those who
> survived and those changed forever. May all who leave here
> know the impact of violence. May this memorial offer comfort,
> strength, peace, hope and serenity.
> —Oklahoma City National Memorial
> and Museum mission statement

The murder of Cameron Crawford's sibling in the Oklahoma City
bombing opened deep fissures in his life. Not only did Crawford have to
deal with the death of a beloved sibling and adjust to the idea that a terrorist attack had struck Oklahoma City of all places, but Crawford's family
began to disintegrate shortly after the attacks. His parents, both very private people, remained segregated from other families even in the bombing's aftermath. Crawford struggled with a profound need to talk to others about his murdered sibling, but with his family relations closed down,
he was unsure of where to turn. One day in late May 1995, Crawford got
a call from a friend who belonged to the "habeas group," an organization formed in the wake of the bombing dedicated to shortening capital
offenders' lengthy legal appeals process. The group was traveling to Washington, D.C., to lobby for new reform legislation, and a seat on the plane
had become available at the last minute. Would Crawford be interested
in going? Thoroughly frustrated with his family, Crawford jumped at the
chance.

This decision was life-changing. Though Crawford certainly supported
the group's efforts to reform the death penalty appeals process, his attach-
ment to the group was not predicated so much on an ardent commitment to
that political goal as it was on his devotion to other group members. "These

This chair commemorating bombing victim Cynthia Brown is one of 168 that stand on the Field of Empty Chairs in the Oklahoma City National Memorial. Handcrafted of bronze, glass, and stone, the chairs are arranged in nine rows to symbolize the nine floors of the Murrah Building. Image courtesy of the Oklahoma City National Memorial and Museum Archives.

wonderful people became my second family," Crawford explained. For Crawford, this new "family" became a critical basis of support and fellowship:

> I became a part of that group, not so much to change legislation but because I was looking for a new family. And so these people were really into the legal aspect of it. I mean, they followed the news, they could tell what every legislator thought about everything, and so it's pretty much, you know, whatever they said. . . . whatever the consensus of the group, that works for me because I just want us to be one happy family.

For family members and survivors such as Crawford, one of the most immediate and palpable effects of the Oklahoma City bombing was its impact on human relationships. Some existing relationships were destroyed; Robin Brown described the devastating impact of her father's death upon her family: "My dad was not a perfect person, but he was our wisdom. . . . when we would find ourselves where we needed to make decisions, like job changes or thinking about buying a house . . . we'd go okay, let's call dad tonight and we'll see what he says. . . . And now we're without all our wisdom." Although the perpetrators' unwelcome presence(s) became a new—and involuntary—part of participants' lives, the bombing also planted the seeds for more enduring and positive relationships to germinate and flourish. Existing relations between friends and family were strengthened, terminated, or radically redefined, and deep ties were forged as individuals who were formerly mere acquaintances or even strangers quickly became soul mates. Social contact mediated stress,[1] and companionship became an instinctual need, rendering social support necessary for recovery.[2]

Forming community groups in the wake of the bombing, working closely with one another to accomplish meaningful group goals such as working toward legal reform or building a national memorial, family members and survivors renewed old ties and forged new ones. Survivor Beverly Rankin, who worked for the Social Security Administration and was at her desk when the bomb went off, explained, "We were close before, but we became a tight-knit family. . . . when one person was down you can bet somebody else would be there to give them a hug. . . . And it just helped us tremendously." Driven by an urge to meet and talk with others who were "like them," family members and survivors joined these groups to seek out those the bombing had impacted in comparable ways. But in seeking similarity, they encountered difference. Disparities in experience and ideology initially had disturbing and destabilizing effects on group formation, threatening interpersonal engagement and therefore reconstruction. But group members committed themselves to confronting, negotiating, and ultimately moving past these distinctions, reconceptualizing diversity as a benefit that greatly enriched the membership experience, that spurred instead of stunted members' camaraderie and group productivity. Relationships between group members helped victims to make sense of the bombing and to ascertain their own relationships to it. These relationships stood in direct contrast to the perpetrators' toxic presences.

"This Is My New World": Understanding Victims' Emotional Landscape

One can best understand how group membership benefited survivors and family members by exploring the profound emotional and psychological suffering that participants experienced in the bombing's aftermath. Many family members and survivors of the bombing were diagnosed with post-traumatic stress disorder (PTSD), and such symptoms had a very real effect on individual memory work and group processes. As Charlie Younger remarked, some family members with PTSD were "very angry [at survivors], quite often said you don't belong in the same room with us. . . . It was their anger toward us because we survived and their family member died, . . . it was more difficult to deal with that than it was the bombing itself at times."

But examining victims' responses solely through clinical terms is inadequate; it not only implies that there is a "cure" but also fails to capture the emotional realities of postbombing life. Memory work—and trauma—must be understood as something broader than clinical diagnoses.

For decades, grief research lacked a vocabulary and framework for effectively conceptualizing "traumatic grief." Research on traumatic grief began in 1917 with Freud's portrait of grief pathology in *Mourning and Melancholia* and continued throughout that century; researchers focused upon the grief stages that an individual would pass through and not on mass or collective grieving.[3] Perhaps the best-known example of this trend is Elizabeth Kubler-Ross's wildly popular *On Death and Dying*, which proposed that terminally ill individuals were supposed to proceed through five stages in coming to terms with their impending death.

Attempting to systematize emotion in this manner is something of a fool's errand; even if there was some logic to identifying grief stages, such schemes would not likely apply to the traumatic grieving experienced in the wake of sudden and violent death. Contemporary research still focuses on grief "syndromes" but has also shown that grief does not progress through predictable stages and does not last for any certain time period,[4] confirming that grieving is messy work.[5] A growing body of literature even focuses on psychological response and adjustment to murder, including an intense three- to five-year "complicated mourning" period,[6] in which individuals suffer from anger, self-blame, shattered assumptions,[7] reexperiencing the trauma, diminished responsiveness, exaggerated startle response, disturbed sleep, difficulty in remembering, survivor guilt, and avoidance of activities that may recall the traumatic event.[8]

Significantly, family members' and survivors' grief was necessarily different from that identified by prior researchers who focused on individual grief syndromes; it was not only combined with psychological trauma but also bound up with other institutional processes altogether separate from them such as news media coverage and legal proceedings, the timing and outcome of which they could not control. Survivors of traumatic events also often felt increasingly isolated and estranged, either because of others' distanced reactions or because one felt set apart by authentic but unwanted expertise in suffering.[9]

Participants sometimes felt as if they were strangers in their own lives. Marsha Kight, whose murdered daughter, Frankie Merrell, was a teller at the Federal Employees Credit Union on the third floor of the Murrah Building, remarked, "It's almost like you know you're being beamed up and then you're put down as somebody else and your whole world just changes." Many also felt as if the bombing suffused their identity. Diane Dooley recalled:

> People were curious and naturally wanted to hear . . . how I was doing and which led to what happened. And you sort of became identified with that event too. And you couldn't go anywhere without feeling like the spotlight was kind of on you. . . . you just would think, "I don't want to be known and remembered for this the rest of my life."

The bombing's aftermath was also hardly conducive to the maintenance of old social ties or the formation of new ones; it was a time of structural disorder in which victims were more likely to focus intensely on murdered loved ones rather than maintaining social ties with living friends and relatives. Some found that friends and acquaintances imposed an interpersonal distance when they tired of hearing about the bombing, felt that healing was taking too long, or felt unequal to the task of responding appropriately to victims' suffering. These forms of withdrawal could produce feelings of shame in family members and survivors. Marsha Kight remembered, "I'd come in and talk about the memorial committee and all this kind of stuff or the pretrial hearings and people started to avoid me. . . . I'm sure they did get tired of hearing about it. You know, their lives were going on, this is my new world and where I was and [it was] very different." In addition, grief itself often opened chasms between family members who were grieving in different ways.

Most family members and survivors also reported a loss of control following the bombing. Murder transports people into radically different experiential worlds.[10] There can be no readiness or anticipatory mourning.[11] The murders in the Oklahoma City bombing were deaths outside of the natural order; there was no leave-taking, contributing to a sense of unfinished and unfulfilled relations with the dead. Loss of control sometimes accompanied physical breakdowns, an inability to control one's own health or mannerisms. Doris Jones recalled being unable to control grieving behavior at work: "My boss had another person come and work with me because, I mean, I would start crying every time someone would say, 'Hi, Doris.' And I would bawl. You know, I'd fall apart." Jones was even unable to speak her daughter's name out loud in public without breaking down. Loss of control also stemmed from exacerbated fears of violent crime. Because victims were powerless to prevent the first death, thwarting future harms seemed impossible.[12] Ernestine Hill Clark, for instance, spoke of her "unnatural fear that if I told what

I saw that day [of the bombing] I was convinced in my head that we were going to be bombed again."

In an effort to restore control and prevent future losses, survivors often felt a sense of "keeping vigil," which maintained the traumatic pitch of post-disaster life: a determination to maintain control and meaning, to never be caught off guard, to never relax or feel secure. Dot Hill described this "hyper-vigilance" as stemming from "mostly the lack of control that we all felt. And then second to that was the fear of another instance of it happening again, soon." Vigils could hinder recovery in numerous ways: protesting injustice could lead victims back into the trauma without resolution, resisting a loss of meaning could lead to depression and despair, attempts to protect others could prevent deeper interpersonal contacts, and survivor guilt could lead victims to feel that they did not deserve therapy or even to be alive—that their suffering or pain was insignificant in relation to the great suffering of their loved one.[13]

Perhaps the most significant disorder that murder ushered into victims' lives was a collapse of meaning.[14] The bombing destroyed victims' moral order, and as a result of this moral loss, family members and survivors struggled to answer new, unfamiliar, terrifying questions: "Why us?" "What now?" As Diane Leonard remarked, "Any crime victim feels helpless, hope-less; someone's walked in, taken control of your life, and the way I describe it is I felt like my life puzzle had been blown apart and I needed to get as many pieces of that puzzle back together in order to be able to go forward."

For these reasons, the reconstruction of moral order became tremen-dously important for family members and survivors. Complex moral sche-mas could devolve into radically simplified and absolutist moral systems. New schemas were often binary and adversarial, pitting innocent victims against the criminal other. Another very common reaction was a desperate need for information with which to lay a reconstructive foundation. Because one could not move forward without thoroughly understanding insofar as possible the circumstances of the murder, information about the crime and perpetrator was precious, as was information about other crimes, perpetra-tors, and survivors.[15]

Ultimately, participants slowly realized that trying to regain control by attempting to exert control only left one feeling spread thin and person-ally and spiritually diminished. Susan Urbach gradually realized that it was important to "let go" sometimes: "You can talk about trials and all that kind of thing. . . . part of healing is recognizing those things and trying to do what you can and releasing what you don't have control over." One palpable way of wresting back control was reclaiming possessions from the Murrah Building. Janet Beck described how she felt when she was able to salvage one rather appropriate souvenir from the Murrah ruins:

> I ended up getting one magnet back [from my desk] and it was the rainbow and the dove. And I thought, how appropriate . . . for that one to be the one that got found. But it was just, any little thing you could get out of there that was personal, it was like one more thing you could pull back out of that building and not let them take that away from you too.

Many participants also found solace in the act of writing. After she was told by a counselor that she either had to talk or write about the bombing to avoid PTSD, Ernestine Hill Clark bought a computer and began to type, composing a journal of more than 100 pages. Clark has taken smaller pieces of this journal and transformed them into poems; two years after the bombing, her sister, liturgical music composer and conductor Nancy Cobb Lippens, asked her to write a poem about her experiences for a composition on grief. The resulting poem, "Through a Glass Darkly," was set to music, and the result, "Threnody," a work for chorus and orchestra, has enjoyed critical acclaim and multiple performances. Similarly, Susan Urbach recalled, "I wrote a ton, a ton. . . . I'd almost call them vignettes, chapter[s]; things would happen and I'd have to go away and ponder on it." Sharing these writings enabled Urbach to communicate with herself and others on a much deeper level: "What I found is that people would read those and it would remind them or it would bring up stuff for themselves . . . and the interesting thing is to go back and read those things because you literally can see how you deal with devastation and chaos." Sometimes the gift of fluency took a nascent author by surprise; as Marsha Kight recalled, "I had never written before but I just picked the pen up and it was just like it almost, somebody else had a hold of it. It was very cathartic, very good for me, but I would read it and I'd be amazed that I wrote it."

Finally, anger was the prototypical victim response; as sociologist Paul Rock has emphasized, it refers not only to a "mass of turbulent and contradictory experiences" but to an emotion that established a new relational web that "embrace[d] the survivor, the victim, the killer, and others around the self as an expressive unity."[16] Anger was not only an emotion but a productive activity that organized and directed victims' attention and energies, such as eliciting victims' determination to see something positive come out of the bombing. It motivated victims, prompting them to once again assert control.[17] Family members and survivors performed anger and lived in its experience. Their anger was self- and world-defining. This constructive capability inherent in anger was tremendously empowering in reconstructive efforts, helping victims to build new self-identities upon anger's performances and relying upon anger as a talisman of the justness of their advocacy.[18]

This emotion could, however, alienate bombing victims from themselves and others. Feeling a sweeping anger that was out of character could lead victims to question their sanity and normality, and engage in self-blaming. Critically injured survivor Stan Mayer recalled that after the bombing his personality "shifted": "For the first time in my life I wanted to kill people. I had never wanted to kill anyone, I've never been a violent person, and now all of a sudden I had violence, I had anger." In addition, victims feared that others' reactions to their angry displays might prompt others to view them as vicious or consumed by hate.[19]

Thus, survivors and family members endured traumatic grieving, alienation, loss of control, and anger. These disturbances, however, made the integration into groups and the invocation of group memory potentially all the more worthwhile.

Oklahoma City Community and Memorial Practices in the Wake of the Oklahoma City Bombing

While several small groups were formed after the bombing, four dominated the landscape and served as homes to the bulk of participant family members and survivors: the Oklahoma City Murrah Federal Building Memorial Task Force, charged with building a national memorial; a "habeas group" of victims' families and survivors seeking to curtail legal appeals for condemned offenders; the Oklahoma City Murrah Building Survivors Association, founded with a community service mission; and Families and Survivors United, which sought to secure assistance for bombing victims.

These groups were not independent organizations but were interdependent, clustered around the bombing. Each chose a different path for making sense of the bombing as a traumatic event, and each was oriented toward a different institutional space—the memorial group to the museum and the monument, the habeas group to the courtroom. These groups produced lasting memorial products—the Oklahoma City National Memorial and Museum, legislation such as the Antiterrorism and Effective Death Penalty Act of 1996 and the Victims Rights Clarification Act of 1997, and publications such as *Forever Changed: Remembering Oklahoma City, April 19, 1995*—that acquired meaning independently of the group and yet continued to reflect group visions and creative priorities.

The Oklahoma City Murrah Federal Building Memorial Task Force

Several weeks after the bombing, in the summer of 1995, Oklahoma City mayor Ronald Norick appointed Robert Johnson, an Oklahoma City attorney, to "organize and direct" the community memorial process, founding the Oklahoma City Murrah Federal Building Memorial Task Force (the "memorial group"). Johnson selected a dozen others to identify "different constituencies" who would have a stake in the memorial process and committed to giving family members and survivors a primary voice. The resulting task force was composed of 10 operating committees, a 160-member advisory committee, a coordinating committee, and an executive director. On July 17, 1995, between 50 and 75 members of the Victim's Families/Survivors Liaison subcommittee held their first meeting. In its early stages, the memorial group negotiated several issues, including tensions between family members and survivors, suggestions that the memorial privilege the children murdered in the bombing, and what the memorial should look like.[20]

The first activity that memorial task force members undertook had the effect of uniting the group around a common vision of memorialization. Through various forms of research, including public surveys and meetings as well as meetings with family members and survivors, the task force gathered opinions on what visitors should "think, feel, or experience." In the spring of 1996, a committee began to write the mission statement, whose preamble captured the heart of the memorialization project: "We come here to remember those who were killed, those who survived and those changed forever. May all who leave here know the impact of violence. May this memorial offer comfort, strength, peace, hope and serenity."[21] This goal was centered around creating and ensuring a lasting memorial *presence* within and around the footprint of the Murrah Building to counteract and defy the absence of life the bombing had wrought.

Memorial task force members felt that this group fulfilled remembrance functions; Doris Jones, for instance, stated the memorial group allowed her to remember her daughter and her unborn grandchild: "In the memorial group, I was remembering Carrie. And I was remembering, making sure her baby was not forgotten. And I got really wrapped up in that too, because you had this fear that they would be forgotten." Richard Williams stated that group members knew "very early on" that the memorial was going to be a very unique and special achievement due to "the Oklahoma standard and that's the response that people all over the nation and the world literally gave to Oklahoma City that there was something there that we had never dealt with before."

The task force undertook the difficult responsibility of determining who was a survivor, using examples like the Holocaust to elucidate a definition of "survivor" and resolve the claims-making of diverse survivor groups. The survivor definition committee created a "primary zone of danger and a secondary zone of distress"; those in the primary zone included those who suffered injury severe enough to warrant being held in the hospital regardless of their physical location at 9:02 a.m., and were to be identified on the building site and inside the Memorial Center, while those in the secondary zone would be represented in the Memorial Center. On March 20, 1997, a total of 624 submitted designs were put on public display in Bricktown, Oklahoma City's entertainment district.

The Oklahoma City National Memorial and Museum opened on April 19, 2000, the fifth anniversary of the bombing, and consists of an outdoor monument and an indoor museum. The outdoor monument is nestled within the

The Oklahoma City National Memorial and Museum at twilight. The Gates of Time bookend the reflecting pool, with the Field of Empty Chairs in between. Image courtesy of the Oklahoma City National Memorial and Museum Archives.

The Journal Record Building, now home to the Oklahoma City National Memorial Museum. To the right of the museum is the Survivor Tree, an American elm that was heavily damaged by the bomb but survived, although evidence was trapped in its branches and embedded in its bark. Image courtesy of the Oklahoma City National Memorial and Museum Archives.

footprint of the Murrah Building and incorporates numerous symbols, as described on the memorial's website.[22] The Journal Record Building, directly across the street from the Murrah Building, houses the memorial museum, which "takes visitors on a chronological, self-guided tour . . . through the story of April 19, 1995, and the days, weeks, months and years that followed the bombing of Oklahoma City's Alfred P. Murrah Federal Building."[23] The indoor museum has been manifestly concerned with representing the bombing as an experience of chaos and recovery.[24] While visitors "see" the investigation in exhibits that display key pieces of evidence and describe investigative techniques, they are actually meant to become *immersed* within the experience of the bombing itself. The memorial museum is designed so as to marginalize the perpetrators' presences as much as possible.

The "Habeas Group"

Many other participants belonged to the "habeas group," so called because its members sought to alter a death penalty appeals process members deemed interminable and unjust.[25] "Habeas" is short for the Latin phrase *habeas corpus*, meaning "you have the body." Individuals in government custody can petition a court for freedom in a writ of *habeas corpus*, a judicial mandate requiring that a prisoner be brought before the court to determine whether the government has the right to continue to detain him. Criminal defendants who are convicted of capital crimes and sentenced to death routinely file such writs in state and federal courts in the course of appealing their conviction and death sentence; thus, the appeals process is often referred to as "habeas appeals."

The habeas group was begun by Glenn Seidl, whose wife, Kathy, was murdered in the bombing. Its members were largely pro–death penalty family members and survivors who also wanted to protect victims' rights through political advocacy; they believed that shortening the time between death sentence and execution was important for victims' families and essential to capital punishment's efficacy. In contrast to the memorial task force, the habeas group was not about remembering but achieving justice; as Doris

Representatives of the "habeas group" gathered in Washington, D.C., for the passage of the AEDPA. Back row, left to right: Senator Don Nickles, an unidentified man, Bob Denison, Alice Maroney-Denison, Dan McKinney, Diane Leonard, Beverly Rankin, Kay Ice, Senator James Inhofe, Suzanne Britten. Front row, left to right: Michael Reyes, Clint Seidl, Glenn Seidl, Gary Bland, Jason Smith, Earl Adams. Image courtesy of the Oklahoma City National Memorial and Museum Archives.

On April 24, 1997, President William Jefferson Clinton signed the Antiterrorism and Effective Death Penalty Act into law. Image courtesy of the Oklahoma City National Memorial and Museum Archives.

Jones explained, it focused on "making sure that who did this was punished and [received] the right judgment, the right justice." Unlike the memorial group, then, the habeas group pursued an *absence*, ensuring timely accountability and an offender's removal from victims' lives.

The first political problem that habeas members chose to address was the lengthy period between a capital offender's death sentence and execution. The habeas group met in the offices of the Oklahoma attorney general, which also provided informal assistance in drafting legislation to reduce habeas appeal opportunities for capital offenders. The resulting legislation was supported by the attorneys general of several other states, including California, Alabama, Pennsylvania, Texas, Colorado, Montana, Nebraska, Louisiana, Arizona, Idaho, and Mississippi. Group members made several trips to Washington to lobby for the law's passage and were received with open arms by most legislators. During Senate hearings, Senator Orrin Hatch observed, "Rather than exploiting the devastation of Oklahoma City, I believe that by including this provision in the antiterrorism legislation, we are *protecting* the families of victims."[26] President Bill Clinton signed the Antiterrorism and Effective Death Penalty Act (AEDPA) of 1996 into law on April 24, 1996. This was an incredible moment for those who had worked so tirelessly to bring it about. "We felt good. We felt really good. 'Cause we had worked really hard," Beverly Rankin recalled.

The habeas group members who lobbied for the passage of the AEDPA embedded their representations of the bombing in letters sent to legislators, reprinted in the *Congressional Record*.[27] Here, members shed their status of victims of terrorism and instead represented themselves as *murder* victims' families. In keeping with the political platform of the victims' rights movement, these letters tied a loved one's death to the need to execute the offender in a timely manner. Several letters mentioned that the murdered victims did not have 15 to 20 years to prepare themselves for death, and that family members did not have the chance to say good-bye. As Wanda Fincher, sister to Kathy Seidl, noted, "Kathy wasn't allowed to say goodbye to her family or to share any more of her wonderful presence with us. If the murderers are sitting in federal prison for 10–20 years they will be given the right to visit with their families and to say their good-byes. How does this give justice to us?"[28] Other letters intimated that a swift execution was needed for "healing" to begin. Glenn Seidl wrote, "We need change, my family wants justice. . . . When the people responsible for this terrible act are found guilty and executed, our families can begin a very important step of the healing process." Clifford Davis, the brother of Kathy Seidl, explained, "Now the only way I can focus my anger, loneliness and the piece of my heart that is now empty, is to try to get the Hatch/Spector bill passed."

The Oklahoma City Murrah Building Survivor's Association

The Oklahoma City Murrah Building Survivor's Association was founded by Dr. Paul Heath, a psychologist with the Veterans Administration, using $1,200 of his own money and running it out of his own small private practice office and later his home. Despite its name, the group was open to everyone, but it was targeted toward survivors, whether or not they had been in the Murrah Building at the time of the bombing. The Survivor's Association held its first "help fair" meeting at the First Methodist Church in July 1995, which provided opportunities for survivors to have their hearing, eyesight, and mental health evaluated by local officials. The founders of this group wished to instill a community service ethic into its activities, connecting bombing victims to social resources, encouraging Oklahoma City residents to help themselves through helping others.

Families and Survivors United

Families and Survivors United was started by Marsha Kight after her adult daughter, Frankie Merrell, was murdered in the bombing, leaving a two-year-old daughter. Kight conceived the idea for this organization after she began to meet and speak with family members and survivors at memorial committee meetings who felt overlooked by the bureaucracy and were especially frustrated by financial assistance applications. "Our goal in Families and Survivors United was to help each other help ourselves," Kight explained. She sent letters to different agencies inviting them to meet with bombing victims in order to explain guidelines and application processes. Families and Survivors United also commissioned a commemorative angel figurine, the sales of which earned enough money to allow 19 people to attend the Denver trials of McVeigh and Nichols, and produced and sent a "thank-you" video to rescue units across the country. Kight also edited a collection of family members' and survivors' stories entitled *Forever Changed: Remembering Oklahoma City, April 19, 1995*. To Kight, a book would be comprehensive, permanent, and safe—perfect for bombing victims who wanted to tell their stories, but not via the media.

From the earliest meetings, Kight played what she called a "watchdog" role in community and advocacy group meetings, "trying to make all the meetings and I was rustling feathers," attempting to ensure that family members' and survivors' concerns were noted and addressed. After more family members and survivors became involved in the memorial, Kight turned to other matters, including the upcoming trials of McVeigh and Nichols. She first stepped into the role of victim advocate after U.S. District Judge Robert Matsch's pretrial ruling prohibiting family members and survivors slated to give victim impact testimony during McVeigh's sentencing from attending the guilt phase of his trial. "Well, that put me on my heels, and I thought, I'm staying here [in the courtroom], but I'm going to go back and I'm going to find a way, that's not right," Kight remarked. "So I got on my computer, I found NOVA [the National Organization for Victim Assistance]," where personnel put her in touch with others who could help overturn this ruling. Ultimately, she became a well-known victims' rights spokesperson. Kight testified before the Senate Judiciary Committee several times and eventually went to work full-time for NOVA in Washington, D.C., in 1999. "My world had opened me up to experiences that I never in my mind thought would be there, and connecting me with people that I never dreamt of [meeting]," she emphasized.

Functions of Groups Formed in the Wake of the Oklahoma City Bombing

Groups fulfilled numerous functions, including providing companionship, spurring a gravitation toward group narrative, and organizing members around chosen reconstructive goals. Each of these functions served important roles: companionship provided support and enabled members to recognize that others were going through similar ordeals, group narratives helped members with narrative and norm construction (building and maintaining social frameworks of memory), and group goals oriented members toward positive goals and gave concrete form to these evolving memory frameworks.

To Join or Not to Join

The story of group membership is largely the story of how bombing victims struggled to become survivors, a journey that took years to traverse. Some did not join *these* community groups but instead elected to follow different paths, either alone or with other companions. Those who joined not only had to work through the challenging task of beginning to make sense of what had happened and what it meant, but also had to learn how to speak with others about these issues, sharing their stories with people with very different experiences of loss. Sometimes these differences created tensions that were difficult for members to surmount. But working to explicate and eradicate these tensions often made groups into more cohesive social units. Group relations were also strengthened by members' commitment to achieving intimidatingly large goals. These bonds, forged through the crucible of interpersonal conflict and resolution, strengthened commitment to group projects and were crucial to these groups' success.

Not all participants became involved in groups. The choice not to become involved with a group was often precipitated by discomfort or dislike of a particular group's evolving theme or purpose—what we might term a "social framework." For some, it was not healthy to be around others who were not at comparable points in recovery or reconstruction; exposure to the memory practices of these individuals carried risk, threatening to undermine personal progress. As Jordan Holt recalled, "I couldn't risk being around people who were still hurting so much, and so I stayed away from the large group."

Many participants who were searching for a group to join recalled feeling discomfort at times with a group's social framework; they responded by either attending various group meetings until they found one that accommodated their needs, or curtailing their search for a group. Merely making the physical effort to attend a group meeting was an assertion of identity, of a right to be present and of a sense of belonging, even if members were ascertaining group dynamics and orientation. At this stage, both family members and survivors felt alienated if their relationship to deceased victims or to the bombing event was atypical. Ernestine Hill Clark remarked, "I felt like I didn't belong anywhere because I hadn't lost a family member and I could not call myself a survivor because I wasn't in the Murrah Building." Similarly, Faith Moore "just didn't feel comfortable" at early memorial meetings because her story earned an "oh" reaction, since it was her former and not her current husband who had been murdered in the bombing.

There was also little incentive to join a group if one's social support needs were being met elsewhere. Diane Dooley explained that because she had tremendous support from her family and church, she felt no need to attend a group at first, believing that her survivor status and other members' anger were both alienating: "I had family, a lot of family and friends and my husband [who were] very supportive and I could talk to them any time. So I didn't feel the need to go."

For those who did join groups, membership in a particular group was often more "a matter of contingency than of deliberate choice"[29] and came about when individuals decided to attend meetings that they had learned about through friends or contacts from group members. Another influential factor was the level of comfort individuals had with a particular group; some family members and survivors joined groups very quickly, but others took more time to find a comfortable environment. Susan Urbach recalled, "It was maybe a year or a year and a half before I felt that I wanted to get involved . . . and then it's like so which group do I want to get involved with and I kind of visited a couple. . . . I went to one here and thought, ooh, they're really mad, oooh, bad vibes here." As Urbach's words reveal, the search for a group "home" was a unique and personal process that differed greatly from person to person.

Searching for Similarities

Family members and survivors learned firsthand the therapeutic benefits of telling and listening to one another's stories. Vicki Hamm stated that she could not stop talking about the bombing once she began to attend meetings of the Murrah Building Survivor's Association: "What we would do is sometimes we would go around the room and each person would tell their story.

And that was healing for me. And I found that the more I talked about it, the more I wanted to talk about it. And I just couldn't shut up." Talking was a way of accomplishing memory work by validating personal memory and interpretations, and sharing memories allowed members to build new social frameworks of memory and therefore new structures of meaning.

One of participants' primary requirements for sharing stories with others immediately following the bombing was similarity of loss. One's willingness to encounter different loss experiences often occurred in stages; victims were most inclined to empathize first with others whose losses were similar to their own. Stan Mayer spoke of the difficulties of sharing his story with others who had not sustained such extensive physical injuries: "I always went last, I always hated to say anything because they would all either start crying or cringe when they'd hear about my week or what was going on with me."

In the wake of the Oklahoma City bombing, grief provided the impetus to talk—about the bombing, about murdered loved ones—and through talk came catharsis. As Cameron Crawford recalled, "This is the therapy that I need. I can tell people about [my murdered sibling]. I can talk about what happened to me." There was an imperative for survivors and family members not only to see, interact, and form relationships with one another but to share their stories. As Priscilla Salyers noted, "I would go to the weekly [memorial] meetings, and I shared my stories with various places, even at churches and things and [with other] survivors, we would get together and we would share stories." Participants emphasized that one of the primary benefits of group membership was the chance to exchange experiences with one another.

More specifically, group meetings became a forum for people to talk about the bombing. "Well, they first started forming the group, that's when everybody would go and start talking about where they were and their problems," Ray Washburn recalled. Individuals were initially driven to exchange stories by a need to find others who could understand the physical and emotional complications they were experiencing. Group "gelling"—members' sense that the group was becoming a coherent and cohesive body—created additional foundations for interpersonal understanding, to the point that sharing meaning (and memory) was a nonverbal process. Diane Leonard stated, "When you're in a group like that you know you don't have to explain if you just start crying, they understand. . . . it's hard to function, but they got it and you knew they did."

The urge to meet with one another was so strong that individuals did not wish to continue to attend groups not oriented around dialogic behavior. Dr. Paul Heath, one of the founders of the Murrah Building Survivor's Association and the group's first president, remarked that group meetings provided an atmosphere in which people could talk. This imperiled the mission that Heath had originally envisioned for the organization:

> When I tried to guide the organization to become a service organiza-tion . . . I found that to be almost impossible because people need to verbal-ize and unload and talk about their bombing experiences. . . . the people who needed to talk, maybe they couldn't talk at home. They'd come to the meet-ing and that's all they wanted to talk about, and that began to be a divider rather than something to bring the group together. . . . the presidents that followed me tried to organize these meetings could not, they were not any more effective than I was to get people to catch the idea of the organization.

As one of the people who attended this group briefly, Stan Mayer felt it was unfortunate that such conversations were not allowed to continue: "We could've helped each other. . . . we could've really relied on each other." Pris-cilla Salyers echoed this sentiment:

> In the very beginning there was a group of us that met because we wanted to come together. I mean we all worked in this Federal Building. . . . . We saw each other in the snack bars and credit union or the elevators. And when we went to this meeting, it started out very good and Dr. Heath wanted to set up a big place where we could just all meet. . . . And he started giving ideas of what he wanted to do. And there were a couple of us that said, we don't want to do all that. We just want to come to one big room and see each other and hug. . . . it wasn't what we needed at that time. It was too early. We just wanted to see each other.

Because they perceived it was too early for additional concerns that would detract from supportive conversational exchanges, some, like Salyers and Mayer, left to join groups in which dialogue could flow more freely.

Growing, Together: Overcoming Differences

In seeking those with similar experiences, it was inevitable that family mem-bers and survivors would also encounter profound differences. As effective as groups were in cultivating a sense of companionship, certain group dynam-ics—interpersonal frictions generated by bringing together individuals with diverse political opinions and radically different experiences of loss—were very difficult to work through in the first months following the bombing.

Initially, group members' differing bombing experiences were as likely to isolate group members as they were to unite them. The fact that group normative frameworks were still under construction in those early days meant that social insecurity and negotiations for whose voices would carry what types of memorial power were natural. Some time had to pass before survivors or victims' family members could become accustomed to and secure in their own perspective to the point where they could understand and validate others' perspectives. Sharing stories very soon after the bombing with others who had different experiences of loss may actually have been harmful.

It was commonly assumed that a victim's relationship to the bombing carried an implicit valuation in terms of one's stake in the task of making meaning and memory. This produced a perceived hierarchy of victimization that prioritized family members—particularly those with murdered children—and relegated survivors to a bottom rung. Initially, those whose family members had been murdered were thought to deserve a louder voice in constructing group dynamics and collected memory than survivors who actually had a much closer physical proximity to the blast. "I do feel like, especially in the media, the families were given more attention. And I'm sure that was hard [for survivors] because their suffering was on many levels," noted Marsha Kight. In this way, various loss groups attempted to transform memorial claims-making into an exclusive privilege.

Profound interpersonal tension existed between survivors of the bombing and family members whose relatives had been murdered in the explosion, between injured survivors and apparently uninjured survivors who experienced survivors' guilt and other forms of mental trauma, and between those who supported the death penalty and those who opposed it. Dr. Paul Heath observed:

> It became very apparent to me early on that [victims' family members] did not feel that survivors, especially early on, had any right to think about, talk about, or in any way be involved in decision-making processes, where we were collectively gathered together. . . . And I, very early, I learned that if you were an injured survivor, they had a perspective and the more injured they were, the more intense the feelings that sort of tried to separate people's involvement in a collective way in meetings. If you were not an injured survivor, they wondered why you were even willing to open your mouth.

Survivors' geographic proximity to ground zero at the time of the bombing was also a source of tension; as Richard Williams stated, "Some people would look at you like, well who are you and why are you here? You know you were two blocks away and I was right there."

For survivors, memorial group meetings assumed a hostile air as family members who resented the presence of the living sought to limit or altogether terminate their participation. Charlie Younger recollected that these tensions rose to the fore when the survivors and family members met together during memorial group meetings: "There were *strong* feelings among family members who had lost someone, in the bombing, . . . [they] had a lot of bad feeling toward people who survived the bombing. . . . And the family members were very abusive in a lot of cases toward survivors. . . . Very angry, quite often said you don't belong in the same room with us." Dot Hill recalled being told that "you don't have a right to be here, you didn't die, you don't have a right to be here, you don't have a right to say anything." Other participants, such as survivor Jamie Blansett, experienced outright rejection from family members immediately after they learned she was a survivor: "This one mother . . . I don't know what her name is, but I know whose mother she was, and she walked up and [said], 'Oh, who was your family? Who did you lose?' I go, 'I didn't lose anyone. I'm a survivor.' She just immediately turns around and just walks off."

Family members felt as if survivors did not understand the pain of death or loss and so privileged a loved one's death over the physical and emotional trauma of survivorship. This is indicative of what researchers have termed the "trauma membrane" phenomenon, which is "characterized by the passive or active exclusion of people who are perceived not to have experienced the same, or similar, dramatic events."[30] Family member Jessie Sternburg explained that the sight of other survivors, especially coworkers of her murdered best friend, was incredibly painful because she could not understand why others had lived when her friend had died: "There was one girl that worked with [my friend] that survived and I just could not stand to see her. . . . It's terrible." I wouldn't want her dead, but then I'd look at her and go, well why her, you know, is she different? Is she special?"

This animosity retraumatized survivors, exacerbating survivor guilt and causing additional emotional turmoil just when survivors were most vulnerable. Jamie Blansett recalled, "A few of them hurt my feelings, and at that time I was really raw and I'd cry a lot." According to Ernestine Hill Clark, this animosity, together with the pain of recovery, made some critically injured survivors feel guilty that they had survived:

Some of those people had over 24 to 29 operations, and there were times when some of those people felt early on with all the pain they were going through, it might have been better if they had died, and to hear a family member say you aren't going through anything . . . [that] just exacerbated that hurt and anger and pain.

Many survivors also experienced survivor guilt just from encountering family members, even when family members were not overtly hostile. As Priscilla Salyers recollected,

I had so many people even in the hospital, you know—[that said] you are special, you must be special, you know God has a special purpose for you. And I was so overcome with—I was scared to death. If I am so special, what is it I'm supposed to do. . . . I had heard about survivors' guilt, didn't understand it. . . . probably about two weeks after the bombing they were going to take families and survivors down to this site. And we were all supposed to meet. . . . And they had buses and they took you down there. . . . as we got to the site, survivors' guilt hit me because I am, like, here I am with all these families who lost somebody and I am alive. And it hit me and it hit me hard. It's a horrible, horrible feeling [when] you feel guilty for living. I felt guilty when family members would come around; it took me probably two or three years to really start getting over that.

Perhaps this was because reconstructing one's own life and integrating the bombing into new routines was a demanding enough task without being physically reminded of and confronted with what family members had to cope with. Survivor guilt, then, was testament to the fact that survivors' individual memory reconstruction processes may have been more collective than that of family members because they included an awareness of perceived disparities between their own and others' traumatized positions. Meeting with family members exacerbated survivor guilt, as Priscilla Salyers noted:

I can remember the one [memorial task force] meeting in particular. I am sitting next to a man who almost bled to death in the building and we were there, and we were talking—they were talking about putting survivors' names on something. And the woman got up and said, this is not for survivors this is for [family members]. She lost her daughter and she was very vocal. And it hit me and this other man hard. And after the meeting I looked at him and I said, . . . she doesn't realize that if it was humanly possible I'd trade places with her daughter.

Such exhibitions of hostility forced survivors to modify their behavior. As Salyers explained, "You have to be very careful not to—around certain people. You have to be very careful that you couldn't voice how you were hurting because they lost a loved one, you know. It was hard, it was very hard."

Gradually, these hostilities diminished; empathic understandings of others' losses became more common, and family members and survivors began to appreciate and validate each other's experiences. Marsha Kight worked actively to defuse such tensions in Families and Survivors United. "There was a little bit of, 'Well I lost a child, you had 23 years with yours,' but that's trying the 'your grief is worse than my grief thing,'" she observed, continuing, "I would try to address, this is not what we're about, it's about helping each other, and that's hurtful." At this point, it became apparent to members that this animosity was itself a symptom of trauma. Unfortunately, some survivors had already ceased to attend. Dot Hill, who was one of them, explained:

I took it deep to my core and I distanced myself. Okay fine, I won't be around them, I don't want to inflict this on them, so I, I wouldn't. I dropped out early on. . . . I thought, okay, I'm not gonna put myself through this. I'm not gonna harm them by being in their presence. So I pulled myself and I didn't get involved until years later.

Other members, however, persisted in attending groups despite this acrimonious behavior, mindful of the need to fulfill a higher calling; Priscilla Salyers recalled, "[At first] I was not going to go back to the meeting and then I was like, no, I came here for a purpose and I am going to continue."

Significant obstacles had to be overcome in order to understand and validate others members' experiences of loss. Some potential members felt so alienated in the early stages of group formation that they elected to forgo membership activities altogether. But those who stayed within groups long enough to surmount experiential differences and take part in the construction of common norms, goals, and group identities soon found that the experience of "growing together" was healing and reconstructive.

"Making a New Family": The Importance of Companionship

Coming together as a group was sometimes easier said than done, but working through group tensions helped to build solid foundations of trust, friendship, and commitment to one another and to the group. Family members and survivors learned to rely on fellow group members as faithful companions and as individuals who would attend to, understand, and share thoughts, feelings, reactions, and stories. At times a group's companionship function was more attractive than the group goal; as Priscilla Salyers recalled, "In the beginning it wasn't really for the memorial; it was so I could be around other people."

Attending group meetings was the first time in which many participants took stock of their social network, seeing who else had survived the bombing and how everyone was faring physically and emotionally. Vicki Hamm recalled a powerful group "reunion": "That's where you saw who was alive. You know, some of the people that I thought were dead were alive." Groups enabled survivors and family members to continually keep tabs on one another. Ray Washburn emphasized that he came in contact with and visited "a lot of people" at Murrah Building Survivor Association meetings and felt that this group was "more helpful because I got to visit with everybody, talk to them, see how they were doing." Keeping apprised of others' progress allowed members to regain a sense of control and provided further details that helped them in their own memory work.

In addition to reconnecting with old friends and acquaintances, group membership allowed participants to connect with others who soon became dear. For family members, meeting new survivors who had known or worked with their murdered loved one was tremendously meaningful, permitting them to hear others' memories of their loved ones. When Doris Jones met Priscilla Salyers, she was thrilled to learn that she had known her murdered daughter, Carrie: "Priscilla was the first person that was a survivor that I met that knew Carrie . . . she was the proof, she was like, 'Oh yeah, Carrie was fun. She was just a character.'" From that moment on, Jones noted, "survivors became crucial, [it was] so important to meet and find people that knew Carrie."

Jones's reaction to meeting others who had known her daughter illustrates how group meetings allowed victims' families to reconnect to their past and that of their loved ones, to recover something of what was lost. This is akin to "prosthetic memory," a concept that denotes how one comes to acquire memories of unexperienced historical events through visiting museums, monuments, and other such places. Surviving coworkers kept murdered victims alive in memories that family members could access by initiating new relationships. For their part, coworkers also felt that forming relationships with family members reconnected them to their deceased colleagues and friends. Thus, interpersonal relationships literally became social frameworks of memory.

In addition, many individuals employed in the state and federal government offices within the Murrah Building still relied extensively on surviving coworkers. Because the devastating events of that morning had irrevocably changed group dynamics among workers, it became important to preserve and re-form, not abandon, those former social frameworks. To these ends, survivors regarded new hires who replaced murdered employees as outsiders. Over time, the survivors who had "been there" on April 19, 1995, found themselves in the minority. By this time, survivors had jelled into new groups and did not often admit others into the circle so as to preserve group identity despite the presence of new workers. As Germaine Johnston recalled:

> [We] had a "bombing group" of employees. . . . It was very cliquish for a while. The new people didn't understand. We didn't expect them to understand. And the survivors were the majority for a while, but it didn't last very long. It was only a year or two because they replaced all the people that were killed. . . . But we still, you know, had things together. We always had a memorial service every anniversary in the office.

For some participants, the bonds of companionship offered so much that it seemed as if fellow group members became extended family. Sources of companionship could arise from physical ties to the bombing site or because members fulfilled familial support roles. For survivor Morgan Scott, membership in the memorial group was family-like, since the memorial's proximity to the bombing location made it feel like home: "It's kind of like going home [to the place where it happened] or something. It's hard to describe it, but it's really helped." Scott's remarks illustrate the crucial link between memory reconstruction and physical space. In fact, ties to physical space were implicit in the categorization of certain groups, such as surviving coworkers, that defined themselves by their relationship to their former workplace. Angela Richerson and Vicki Hamm both stated that members of the memorial group functioned as family members, with Hamm noting, "We felt like that was your family from the Murrah Building."

These familial roles were especially important for members who did not have a base of support in their own families. Cameron Crawford felt that he had "lost" his family in the bombing, since they did not talk about it: "I mean, that just compounded this horrible hurt that you're going through. I started to see my family fall apart. . . . we're dealing with first the death of someone you love and then second a terrorist attack and then your family starts to disintegrate." For Crawford, the habeas group became another outlet: "That was their appeal for me, to be able to talk to other people outside of our family." This fellowship was ultimately more important to Crawford than death penalty reform: "More than the political, it was more the contact with making a new family since I had lost mine and [the group was] kind of a way to get my head off what was going on with my own family."

Unfortunately, several participants, both family members and survivors, described their families as being unable to understand the full extent of the bombing's impact upon their lives. Often, survivors' family members expected them to be the same people they had been on the morning of April 19, 1995. This gave rise to tremendous emotional alienation as survivors faced loved ones' expectations that nothing had changed. As Priscilla Salyers described:

> My family was not understanding what I was going through. . . . they didn't realize that I am not the same person. . . . My husband was the type who wanted to just pretend like this didn't happen and we'll be fine. And I couldn't, I had to face what happened. . . . And the only place I could get that was to go and be around other survivors and families.

Many described how the bombing did not seem to exist for their families, rendering it impossible to talk to them about the event and its aftermath. Several were also offended when family members did not call on the bombing's anniversary. Doris Jones acknowledged that her family might not know that talking about the bombing was actually healing for her: "Maybe they don't want me to get upset. Maybe they think I'll be talking to them just like to you. But they just think, they don't want to upset me. But they don't know that that's what's healing. . . . your family should be helpful when you're healing."

As a result, several participants did not talk to their families about the bombing. "I would just try to reassure them that I'm doing okay. I guess I didn't want to upset them anymore and I would only tell them the good, positive things that were happening. . . . I didn't want to put any more burden on them. I mean, they had been through it too," explained Janet Beck. Taylor Rickel shared more with coworkers than with family because they intuitively "understood" in a way that family could not: "They understood, but they didn't go through [it] like my coworkers that were there went through it so we had like a bond. Whereas my family, I had to explain it to them. It was better at work." Thus, boundaries of "family" in the wake of the bombing became an elastic concept, more flexible than blood relations or legal kinship.

"A Whole Lot Inside": The Narrative Benefits of Companionship

Group membership fostered trust in and respect for fellow members, which in turn made it easier for family members and survivors to truly open up to others. Group bonds, then, were built on and in turn facilitated interpersonal engagement and narrative exchange, transforming groups into "storying" sites where narratives of the bombing and of the identities of its perpetrators were continually constructed and revised. Narrative formation is an essential element of Freud's processes of "working through,"[31] and others have noted its importance in overcoming traumatic discontinuities and ruptures.[32] Sharing stories facilitates the development of social bonds and sensemaking.[33] Significantly, narrating grief is a collective experience, and sharing stories created a set of normative expectations or assumptions regarding who a group was and what it stood for.

Participants often discussed the benefits of exchanging stories in abstract therapeutic terms such as "healing"; Doris Jones even explicitly described talking through trauma as the only form of counseling she had. Diane Dooley stated that talking held healing potential, and for Priscilla Salyers, fellow group members were a "support base" and group participation was "cathartic." Even the physical act of speaking could result in emotional healing because telling one's story made one more *aware* of traumas. Ernestine Hill Clark recalled one moment when she unexpectedly broke down:

In the first families and survivors meetings that I went to and they had everybody around tables and they asked you to talk about something. I thought I was there to listen and facilitate, right, but as they came around the table to me, well, I started talking, I started crying just like I did today, and realized I had a whole lot inside that was going to need to be taken care of.

Storytelling, then, illuminated what victims still needed to work through in regard to the bombing. As one therapist has explained:

There is typically a key point in the story where each individual's composure changes, the ability to proceed is disrupted, and, typically, crying occurs. Remarkably, these moments do not typically occur at the moment in the story where the most "objectively" horrific or distressing aspect of the event is told. Rather, such moments typically reflect the difficulty the individual is having in coming to terms with the way the events unfolded. At these moments, the conflict is most clearly presented.[34]

Recalling one such moment of conflict, Doris Jones discussed how talking about her daughter before other members of the memorial group was important to her recovery:

> Each time we met, a different person would stand up and talk, be the representative of that table. . . . it was my turn. I had to get up and I got my name [out] and I couldn't say Carrie's name. I just, you know, the tears just began to pour. And I finally got out Carrie's name. . . . the next time I had to do it, I was able to say Carrie's name, and then I began to cry again. But each time I went, I would get a little bit better.

Jones's narrative illustrates how memory work is a sense-making process whereby one learns how to structure the bombing and its effects, the first stage of which is pronouncing what has happened and, most important, to whom it has happened. Jones had to verbally situate her daughter, Carrie, within the bombing in order to begin the profoundly important process of telling others her story.

Narration enabled bombing victims to gain critical distance from and therefore perspective on the events of April 19, 1995, and their aftermath. As Diane Dooley noted, "You would talk and talk and talk that first year and tell it over and over and over and over again. And so I think, naturally, . . . you sort of become desensitized to it, to what you went through in a way." The importance of being able to speak to other group members after most others had "moved on" from the bombing was especially valuable. Oklahoma City groups retained the bombing as the nucleus of their social frameworks of memory long past the time when it was publicly eclipsed by other events. Ernestine Hill Clark stated that she and others felt as if they had to conceal their own feelings outside of groups: "You had to be real careful because after six months a lot of people felt like people shouldn't be talking—that you should've gotten over it, so a lot of us had to hide our feelings."

Story sharing and the extension of insider status to others continued for years after the bombing. As time passed, group social frameworks grew flexible enough to allow in those who became affiliated with the bombing much later. As late as five years after the bombing, for instance, park rangers became part of the memorial group "family" when the National Memorial opened and was staffed partly through National Park Service personnel. Ernestine Hill Clark noted that the rangers were accepted into the memorial group after meeting volunteer survivors and family members by sharing stories:

> So we went through training with those rangers and we became like a family because, once again, at that point, which was at four years for a new group of people we were asked to tell our story. . . . And as the rangers sat there and listened to us and [we] saw the tears, [those] tears also softened my four years of healing, they became close to us. We volunteered weekly with them. . . . We had private parties where the rangers and the volunteers got together. So they watched us really grow and heal. By the fifth anniversary where we had that big celebration they were like brothers and sisters to us, so they became family.

From Narrative Engagement to Agency and Advocacy

Some survivors and family members directed their intense emotional passions into advocacy to such an extent that they became "career" advocates and were still involved in advocacy work many years after the bombing. Group affiliation was a key factor in many survivors' and family members' transitions from narrators to advocates. Bud Welch and Marsha Kight both became career advocates for a time; Welch serves on the memorial's board of directors as well as on the boards of several national anti–death penalty organizations, and Kight became a nationally known victims' rights advocate following the trials of McVeigh and Nichols, at one point working for the National Organization for Victim Assistance.

Participants frequently described active involvement in group teamwork—communally accomplishing goals—as reconstructive and therapeutic. In addition to being vocationally interested in the memorial as a project, Charlie Younger found the building process "healing": "My office being right across the street from it and watching it go up, it was like, you know, a little pet project of mine. That was probably as much healing as anything watching the memorial be built." Similarly, Dr. Paul Heath related that group participation enabled him to channel PTSD symptoms such as hypervigilance into positive activities. Other therapeutic benefits of communal activity were staying active and not surrendering to despair; Diane Leonard described involvement in the memorial task force and habeas group as "healing" because it satisfied the need to "do something." Although this need could also evolve to the point where participants literally wore themselves out, Cameron Crawford stressed that exhaustion was also a blessing: "I think for me, it was [healing]. It was that partly it was having to do something, and the other part was having to keep myself busy night and day so that I was just so exhausted that I just could kinda go home and fall into bed. You didn't really just sit and think about it."

Accomplishing group goals also helped group members regain a sense of control and overcome helplessness. Susan Urbach felt empowered by the habeas group's successful lobbying for the passage of habeas reform. Sometimes members' immediate needs were directly fulfilled by the group; Stan Mayer, a critically injured survivor, was in danger of being fired from his job because of the extensive leave time required by a succession of surgeries and periods of recovery, and the habeas group helped him to keep his job.

Occasionally group members took on additional advocacy responsibilities in pursuit of a group goal. Richard Williams, an injured survivor who had also been the assistant building manager for the Murrah Building at the time of the bombing and who knew it and its occupants intimately, assumed the mantle of survivor advocate to ensure that survivors were accorded an appropriate place in the memorialization process, and to continually emphasize that survivors as well as family members had been injured and traumatized:

> I always felt like that I spoke for those who were in the building and survived and those who were, maybe not at work that day, who worked there and as it turned out even those who were in the other buildings outside of the Murrah building. . . . I felt like that it was my purpose because of my connection with the building, my connection with the people, most of the survivors for that matter.

Group members themselves were intensely proud of what they had accomplished. Charlie Younger characterized the passage of the Antiterrorism and Effective Death Penalty Act of 1996 as "a miracle in most of our eyes" and described being part of the memorial process as "quite an honor." Diane Leonard, who was present on the stage when President Clinton signed the

AEDPA into law, recalled, "What an amazing day that was. It was incredible to see those initials going on that piece of paper." Richard Williams described the memorial as a tremendous accomplishment as well: "You know whether it's gonna be a stone in the ground or, you know, and obviously I don't know that any of us really thought it would end up being what it is today. That's the miracle about the whole process." Vicki Hamm believed that she felt most whole the day the memorial opened:

> When I walked down the steps I could feel . . . something being lifted from me. And I felt lighter and I felt relief. And when I thought about it later, I could describe it as I had been wearing an overcoat for five years and had all these feelings of depression, anger, sadness, guilt, despair. . . . And now I had a place to hang that overcoat and leave those feelings there. I didn't need to carry them with me anymore. . . . It was very liberating.

Many even remarked that members' efforts were guided by divine energies; as Beverly Rankin observed, "It just seemed like God had a hand in it."

As beneficial as the accomplishment of a collective goal was, there came a time when some members felt that involvement was no longer necessary. For some, moving forward created the incentive to cease intense involvement. As Diane Dooley stated, "After about the fifth anniversary, when they opened the memorial, and the memorial got off and running, I sort of didn't feel like it was as therapeutic anymore."

As sites of memory work, community advocacy groups mediated members' lived experience in the aftermath of the Oklahoma City bombing, providing camaraderie, conversational exchange, ideological engagement, and the chance to effect transformative goals. These groups were certainly not the only institutions that fulfilled a mediating function; news media organizations and the criminal justice system also played formative roles. Many family members and survivors became actively involved in more than one of these institutions and had to simultaneously learn, negotiate, and manage a plethora of norms, perspectives, and objectives.

Like other forms of institutional participation, the experience of group membership was fraught with the tension between passivity and agency, defeat and accomplishment, accepting the status quo and effecting change, stagnating within anger and moving forward. But joining a group was unique among these myriad possible opportunities for institutional involvement. Community advocacy groups were initially the only institutions that family members and survivors actually created or helped to create from scratch. In founding a group, family members and survivors negotiated and established group norms, routines, means, and ends, determining what a group would be about, what it would accomplish, and how it would achieve these goals. Essentially, these groups were institutions with human faces, where one was most likely to *join with* familiar others instead of temporarily working within a preexisting institution and having to adopt to its strange, professionalized norms.

Created and populated by family members and survivors, community advocacy groups were perhaps the institutions most receptive to and accommodating of the unique demands of members' memory work. Because groups' goals were more localized and discrete than those of the news media and the criminal justice system, they enjoyed greater flexibility and freedom to change over time and so could easily respond to new developments and adopt new priorities once old purposes were obviated or accomplished. Therefore, group membership was a very different form of institutional involvement than working within a preexisting juggernaut like the news media or the criminal justice system, where family members and survivors were confronted with foreign cultures of strange norms, jargon, processes, and priorities that may or may not have mapped onto the memory work that they so desperately wanted and needed to accomplish.

5

"God Bless the Media"

Negotiating News Coverage

In the bombing's aftermath, the media were largely responsible for piecing together the fragments of its evolving story, investigating the suspects, their motivations, their families, and their life histories, repeatedly airing photographs of McVeigh's perp walk and the Murrah Building ruins. McVeigh chose the Murrah Building in part because its open design would afford news organizations ample opportunity to obtain the photographs and television footage necessary to adequately convey the full extent of the damage.[1] In essence, McVeigh was counting on the media to cement the bombing's place in American memory. And they did not disappoint.

But the media also fulfilled new, unforeseen functions and roles. Paradoxically, news media both constituted part of the traumatic problem and proffered new opportunities and solutions to combat its effects. Endless parades of stories on the bombing could simultaneously be fonts of information and painful reminders of loss. Media coverage prompted national and international demonstrations of support, solidarity, and compassion. It provided crucial information to family members and survivors concerning the bombing site's status and documented others' reactions. It cast family members and survivors as helpless bystanders to tragedy and trauma but also aided them in activist ventures. It introduced them to the perpetrators and acquainted them with their life histories, family relationships, personalities, and alleged motives. Yet, the perpetrators could manipulate this same medium, and news stories also played a significant role in creating, maintaining, and strengthening the impression that McVeigh, Nichols, and Fortier were unwelcome presences in participants' lives. Finally, the media allowed victims themselves to take center stage, if only temporarily, thereby providing outlets for their voices, energies, and opinions and a forum where they could advocate for change, explain community developments, remember murdered loved ones, respond to prior news stories, or simply provide their perspectives.[2] As an institutional site of memory, the mass media were a venue of contestation and negotiation, resolving issues such as who could and should tell which types of stories, who should be visible in the media spotlight and when, and what it meant to exercise agency or remain passive.

The mass media almost immediately regarded the Oklahoma City bombing as a traumatic event.[3] Media coverage catalogued the latest developments in rescue efforts and law enforcement investigations and encapsulated and disseminated diverse experiences of loss, injury, pain, suffering, victimhood, and survivorship.[4] At the same time, the mass media unified and galvanized the Oklahoma City community, becoming a site of shared knowledge and cultivating shared impressions of the perpetrators, documenting shared ties with and support for victims, and shared frustration over the event's inconceivability.[5] They demarcated and packaged the bombing as a culturally and collectively traumatic event. Therefore, participants found that local and national media coverage of the bombing simultaneously helped and hindered their memory work

Reporting Stories, Recording Stories:
The Mass Media and Memory Work

Confronted with the Oklahoma bombing crisis, journalists attempted to structure, control, and thereby defuse the threats that it and its agents posed to the existing social order, normalizing what could be normalized and marginalizing the remainder in the hope that transforming the bombing into a spectacle would establish it as an outlier, lessening its threat.[6] Therefore, journalists labored to problematize, construct, organize, and resolve the bombing as a social dilemma. They recycled narratives and images so that the disturbing became routine, rendering the bombing more familiar to viewers and thus potentially less distressing and ominous.[7]

To these ends, journalists used narrative to construct and reaffirm their own professional and cultural authority in the bombing's wake.[8] News stories re-presented individuals and events according to narrative conventions: assigning family members and survivors a protagonist role to personify events, describing relationships and conflicts in a rising action segment, and then concluding by restoring harmony and balance to the extent possible.[9] Through these conventions, journalists became agents of social cohesion; cued audiences in to appropriate interpretations;[10] ensured that stories were "culturally consonant" with readers; strengthened existing cultural, social, and political norms and respect for authority;[11] constructed new social identities and facilitated social action;[12] and chronicled individual and collective progress.[13]

By determining what was "newsworthy," the media also acted as gatekeepers, turning dilemmas into crises and moments of discord into movements. Stories about certain types of events—from rescue and recovery to advocacy processes of memorialization and legal reform to investigation and prosecution—became essential to redefining personal and public priorities, commitments, and communities. With routines and norms disrupted, attention was now focused upon more metaphysical consequences—what the events of April 19, 1995, had revealed about victims,' responders,' perpetrators,' and citizens' humanity and morality as well as their repercussions upon these individuals, Oklahoma City, the state of Oklahoma, and America.[14]

The "News" Normal: Family Members and Survivors in the Media

Key to the bombing's framing and interpretation were victims and perpetrators, the news makers who most centrally embodied or threatened cherished social institutions, norms, and values. As part of this stabilization, news coverage of the bombing molded victims and perpetrators into stereotypical character types. Antiestablishment villains who disturbed social order to get undeserved media attention were juxtaposed against advocates who did not disturb social order to publicize their messages and heroic protagonists who overcame adversity to restore public peace and safeguard enduring values and institutions.[15] Coverage of crime emphasized predictable binary oppositions—good versus evil, victim versus offender, moral insiders versus moral outsiders, moral acts versus immoral acts, justice versus injustice.[16] These stories invoked contests between victims and perpetrators that were mediated by police, prosecutors, and judges who adjudicated and enforced moral superiority and moral control.

Despite being championed by aggressive-sounding movements such as "victims' rights," crime victims typically appear passive in news coverage, as individuals powerless to prevent their violation, as weak, helpless, or blameless individuals engaged in a respectable activity when attacked who were powerless to prevent their violation.[17] Bombing coverage, however, did not necessarily portray grieving family members and survivors in a passive light. News stories covered bombing victims' memory work, recording the evolution of a transformative narrative and chronicling their progress from victim to survivor.

In the wake of the bombing, family members and survivors heard talk of finding a "new normal"—the need to find comfort and stability in the radically altered, scarcely quotidian social, emotional, financial, and physical landscapes of their lives. For many participants, giving media interviews became part of this new life, giving rise to a "news" normal. Family members' and survivors' willingness to grant media interviews—and the news media's embrace of them—accords with popular culture's enthusiasm for victims and victimization stories and the importance of talking about trauma when working through its effects. Even when media stories highlighted how the bombing victimized family members and survivors, even as they were portrayed as all but crushed by its emotional, physical, financial, or social impacts, their media appearances evidenced a strategic agenda toward remembrance, reconstruction, or even revenge.

Family members' and survivors' media participation could thus be regarded as identity management—efforts to evolve, express, and maintain personal identities that accorded with a healthy self-understanding, along with offering public eulogies for murdered loved ones.[18] Individuals sought to portray themselves as survivors of crime moving forward and not crime victims mired in the past, as a mobilized and memorializing community and not a pessimistic and bitter enclave. These individuals had been powerless to predict or prevent their victimization on April 19, 1995, but now they could control how they responded. Together, their personal stories of victimization became collective representations of individual and institutional perseverance, dedication, and transformation. Indomitable as individuals and unstoppable as organized groups, family members and survivors created narratives that were perfect capstones to media stories that ended with a dollop of normalcy.

Through media appearances, family members and survivors staked moral claims, told their own stories, and publicly took control of their memory work, gaining renewed self-control and denying McVeigh a hold over their lives and personalities. Amid media coverage heavily focused on McVeigh and his fellow conspirators, family members' and survivors' narratives emphasized hope, caring, camaraderie, civic engagement, and possibilities for institutional reform. In managing individual and institutional identities through media interviews, victims accomplished memory work by confronting the bombing's impacts on themselves and their community. Participating in media coverage allowed family members to argue for and attain a place for their emotions and emotional needs, benefiting from and reinforcing media norms of emotional propriety that differed drastically from those in the courtroom.

The first requests for interviews came almost immediately; injured survivors were often interviewed in the hospital in the days immediately following the bombing. Survivor Susan Urbach recalled, "They wanted to interview someone hospitalized. I fit that bill. With facial injuries, you didn't even have to say I was injured, they could see it, and it wasn't too horrifying to look at those injuries." Sometimes one's media involvement began somewhat involuntarily. Tom Hall, who began to grant interviews after news media published an unattributed image of him in an injured state taken shortly after the bombing, commented: "Early on I gave a few interviews just to put a name with my picture that was in *Time* magazine. . . . the graphic picture of me in the street and there was no name with it." Others chose to participate in media interviews to further an important goal; Diane Leonard "originally declined interviews" but later began to grant them while advocating for the passage of federal death penalty reform.

Family members and survivors who granted interviews alluded to an unspoken governing "etiquette." Richard Williams noted that it was disrespectful to speak to the media while in the midst of burying friends and coworkers: "I had requests in and around the many, many funerals I attended but refused to do them out of respect for my friends that were being memorialized and put to rest." This unspoken code also demanded that individual family members or survivors not claim to speak for others, leaving room for alternative stories and perspectives. Doris Jones emphasized, "When I did an interview I tried to always state that I was speaking only for me." She also attempted to ensure that media coverage reflected a diversity of opinion: "Another reason [I did media interviews] was that there were some people making statement[s] that I didn't agree with, and they made it sound like everyone agreed with what they were saying."

Once family members and survivors began to give interviews, they often continued to do so for many reasons. Media interviews provided opportunities for advocacy, response, and "setting the record straight." Diane Leonard found the media to be a key advocacy resource: "When we started working on the federal [habeas reform] legislation, it was important that we get as much public support as possible, so I began interviews." Doris Jones granted media interviews to raise awareness that Judge Matsch had ruled "some families and survivors . . . could not attend the trials if we were going to testify." Similarly, Leonard continued to grant interviews "with many members of the media . . . because of the relationship we had built" and other reasons: "I realized how I wanted information . . . and that drove me to give others information [about our issues.] Also, I wanted to assure that the correct information was out there as much as possible. Another thing, I guess, was that I felt so passionately about every subject I was interviewed on and was glad to have a way to express my views." Relationships of trust frequently evolved between family members or survivors and individual journalists. Janet Beck recalled that "we got to know who they were real quick, and who the ones were that really cared and who the ones were that were after a story." And there were ways to protect one's integrity during interviews.

Despite their diversity of opinions, victims' families and survivors were aware that in these media interviews they were seen as representative victims, representative grievers, and even representative Oklahomans, and acted accordingly. As Susan Urbach noted:

> Many of the media had contacted the Greater Oklahoma City Chamber of Commerce about interviewing people. I was a known quantity to the chamber as being someone who was articulate and thoughtful and likely able to deal with national media and present a good image for the city. I [mean that] they knew I wasn't going to sound like a kook or a hick, which is often what it appears that major media from [the] East or West Coast might [think] about a state like Oklahoma.

Richard Williams regarded participation in media interviews as a way to positively influence what the media said about the bombing and those it had most intimately affected; it was important not only "for the world to know each of our stories" but also for "the world to see how someone directly affected was coping, healing, moving on, never forgetting the event but realizing that life has to move on without leaving the pain and suffering behind." Marsha Kight, too, felt that "the media was very helpful in giving the victims a voice as well."

On a related note, participants often agreed to interviews because of a perceived duty or responsibility to convey the possibility of rebuilding lives and communities, to represent murdered loved ones and other survivors, and to represent bombing-related groups. Susan Urbach remarked, "I have felt that I have had a 'role' so to speak that has been more a lay philosopher and theologian," focusing upon "how do you become mentally and emotionally well again." Heavily involved in the memorial task force, survivor Richard Williams felt that giving media interviews was part of his "responsibility to represent my fellow survivors due to my current position with GSA and as a survivor," which gave him "unique connections to everything." Interviews allowed Williams to both represent community groups and convey that key values and interpersonal and institutional bonds had not only endured but grown stronger: "I always felt it was my responsibility to properly represent all of the groups I was working for, representing, and connected to in a manner that the public would see that even in the worst of times . . . I and others could continue our lives."

Cameron Crawford felt a responsibility to represent his murdered sibling:

> With there being so many victims in the bombing, I think I was so afraid of no one knowing who [my sibling] was and how dedicated he was to serving his country, and I wanted everyone to know that they, too, had suffered a loss. I always tried to make sure the focal point of an interview was [my sibling] so he would be remembered by people who hadn't even know him.

Similarly, Doris Jones said, "Some of the first interviews I did w[ere] about the count of 168 [victims] when I knew it was 169 (later to be 171) [taking into account the viable unborn babies, including my daughter's, who were also murdered in the bombing]. . . . And I wanted everyone to know my loss and how the world would never get to know who my daughter was."

For many, media interviews were therapeutic. Crawford found them "cathartic," explaining: "This is the therapy that I need. I can tell people about [my sibling]. I can talk about what happened to me." Marsha Kight also termed media work "cathartic": "I think talking about it, sharing your experience, hope, how things might change is a cathartic process, and it's helpful to know that it is getting to a large group of people. . . . hopefully . . . somebody will glean something that is helpful from what I've said." But media interviews could also be exhausting; Kight acknowledged, "It was emotionally draining, yes. Sometimes I think I expected too much of myself, and . . . I became very tired." And although media participation had its benefits, it could also hinder personal reconstruction and recovery. "I also realized that if not careful one could get caught up in the media hype from time to time, and if [you were] not able to do the interviews for all the right reasons and be able to turn off the cameras and lights afterward, it could become something that possessed you instead of [you] possessing it," explained Richard Williams. "Many family members, survivors, and rescue workers that were the media darlings didn't seem to cope with the tragedy as those who could accept all the attention and turn it on and off and go on with our focus and new normal life," he added. Tom Hall agreed: "I have seen several of the survivors that look like they are being consumed by the interviews and media attention. I actually think that is a way some of them cope with it and use the attention as a crutch."

In addition, sometimes family members and survivors found certain media practices very disturbing. Marsha Kight recalled that, before interviewing her, many television news media programs would air upsetting lead-in segments: "Right before an interview . . . it would show my daughter and then the Oklahoma City bombing and the aftermath, which made me emotional. . . . I got to the point, there wasn't anything I could do about the sound, but I would close my eyes so I wouldn't have to look at those images again and again right before an interview on TV." Kight also remembered individual interviews in which she was treated badly; on one occasion, she terminated an interview after learning that the show intended to pit her against a member of the Nichols jury. Janet Beck, too, recalled that certain reporters were overly demanding: "I know how invasive they were when they'd call and want to do interviews and just almost insist that you be available for them when they wanted you available to talk to them."

For most, media participation has declined over time. "Most of the media I have been on has been through the first six years, and very little after 2001," remarked Susan Urbach. She noted, "I did one more TV interview recently, which was frankly, exhausting. You never know what their agenda is and how they are going to use it. I'm not interested in doing more of that." Tom Hall stated that "around the anniversary time each year, I get several requests for interviews and only agree to one here and there." Hall explained that he will agree to interviews "if it looks like they are using the interview for something worthwhile and they have a little compassion in their request." Hall also is likely to give interviews to foreign reporters and continues to speak at the National Memorial to various groups, including schoolchildren, because "I guess I feel like I owe it to them for coming down to visit the memorial."

A Healthy Skepticism

In general, the media's efficacy as a site of collective memory depends upon the type of crisis they are covering. Most crises are unpredictable, which may pose difficulties for the news media, and particularly for television, a "time-bound" medium with tightly scheduled programming that the bombing profoundly disrupted.[19] To compensate, television news may continuously play and replay certain images, a practice that maintains and enhances the medium's narrative credibility at a time when journalists are actually hastily trying to recoup and get back on top of a fast-developing story.[20] This was certainly true in the bombing's aftermath, when television viewers were inundated with continuous footage of the Murrah Building ruins and McVeigh's Perry walkout. These images packed the most punch because they were intensely emotive, but while they graphically demonstrated the bombing's affective stakes and shaped popular understandings of grief and suffering, they did little to explain why it occurred.[21]

In addition, the news media could misunderstand, misrepresent, or misappropriate family members' and survivors' concerns. Journalists were frequently accused of using victims' grief to get ratings and of not analyzing or addressing suffering's root causes. The potential for exploitation was highest when the media sought to appropriate a victim's story. Like others before them, many family members and survivors asserted that they "owned" their stories as one might possess tangible property. This claim had real implications for news organizations and news practices; victims who "own" their story should theoretically be able to influence or outright squelch certain uses or representations of it, creating ethical conflicts over who does and who should have control over how victims' stories are presented, and whether and to what extent sensitivity to victims' needs and suffering should become a norm of media coverage.[22]

Many family members and survivors had no difficulty with questioning news practices, and they developed serious reservations about how the media represented postbombing reality, problematizing the credibility, accuracy, influence, and quality of newspaper and television coverage of the bombing, the perpetrators, and their victims.[23] Several took issue with the quality of local media reporting and the sensationalized coverage of local and national media; others were reluctant to credit mass media influence on personal opinion. Overall, there was a preference for national media coverage that was perceived as more objective in tone and broader in scope of context and coverage; inadequate coverage damaged the media's credibility as an information source, its cultural authority, and its efficacy as a site of memory work. A handful of individuals distrusted much of the local Oklahoma City bombing news coverage. Ernestine Hill Clark found the *Daily Oklahoman* "fairly provincial" and "trusted the national writers and the national interviewers more so than I did local ones. . . . being a liberal in this state, I think that they have at least a more level viewpoint. They give both sides." Survivor Stan Mayer also preferred national newspapers: "Newspapers outside of Oklahoma City,

I tended to trust. We don't have a newspaper in Oklahoma City that I would call a newspaper. . . . there's no journalistic credibility, whatsoever."

Others faulted the mass media for exaggerating, sensationalizing, or over-reporting information. For some, media coverage was disproportionately downbeat; Janet Beck recalled, "They were trying to make everything nega-tive, negative, negative. . . . I think they've learned now that they need to, but at the time, they were not focusing on anything positive." If anything, this approach could make victims feel increasingly isolated and powerless; as Beck explained, "they just kept, basically kind of rubbing your face in it. . . . any little thing that happened, I think they kind of blew it out of proportion just to get it out there and nothing we could do could stop it. . . . it got to where you just kind of shut yourself off from everything." But the primary concern was sensationalized coverage. As Ray Washburn put it, "I hate to say this, but I think the media kind of exaggerates some." "I don't trust the mass media to give me facts," Charlie Younger said. "The information they dissem-inate in the media is bits and pieces which would totally lead you to different conclusions sometimes than what the facts were." Diane Dooley also com-mented that victims' vulnerability intensified the media's influence, empha-sizing that "the media does paint . . . maybe a distorted picture of events. . . . we probably were influenced by that. You'd have to be."

In particular, many participants felt the media went too far. "God bless the media, we gotta have them, but their problem is sometimes they report too dang much and they keep trying to keep things going," commented Paul Howell. Younger faulted the media for hyping emotion in the bombing's after-math and throughout the perpetrators' trials, characterizing media coverage as emotionally manipulative, not factually informative: "It helps you form an opinion immediately, you hate the guy to start with. . . . the media has a way of trying to sensationalize all of it to the point that in a way they make it a far different feel than it really is sometimes. . . . there's a lot of misinformation. So I don't trust the media a whole lot." Younger was particularly sensitive to the sensationalized coverage during McVeigh's federal trial in Denver. "I could not believe sometimes when I listened to the evidence for one day, go outside the courthouse, listen to the media people interviewing and then hearing it on TV that night and seeing the facts change," he recalled.

Several participants emphasized that they formed their own opinions or made up their own minds about the bombing suspects rather than rely-ing on news media. Richard Williams noted that the media were helpful in forming his personal opinions because "[it] gave me an opportunity to listen, study, read, and learn and form my own opinions. . . . to reach out to more than one source and try to gather as much information as I thought I needed to try to determine for myself how I felt about it." Other participants even saw the media as profoundly useful tools. "The mass media . . . have more investigative tools, I guess, and they have the ability to go out and really do research where your family doesn't," noted Diane Dooley. Peggy Broxterman felt the media coverage was a believable source that influenced her opinion of McVeigh: "It didn't lie about him. It just told what was going on and so forth and so on."

Consuming, and Being Consumed by, Media Coverage

Participants also differed in their assessments of media coverage's overall usefulness, as well as what it helped them to accomplish. For some, media coverage was not an effective reconstructive tool. Tom Hall confessed he did not pay that much attention to it: "I'd skim over the headlines and read a little bit on it and maybe every now and then read the whole story, but I didn't allow myself to be consumed by it like some people did."

Many participants felt that they had to devour as much coverage of the bombing and the perpetrators as they could. "If there was anything on I watched it," recalled Ernestine Hill Clark. "I videotaped everything that came on. . . . I was just obsessive compulsive about having all the information I could." Hearing news reports and reading articles "were the only ways that I had of forming any opinions at all," emphasized Faith Moore. News coverage allowed participants to grapple with the compelling question "Why?" Diane Leonard noted, "I was driven to get everything I could":

> Until we had the trial . . . that was your major source of information about "why," you know, and "why" is the major haunting question. At least it was for me and it was for many others. . . . I read every shred of anything I could get hold of to try to understand why. . . . I couldn't wait to get to the newspaper every morning to see what new little tidbit there was.

Others felt that they learned much from the media, but nothing that actually improved their comprehension of events and the perpetrators. As Richard Williams noted, "There was a lot of information out there, but it never really told you who they were. Or how they thought or why they thought the way they did."

Individuals' media consumption habits often changed over time. Initially, Doris Jones did not utilize the media to cope. "[I was] consumed with grief," she recalled. "I don't think I really paid that close attention to what I was listening to." At some point, however, this changed: "[Now] I can't seem to get away from the news. I watch it and I'm almost obsessed. I have to watch it. . . . And I didn't used to be that way and I am now, so, yeah, I think media probably did a lot to me that I didn't realize." For the first two years, Vicki Hamm remembered, the bombing "dominated news here in Oklahoma. . . . I was immersed in it and that's where I wanted to be. I wanted to learn everything that I could." But eventually Hamm looked forward to business travel outside of Oklahoma City, where "you wouldn't hear anything about the bombing at all on the news. And that was a relief. I was away from it." But whether or not individual participants found media coverage useful, its constancy made it a presence that could not be easily ignored or avoided. "You can't shut it off, you can't put yourself in a vacuum because it's not gonna go away," emphasized Richard Williams.

Ordinary Faces, Extraordinary Malice: Perpetrators in the News

Another key step in authenticating the bombing as a culturally traumatic event was constructing and managing the perpetrators' identities. Participants faulted the media for their ceaseless coverage of the bombing conspirators, in particular McVeigh and Nichols. Such stories were a primary focus of much early media coverage, as well as the majority of coverage in later years. Many felt that the perpetrators' ubiquitous media visibility was just another factor that they were powerless to change, forcing them to bide their time until the conclusion of legal proceedings, after which, they hoped, news about McVeigh and Nichols would slow to a trickle. As survivor Dot Hill emphasized, "Just about every day I didn't want to hear his [McVeigh's] name anymore. I was sick of him, but I didn't have any control over that." Hill was sure that "there was no way that he was going to ever be out of daily conversation in the news or anywhere else until after he was dead," and so she told herself that "one of these days he'll be dead and gone and he won't get this media circus anymore."

Meeting the Trigger Man: Media Coverage of Timothy McVeigh

> All you heard about was McVeigh, McVeigh, McVeigh, but what about all the people he killed and their worth? We lost

some very smart, wonderful people in our office and in the building. . . . what about them?

—Beverly Rankin

From his arrest to his execution, Timothy McVeigh was always in the media spotlight. The news media familiarized audiences with his physical appearance and demeanor (see chapter 2) and provided biographical information that they found simultaneously enlightening and helpful, troubling and destructive. Reporters unlocked treasure troves of information about his motivations, military service, childhood, family life, and personality—all elements of the "why" question that haunted family members and survivors. Several were fascinated by coverage of McVeigh's strong opposition to the government's actions at Waco and Ruby Ridge and recalled a photograph of McVeigh seated on his car at Waco, staring at the burning Branch Davidian compound. Susan Urbach appreciated in-depth newsmagazine coverage of McVeigh's life before the bombing, which helped to explain why a "smart kid" and U.S. Army veteran had carried out such a heinous act. Certain types of media coverage could also be painful. Survivor Vicki Hamm recalled one particularly troubling newsmagazine interview (probably David Hackworth and Peter Annin's interview, published in *Newsweek* on July 3, 1995) in which McVeigh's defense attorney, Stephen Jones, "wanted to make Timothy McVeigh appear as a real person so people could relate to him." Hamm was angered because the article "had pictures of him smiling, laughing, and that stands out in my mind. . . . they made me feel angry because what difference does it matter how real a person may seem after they've committed such a terrible, terrible thing?" Diane Leonard read the same interview and found that "just seeing him there talking and looking comfortable . . . was just a really difficult thing to see"—so difficult that it "really ripped me to shreds."

The Sidekick: Media Coverage of Terry Nichols

Just as media images of McVeigh emphasized his youth and ordinary appearance, those of Nichols belied his dangerousness. To Ernestine Hill Clark, Nichols's innocuous picture did not match his deeds: "When you just look at a picture of Terry Nichols he looks like a real estate salesman. He looks like somebody very safe. Until you start reading about him." For Germaine Johnston, "Nichols looks like a nicer person" than McVeigh.

Terry Nichols in custody. Image courtesy of the Oklahoma City National Memorial and Museum Archives.

Many participants recalled seeing photographs of Nichols in custody shortly after he turned himself in to authorities in Wichita, Kansas, but most perceived such images to be less influential than McVeigh's perp walk because of Nichols's ancillary involvement in the bombing. "I don't know if that [image of Nichols] had any influence over what I thought like it did with McVeigh," commented Faith Moore. "But it didn't impact me like the one with McVeigh did." When Charlie Younger first saw Nichols's image, he explained, "Just seeing his picture didn't trigger any response for me as much as McVeigh's did. Because I knew who tried to blow me up."

Participants recalled many informative media stories about Nichols. Susan Urbach remarked that many articles, such as those reporting Nichols had renounced his American citizenship, did not seem to be written about the humdrum man with square wire-rimmed glasses. Several were struck by media stories that described how Nichols had turned himself in to the sheriff's office in Kansas "holding his child in front of him," "almost us[ing] his family as a shield." "That really gave me an enormous impression of what a coward he was," Leonard remarked. Many remembered stories reporting that Nichols told the FBI he had purchased great quantities of ammonium nitrate to fertilize his yard. For Richard Williams, media coverage of Nichols still "raised more questions than it gave me answers"; he most appreciated stories about where Nichols had lived and why he hated the government.

In general, then, media coverage of Nichols fostered and reinforced participants' impressions that he was more passive, both in his personality and in his bombing involvement, rendering him a less intrusive media figure than McVeigh.

The Drifter: Media Coverage of Michael Fortier

Family members and survivors recollected that the news media portrayed Fortier and his wife as young, drug-addicted drifters living a rough, redneck existence in a trailer in Kingman, Arizona. "Let's just say he would never be a member of the chamber of commerce," quipped Susan Urbach. "This sounds horrible to say, but when you hear that stereotypical phrase of trailer trash, they were." Several remembered footage of the couple walking in front of their mobile home "out in the middle of nowhere."

Participants unanimously agreed that the mass media were their primary source of information about Fortier. "The only time we saw Fortier was when he was testifying against McVeigh and Nichols," remarked family member Paul Howell. "We didn't get as much information about him through the court as some of the newspaper articles, so in some respects, newspaper articles were more important with Fortier."

Michael Fortier in handcuffs. Image courtesy of the Oklahoma City National Memorial and Museum Archives.

Nearly every participant recalled media reports that McVeigh, Fortier, and his wife had gathered at Fortier's kitchen table in Kingman, Arizona, and watched McVeigh use soup cans to demonstrate how the barrels would be arranged in the rental truck so as to maximize damage. Participants found it hard to imagine what Fortier had been thinking at the time. "They laughed and thought that was funny, and they didn't think he was going to do it and all this kind of stuff," Peggy Broxterman opined, which convinced her that "[Fortier's] almost as evil. . . . What he was encouraging McVeigh to do was wrong. And he encouraged McVeigh by listening to him."

Some victims found Fortier somehow more accessible than McVeigh or Nichols. Diane Dooley explained, "I think McVeigh was a little more of a mysterious figure, I think Fortier was somebody they could really scrutinize" because he was "a pretty simple person . . . more of a lost person that just . . . goes through life without any real purpose or mission or goal." Robin Brown got the impression that he was "just a rebellious teenager who got into some trouble, but I don't think he realized how big of trouble he was going to be in." Janet Beck regarded him as a very selfish young man who took "whichever way is going to be the easiest way out, as long as I can get along in life and as long as I get my drugs, my whatever, I'm happy and life is good, so I don't care." But media details about Fortier's involvement produced a snapshot of Fortier that bewildered Ernestine Hill Clark: "I don't know whether he was so young that he'd thought they were just playing war games or what the deal was." Thus, as with Nichols, media coverage of Michael Fortier created the impression that he was a less threatening figure who played a more minor role in the conspiracy, but could most easily have taken steps to thwart it.

Blood Relations: Perpetrators' Family and Personal Lives in the Media

In addition to media coverage of the perpetrators' personalities, motivations, and ultimate fates, participants were extremely interested in media coverage on a very different subject: the suspects' childhood years and familial relationships. Participants sensed a profound gulf between McVeigh's childhood photographs and the knowledge of what he would grow up to become. "I remember seeing on TV some pictures of him as a young child and as a sweet child," recalled Ernestine Hill Clark, "and thought how tragic it was that whatever had happened to him . . . turn[ed] him into a killer." Ultimately, however, participants regarded McVeigh's childhood experiences as an influence but not an excuse; as Morgan Scott observed, "Thousands, millions of other people have messed-up childhoods too, and they don't go out and do these things."

Participants were also intrigued by media coverage of McVeigh's and Nichols's family members. Susan Urbach observed that "there was much more empathy toward [McVeigh's] father than the mother," in part because Bill McVeigh "looked like he had the weight of the world on his shoulders. . . . he looked like he loved his son immensely and he was so crushed by what his flesh and blood had done, and how does that poor man reconcile loving his son who did this?" McVeigh's mother, Mickey, on the other hand, was not a sympathetic figure, and at one point she even urged victims to "get over it."[24] James Nichols's brother also attracted much attention and speculation. Most participants, including Ernestine Hill Clark, wondered if James Nichols "knew more than he talked about." Some were upset that James and other members of Nichols's immediate family would grant media interviews. "James Nichols was right out there . . . he just kept spouting off for a long time," Janet Beck asserted. "They were able to get their message out, and they were using the media just like the media was using them," she continued. "Their antigovernment views and militia views and everything were really coming out. For them that was a good outlet, and they took advantage of it."

One of the most spectacular participant experiences with perpetrators' family members arose out of a media interview with McVeigh's father. Bud Welch was struck by a television interview with Bill McVeigh about a year after the bombing in which he was "physically stooped in grief"; Welch explained, "He had a deep pain in his eye that I recognized immediately because I was living that same pain at that same moment." Then and there, he said, "I knew that someday I needed to go tell that man that I truly cared how he felt and did not blame him or his family for what his son had done."

Welch finally got this opportunity in September 1998, when he journeyed to the Buffalo/Niagara Falls area of upstate New York to speak against the death penalty. The two men spent the first half hour of the visit literally finding common ground in Bill McVeigh's garden. When Bill invited Welch into his house, Welch met McVeigh's sister Jennifer, and the three sat around a kitchen table that was pushed up against a wall upon which hung family photographs. One particular photo of Tim soon caught Welch's attention, and his gaze was repeatedly drawn to that image. He eventually realized that he had to say something about why he was drawn to the picture. "Finally I just said, 'God, what a good looking kid,'" Welch recalled. His comment was greeted by silence; finally, Bill McVeigh looked at him and said, "That's Tim-my's high school graduation picture." At that moment, Welch related, "There was this big tear that rolled out of his right eye, down his cheek. And I could see at that moment that this father could cry for this son." Reflecting back upon this meeting, Welch said, "I think what happened that Saturday morning in western New York is I found a bigger victim of the Oklahoma City bombing than myself." While Welch has had numerous opportunities to talk about Julie, he emphasized, "Bill doesn't have a chance to ever say anything positive about Tim."

The conspirators' romantic and familial relationships also received media attention. A comparison between coverage of McVeigh and Nichols was a study in contrasts. As one article noted, "While McVeigh imprinted himself on the public consciousness as an angry, unrepentant loner, Nichols has made a less emphatic impression: antigovernment, yes, but also somewhat timid and confused."[25] McVeigh apparently did not date or have a girlfriend even while in high school, and although he may have traveled to Wichita a couple of times to see a girl while he was in the army, he allegedly was very nervous around women and would "literally blush."[26] In contrast, Nichols had been married twice and fathered three children; his eldest son, Josh, was born in 1982 to his first wife, Lana Walsh (now Lana Padilla), and he had conceived two others with his second wife, Marife: a daughter named Nicole, born August 1, 1993, and a son, Christian, born in late 1995.[27] Both Marife Nichols and Lori Fortier were pregnant at the time of the bombing.[28]

The media made much of Nichols's family ties. In the days immediately following the bombing, "friends and neighbors in Decker, Michigan," described Nichols as a "decent, hard-working" man, albeit one with a "deep distrust of government."[29] According to some, Nichols was an upstanding family man and doting father who tolerated his second wife's infidelity and accepted the child of that union.[30] But other sources revealed a darker side to Nichols's family life. Evidence suggests that he was a controlling and misogynistic husband; his second wife, Marife, "confirmed under cross-examination that she once quoted her husband as saying that 'Young ones [wives] were easier to train.'"[31]

Whatever the truth, the media took notice when Nichols's defense team chose to capitalize on their client's family-friendly image during the sentencing phase of his federal trial, attempting to "portray him as a loving family man who was unknowingly manipulated into performing innocent favors for his dangerous friend McVeigh."[32] Defense attorney Michael Tigar characterized Nichols as McVeigh's foil, a man who "baked bread, raised fawns, and received a hardship discharge from the Army in order to care for his 7-year-old son."[33] Nichols's behavior during sentencing supported this image; news stories reported that he "wept silently as his friends and relatives told how he made flash cards and greeting cards out of the file folders and toothpaste he was given in prison."[34]

Like Nichols, Michael Fortier was married with children. At the time of McVeigh's trial in 1997, the couple had two children, 4-year-old Kayla and 16-month-old Michael. But unlike Nichols, whom acquaintances had described in media interviews as serious and quiet, Fortier was deemed a "happy-go-lucky guy" by "former employers, teachers, friends, and Army chums."[35] Though others noted he was "suspicious of the government," the media reported that Fortier had returned to his hometown of Kingman, Arizona, to "raise a family, and, some say, start a business,"[36] but was sidetracked by his habitual use of crystal meth and marijuana[37] and his subsequent involvement in the bombing.

In August 1995, Fortier pled guilty to reduced charges in exchange for his cooperation and testified before a federal grand jury, along with his wife, Lori, who was granted immunity from prosecution.[38] Media sources reported that Fortier took this deal in order to preserve his family; a *Los Angeles Times* article from June 1995 stated that cooperating and agreeing to a plea bargain could allow his attorney to "negotiate a deal to salvage some of his life with his family" while refusing would mean that "he could be executed by lethal injection, leaving his child fatherless."[39] Journalists knew that Fortier's daughter, Kayla, was his "soft spot."[40]

Family members and survivors knew, of course, that the fact that Nichols and Fortier were husbands and fathers did not necessarily mean that they were successful in those roles and relationships. Nichols likely had difficulties in maintaining romantic relationships with women, if his choice of a Filipino mail-order bride is any indication. And it is difficult to believe that the Fortiers's marital and familial relationships were not affected by the fact that both were drug users, habitually using marijuana, crystal meth, and LSD.[41]

But setting aside telltale symptoms such as mail-order brides and meth addictions, even the bare presumption that Nichols and Fortier loved their families made their involvement in the bombing harder to understand. As family member Cameron Crawford stated, "We learned about McVeigh's father and sister, but you know, McVeigh stood out to me as [having] a . . . single focus against the government, Waco, whatever. But I mean, Terry Nichols had a brother and a mom and a wife and a son . . . but he still got involved with this, but aren't you thinking about your family?" Robin Brown thought Nichols's participation "rather strange because he has kids."

Many felt that these suspects' family ties somehow made them more human than McVeigh, the stoic loner with so few emotional encumbrances. While having a family was not a mitigating factor per se—indeed, it meant that Nichols and Fortier had more to lose and rendered their involvement even more inexplicable—it did serve as a proxy for their capacity to engage in meaningful human relationships and normative emotional interaction.

Keeping Up with Jones: Links between Media and Legal Narratives

We have seen how the media attempted to manage the identities of bombing victims and perpetrators, and how family members and survivors also used the media to engage in identity management, combat the perpetrators, set the record straight, and appear active and engaged instead of passive and disconnected. But the perpetrators, too, used the media to similar ends, with potentially harrowing consequences for family members and survivors.

In pretrial proceedings, McVeigh's defense attorney Stephen Jones faulted family members and survivors for making emotional comments about McVeigh in media interviews, alleging that their remarks demonized him before his federal trial and necessitated that McVeigh be allowed to grant media interviews to counteract that negative publicity. This illustrates how the media's acceptance of emotionality and public catharsis are at odds with legal emotive norms. In the courtroom, emotion should be private, not public; adjudication must utilize reason, not passion, with control prioritized over catharsis. Jones's claims invert typical "rights" arguments; it is customarily crime victims, not criminal defendants, who appeal to judges for increased participative rights. In addition, these contentions demonstrate Jones's willingness to strategically manage McVeigh's identity by forsaking restrictive legal norms of emotionality for the more liberal norms preferred by popular culture.

The drama began in August 1996, when Jones filed a motion to expand McVeigh's access to media outlets. In his supporting brief, he noted that to date McVeigh had given four print media interviews; that he had permitted journalists to talk off the record with McVeigh while he was incarcerated in El Reno with the caveat that these conversations would not be recorded, published, or made part of the public record; and that he allowed Tom Brokaw from NBC and Scott Pelley from CBS to "meet, film and record a very brief casual meeting" with his client, resulting in short news segments.[42]

Jones alleged that he agreed to these media appearances to "humanize" McVeigh and to "stop the rush to judgment of guilt by undermining the inaccurate impression of Mr. McVeigh conveyed throughout the world by incessant repetition of . . . walk-out footage . . . that cast McVeigh as an anti-government killer, a 'marginalized' figure, an 'aberration,' a 'person who lived alone and embittered,' and as a 'loser' whose own inadequacies produced the tragedy."[43] Additional media interviews with "respected" national media sources were necessary, Jones asserted, to counteract inaccurate information as well as to "offset the continuing parade of survivors who speak about 'clawing out his eyes' or 'coming over the bar and hitting him.'"[44] Thus, the defense attorney contended, "Timothy McVeigh has a right to appear in Court as an accused defendant in something other than sackcloth and ashes" and "to soften the less than human sculpture that the Government has chiseled into the consciousness of the nation."[45] The prosecution opposed Jones's request, arguing that McVeigh did not seek media access but an image makeover—"an extraordinary attempt to manipulate the news media to produce a favorable impact on the potential jury pool."[46]

Matters grew even more heated when Judge Matsch adjudicated the matter at a motions hearing on October 4, 1996. In the hearing, Jones asserted, "We don't have victims speaking up for us, we don't have the press speaking up for us, we don't have former prosecutors speaking up for us; and there is very little sympathy" for the defense.[47] Arguing that media interviews were necessary to show that "no matter how thin you make your pancakes, there are always two sides," Jones again emphasized that McVeigh wished only to "present an image of himself smiling, chatting informally and coming across as a regular guy" to "offset to a modest, appropriate, professional degree a year and a half of people who have constantly gone on national television and talked about killing my client, clawing out his eyes, he's a monster, he's an introvert, he's a lunatic, he's a right-wing nut, he's a racist."[48]

Prosecutor Joe Hartzler, however, responded to Jones's comments by insisting that Jones wanted to produce an "infomercial about Timothy McVeigh" and would give preferential treatment to networks that "will present the most favorable image of Mr. McVeigh, the ones who will not ask the hard questions, the ones who will not portray him refusing to answer questions, the ones that will not depict him unfavorably wearing handcuffs or otherwise."[49] Hartzler, who predicted that these interviews would themselves become "news event[s]," asked Judge Matsch to try the case in the courtroom instead of the court of public opinion.[50] Jones, in turn, explicitly blamed fam-

ily members and survivors for organizing a campaign to ruin McVeigh's public image:

> The victims' association lobb[ies] for a single trial, they lobby Congress,
> and they are lobbying for a death penalty. And the facts—they don't want
> to be bothered with the facts. They have already formed their opinion.
> Now, the reason they formed their opinion, I understand. From my soul, I
> understand what they've been through. But let us not kid ourselves: There
> is an organized public effort to use every vehicle in the media to convict
> my client before the first jury member has been empaneled, and that will
> continue throughout the trial.[51]

Jones warned that "if the Court denies this motion, the champagne bot-
tles will break out in the prosecutor's office figuratively and in the victims'
association, and they'll start working the network of telephones and the press
and they will continue."

Though Judge Matsch ultimately denied McVeigh's request for increased
media access, Matsch acknowledged that he did not "exist in a vacuum" and
understood the "publicity and the commercialization of not only the case
but the incident upon which the case is based." Nonetheless, Judge Matsch
affirmed that he was there "not for the defendants but for the process and the
integrity of it,"[52] guaranteeing that he, not the media, would stand guard over
due process to ensure that the defendants received a fair trial.

This legal exchange embodies a fascinating interplay of clashing emotional norms, pitting public enthusiasm for confession and catharsis against
legal reticence. Jones attempted to counteract media coverage "demonizing"
McVeigh by seeking a change of trial venue and requesting increased media
access for his client. He actually succeeded in the first instance, establishing
to Judge Matsch's satisfaction that press coverage of the defendants in Oklahoma was too sentimental, too suffused with emotionality for legal comfort.
There, Jones comported with legal emotive norms by *opposing* popular culture's enthusiasm for confession and catharsis.

But in advocating for McVeigh's increased media access, Jones actually
urged that these same pop culture norms be *embraced*. Though he continued to condemn emotive media coverage of McVeigh as inappropriate, he
essentially requested permission to strategically use and work within these
same norms favoring open emotionality. In an "if you can't beat 'em, join 'em"
move, Jones asserted that McVeigh's cause would be sunk if he were demonized and thus too "hot" to handle, but that favorable media coverage could

"cool" off his client, rendering him the sort of ordinary, approachable, easy-going fellow who might be invited into every audience member's den. Jones essentially urged that it was necessary to adopt mainstream emotive norms in order to reach and influence potential jurors. Therefore, while cultural norms favoring open emotionality had to stop at the courtroom door, individuals' normative expectations and personal emotional practices did not, putting emotion and its propriety on trial along with McVeigh and Nichols.

Jones is scarcely the first or last lawyer to attempt to influence public representations of his client. Like journalists trying to sell publications or increase ratings, lawyers are engaged in advocacy and attempt to "sell" legal narratives and favorable interpretations of defendants' actions. Unlike media stories, attorneys' wares are not for sale to the general public so much as to its representatives—the jury. In their marketing efforts, lawyers make use of many of the same narrative conventions as the mass media—a criminal protagonist with free will, certain story formats, featuring rising and falling action, an interpretation of events that effectuates justice and restores the status quo, and cultivation of professional authority.

Too often, these processes remain hidden from audiences, although the jury is at least charged with critically evaluating competing narratives. Sometimes, however, these constructive processes are too obvious to miss, such as when defense attorneys advocate or facilitate reputational repair, as Jones did for McVeigh, or when lawyers work aesthetic miracles for witnesses, as the prosecution did to transform the Fortiers into responsible-looking professionals prior to their testimony. In fact, McVeigh, Nichols, and Fortier were all targets of "repackaging" efforts by either prosecution or defense attorneys; McVeigh went from the mad bomber to the guy next door, Nichols from a militia member to a devoted family man, and the Fortiers from drug-addicted "losers" or hippie types to sober government witnesses. Participants were frequently uncomfortable with these legal marketing strategies, although they trusted that the prosecution was merely attempting to marshal all of its weapons to convict McVeigh and Nichols. It is to how family members and survivors negotiated these processes of law, narrative, and memory that we now turn.

6

"Making Sure Justice Was Served"

Pursuing Accountability

In the years preceding McVeigh's trial, family members and survivors anticipated the day when "justice would be served." All could agree on the need for accountability; all wanted McVeigh to be held responsible for his role in the bombing. However, beyond the threshold issue of the need for accountability, family members and survivors negotiated the criminal justice system in different ways and held diverse opinions on participation, appropriate sentences, the desirability of state trials as supplements to federal proceedings, and the necessity of attending trials and McVeigh's execution.

When opening statements began in *United States v. Timothy McVeigh* on April 24, 1997, family members and survivors were at many different places in their reconstructive efforts. Only a few, such as Ernestine Hill Clark, declined to attend trial proceedings, most often out of fear that attendance would undo what healing they had accomplished. Most, like Charlie Younger, felt that attending the trial was integral to their recovery efforts and were in attendance that very first day. Why was McVeigh's trial so important to family members and survivors, who had already been inundated with information about and images of the bombing for nigh on two years?

Accountability and Bearing Witness

In contemporary American culture, there is a perception that the dead "are nourished by judgment," and that criminal law is a "means of recompensing the slain through a deliberative act."[1] In television and other entertainment media, law is depicted as a site of memory work and closure. Episodes of shows from *Perry Mason* to *Law & Order* are structured to effectuate "patterned closure," much like detective stories: the truth is uncovered, innocents are exonerated and avenged, and order is restored through legal procedure.[2] Offscreen, legal professionals and parties attempt to redress traumatic injuries and preserve certain moral truths for collective benefit. According to popular culture, legal proceedings are just right for redressing wrongs; justice and accountability are integral to reconstructing lives after culturally traumatic events.

But what does it mean to say that law is a site of individual and collected memory work? What qualities of legal proceedings make it especially suited for reconstructive behaviors? And how do victims use the law to achieve such ends? Like the mass media, legal proceedings served as a forum for narrative contestation and negotiation, only now with life-or-death outcomes. Essentially law, an institution adept in operationalizing and adjudicating narrative conventions, provided the courtroom venue in which victims and survivors became active, vocal, and visible participants in adjudicating the perpetrators' guilt and holding them accountable.

In actuality, although attending and testifying at McVeigh's trial allowed family members and survivors to engage in memory work, it also satisfied an additional obligation: bearing witness. To bear witness is to testify, to explain an experience to listeners so as to authenticate, represent, and preserve it. Bearing witness is at once a compassionate activity, a form of commemoration, and a courageous act performed in defiance of social forces, informational distortion, and time and forgetfulness. Those who provide such testimony may *bear* witness in many senses—as burden, opportunity, protest, political or personal statement, act of remembrance, social cause. But one always bears witness out of dedication to a purpose, which may be a moral truth, a beloved person, or simply "doing justice."[3]

In Oklahoma City, family members and survivors engaged in bearing witness to cry out for justice and to mourn and commemorate all that had been beloved, comfortable, and safe, and was now lost. Their perceived needs to remember and give voice to murdered victims, to recognize survivors and commemorate first responders were very different from their perceived needs to silence and banish the perpetrators. In this context, silence acquired new semantic dimensions; it was a profound injustice to mute an innocent victim and by extension that victim's family members, but profound justice to silence perpetrators. Determined not to be silenced, family members and survivors struggled for the legal and moral standing to speak, through either actual testimony or active courtroom presence.

Family members' and survivors' urge to bear witness also entailed conflicts between cultural and legal norms of standing—whether and where they had the right to speak. Outside the courtroom, the public's embrace of victims and their stories ensured that bombing victims, not the state, possessed cultural standing as aggrieved parties. However, the requirements of legal standing are very different from those of popular culture. In federal courts, standing as defined by Article III of the Constitution has three requirements: an "injury in fact," or an invasion of a concrete and particular legally protected interest that is actual or imminent, and not hypothetical; a causal relationship between the injury and the defendant's challenged conduct; and a likelihood that the injury will be redressed—that legal "relief" will be obtained—by a favorable decision.[4]

In a criminal trial, the state claims (or, historically, has usurped) the role of the injured party, with the rights of other injured victims receiving at most ambiguous legal protection. The state's legal standing as the wronged sovereign ensures that legal proceedings will fulfill therapeutic functions for the state-as-victim, restoring and affirming sovereign authority through trying those suspected of wounding that authority and performing the institutional memory work of trying, acquitting, convicting, and potentially banishing them through imprisonment or execution. But the state's claim to the status of primary victim always threatens to marginalize human victims. For this reason, family members and survivors were understandably put out by the Tenth Circuit's finding that they would not be accorded legal standing to challenge Judge Matsch's rulings that would have effectively silenced their demands for inclusion.

Trying Stories, Stories on Trial

In an unusually pointed and intense manner, the trials of McVeigh and Nichols became struggles for "the privilege of recounting the past."[5] The relationship of a trial to past events is complex. Trials invoke the past both for the sake of the present and to move past the present—to rewrite accountability into past narratives, and to restore justice to the extent possible.[6] The trial as a form of witness and a forum for bearing witness does not merely contextualize past facts but unites the perpetrator with the victim or her representative "under the gaze of the law."[7] Thus, the trial attempts to erase the distance between past and present in an effort to unify the two into a justiciable whole. These erasures and mergers are accomplished largely through narrative convention.

Like other institutions, law has its own collected memories and relies on its own archives of knowledge, procedural systems, and rituals that display, consolidate, and affirm its professional and cultural authority.[8] One of law's chief institutional aims is maintaining boundaries between legal professionals and laypersons, enforcing distance through bar membership, clothing, and courtroom design that separate spectators from litigants and litigants from adjudicators.[9] The "rule of law" is itself a narrative concept, broadly understood as the safeguarding of rights and enforcement of responsibilities through legal proceedings instead of violence.

Through narrative, law endeavors to heal social ruptures. Crimes alter social life and receive social attention because they violate norms and imperil order.[10] Crimes that are so disturbing to a collective that they become culturally traumatic events may trigger not only social evaluation but also institutional teardown and reconstruction,[11] prompting what Victor Turner termed "social dramas," collective processes that allow a community "to scrutinize, portray, understand, and then act on itself."[12]

Trials, including criminal prosecutions, are social dramas and, as forums for resolving narrative conflict, sites of memory work. Both criminal law and memory are future-oriented toward greater social solidarity, and past-oriented, where narrative content and the criminal acts in question may be found.[13] In criminal trials, prosecutors chronicle a crime's effects upon directly impacted victims and indirectly affected social collectives in narratives that emphasize the perpetrator's immoral exercise of free will and individual rights.[14] Precedent (court decisions enunciating standards that constrain courts deciding subsequent cases with similar factual or legal issues) ensures that the rule of law and legal narratives are for the most part consistent and continuous through time.[15] Legal precedents become part of national, legal, and social collected memory; they constrain future adjudication and contextualizing and reinforcing social norms.

Juries and judges evaluate parties' narratives against each other and precedent, and apply legal and cultural principles to determine how to prioritize narrative interests and discern "winning" parties. Ideally, the winning narrative will seem the "natural" choice because it comports with both cultural experience and binding legal principle.[16] Otherwise, the case outcome will seem "arbitrary and illegitimate," perhaps prompting discord or defiance.[17] A guilty verdict confirms the statuses of perpetrator, victim, and victim's family member, legitimating the conscious remembrance of the victim and the willed forgetting of the perpetrator. After the verdict, "losing" parties must acclimate themselves at least temporarily to a legal outcome that is inconsistent with their narrative perceptions.[18] Punishment reinforces social norms and collective awareness that certain acts are unacceptable.[19] The ability to enunciate and fix stories in legal frames, then, is an important exercise of sociocultural authority.[20]

"Doing Justice": Attending and Testifying as Memory Work and Witness

Historically, crime victims played a much more important narrative role than they currently enjoy. In medieval times, victims prosecuted their own cases, but today's victim no longer manages how her story is constructed or delivered.[21] Moreover, the defendant's narrative has come to enjoy a place at the heart of the criminal trial; as legal scholar Paul Gerwitz has observed, murder victims and their relatives are at a "narrative disadvantage" because the outcome of their story is well known and indeed justifies a murder trial, while the outcome of the defendant's story is still unknown.[22] Determining the most appropriate ending for the defendant's story threatens to obscure victims' perspectives, and so it is especially important for family members to retain narrative agency through trial attendance and testimony.

By 1997, the victims' rights movement had succeeded in enshrining many of its core principles in state and federal law; the Victims' Rights and Restitution Act, for instance, allowed victims "to be present in all court proceedings related to the offense."[23] Bolstered by this statutory support, the Oklahoma City family members' and survivors' community believed that institutions such as the criminal justice system should privilege their needs, which they framed as "rights." Diane Leonard referred to both "our right to testify" and "our right to attend," and Doris Jones asserted that family members and survivors had the "right" to attend McVeigh's execution if they wished.

These demands channeled victims' and survivors' expectations and hopes into the criminal trial, an institutional product that was not victim-centered in either its focus (which is upon the defendant's actions) or its inquiry (which centers upon guilt or innocence). Victims' claims constructed trial attendance and participation as entitlements and are a crucial part of understanding how participants came to link attendance or participation in legal proceedings to memory work, healing, and reconstruction. To exclude family members and survivors from the courtroom was not only a denial of key sense-making and commemorative opportunities; it was also a denial of perceived legal rights, a denial of their victim status, and a gesture that disrespected and trivialized their losses.

In the aftermath of murder, the murdered victim's absence and the incompleteness of relatives' lives is linked to the absence and incompleteness of justice.[24] While a trial may acknowledge a victim *as* victim, the affirmation of victimhood and the accomplishment of justice is only effected by declaring perpetrators accountable and determining and carrying out an appropriate

In the bombing's aftermath, many rescuers left messages like this one, which Oklahoma City Bomb Disposal Unit Team 5 spray-painted on the wall of the Journal Record Building. Image courtesy of the Oklahoma City National Memorial and Museum Archives.

sentence. Thus, bearing witness not only ensured justice for murdered victims, family members, and survivors but also ensured justice *against* the perpetrators. While neither justice *for* murdered victims nor justice *against* the perpetrators could atone for the utter absence and incompleteness of justice on April 19, 1995, both forms of justice were necessary to avoid an unacceptable void in the memory of the bombing, and thus to ensure a coherent narrative[25] and facilitate memory work.

"Doing justice" invokes the past to salvage the present, using relevant social norms in order to punish bad conduct.[26] Memory as a guarding mechanism must provide sanctuary for victims while denying sanctuary to perpetrators. Bearing witness by trial attendance or testimony can be seen as retributive behavior, efforts to reestablish a just world by quashing perpetrators whose presences and deeds threaten reconstruction.[27] There is a sense that justice, not time, must be applied first to salve these wounds.[28]

"Doing justice" in McVeigh's trial also arguably satisfied obligations of democratic citizenship. It was one of the great ironies of the bombing that

McVeigh, Nichols, and Fortier, all former soldiers and therefore supposed agents of democracy, espoused antidemocratic principles in adopting violence to effect social change. McVeigh's trial—a lawful adjudication of rights and responsibilities—stood in opposition to his unlawful and irresponsible usurpation of others' rights, reinforcing the idea that a democratic government must be responsive to citizens' needs by redressing these wrongs.[29]

Of all possible sites of memory work, the criminal justice system is the only institution that can fulfill demands for accountability, retribution, and vengeance. Its ability to hold McVeigh accountable rendered it an important mediating entity for every family member and survivor whether or not they attended the trial. In essence, for most bombing victims, legal proceedings both created a new reconstructive duty—a duty to themselves or to murdered victims to be present as McVeigh was held accountable—and provided a venue in which that duty could be satisfied.

Taking the Stand for Justice

Testifying in open court was the most obvious way that bombing victims could satisfy a duty to participate in legal proceedings. The witness called to the stand at trial is literally a vehicle for memory, charged with illuminating past truths.

A trial witness who takes the stand fulfills three roles simultaneously: "giving evidence, telling the truth, and doing justice."[30] In these ways, the witness functions as a porter for things past and an ensurer of things to come, exercising fidelity both toward the accurate recollection of events and representative loyalty to deceased victims.[31] Its moral obligations notwithstanding, bearing witness is a voluntary act, which only underscores its moral qualities; if one has a choice, then choosing to testify affirms that the witness is electing to remember the victims, and not helping to "complete[] the perpetrators' work of effacement."[32]

Significantly, two participants who were called as witnesses at McVeigh's trial but who did not otherwise feel a duty or responsibility to attend felt a moral obligation to testify. Prosecution witness Richard Williams affirmed, "I felt like it was my responsibility because I was asked by the U.S. Attorney to . . . be the government's witness for GSA for the building. . . . I felt a tremendous responsibility to my friends, my coworkers, my community, to make sure that my testimony was a part of helping to prosecute those people." Tom Hall, who was slated to give victim impact testimony but whose testimony was canceled at the last minute, also spoke of a duty to help sentence McVeigh to death:

The way I looked at it was . . . my story and my case and injuries . . . could make a big impact and if it could help to get him the death sentence then . . . I'd do my part, you know. . . . they were gonna pay my way up there for the trial and pay the lodging and all that, but if I thought me being there would help him get the death sentence, I'd've paid my own way.

Marsha Kight, a victim impact witness at McVeigh's trial, said that she felt a different responsibility to share her story with those who would decide his fate:

It was also sharing with the judge and reinforcing the fact that I'm here to give an impact statement, that's how my life and the lives of my family had been changed. So, I wanted the judge to hear it. I wanted the jury to hear it. . . . but part of it was asking, not telling the judge what to do, but just saying that this is my sentence.

Similarly, witness Susan Urbach described her physical wounds to the court, relating that her "ear was totally cut in half, all the way through the cartilage," that she had "almost four feet of stitches," and that her face looked like "fresh-stitched meat."[33] She was proud of the story these injuries told; her poignant description of a scar on the left side of her face was reprinted in national news coverage of the trial:

Q. And how do you feel about your scar today on your face?
A. Well, it's my badge of honor.
Q. What do you mean by a "badge of honor"?
A. Well, to me, you see, a scar—and any scar, tells a story. And the story it tells is it tells a story of a wounding and a healing that goes along with that wounding. And the more deeply you're wounded, the more healing that must come your way; that you must experience for that wound to close up and for you to get your scar. I mean, you don't get your scar unless you've been wounded and you have been healed. And I've got my scar.
Q. So you're proud of your scar?
A. Yes.[34]

Family members and survivors were willing to go through a tremendous ordeal in order to satisfy a complex system of responsibilities to individuals localized and dispersed, dead and alive, known and unknown, as well as to answer the deeds of McVeigh and Nichols. As witnesses, they injected a very different quality into impersonal trial proceedings, proudly raising their voices and joining others in a chorus of protest against loss in a forum where they were otherwise bystanders.

"You Want to Be There for Them": Attendance as Bearing Witness

One did not have to take the stand in order to be a trial witness, however. Physical presence, though silent, was a profound reminder that others stood in for deceased victims out of love and duty or to gather information to understand what had happened. To attend a trial was to experience justice. By a small margin, most participants reported that they did not feel a duty or responsibility to attend McVeigh's trial, but most did feel that trial attendance was an important step in being involved in the process. Being there—seeing justice done—mattered, and bearing witness was a progressive behavior that assisted memory work.

Family members and survivors who felt a duty or responsibility most frequently described it as a need to represent murdered victims. Dot Hill explained, "I thought it was critical for me to be there as a representative of the friends that I lost and for their families that couldn't [be there]." Diane Leonard also attended to represent her murdered husband: "So many of us want to, and I'm included in that group, you want to represent your loved one. They can't be there. You want to be there for them." Sometimes participants' need to represent individual victims stemmed from a perception that that person would have wanted participants to attend, a need to keep others from forgetting the victim, or a need to be a spokesperson for the victim. Doris Jones commented, "I felt I did [have a duty] for . . . for my daughter. I felt . . . she can't be there. And believe me, she would have been there. If it had been the other way round, if it had been me, she'd be there. . . . She would have been very vocal." Attending legal proceedings to represent a deceased victim served to somehow keep alive that person's presence and invoke it within the forum of accountability.

Family members and survivors who were distrustful of media coverage also looked to legal proceedings to fulfill their needs for *unbiased* information. They believed that the trials would provide a much more complete picture of the defendants and their motivations, one not composed with an eye toward increasing profit margins. As Janet Beck explained, "You cut out the middle man, I guess, so to speak. The legal teams were there to do their job, . . . they weren't focused on how they were going to be perceived by the public, and they weren't worried about their ratings, so to speak, with the public." Marsha Kight wanted to hear everything in person, not "snippets" of the "most sensational part of the day in the courtroom."

Accurate information was regarded as a precious commodity. Angela Richerson attended to learn why the bombing had occurred: "I went, for some insight, to see if I could . . . figure out why he could do something like that, you know, why people would not report it. . . . I never got any insight to it, but I felt better." This craving for information could be an all-consuming need; as Paul Howell remarked, "I needed to find out everything that went on, how it went on, how they w[ere] able to prosecute or catch him and all these things. The more I knew about what was going on and in that case, the better off I was as far as myself and my family was concerned." Dr. Paul Heath craved accuracy "so that when I spoke about it, when I thought about it, it was based on facts and rule of law and not just driven by rumor and emotion."

The "duty" to attend in representation of murdered victims was closely related to a duty to pass information on to others. A few who attended to represent decedents also felt responsible for sharing information with those unable to attend, demonstrating not only the significance of information in memory work but also proving that these processes were above all *social*. Dot Hill attended to share information with coworkers who "didn't want to go, . . . didn't want to get that involved, didn't want to be reinjured, whatever their reason." This in effect created a liaison role where one person from a family or group would be designated to attend and report back. Paul Howell fulfilled this role for his family: "My family expected me to be the one who would come back and tell them what was going on, if they had any kind of questions or so forth." Participants who attended out of a duty to represent the dead also likely felt a corresponding duty to represent the living. Other individuals explained that they felt a duty to attend because they wanted to be supportive, represent an organization, or confirm in person that McVeigh was guilty.

Many acknowledged a desire to bear witness to justice live. Survivor Charlie Younger not only went to see "justice" accomplished but also wanted the jury to see him and know that he and others were very concerned about the trial's outcome. Several needed to know that the right men had been arrested. "I didn't want the wrong person to be convicted, and after going to the trial at the FAA Center I was certain," Beverly Rankin emphasized. Lane Wharton tied attendance to participation and the need to confront the accused: "I don't think I felt a duty or responsibility as much as just wanting to know that I was there and a part of it and was able to look him in the face, you know, and call him a creep. Which I did." Seeing justice done, according to Janet Beck, "was definitely important to me as far as healing for the reassurance that everything was like it was supposed to be."

Finally, participants also attended the trial out of a desire to observe the defendants' physical behaviors, nonverbal expressions, and reactions. Lane Wharton, who remembered seeing McVeigh and others in the Journal Record Building before the bombing, stated:

> I always wondered when he was looking at us in the courtroom too. If he ever recognized any of us, like, when he came to my office. Do you know that you came to my office, that I'm a real person, you know, and you hurt me? And I don't know, . . . that was one reason I wanted to be there, to look him in the face.

Not everyone who attended the trial found it a positive experience. A handful of participants attended for at least one day and decided not to return. A few physically uninjured survivors felt that they should not attend because they felt only minimally involved in comparison to family members and injured survivors. If they attempted to attend legal proceedings, these individuals became emotionally devastated and felt profoundly guilty for what they perceived to be taking seats that others deserved to occupy. Attendance was also not a priority for some participants who felt they could perform memory work more effectively elsewhere; they believed that others' angry demeanor or the tedium of evidence presentation detracted from the trial's reconstructive significance.

A handful of participants did not attend any legal proceedings at all because of a need to protect themselves and their hard-won well-being or because they had moved on and chose not to get wrapped up in proceedings. Jordan Holt explained, "I felt for my own mental health that I had a duty to stay away from it," and Richard Williams decided "that's not something that I needed personally . . . to be able to move on in my process."

In summary, willingness to attend the trial was connected to the expected role that attendance would play in memory work; those who expected trials to play an essential role in recovery were most often participants who felt a duty to others deceased or living, who craved information, or who needed to satisfy personal desires for completion or justice. Participants did not attend the trial or ceased to attend when it became apparent that attendance would not assist memory work, or worse, would hinder such tasks.

"I Think I Would Have Been a Basket Case":
Trial Attendance as "Doing Justice"

As a practical matter, it was not easy for family members and survivors to attend the trials of McVeigh and Nichols. Those who wanted to view the closed-circuit trial broadcast at the FAA Center had to juggle that activity with a host of others, including work and family life. To make matters more difficult, those who attended the trial live in Denver found that seats were reserved for only ten victim witnesses, and none for their support persons; each morning, volunteers in Denver stood in line outside the courthouse so that attendees' support persons could accompany them into the courtroom.

Nonetheless, participants confirmed that attending the trial was an important step in being involved, a core component of bearing witness. Maintaining a testimonial presence in the courtroom required seeing and being seen during the processes of narrative enunciation, negotiation, and selection that culminated in McVeigh's guilty verdict and death sentence. The memory work that attendance facilitated revolved around participants' needs to achieve "completion" and "justice." Diane Leonard remarked, "I don't think . . . had that legislation not been passed and . . . I had not been able to view and learn what had occurred I think I'd be a basket case. I don't think I could've stood it." Such involvement was particularly important for individuals who lived outside of Oklahoma City, such as Robin Brown, who explained:

> We live in Florida, and I mean, you're talking Oklahoma and then Colo-
> rado, so you were so far away from it, so getting to go for a week and sit in
> trial and be part of that process, I think it helped to deal with all the stuff
> that was going on because you were part of the process of justice being
> served.

Several also mentioned "justice" as a reason why trial attendance was so important. Charlie Younger described "a desire to see that justice was served and witness it so that if it didn't come out the way I knew it should've I could understand why it didn't." Justice was the only proper response to the victims' murders; Jessie Sternburg noted, "We didn't have our loved ones, I mean, at least we could see that we got justice." Some survivors felt that the trial was the rare forum in which they received justice; Jamie Blansett remarked, "It was like, there is justice and there w[ere] a lot of times when we didn't feel like we had any, there was not any justice for the survivors."

Testifying and attending McVeigh's trial, then, exemplified family members' and survivors' vigilant commitment both to the projects of "doing justice" for victims and against the defendants, and to the reconstructive process of self-healing. These forms of bearing witness implied not detached voyeurism but an interactive experience.[35] Such participatory opportunities enhanced family members' and survivors' experience of "doing justice," recognized their suffering, and afforded them some degree of power and control in a system that primarily relegated them to bystander status.[36] Participants wanted to live once again in a world governed by moral principles and civilized norms; some even took pride in the trial as a civic act, in generously extending rights to a murder suspect that his victim did not have.[37] Family members and survivors respected the criminal justice system's authority to try the defendants, and so tacitly agreed that due process rights should be extended to them. But this did not mean that they had to like it; it did not hurt that trial participation was also perceived as a direct blow to the defendants.[38]

Legal proceedings enabled family members and survivors to bear witness through their presence and their testimony. Bearing witness, in turn, facilitated memory work. What family members and survivors were able to accomplish, however, was very dependent on how law regarded itself as a site of memory work—how it perceived, incorporated, and packaged victims' emotion, including explicit rules and implicit norms governing emotion's propriety within the courtroom. Their desire to bear witness prompted family members and survivors to fight for their right to both attend proceedings either live or via closed circuit and testify—in essence, to attain and preserve these witnessing opportunities for themselves and for others facing similar challenges in the future.

The Road to Execution

Emotion on Trial

Prosecuting Timothy McVeigh

Family members and survivors had yearned for Timothy McVeigh and Terry Nichols to be put on trial ever since their arrests. They longed to hear the evidence against the suspects, gather information, make their presence felt in the courtroom, watch the defendants' reactions and behaviors, and most of all, "see justice done." But in the months leading up to these proceedings, U.S. District Judge Richard Matsch, charged with overseeing the trials of McVeigh and Nichols, transferred the trial from Oklahoma to Denver, Colorado, refused to permit the trial to be broadcast via closed-circuit television back to Oklahoma City, and announced his intent to exclude bombing victims who planned to give impact testimony at sentencing from attending the trial. It became readily apparent that the perpetrators' prosecutions would be "trials" in more than one sense.

The groundwork for the conflict between Judge Matsch's decisions and the families' and survivors' desires had been laid many years before the Oklahoma City bombing, in the turn to conservatism and the growing popularity of the victims' rights movement beginning in the 1980s. In 1996, when pretrial proceedings in *United States v. McVeigh* began, criminal defendants' due process rights had long been in tension with participatory rights claimed by crime victims. As President Clinton once remarked:

> When a judge balances defendants' rights in the federal Constitution against victims' rights in a statute or a state constitution, the defendants' rights almost always prevail. That's just how the law works today. We want to level the playing field. This is not about depriving people accused of crimes of their legitimate rights, including the presumption of innocence; this is about simple fairness. When a judge balances the rights of the accused and the rights of the victim, we want the rights of the victim to get equal weight.[1]

At that time, a new emotional equilibrium was evolving, spurred in large part by the U.S. Supreme Court's decision in *Payne v. Tennessee* (1991) allowing states to permit murder victims' family members to deliver victim impact testimony during the sentencing phase of the accused's trial. This new equilibrium took hold through a controversial series of judicial struggles in which those determined to champion crime victims' participatory rights— prosecutors, legislators, and victims, bolstered by emotive norms prevalent in popular culture and therapeutic discourse—arrayed themselves against others who felt such claims undermined defendants' constitutional rights.

It did not take long for *United States v. McVeigh* to become a prominent battleground in this conflict. Judge Matsch and bombing victims each hoped to achieve different goals through McVeigh's criminal trial. Judge Matsch strove above all else to conduct a fair trial, and so was concerned with emotion's potential effects on the jury. To this end, he carefully monitored its presence so as to avoid prejudicial imbalance, safeguarding both defendants' due process rights and the proceedings' integrity. Family members and survivors also wanted the defendants to receive a fair trial; they realized that everything had to be aboveboard to ensure that any trial convictions would

McVeigh reviews court documents, flanked by defense attorneys Robert Nigh (left) and Stephen Jones (right). Image courtesy of the Oklahoma City National Memorial and Museum Archives.

not be overturned on appeal. But they also wanted to accomplish something further. They wished to utilize the trial as a site of memory work and so were focused on its emotional consequences and on the defendants' behaviors. Prior to *Payne*, such desires would likely have merited little to no judicial consideration. But after that decision, and particularly after Congress intervened to facilitate a closed-circuit broadcast of McVeigh's and Nichols's trials and to ensure that family members and survivors could both attend these proceedings and deliver victim impact testimony, it was clear that judges now had more to worry about than safeguarding defendants' due process rights.

As a result, the dynamics of criminal trials were irrevocably altered. Constitutional protections for criminal defendants often prescribed one set of actions and priorities, and victims' rights highlighted distinctly different, and often conflicting, demands. The judicial spotlight became crowded and chaotic, with both defendants and victims claiming priority. In this new equilibrium, emotion and emotional work had become legitimate aims of criminal prosecution—ones that the U.S. Supreme Court and legislators had deemed important—but it was unclear how these competing needs should be balanced and incorporated into legal proceedings.

In opposing and ultimately overturning Matsch's rulings, family members and survivors forged new paths, helping to create new roles and rights for victims and cement established ones. But this advocacy was not only about advancing victims' rights; it was also about recognizing, respecting, and resolving victims' emotional needs. With victims came their emotions, their ardent desire for memory work, and their yearning to accomplish this labor through physical presence and participation at legal proceedings. Thus, "victims' rights" struggles also concerned the proper place of emotionality in legal proceedings. Throughout these contests, Judge Matsch, his peers on the U.S. Court of Appeals for the Tenth Circuit, and the defense team often occupied one camp, while the prosecution, bombing victims, and Congress occupied the other.

Family members and survivors viewed emotion as an inherent part of holding McVeigh and Nichols accountable, asserting that the failure to incorporate both victims and their emotionality into proceedings would undermine justice, imperil judicial integrity, and endanger legal authority, rendering justice an impoverished concept that was only "for" the defendant and not bombing victims. In order to understand how bombing victims accomplished memory work, one must closely examine the inherent conflict between victims' conceptions of emotion and its legal propriety and those espoused by Judge Matsch. The clashes that ensued over each of Judge Matsch's three key pretrial rulings—the change of venue, the closed-circuit trial broadcast, and the exclusion of victim witnesses from proceedings—can be understood as important contests not only over victims' rights but over emotional proprieties, and ultimately a negotiation of how law would and should serve as a site of reconstruction and memory work.

It is imperative to emphasize, however, that the fact that family members and survivors occasionally felt disappointed or silenced by Judge Matsch's approaches to these trials does not mean that his decisions—difficult determinations of how to resolve novel and thorny issues—were incorrect, particularly when the "correctness" of his decisions appeared very different from a legal vantage point than from a victims' rights perspective. Indeed, in ensuing years, both legal professionals and family members and survivors have commended Judge Matsch for his admirable, professional, and sensitive handling of both McVeigh's and Nichols's trials. Despite their frustrations with his early rulings, family members and survivors have always known that Judge Matsch's goal—ensuring fair trials for McVeigh and Nichols—was also their first priority.

Competing Perspectives on Emotion, Emotional Needs, and Emotion Work

Legal perspectives on emotionality affected courtroom conduct, trial strategy, and trial outcome. To avoid the possibility that emotional displays would bias the jury, Judge Matsch banned many potentially emotionally provocative and thus prejudicial items from his courtroom, such as jewelry with religious symbols or photos of the victims; warned spectators that "this is not theater, this is a trial"; and cautioned them to "conduct themselves with appropriate demeanor and courtroom manner," including refraining from untoward emotional displays such as crying.[2]

Judge Matsch viewed emotion as a potent force to be quashed to the extent possible lest it prejudice jurors' adjudications of guilt and innocence:

> What jurors have to do, what people who make decisions about evidence have to do, is take it in steps and not jump to any conclusions because what happened is horrible or is sad or makes us angry. Those are emotional responses. And of course, emotion is part of us; but you have to set aside emotions like anger and sadness in deciding whether other evidence in the case connects up the accused person with the horrible event.

And that's what we're exploring with you, whether your emotions would be such that you couldn't use the discipline to separate the horror of what happened with the evidence as it may or may not show any connection with the defendant.[3]

Similarly, instructing the jury on how it should interpret victim witness evidence, Judge Matsch asked jurors to separate their reactions to impact testimony from their "moral judgment":

You're going to have to make a decision based on reasoning, and it must be free from the influence of passion, prejudice. . . . what you have to attempt to do is free it from the influence of the human emotions that testimony like this generates in us; and that is anger, rage, a number of other emotions, including grief and sadness. People have been on this stand sharing moments of grief with you. We have tried through some rulings and also some instructions and cautions to witnesses to try to be careful so that you can hear the important parts, the more objective aspects of loss and impact. But you understand that these are people. And when they come in here and testify and answer some of these questions . . . it's only because they are human that they come forward with some things that really are not relevant. And I mention some things like the last moments that some of these women have had with their children or with their husbands. They cried and you cried. But that's—you know, those most poignant moments in their lives, they want to tell you about it; and it's hard for them to discuss the impact of this loss without going into that. But those images that have been created by that testimony are not the things for you to consider. We're not here to seek revenge on Timothy McVeigh. We're here to consider these lives and what's happened to these people and also, as you will hear later, his life. And so, hard as it is, you must wait now and withhold judgment. Don't overreact. And I know you are human beings, too, and so am I. So is everybody here. And we have to be careful and not let ourselves be overly stimulated by some of the testimony that we've heard here and try to suppress some of the emotional reaction that it's natural to have. . . . I can't expect you to sit here and listen to some of this testimony and not have some reaction to it. It's impossible to ask that of you. But don't let that reaction become the measure of the moral judgment that you will make.[4]

Judge Matsch's conception of emotion is scarcely unusual; that is exactly how esteemed jurists are expected to think about matters of the heart.[5] In death penalty cases, the Supreme Court has repeatedly affirmed that the decision to impose the death penalty must be a "reasoned moral response . . . rather than an emotional one."[6] Emotion, then, is not typically regarded as a component of moral judgments.[7]

Nevertheless, emotion is inherently part of the jury's punishment determination.[8] It may not even be consistently applied; according to legal scholars, the Supreme Court has been "blatantly inconsistent" in its handling of emotion, "invoking the notion that law is reason, not emotion, only when it is convenient to do so."[9] Judge Matsch relied upon his own emotions as a radar system; if any blips on screen during trial indicated the possibility for juror prejudice, he could rely upon jury instructions to protect the proceedings' integrity. Nonetheless, the criminal justice system forced both bombing victims and jurors to learn and adopt new, foreign techniques of emotion management. Family members and survivors willingly attempted to abide by these public, institutional modifications of private, individual feeling rules, even though many times they contradicted normal human reactions to inherently emotional subject matter.[10]

Victims' understanding of the propriety of their emotions—and thus of themselves—was eloquently captured by President Clinton in remarks he made upon introducing efforts to pass a victims' rights constitutional amendment on June 25, 1996: "When someone is a victim, he or she should be at the center of the criminal justice process, not on the outside looking in. Participation in all forms of government is the essence of democracy. Victims should be guaranteed the right to participate in proceedings related to crimes committed against them."[11]

Being "at the center of the criminal justice process," according to bombing victims and their supporters, was therapeutic and cathartic. They viewed trial attendance and participation as precious opportunities for gathering information, fitting puzzle pieces together, watching the defendants' behaviors and reactions, bearing witness to loss through presence or testimony, representing lost friends and relatives, and "doing justice." For bombing victims, then, emotion provided a way of "knowing about the world" and "testing reality."[12] Emotional reactions were often reasonable reactions; to lack emotion was to be inhuman, to be like McVeigh.

Although the trial was likely to be traumatic, its unique potential to determine culpability and produce accountability was a necessary part of the healing process. For victims, the horror of a crime and the awful emotions it evoked could be masked, but never banished entirely from the courtroom; attempts to do so merely compounded that horror by attempting to divorce it from accountability. Thus, raw emotion did not portend a lynching but could be part of a just and equitable—and moral—response.

With these conceptions of emotionality in tow, it becomes easy to see how disputes over whether to broadcast the Denver trial back to Oklahoma City and whether to allow victim impact witnesses to attend the trial devolved into contests between victims' emotional needs and priorities and defendants' due process rights. These struggles were resolved through congressional intervention that demonstrated that emotion—and those who bear it— could not be exorcised from legal proceedings.

Escaping Emotion: The Change of Venue Ruling

Emotion had much to do with why lawyers for both McVeigh and Nichols sought to relocate the trial venue outside of Oklahoma. In granting the defendants' change of venue motion, Judge Matsch linked media coverage to the construction and maintenance of the bombing as an emotional experience, noting that national media coverage of the bombing had become less emotional and more factual over time,[13] while local coverage continued to feature victims and their families and "individual stories of grief and recovery,"[14] emphasizing victims' innocence, the impact of loss, and symbols such as angels, teddy bears, and purple ribbons.[15] Judge Matsch expressed concern that media coverage would encourage jurors to identify with victims, undermining trust in their impartiality if they felt "a personal stake in the outcome" or "a sense of obligation to reach a result which will find general acceptance in the relevant audience."[16]

Judge Matsch was also worried about the presence of a "citizens' movement in Oklahoma" to limit death penalty appeals and took note of a media interview in which Oklahoma residents discussed the importance of a guilty verdict and implied that a death sentence was appropriate.[17] In contrast to the media's "humanization of the victims in the public mind," Judge Matsch determined that the defendants had been "demonized," in part because "the videotape footage and fixed photographs of Timothy McVeigh in Perry have been used regularly in almost all of the television news reports of developments in this case."

Judge Matsch's remarks not only identified victims' emotionality as a potent force but confirmed that it could endanger the integrity of legal proceedings. The problem was not only media coverage per se but also families and survivors themselves, who not only appeared in the media but also were vocal advocates seeking legal change. This perceived threat was so great that there was no solution less drastic than removing the defendants—and legal proceedings—from Oklahoma. Indeed, Matsch's change of venue ruling has set the blue ribbon standard for safeguarding a defendant's constitutional rights; in oral arguments in *United States v. Skilling*, counsel for Jeffrey Skilling noted that Matsch not only granted the change of venue but also conducted a painstaking jury selection that lasted 18 days, with each potential juror being interviewed for one hour on average.[18]

It was at this point that victims' attempts to insert emotion into criminal proceedings intersected with judicial attempts to keep it out. In the Oklahoma City context, claims that victims, their emotions, and their emotional needs should be prioritized in criminal proceedings became most concrete in two separate incidents when victims and survivors went to Congress to override a decision by Judge Matsch that would limit or prohibit attendance at McVeigh's trial.

Airing Emotion: The Struggle over the Closed-Circuit Trial Broadcast

Judge Matsch's February 20, 2006, ruling moving the trial venue from Oklahoma City to Denver presented a colossal dilemma for family members and survivors who wished to attend but could not afford to travel to Denver or had other obligations. Federal courts had traditionally banned cameras in federal courtrooms. Determined to fight this ruling, family member and legal secretary Rhonda Bartlebaugh enlisted her boss, Karen Howick, for assistance in their struggle for a closed-circuit trial broadcast. Howick filed motions in federal court, ultimately appearing before Matsch to request the closed circuit broadcast.[19] Matsch heard Howick's arguments but ultimately refused to permit a closed-circuit broadcast.

Howick then turned to Oklahoma congressmen, who helped to add an amendment mandating the closed-circuit broadcast to the then-pending Anti-Terrorism and Effective Death Penalty Act (AEDPA). Encapsulated in Section 235, this amendment required federal courts to permit closed-circuit broadcasts if a trial was moved more than 350 miles from its original location and placed restrictions on who could view these televised proceedings, granting federal judges discretion to determine "who has a 'compelling' enough interest to attend and who would be unable to do so 'by reason of the inconvenience and expense caused by the change of venue.'"[20]

Following the passage of the AEDPA, Judge Matsch heard hearings on the constitutionality of Section 235; the prosecution supported a closed-circuit trial broadcast, while the defense opposed it, largely on emotive grounds.

The prosecution emphasized the therapeutic value of trial attendance for family members and survivors:

> While the nation as a whole has a great interest in this case, there are certain individuals who have a much greater than generalized interest in satisfying themselves that justice is served. They are the hundreds of persons who were in the Murrah Building at the time of the explosion, and the many more who lost loved ones and suffered personal injuries in the bombing. . . . Part of their recovery depends on their seeing—first hand, if possible—our system of justice at work.[21]

The defense, however, spoke of traumatization, not therapy, citing the victims' "inflamed emotions" as a reason that a closed-circuit broadcast would "inevitably interfere with the administration of justice."[22] Asserting that victims' strong emotions would attach to McVeigh's person, the defense argued their actual and implied presence would distract the jury:

> Courtroom cameras will remind the jurors daily that, in addition to those victims certain to pack the Denver courtroom as spectators and potential witnesses, a large, faceless group of grievously injured persons are depending on the jury to return the only verdict (guilty) and sentence (death) this group will find acceptable. The enormous psychological pressure brought to bear on jurors is certain to create bias against Mr. McVeigh. . . . The risk is that a juror possessed of reasonable doubt at the trial's conclusion nonetheless may feel intimidated into returning a guilty verdict by the invisible hand of Oklahoma victim-spectators.[23]

The defense also asserted that trial witnesses might be reluctant or refuse to testify when their testimony is "broadcast to thousands of unseen spectators, virtually all of whom are antagonistic to the defendant."[24]

Moreover, in a strategic move that reversed the victims' rights claim that defendants receive too many protections while victims receive too few, the defense argued that Section 235 suggested that "the victims and their families are entitled to preferential treatment over all others, but particularly over defendants Timothy McVeigh and Terry Nichols, and their families and friends."[25] Alleging that this "burden[ed] this Court with the responsibility of attending to the victims' recovery," the defense posited that the amendment "forc[ed] courts to attend to the emotional well-being of victims" and queried "how is a Court expected to assist actively in the victims' recovery while remaining absolutely fair to the person presumed by most of those victims to be guilty and deserving of death?"[26] They even attacked the idea that trials could be cathartic for victims, urging that this notion was refuted by the "tortured expressions" of the families of Nicole Brown Simpson and Ron Goldman during the O. J. Simpson murder trial.[27] Finally, the defense intimated that the closed-circuit broadcast would provide an access point for journalists to tap the boiling rage of remote victim attendees:

> A gaggle of media representatives will converge at the Oklahoma site to report the reactions of the victims and their families. . . . Interviews granted by victim-spectators in Oklahoma will inevitably resonate with passion and fervor, virtually all of which is likely to be directed against Mr. McVeigh and Mr. Nichols.[28]

These defense arguments are problematic for two reasons. First, they presume that victims would be the population most likely to be excluded from the courtroom; in reality, victims had much to lose from ejection, and thus carefully monitored their behavior. In addition, even assuming that unruly victims were ejected from the courtroom, it is unclear how they would have left other than through courtroom doors—placing them in a prime position to be targeted by media camped outside.

Out of this fracas came a distinct picture of how the prosecution, defense, and Judge Matsch believed the law should function as a site of memory work. While the prosecution linked trial attendance and "recovery," the defense linked trial attendance to trauma. This latter characterization, however, ignored the fact that memory work involves real labor; forming crises' emotional rawness into a more structured narrative is at best a distressing and difficult process.

On July 15, 1996, Judge Matsch upheld the constitutionality of the AEDPA amendment but placed restrictions on the broadcast, including placing only one stationary camera on the courtroom's back wall.[29] This ruling was not so much a victory for trials as therapeutic vehicles, however, as the prioritization of legal expediency. To do otherwise, Judge Matsch feared, would delay the beginning of Timothy McVeigh's trial.

On March 31, 1997, the first day of jury selection, Judge Matsch explained the procedures for the remote closed-circuit viewing. A fixed-position, fixed-focus camera in the back of the Denver courtroom would broadcast an image of the courtroom to a 320-seat auditorium in the FAA Center in Oklahoma City. Remote viewers would always see the well of the courtroom (including the bench, the witness box, and the defense and prosecution tables), the attorneys, McVeigh, and Judge Matsch; they would not, however, see jurors. This shot would never be altered, foreclosing close-ups or changes in focus. Remote trial witnesses were asked to make reservations two days beforehand. Retired Colorado state judge Gaspar Perricone, who was assigned to maintain decorum at the Oklahoma City remote viewing site, relocated to Oklahoma City for nine months to preside over the FAA Center auditorium, which, per Judge Matsch's orders, was "recharacterized as a courtroom."[30] Remote witnesses were to be bound by the same code of conduct as those attending the trial in Denver, with Judge Perricone on hand to enforce the court's orders.[31] Judge Matsch informed attendees that he was also able to view proceedings back in Oklahoma City via a return closed-circuit signal. By the opening day of jury selection, 1,200 people had requested credentials to attend the closed-circuit viewing, and the U.S. Attorney's Victim Assistance Unit had credentialed more than 832 of them.[32]

Expressing Emotion: Allowing Testifying Victims to Attend the Trial

> I was attending pretrial hearings when Judge Matsch invoked [Federal Rule of Evidence] 615, and it was in the morning. We were in Denver, and we had the lunch hour to decide whether to give up our right to testify by attending or to give up our right to attend by testifying. It was an enormous decision. Everybody . . . that was in the courtroom that day was [thinking], it was a terrible decision just to have to make on your lunch hour. I decided to stay out of the courtroom to maintain my right to testify, but I felt that it was so wrong that the damage is done the day of the event and . . . there's nothing that is going to be heard in that courtroom that's going to affect that.
>
> —Diane Leonard

The therapeutic effects of trial attendance and the need to fulfill family members' and survivors' emotional needs also provided a motivation and argument for the prosecution to challenge Judge Matsch's initial rulings excluding victim impact witnesses from the trial's guilt phase. Federal Rule of Evidence 615 allows judges to exclude material witnesses from court proceedings—traditionally, those testifying to factual matters, not victim impact witnesses—to ensure that their testimony is not affected or altered. In keeping with Rule 615, Judge Matsch twice ruled that survivors or family members could not attend the trial if they wanted to testify in its penalty phase. On June 26, 1996, he gave a number of bombing victims and potential sentencing witnesses the option of foregoing testimony in order to remain in the courtroom during a pretrial hearing and refused to reverse this ruling on October 4, 1996.

The interplay between Judge Matsch and attorneys for the prosecution and defense revealed that neither side was exactly sure how to incorporate family members' and survivors' emotional needs into courtroom proceedings while still protecting proceedings from emotive influences. The easiest option appeared to be the most drastic—excluding individuals of a certain "emotive category" from proceedings unless they agreed not to testify. Usually, witnesses are not excluded under Rule 615 because the *emotionality* of a trial's subject matter in particular may impact their testimony, but rather because their testimony could be altered by *any* information they heard. But due to the proceedings' disturbing content, Judge Matsch was concerned with the emotion's prejudicial effect upon witnesses' recollections. He believed that these trials would inevitably cultivate emotionality, remarking, "I don't think that it's news to anybody who has participated in a trial that there are traumas to trial," including "the presence of the defendants, their reaction to being in the same room with these two men."[33]

For Judge Matsch, the trauma of the trial was merely an extension of the trauma of the bombing itself. He accepted that trials were therapeutic, as evidenced by victims' media comments about attending preliminary proceedings, acknowledging that it "probably helps . . . to express their views, including negative opinions of the court's rulings and all of those things."[34] But he remained concerned that these emotions would bleed over into courtroom proceedings, affecting victim impact testimony: "But I don't see any way in which you can cabin that kind of emotion and feeling and reaction to what they see and hear and say, well, that has had no effect or could have no effect on their testimony . . . as to what has happened to their lives as a result of these alleged crimes."[35]

As Judge Matsch saw it, any change in victims' emotional status because of the trial would be a change that affected their testimony.[36] What Judge Matsch failed to account for, however, was that victims' emotional status was changing every day, influenced by many other factors besides trial attendance. Time itself altered victims' physical, emotional, and mental status. Admittedly, some influences were more prejudicial than others, including media coverage of the defendants' trials. Victims who consumed media coverage of McVeigh's trial would get a dose of opinion with their news from journalists who, even unconsciously, added interpretive layers to their coverage. Thus, the emotional status of victims—even those who would elect not to attend the trial in favor of delivering impact testimony—would inevitably be affected by potentially prejudicial information. Perversely, this supported a decision to ban all victims from testifying.

Defense attorneys realized this and used this point to strengthen their arguments, although they stopped short of asking the court to exclude all victim witnesses. Attorney Richard Burr hung his argument on the peg "that going through the trial process will be retraumatizing on the victim witnesses who are here and, indeed, to the victims who are here who are not witnesses,"[37] distorting victims' memories. Defense attorney Reid Neureiter in effect advocated for asking the victims to choose not between attending and testifying, but between "healing" and testifying (there was no consideration of whether testifying itself was also therapeutic):

> The last thing we would want to do was to hinder the healing process of the people and the victims who have suffered so much. What we are asking, however, is that they make a choice, a choice between going through the healing process while sitting as—in the pews behind me, watching the trial, or deciding to testify at the penalty phase. That is a choice that we believe the law and the Constitution require.[38]

In explaining his decision to exclude victim witnesses from the trial, Judge Matsch remarked:

> It is impossible for me to believe that that extension of experience [of attending the trial], which I think is not a part of the admissible evidence, can be separated out from the experience that otherwise has followed from the loss and the grief and the other emotions. We're talking about emotions. . . . there are emotions from being in the courtroom, from everybody who is in the courtroom. So in my mind, there is simply no way to separate it.[39]

Matsch emphasized that he was not ruling against the victims or for "defendants' rights" but to preserve the trial's integrity:

> The reference is made here that Congress did not pass a defendant's Bill of Rights. Of course, it's not necessary. . . . That's what the Constitution does in the Bill of Rights amendments in the Constitution. But, you know, I think it is often misunderstood when they talk about "defendants' rights."

We're not talking about defendants' rights as such. We're talking about the protection of the integrity of the process by which defendants are judged and the evidence is judged. And that's the responsibility of a judge, and that's the responsibility I'm attempting to meet by what seems as a very hard-hearted rule.[40]

Thus, for Judge Matsch, emotionality threatened, not enhanced, the integrity of a criminal trial. And so "pure" victims—those who had not attended the trial—could step into the heart of the courtroom, its gallery, to testify, but "tainted" victims who had attended the trial could not.

Judge Matsch's ruling had two invidious consequences. First, it imposed a terrible dilemma upon family members and survivors: they could attend McVeigh's trial, with the knowledge that doing so could give McVeigh an argument that on appeal could lead to reversal of his conviction and sentence. Or they could forfeit their right to attend or provide impact testimony—both opportunities that many held dear. "The victims are confronted with an excruciating dilemma," the prosecution asserted. "There is no legal basis for forcing the victims to make this heartrending choice."[41] In addition, according to this precedent, defendants in other cases could list victims' family members as prospective witnesses in the sentencing phase of their trials and then not call them, thus excluding them from both attending the trial's guilt phase and testifying in its penalty phase.

Predictably, family members and survivors reacted to these rulings with shock, indignation, frustration, and anger. Diane Leonard described her confusion over the logic of excluding victim witnesses: "The impact that this crime has had on our lives has already happened. . . . And it's not going to be influenced by seeing the defendant in the courtroom and hearing the testimony. We may be angered and upset by what we hear in the courtroom, but that does not change the life-changing impact this crime has had."

Because of their efforts to pass the AEDPA, family members and survivors were already organized and knew how to tackle legal reform. Soon after Judge Matsch's second refusal to allow testifying victims to attend the trial, a coalition of 89 bombing victims appealed his ruling to the U.S. Court of Appeals for the Tenth Circuit. Their petition, filed by University of Utah law professor Paul Cassell, asserted that the federal Crime Victims' Bill of Rights gave them certain rights, including the right to be present at all related public court proceedings.

At the time of Judge Matsch's ruling, attorneys for both McVeigh and Nichols had opposed allowing victims slated to testify at sentencing to attend court proceedings. McVeigh's attorneys had even gone so far as to use victims' words against them, asserting that comments such as "I felt so much rage and anger today that I could have just clawed his [McVeigh's] eyes out" meant that this ruling was correct.[42] Defense attorneys argued that this ruling was not subject to appeal, and so the Tenth Circuit had no jurisdiction to review the ban, and that victims had no legal right to intervene.[43] Before the Tenth Circuit reviewed Matsch's ruling, however, Nichols reversed his earlier opposition to banning victims from the courtroom and filed a 200-word statement with the court, stating, "If any of the victims can get some peace of mind or relief of pain by attending the trial, then I waive my right to have the victims barred from the court."[44] Victims largely perceived this move as self-serving, a way of polishing his image.[45]

Matsch's ruling was upheld on February 4, 1997, by a three-judge panel of the Tenth Circuit, which held that prosecutors had no right to appeal that kind of judicial ruling and that victims had no standing to take legal action under the Crime Victims Bill of Rights.[46] Unwilling to accept this outcome, the victim coalition filed an en banc appeal asking all 12 judges on the Court of Appeals to reconsider the ruling. Numerous congressmen and others agreed to support the request as friends of the court, including Attorney General Drew Edmondson of Oklahoma and attorneys general of other states. Nonetheless, on March 11, 1997, the full Tenth Circuit declined to hear the case en banc and affirmed the panel's original decision.

With nowhere else to turn, family members and survivors once again sought assistance from Congress. Help arrived within two weeks in the form of the Victim Rights Clarification Act (VRCA) of 1997, which passed with great support; only nine members of the House of Representatives voted against it, and the Senate passed it unanimously. The act stated in part that "a United States district court shall not order any victim of an offense excluded from the trial of a defendant accused of that offense because such victim may, during the sentencing hearing, testify as to the effect of the offense on the victim and the victim's family." The act was signed into law a mere 11 days later on March 20, 1997, by President Clinton.

Members of both the House of Representatives and the Senate were aware of these justice needs; as Representative Bill McCollum of Florida acknowledged, "While we all understand that the guilt or innocence of the defendant must be of primary concern to the Judiciary process, we become increasingly sensitive of the need to include the victim and victims' families in the criminal justice process in appropriate ways that they too can feel that justice has been done for them."[47] More specifically, Representative Frank Lucas of

Oklahoma described the "healing process" in narrative terms, stating that victims not only "desperately want to know what activities led to this terrorist attack" but also "want the opportunity to express the pain and devastation this act has brought to their lives. They want the chance for their story to be heard; to know they played an important part in ensuring a punishment equal to the crime. They want, and need, to express their loss in their own words."[48]

Similarly, in the Senate, former prosecutor Patrick Leahy of Vermont stated that victims' stories could bring "reality" to the courtroom, unlike defendants' arguments, narratives, and behaviors:

> I found many times when the person being sentenced had suddenly gotten religion, had suddenly become a model person, usually dressed in a better suit and tie than I wore as a prosecutor and was able to cry copious tears seeking forgiveness and saying how it was all a mistake, sometimes reality came to the courtroom only when the victim would speak.[49]

Senator Orrin Hatch of Utah agreed, asserting that the legislation would ensure that victims could "alleviate some of their suffering through witnessing the operation of the criminal justice system."[50] These perspectives vindicated the emotive norms embedded in popular conceptions of "justice" for victims, including the opportunities for confrontation, confession, and catharsis.

A few opposed congressional intervention. Representative Bobby Scott of Virginia asserted that the act violated the constitutional doctrine of separation of powers preventing Congress from interfering in judicial affairs, termed the act "unseemly"[51] and warned that "tinkering with the judicial process could jeopardize the prosecution's case, and undermine the integrity of both the legislative and judicial branches, holding the entire process up to ridicule."[52]

Congressional intercession on bombing victims' behalf transformed the defendants' trials into hybrid proceedings in that the trials' key aspects—who would be able to witness them and where, and who could testify—were determined in part by extrajudicial actors. Jurors were asked to apply legal standards that had been recently authorized by legal precedent but that embraced popular cultural emotive norms. Victims' advocacy and congressional involvement did not alter legal emotive rules per se; rather, they carved out a place for victims, their emotions, and their emotional needs, thus affirming that such emotions should—and inevitably would—be present in the courtroom. Victims' emotions were now inextricably conjoined with "doing justice." Congress, then, opened up the trial to family members and survivors so that closure—memory work—could more readily occur.

Following the VRCA's passage, defense attorney Randy Coyne asked Judge Matsch to consider its constitutionality and again characterized the victims as emotional individuals:

> When victim/witnesses are exposed to the type of inflammatory, emotional, heartrending testimony permitted during the guilt phase of this trial, passion, prejudice, and perhaps even mistake are as inevitable as they are understandable. This Court did not rule in a vacuum. Indeed it had before it several examples of emotional outbursts by victims in direct response to attendance at proceedings in this case. . . . Those are the types of effects, your Honor, that we can't cabin off. Those are also the types of effects that are very difficult to detect.[53]

Judge Matsch, however, declined to address the constitutionality of the VRCA because doing so would have delayed McVeigh's trial. On March 25, 1997, Matsch ruled that if McVeigh was convicted, the court and prosecution and defense teams would question testifying victims outside the jury's presence to determine if they had been influenced by earlier testimony, after which he would determine whether that victim could testify. This allowed him to continue to exercise judicial authority over victim impact testimony while complying with the VRCA.

"Why?"

Participants hoped that the trial would answer what they felt was perhaps the most compelling question: "Why?" This was described as an unanswerable query that encompassed not only a deep inquiry into why McVeigh committed the bombing, but also the question of "Why us?" Diane Leonard described "Why?" as an incessant question that "just drives you crazy the first several . . . months, I guess it was. . . . all day, that question, why, why, why, why, why, why. It drives you nuts. . . . You need an answer." "Why?" included McVeigh's motives for harming innocents. Dot Hill described the question "Why?" in terms of the bombing's impersonality:

> Why? Help me understand your thought process in this. I understand vengeance. . . . Help me understand why you thought this would serve your

need for vengeance. What did I ever do to you that makes me die, pay for those people dying in Waco? . . . . these are strangers to him, just as we were strangers to him. What was it about this that made him think we should be the ones to suffer for them, those strangers dying, what made the connection there?

Coming to terms with this impersonality was a necessary accomplishment of memory work. Janet Beck observed that "you had to figure out that he was mad at an idea or mad at what he perceived the government stands for. . . . it wasn't anything directed at me, that it was just because I was a part of a [target] group."

Jamie Blansett described "why" as what made McVeigh choose to blow up the building when people were inside: "If you wanted to blow it up, why didn't you blow it up when there wasn't anybody there? You're still making a statement; you're still costing the government lots of money." Diane Leonard described "why" as "why in the world he thought this action would cause the reaction that he thought it would." These statements reveal participants' belief that understanding how and why a traumatic event occurred is necessary for memory work.

These remarks also illustrate that one of victims' hardest tasks was reconciling the very *personal* impact of the bombing's aftermath with McVeigh's impersonal, terroristic decision to murder unknown innocents. Participants sought a rational reason why the Murrah Federal Building was bombed, but they felt none was given; McVeigh's hatred of the government seemed too superficial. As Diane Leonard explained, "We were given a reason. You know, Waco. But for, for those of us who think fairly normally, that's not enough of a reason to do what he did." Leonard affirmed that the trial did not answer every question: "I knew going in that you don't get every question answered, but that's the place that you can get more questions [answered] than anywhere else. So I didn't expect everything to be answered."

Other participants were quick to note that they disagreed with the federal government at times but worked to change the system through legitimate means, not murder. Family member Ron "Tony" Brown, whose father-in-law, Special Agent Robert Westberry, was murdered in the bombing, quipped, "I just paid my taxes. I don't want to pay my taxes. But that's my responsibility, you know? I get to live in a free country. . . . I guess he was just playing God." But information revealed at trial about McVeigh's childhood allowed many to infer psychological bases for his motives; for Diane Leonard, "needing to understand why for me went, you know, I just kept trying to go further back and further back and figure out why." Inevitably, part of the process of coming to terms with the bombing included learning that there was no perfect answer to "Why?" This is what Dot Hill concluded: "And it never will be [answered]. . . . I honestly don't think he would be capable of giving an answer that a human being with a heart would ever be able to understand."

"It Was Just like a Stone Sitting There": Assessing McVeigh's Courtroom Conduct

Opening statements in McVeigh's trial began on April 24, 1997. McVeigh faced 11 counts: one count of conspiracy to use a weapon of mass destruction, one count of use of a weapon of mass destruction, one count of destruction by explosive of a federal building, and eight counts of first-degree murder for the deaths of eight federal law enforcement officers. While Judge Matsch and attorneys for the prosecution and defense exercised hypervigilance over family members' and survivors' emotionality, family members and survivors themselves were more concerned with the reactions of those on trial for their lives. For them, it was profoundly important to bombing victims to see McVeigh and Nichols in person, to gauge the depths of these men who had allegedly wrought such destruction.

Seeing the offenders' behavior affected the mediated victim-offender relationship, solidifying victims' perceptions of McVeigh and Nichols and providing insight into the defendants' relationship to the bombing—whether they regretted or took pride in it. Family members and survivors had to wrestle with such questions when negotiating the perpetrators' toxic presences; it was necessary to consider personal feelings toward McVeigh and McVeigh's purported feelings about the bombing to integrate him into memory work.

Family members and survivors who attended the trial in Denver constantly scrutinized the defendants' behaviors, and it did not take long for them to realize that McVeigh would not oblige them by displaying sorrow, remorse, or indeed any emotion, and that his conduct was much more likely to disturb than to mollify. This was a tough lesson for those who believed that McVeigh's remorse was crucial to their own recovery. As Susan Urbach noted:

> There were some observers to the trial who expressed a lot of anger in that he didn't react. . . . And it's been very evident from the moment he was arrested, he wasn't sorry. So, if he is not sorry, he's not going to act sorry. . . . my feeling is what victims always want to hear is remorse. . . .

You can't get that with McVeigh. . . . you have to figure it out, how you're going to get beyond. If you're going to make a life, there has to be a point where you understand you're not going to get that. And so if you're waiting on that remorse and that expression of sorrow, and that expression of guilt, . . . it's not going to happen.

Many were disturbed by McVeigh's ordinary appearance. Watching his trial behavior reminded Urbach of Oscar Wilde's classic novel *The Picture of Dorian Gray*:

> With McVeigh and Nichols we look at them and go, "They don't look like guys who would blow up a building and hundreds of people," and what we really expect is that . . . evil is written literally on the bodies of people so that you can look at them and go, "Ahhh, Charles Manson looks like a crazy man that would murder people," and yet you'd look at Ted Bundy and you'd go, "Looks like a nice clean-cut guy."

To Urbach, McVeigh "looked like a kind of a normal young guy, but with a buzz cut." The heightened physical proximity between bombing victims and McVeigh could facilitate new revelations. Ironically, Doris Jones was struck by McVeigh's humanity upon seeing him in person for the first time during the change of venue hearing: "It hit me too, he's just a man. He's a man. You know, in my mind he was a monster. But he really was a man." Stan Mayer found McVeigh's ordinariness terrifying: "I think you would prefer that someone who did something that hideous would be grotesque, you know, would look like a monster or an alien or something, but he didn't." But to see McVeigh in person could also produce what Jones termed "the horror feeling." In the courtroom, Jones recounted, "our eyes connected and I had to turn away. It was just very piercing, it was just like sending a chill up your spine."

McVeigh was most often characterized as an unemotional defendant whose reactions were nonexistent or impossible to interpret. Germaine Johnston affirmed that McVeigh "was always just sitting there expressionless, never showed any remorse. Never showed any emotion. He was just like a statue there." For Cameron Crawford, this impassivity was inhuman: "I mean McVeigh was just [an] automaton almost. Just so—didn't move. Nothing. Just stony. Like I said . . . [he] wasn't even a human being." Marsha Kight believed that this "stoic, ice-man" behavior was "military-like." Often, this impassivity was connected to a coldness of demeanor; Angela Richerson remarked, "McVeigh was a raw, hard person to understand and to get any kind of vibe from; he was just cold and callous." Diane Dooley linked this passivity with a capacity for deceit: "Even if he'd said something, whether you could have trusted that what he was saying was honest or . . . I mean just because he was so stoic throughout the trial and he always had the same look on his face." Two participants connected this coldness to "evil."

Another pervasive characterization of McVeigh was as a proud or arrogant perpetrator who enjoyed attending the trial; for instance, Jessie Sternburg explained, "He sat there arrogant and looking like he was enjoying the show." Several other family members and survivors were angered by McVeigh's apparently casual behavior, perceiving it as perverse relaxation or enjoyment. Lane Wharton recalled, "McVeigh would walk into the courtroom laughing, and joking, and sneering, and looking at the victims . . . like he was just having a good old time until the jury and the judge would come in and then he would settle down and, you know, be more serene." Diane Leonard noted that McVeigh was so relaxed and disengaged when uninterested in testimony that his behavior was more in keeping with a "party." Such behavior greatly angered participants; Doris Jones stated, "He just made me sick, because he would sit up there and talk to his lawyers and smile at the media. . . . it was just crazy."

These moments of inappropriate jocularity and informality contrasted with other moments in which McVeigh paid a great deal of attention to proceedings. Leonard perceived that McVeigh was only interested in evidence of the truck bomb and the harm it had caused: "The things he paid attention to were anyone who was testifying about that had bomb knowledge, how they're built and what works, what doesn't work. . . . and any rescue workers . . . because he wanted to know the damage he'd done. And victims. He wanted to know how much he had hurt everybody." At those points, "he was intent on what was being said, he was forward in his chair." Paul Howell also described McVeigh as "very aggressive" and very involved at times: "He got involved in a lot of it. When they brought out parts and they were talking about the telephones and the chemicals, he looked like he was really interested in it more than Nichols was."

Overall, McVeigh's courtroom conduct created the impression that he was not only guilty but proud of the bombing. Most participants shared Dr. Paul Heath's perceptions of his attitude:

> I'd be looking out at him and he'd make eye contact with me and start smiling real big at me and shake his head yes at me, gave me the impression that he was communicating. . . . "You bet I'm the one that did it." . . . The

way he behaved in the courtroom told you that he was glad he did it and he wasn't backing off from it at all.

McVeigh's defiant courtroom behavior had a particularly profound impact on victim impact witnesses who directly confronted him. Priscilla Salyers lost her composure while testifying:

> I couldn't, I, I looked at him, I mean I was so nervous and so scared and I really don't understand why it was affecting, well it was affecting me emotionally. . . . I just wanted to cry and when I looked over him, it shook me out so bad that I was like I can't look at him or I can't stay focused on what I am here for. . . . So I did not look back over at him.

Similarly, Diane Leonard recalled that "when I testified, we locked eyes and I've never felt anything like that before in my life. . . . I felt there was such a cold emptiness that I felt from him." She continued, "My body absorbed that feeling, it felt like it just washed over me, that cold evil that emanated from him. . . . It was something you physically felt."

"It Worked": Closing Arguments and the Guilty Verdict

At the conclusion of McVeigh's trial, emotion was still a core focus of both the prosecution and the defense, both of which invoked it in closing arguments. Defense attorney Stephen Jones asserted that "the prosecution . . . has based a substantial portion of its presentation . . . through the trial on emotion," composed of both "sympathy for the victims and, on the other hand, repugnance for [McVeigh's] political beliefs . . . and where they allegedly led him."[54] Jones cautioned that these emotions were not properly part of jury deliberations:

> But justice is blind. Justice does not wear a mourning armband. Justice does not show a tear on her face. A criminal trial is not a therapeutic counseling session. It isn't a closure. . . . Its function is very specific and very narrow: Has the Government presented enough evidence to convince 12 people beyond a reasonable doubt that the accused is guilty?[55]

In the prosecution's rebuttal to Jones, Scott Mendeloff agreed that emotion had no place in justice, that only justice could heal. Mendeloff's justice was not only for victims but for the nation:

And your decision in this case is about one thing. Not emotion. It's about justice; hard, cold facts; and proof; justice. Your verdict won't mend aching hearts forever broken. . . . The central tenet of our government is justice. I ask you to deliver the justice that defines this nation, the justice that the nation deserves. I ask you to declare together with a strong, clear voice that our society has no room for one whose seething hatred leads him to kill innocent children; innocent men and women; innocent, dedicated public servants. . . . only justice can begin to salve the wounds that this crime has wrought on the wounded, the killed, and on this nation.[56]

There is an implicit link in Mendeloff's argument between emotion and danger. To be emotional was to be irrational; McVeigh was the one suffused with "seething hatred." Accordingly, Mendeloff urged jurors to respond with a guilty verdict derived through cool moral judgment.

On June 2, 1997, McVeigh was convicted on all 11 counts of the federal indictment. The moment that the verdict was read was tremendously emotional for family members and survivors; Diane Leonard recalled, "I remember sitting there [in Denver]. . . . Makes me cry again. Looking at our flag and being so proud of our judicial system. It worked. I kept saying it worked, it worked, it worked. It went like it was supposed to." Diane Dooley just happened to be on vacation in Colorado at the time that the verdict was handed down, and she decided to take one day of her vacation to attend proceedings. She felt that it marked the "end":

Just a sense of relief when they found him guilty. Just a sense that he wasn't going to be able to do it to anybody else or get off, you know. . . . I remember sobbing when they read the guilty verdict, just because it was just such a sense of—okay, it's done. For me it was done. . . . I don't want to say closure, but I got a huge, I mean I moved very fast-forward.

Emotion Takes a Stand: Policing Affect in Sentencing Phase Testimony

With McVeigh convicted on all counts, the court's focus turned to determining his sentence, literally a life-or-death matter. In presiding over McVeigh's sentencing, Judge Matsch had to walk a fine line to ensure as neutral an atmosphere as possible. Adhering to the creed that "a penalty-phase hearing cannot be turned into some kind of a lynching," he set out to prevent "testimony which would inflame or incite the passions of the jury with respect to vengeance or the passions of the jury with respect to empathy for grief"—emotions "inappropriate in making a measured and deliberate moral judgment as to whether the defendant should be put to death."[57]

To this end, he barred prosecutors from presenting home videos of victims' wedding photos and records of credit union activities, a victim's father's poem, and a photo of a mother releasing a dove in lieu of a funeral, but permitted them to introduce more representative but still emotional evidence like "photos of maimed survivors and of victims in hospitals and coroner testimony about the various causes of death, including slow suffocation from gravel in the lungs."[58] He also permitted a 10-year-old boy to read a statement about his mother's loss after prosecutor Patrick Ryan assured he would not cry.[59] Judge Matsch accepted that the introduction of some graphic evidence was inevitable, noting, "We can't sanitize this scene. Some of the photographs, although they are disturbing, of course, are representative of what occurred."[60]

Nonetheless, testimony and evidence were so heartrending that sentencing proceedings were fraught with emotion. Reporters observed that prosecutor Joe Hartzler "stood at the podium on one occasion wiping a tear from his eye," "family members sobbed quietly in the back rows of the courtroom on a regular basis," and even Judge Matsch "was observed moist-eyed at times."[61] All told, prosecutors called 38 victim impact witnesses, including 26 family members, three injured survivors, a day care center employee, and eight rescue workers. These poignant, agonizing impact narratives dominated the sentencing phase of the trial.

On June 13, 1997, the jury sentenced Timothy McVeigh to death. McVeigh's behavior at trial was a nail in his coffin, cementing family members' and survivors' initial impressions of him as a defiant, remorseless, arrogant offender. Moreover, his behavior set the tone for the years between his death sentence and execution, cultivating the widespread impression that he wished to further wound families and survivors through media appearances, as well as the perception that he could only be silenced through execution—a justification that was never given for Nichols.

Law's Efficacy as a Site of Memory

Most families and survivors viewed McVeigh's trial as triumphant proof that the "system worked," believing that it validated the impartiality of American justice and thereby enhanced the criminal justice system's cultural authority.

Victims felt they had contributed to "doing justice" by working with the jury and the prosecution to hold McVeigh accountable. Thus, McVeigh's trial provided tremendous opportunities for memory work, demonstrating that legal proceedings' reconstructive usefulness depends upon trial outcomes and how victims perceive judicial disruptions. Paradoxically, the judicial rulings that had initially threatened the McVeigh trial's ability to facilitate memory work ultimately heightened its capacity to do so, forcing family members and survivors into close and creative collaboration to protect their perceived rights of attendance and testimony.

But we must not lose sight of the fact that, historically, criminal proceedings have not been ideally suited to memory work. Despite the reconstructive expectations and demands now placed upon them, criminal proceedings were originally designed as specialized inquiries into whether a suspect committed a criminal act, with a narrow adjudicative focus on an individual's behavior that likely excluded its social implications.[62] The recent imposition of new therapeutic aims has required that they be retrofitted to achieve such goals. Thus, even when victims enjoy participative opportunities, the efficacy of legal proceedings as a site of memory work can be imperiled by several factors, including judicial modesty, differences between legal and lay norms and decision-making processes, adverse legal outcomes, legal practitioners' constant anxiety over law's legitimacy and authority, and their corresponding desperation to safeguard its professional and cultural influence.

Courts answer weighty questions at the heart of public life and popular culture, and to this end they gather and assess volumes of evidence.[63] However, courts sometimes protest that they are ill-equipped to serve as sites of memory on the grounds of judicial "modesty," claiming that they lack the requisite authority and that their view of events is at once too narrow and constrained to fully contextualize events for social collectives.[64]

Similarly, law is also often reluctant to acknowledge its socially constructed nature, perhaps out of its desire to safeguard the stability and authority of its principles and rulings. According to legal scholar Mark Osiel, legal doctrines such as "res judicata, collateral estoppel, stare decisis, double jeopardy, mandatory joinder, statutes of limitations, and restrictive standards of appellate review" are designed to discourage courts from overturning precedent.[65] In law, the past most often informs the present by binding it. Only in legal interpretation do practitioners readily acknowledge constructive processes.[66]

Moreover, although legal and social norms and decision-making processes overlap to some extent, there are also important distinctions between them that threaten law's efficacy as a site of memory work. What is legally relevant may not be socially meaningful, making "good law" but "poor history."[67] Specialized legal practices may not translate into or be meaningful within the social collective. Legal facts are divorced from subjective experience and social context.[68] Victim witnesses' testimony may be viewed as sacred and untouchable, creating tension with the need to conduct effective cross-examination.[69] A defendant's proffered motives may seem insufficient; McVeigh's statement that he committed the Oklahoma City bombing in anger over Waco and Ruby Ridge neither exculpated him from criminal responsibility nor satisfied many family members and survivors.

In addition, unanticipated and undesired legal outcomes can profoundly affect memory work. Just because a murder defendant is charged and tried does not guarantee that he will be convicted; an acquittal not only stops memory work in its tracks but appears to devalue the murder victim and her family members. Nichols's sentence of life imprisonment without parole, for instance, was legally acceptable but seemed socially indefensible, a "morally compromised" travesty—and trivialization—of justice.[70] For these and other reasons, translating legal proceedings and judgments into collected memory can be troublesome. Thus, legal proceedings very rarely, if ever, provide the "official history" of a crisis.[71]

Nor are legal proceedings often the dramatic, spine-tingling sites of closure and memory work portrayed on crime dramas. At trial, proceedings focus upon minute evidentiary details that may seem meaningless to a public hungry for dramatic developments, making them boring to the social collective and thereby diminishing their impact.[72] But boredom can be a boon as well as a burden to memory work. Just because a trial is dull for citizens unconnected to the events in question does not mean that individuals who *are* intimately connected will find it boring. Some participants believed that McVeigh's trial, although dry at times during the detailed evidence presentation, was still momentous because they could simultaneously watch the jury, scrutinize McVeigh's behavior, and gather information. Indeed, many participants saw dullness as a necessary characteristic of proceedings, an inherent result of the detailed and methodical prosecutorial labor required to obtain a conviction. Thus, for some, dullness is a *professionally* necessary as well as a *morally* required quality of an effective criminal prosecution.

Law's ability to influence collected memory may also depend upon the factual situation being adjudicated; some cases demand the evolution of new legal principles or the creative application of existing principles to unusual contexts. Trials reinforce social solidarity only when the legal foundations and social norms upon which a decision is based are not themselves subject to challenge. When they are, authority may be compromised; if there is no consensus on what social norms should apply, these norms cannot be reinforced.[73]

Law is innately subjective; there is rarely one "correct" reasoning underpinning a judicial decision, or even one "correct" outcome. Trial judges' determinations are always subject to review. Law's professional and cultural legitimacy, authority, and influence are therefore a constant source of anxiety to practitioners, who struggle over how best to protect and enhance these attributes. In general, law's authority derives from practitioners' strict adherence to legal convention and the rule of law and from proceedings' procedural stability and neutrality.[74] Conservative jurisprudential rulings enhance a trial's authority and legitimacy and remove grounds for cases to be overturned on appeal. Thus, confronted by the specter of the O. J. Simpson murder trial and its circus-like atmosphere, it is no wonder that Judge Matsch ruled conservatively in favor of the defendants' motion for a change of venue, against a closed-circuit broadcast, and for excluding testifying victim impact witnesses from the courtroom. But while altering legal proceedings to satisfy unprecedented justice demands can sometimes undermine law's authority, legal proceedings may also lose their authority and even their relevance if they are too inflexible to adapt to culturally traumatic events meriting novel legal responses, including unprecedented criminal behaviors, horrific twists on existing offenses, and mass victimage.

But to acknowledge that law is an incomplete and imperfect site of memory does not diminish its significance; it achieves essential goals that no other institution can. How law accommodates memory work—and how well it does so—changes with the evolution and application of legal principles. Although law has been charged with satisfying new therapeutic responsibilities to suffering parties, it may yet be reluctant or unwilling to admit to such a role. But as more legal practitioners come to regard it as an institution with the potential to shape collected memory, the law will become changed by that potential and evolve to accomplish therapeutic goals.

Revisiting *United States v. McVeigh* and *United States v. Nichols*, we see how responding to the Oklahoma City bombing as a culturally traumatic event threatened to jeopardize the rule of law, prompting Judge Matsch to respond through conservative rulings and vigilant policing of victims' roles and emotional displays. In a conflict that illuminated the rift between legal practice and sociocultural norms and values, family members and survivors demanded further accommodations in response to Judge Matsch's conservatism, ultimately finding succor and aid from the political—not the judicial—branch. Thus, in the storm that followed Judge Matsch's adherence to legal formalism, the political branch fell upon and pinned the judicial branch.

If justice—particularly for victims—is increasingly seen as a public good, then law's failure to ensure that victims receive justice could potentially imperil the integrity of legal institutions as well as the law itself. The wider the chasm between the demands of popular culture and the justice that a court delivers (or fails to deliver), the greater the threat to law's cultural authority. Fortunately, as Judge Matsch discovered in the wake of the VRCA, allowing emotion in but maintaining strict vigilance upon its effects can satisfy both judicial desires to safeguard a trial's validity, integrity, and authority and popular desires to accommodate victims and their needs—even (or perhaps especially) their emotional needs.

It is far more productive to consider what limits can and should be placed on emotion—how it should be "bounded"—than whether it can be excluded.[75] Crime victims are representatives of the general public, who tend to picture themselves in the victims' shoes. Excluding victim witnesses from proceedings and even failing to provide opportunities for victims to view trials may diminish the public's confidence in law's ability to "do justice" for anyone but criminal defendants. As legal scholar Paul Gerwitz has noted, "If we wish to keep public confidence in the courts and public faith in the law, and if we wish to allow the courts to play their role of channeling public revenge, we cannot exclude too much of the reality of life—just as we cannot let too much in."[76]

But even after a trial in which all goes as planned, where the defendant is convicted and receives the sentence that most feel he deserves, additional memory work remains. Verdicts and sentences are necessary to but not sufficient for victims' narrative reconciliation to culturally traumatic crimes and their perpetrators. Legal proceedings may introduce more questions than they resolve, and as such, the inclusion of victims and emotive concerns in and of themselves cannot guarantee legal proceedings' efficacy as a site of memory work—a point aptly demonstrated by Nichols's federal and state trials.

8

Reaching Law's Limits

*Trying Terry Nichols and Welcoming the
McVeigh Jury to Oklahoma City*

After the jury convicted Timothy McVeigh and sentenced him to death, family members and survivors felt that they had witnessed the ideal exercise of justice, the outcome of fair, measured, and deliberate processes. But in Terry Nichols's federal trial, many would feel that justice remained elusive, leaving Nichols to dangle like an untied shoelace until his state trial in Oklahoma in 2004. In addition, following Nichols's federal trial, bombing victims worked to bring the McVeigh jurors to Oklahoma City, discovering in the process that memory work left incomplete at trial could be accomplished by meeting and speaking with the 12 jurors and 6 alternates who, for eight weeks, had dedicated themselves to adjudicating McVeigh's guilt with great personal and emotional sacrifice. Both Nichols's federal and state trials and the McVeigh jurors' subsequent visit to Oklahoma City illustrated how the courtroom was an essential but incomplete site for memory work.

Nichols's Federal Trial

As the federal trial of Terry Nichols approached, there was every indication that the prosecution would enjoy the same success it had in McVeigh's trial. But when it came time to try Nichols, his defense attorney, Michael Tigar, put into action the lessons he had learned about emotionality in the courtroom from the McVeigh trial. Tigar was determined that things would be very different for his client.

For starters, Tigar filed a pretrial motion to limit the types of impact testimony that would be permissible in this second trial, declaring:

It is our well-founded belief that the United States plans to use victim testimony to great prejudicial effect in the upcoming trial. Victims and rescuers will take the stand to testify at strategic times during the guilt phase, not for the purpose of establishing any disputed fact, but to divert jurors from legitimate questions they may have had about the government's case and to suppress the deliberative process with waves of emotion and pathos. . . . one of the most important prosecution tactics was the interspersal of victim testimony through weeks of dry testimony in a sort of "sympathy strategy," focusing jurors on the horror of the bombing. . . . It would serve only one purpose for the government, to repeat a similar interspersed procession of pain in the guilt phase of this upcoming trial—to stoke a fire of sustained hatred against Mr. Nichols, while coercing jurors, via emotional manipulation, to overlook any doubts they may have about the government's evidence.

Tigar also went much farther than Steven Jones had, reportedly requesting Judge Matsch to "eliminate all victims' testimony and to eject prosecutor Patrick Ryan from the case for crying too much during the McVeigh trial."[1] He also "promised to cross-examine every witness for the prosecution,"[2] in contrast to Jones, who did not question many testifying bombing victims. Finally, Tigar actively worked to defuse emotion in the courtroom, at one point asking a photographer who had filmed a "video of dazed and blood-soaked survivors if he could identify the type of earth-moving equipment in the background."[3] At Nichols's trial, Judge Matsch did not allow any testimony about visits to grave sites, donated organs from deceased victims, or victims' speculations about bombing motives.[4]

These differences between the two trials were blatantly obvious to journalists covering the Nichols trial. As one reporter observed, "Perhaps the most striking difference between the first Oklahoma City bombing trial and the second is not what's new but what's missing—the tears."[5] The "gripping, gut-wrenching stories" that had characterized victim impact testimony in McVeigh's trial allegedly "got so bad that court guards started stocking the 'listening room' used by the press with boxes of tissues."[6] In Nichols's trial, however, Tigar "forced the prosecution to tone down the victims' testimony to a basic recitation of the facts."[7] Thus, the prosecution's opening statement featured "a methodical summary of the government's case" instead of victims' stories, and victims themselves replaced heartrending details with terse replies.[8] At Nichols's trial, family member Helena Garrett merely responded "yes" when asked whether she got to see her 16-month-old son one last time before his burial; in McVeigh's trial she "gave a heartbreaking account of how she kissed her son's feet and legs at the funeral home because his head and face were so badly injured."[9] And Susan Hunt, an executive with the Oklahoma City Housing and Urban Development office, identified her coworkers on an exhibit that showed only their faces, whereas during McVeigh's trial she had "used a floor plan to place [them] at their desks" and "described their wedding plans and vacations, and later told how she attended 22 funerals in one week."[10]

Judging the Nichols Jury

As in Nichols's federal trial, jury issues made it easy for victims to place the blame in that corner of the courtroom. Family members and survivors closely scrutinized the behavior of the newly empaneled Nichols jurors and most assuredly did not like what they saw. "I don't think the Nichols jury had a clue what was going on," Janet Beck related. Family members and survivors predicted that one female juror in particular would be particularly problematic. According to Beverly Rankin, foreperson Niki Deutchman "spent a lot of time making eyes at Michael Tigar," which was worse than the other jurors who "weren't interested in what was going on."

News media described how Nichols's defense attorney Michael Tigar was permitted to "rehabilitate" "would-be panelists who expressed doubts" about their ability to impose the death penalty, "getting them to indicate just enough willingness to qualify for service."[11] This conduct did not escape the notice of family members and survivors; Diane Leonard, for one, was furious that Tigar was allowed to "badger" jurors by asking them again and again if they could give the death penalty after they initially told prosecutors that they could not. Leonard finally took action:

> I was so livid I couldn't wait to get out of the room where we were watching court on the next break. And I called one of the prosecutors and said, "What in the heck is going on here? You guys cannot allow—you've got to make sure that they are not qualified before you let go of them and hand them over to Tigar."

Family members and survivors also found fault with individual jurors. Leonard believed that "many of them came in with agendas" and felt the foreperson in particular was "against the government." Doris Jones termed the jurors "wimps" for being unable to make a decision, forcing Judge Matsch to sentence Nichols to life in prison without parole.

"You Would Have Thought He Was Asleep":
Nichols's Courtroom Behavior

Most survivors and family members characterized Nichols's courtroom behavior as the opposite of McVeigh's. Nichols was variously described as more emotional, ashamed, nervous, refined, quiet, afraid, sorry, or remorseful—quite literally the converse of McVeigh. For Paul Howell, these differences between the two defendants "made us look at both of them as individuals": "During the court procedures he [Nichols] acted like he was more concerned about what was going to happen to him. . . . He was quiet and paid attention to what was going on, where McVeigh didn't pay attention to anything." And unlike McVeigh, "most of the time he . . . looked like he was a little afraid about what was going to happen."

Some participants reported that Nichols was more sensitive than McVeigh; according to Richard Williams, at times such as during victim impact testimony Nichols was "very emotional." Nichols also displayed more situationally appropriate emotions; Jessie Sternburg stated that he appeared to be "uncomfortable, scared, guilty. . . . He looked very frightened"; Doris Jones described Nichols as "a little more nervous"; and Bud Welch described him as "very definitely remorseful." For Cameron Crawford, these displays of emotion were signs of humanity: "And I hate to give him credit for this, but you kind of see a person in Nichols." Nor was he particularly jocular; according to Jones, "He wasn't the jokester whatever. . . . he did lean over and talk to his attorneys but he didn't do the waving at people and the laughing and, you know, he did not do that. He was much more serious."

Other participants, however, believed that Nichols's conduct was similar to McVeigh's. Peggy Broxterman recalled, "I looked at him as he sat there, and [his attitude was] just like, you know, well, I don't know why everybody's here. I don't know why the attention is focused on me, I'm such a nice guy and I'm so innocent." Tom Hall recalled that, like McVeigh, Nichols "too was very stone cold look[ing], just sat there emotionless, just didn't even hardly blink or turn his head or anything the whole time." When Hall testified, he "tried to make it a point to give everybody equal eye time, being the jury, the spectators, the judge, the attorney, and Nichols himself." Hall recalled, however, how that effort was wasted on Nichols: "I remember each time I would come to him he'd just sit there. If his eyes wouldn't have been open you would have thought he was asleep."

"Nobody Comes Away Unscathed": Courtroom Encounters with Nichols's Family

Personal contact with Nichols's family members led to memorable and often emotional moments for participants. Family members and survivors attending Nichols's trial in Denver were flabbergasted that Nichols's immediate family members sat with them in the courtroom. All attempts to oust them were unsuccessful; Janet Beck recalled that Nichols's family would hold seats for one another, so that family members and survivors could not retake them during breaks as they had hoped. Most participants thought that Nichols's relatives intentionally occupied those seats in order to overhear victims' conversations.

But other participants had more positive encounters with Nichols's family members. Dr. Paul Heath had a moving encounter with Nichols's father in the courthouse bathroom in Denver, which he recalled as follows:

> I put my arms around him and hugged him, and I said, "Mr. Nichols, my family, and I know a lot of other families, don't hold you responsible for what your son did." And he started to cry. And I hugged him, and then he looked up at me when he finally quit crying and said, "This is the most difficult thing that's ever happened to me in my life."

Marsha Kight also appreciated it when Nichols's mother approached her by the elevators one day during a court recess and told her that "she was sorry for my loss." Susan Urbach vividly recalled sitting next to Nichols's family members at the trial, so close that she was "thigh to thigh with his mom." This physical closeness prompted her to realize that "nobody comes away unscathed from any of these things." After Urbach told Nichols's mother that she was an injured survivor, Mrs. Nichols said, "Oh, I'm so sorry," and Urbach replied that "we were on different sides of the aisle, but I know your life was impacted the same day as mine was."

The Conviction That Lacked Conviction

On December 23, 1997, jurors in Nichols's federal trial convicted him of eight counts of involuntary manslaughter and one count of conspiracy to use a weapon of mass destruction. Because the conspiracy charge carried the death penalty, the jury had to determine whether Nichols deserved life or death. However, on January 7, 1998, in the sentencing phase of his trial, the jury deadlocked after deliberating for 13 hours over two days, leaving one question: What happened?

According to Judge Matsch, the jurors "disagreed on the issue that was a legal threshold for deciding on the death penalty—whether Nichols intended people to die in the blast."[12] In one of the few interviews she granted, jury foreperson Niki Deutchman "described a panel tortured by doubts, wracked by dissension and deeply skeptical of the government's case."[13] In stinging remarks, she criticized the government for "dropping the ball," called the FBI "arrogant" and "sloppy in its investigation," and even implied that the government's conduct was actually to blame for the bombing. "I think the government's attitude . . . is part of where all this comes from in the first place," said Deutchman, referring to the conspirators' antigovernment animus. "I think maybe it's time the government be more respectful . . . and not with the attitude that we know and you don't, we have the power and you don't."[14] Another juror reported that members were troubled by the government's "failure to prove decisively that Nichols helped construct the bomb," and felt that he may have been "coerced into helping McVeigh" early on in the conspiracy.[15] Though jurors were aware that bombing victims "wanted Terry punished," they noted that their job was to "review the evidence"; one juror observed, "I can't be their arm of justice if the facts weren't there."

Juror interviews with news media detailed what transpired during deliberations. At the start of deliberation, the jurors took a vote—10 to 2 in favor of acquittal.[16] Those supporting conviction expressed frustration with peers who wished to acquit Nichols.[17] One juror, a geophysicist, stated, "You had people that napped during the trial and couldn't understand what was going on. . . . And then you had really sharp people as alternates and they couldn't be part of the deliberations."[18] Jurors also expressed frustration when their colleagues could not articulate the reasons for their decisions, and were vexed by both those who wanted to convict the defendant but "could not explain why" and with one juror who wanted to acquit after explaining, "I have to go with my heart."[19] Those supporting conviction found the trial and its outcome to be an arduous and traumatic experience; one woman admitted that she felt guilty, as if she had "let everyone down," and another was "very bitter."[20] In terms of the substantive merit of the charges against Nichols, jurors opined that the Nichols case "wasn't as concrete" as McVeigh's, and that "there were a lot more uncertainties," including Nichols's presence in Herington, Kansas, the morning of the bombing and his lack of involvement in renting the truck.[21] Jurors also credited Michael Tigar for his effective advocacy and for portraying Nichols as a family man who was "building a life, not a bomb."[22]

The overwhelming majority of family members and survivors were extremely disappointed in the outcome of Nichols's federal trial. Robin Brown's comment was representative: "You were disappointed that he didn't get what he deserved. He may not have been there that day and may not have put his finger on that button, but he helped plan it, he helped build it, he knew those kids were in that day care." Darlene Welch remarked in a media interview, "The jury failed us. I don't care what the judge says. The jury failed."[23] Others felt let down by the criminal justice system. Charlie Younger was dumbfounded: "Well, I just couldn't believe that our system . . . could allow the guy that was most guilty in this crime [to] get off with life in prison." Younger blamed systemic "flaws," including the difficulty of getting all jurors to agree on the death penalty and the influence of Nichols's purported religious conversion.

Notwithstanding the outcome of Nichols's federal trial, participants had to persevere in the face of their disappointment. "I guess for a little at first, I was maybe a little depressed or let down," recalled Tom Hall, "but I kind of got over it, you know, and went on with things." For many participants, the knowledge that Nichols would likely be tried again in Oklahoma made the outcome of his federal trial easier to bear.

A few participants were satisfied that Nichols received life in prison without parole. Diane Dooley believed that Nichols's sentence was actually harsher than McVeigh's, saying: "It's probably harder for him to be in prison the rest of his natural life and McVeigh really got off pretty easy." Doris Jones was very comforted that Nichols would never again walk free: "In federal prison, life is life. . . . Where you see all the time people get off on parole, get out on a technicality, whatever, and to know that life truly meant life was a good thing to me." But while Bud Welch initially "felt very relieved" that Nichols received life without parole, he eventually regarded this sentence as too harsh: "I think if Terry Nichols would, I think if he were released he would stay as far away from anything like that as he possibly could."

Escaping Death, Again

After Nichols was sentenced to life without parole in his federal trial, Oklahoma County District Attorney Robert H. Macy had vowed to file state charges against him, and in March 1999 he filed 163 counts against Nichols—"160 counts of murder, one count of first-degree manslaughter for the death of a fetus, one count of conspiracy to commit murder, and one count of aiding and counseling in the placement of a substance or bomb near a public building."[24]

When Macy retired in 2001, Wes Lane took up the reins of Nichols's prosecution. Lane was initially reluctant to prosecute the case because "he thought it was all about seeking the death penalty for Nichols."[25] But meeting with victims' families changed Lane's mind: "What I realized is that it was not about the death penalty. . . . this was about all these families truly believed that they never had their day in court."[26]

The decision to try Nichols for the deaths of the 160 civilians—those who did not work for the federal government—was an extremely controversial one. Before the state trial began, statewide polls revealed that most Oklahomans opposed it, favoring a plea bargain.[27] Reflecting back on Nichols's state trial, family members and survivors exhibited a range of reactions. Many had been opposed to retrying Nichols in Oklahoma because it would be very expensive, they did not feel that it was necessary, and he had already been sentenced to life in prison without possibility of parole at the federal level. Others regretted the expense of the trial but thought that it would be justified if it helped family members and survivors to heal. Finally, some participants thought that a state trial was absolutely necessary, if for no other reason than to hold Nichols accountable for the full extent of his crime—to convict him not only for the deaths of eight federal law enforcement officials but for the murders of the other 160 victims as well.

Most who opposed Nichols's state trial did so because of its expense and because it would be a painful experience for family members and survivors. "It was such a waste of Oklahoma's money," remarked Ernestine Hill Clark. "Even people who wanted McVeigh dead thought it was a waste of money. We had already tried him once." "I did not see any point in spending another $5 million in having this trial down here," said Germaine Johnston.

Fewer participants looked past the trial's monetary price tag to its psychological and emotional costs. Many years had passed, and several victims felt that the dust had settled to the point that, in Susan Urbach's words, "it wasn't important to me for him to have the death penalty or not. It simply didn't matter anymore." Bud Welch, too, believed they should have let a sleeping Nichols lie:

> When you have the death penalty this thing lingers on and on and on. . . . Terry Nichols was tried in Denver, he was in Florence, Colorado, he wasn't revictimizing anyone. No one was talking about it. . . . if they left him alone everyone . . . wouldn't have felt revictimized. They started everybody up

again, the victims' family members, they had those opposed to the death penalty for him and those supporting death penalty on opposite sides. . . . I had dirty looks given to me at McAllister after I testified [for Nichols], I walked down in front of the courthouse, and those that I knew supported the death penalty they were giving me these ugly looks, I didn't need that, I didn't need that out of them, and had we not had the death penalty we [would have been] done less than three years after it was over.

Other participants were against a state trial because they saw it as a political maneuver or an attempt to execute Nichols. Ernestine Hill Clark saw Nichols's state trial as political gamesmanship: "It was filed by . . . a local politician who'd been instrumental, who was at the end of his career and was using it . . . for self-aggrandizement, wanted himself seen as the people's person, he was long past that and, in fact, was retired by the time that happened." Clark believed that the money would have been much better spent elsewhere. Bud Welch described the state trial as something of a financial fiasco: "He is in here in [an Oklahoma] county jail for three years before his trial took place. He ran out of money, the defense attorneys went for a year and a half without even being paid until the legislature voted more money in for them."

But for those who were in favor of Nichols's state trial, its benefits were beyond price. They believed it was crucial that Nichols be held accountable for the murders of the other 160 victims. "Accountability" meant not only ensuring that Nichols was formally charged with each victim's murder, but convicted of each murder count and potentially sentenced to death. Family member Diane Leonard, whose husband was one of the 8 included in the federal indictment, stated, "No one had ever been tried for murder in those other 160 deaths. No one. I fought real hard, real real hard to have that happen. Because I wanted them to have their day in court. It's important." "He [Nichols] has 168 names on his charges, and that's something Tim did not have and there's something, that was really important," emphasized Jessie Sternburg. "Tim died for 8 deaths, not 168." As a member of one of these other families, Doris Jones very much appreciated the state trial: "I won't say it was a waste of time, because it wasn't. If for no more than what I've said before, that someone . . . was being held accountable for Carrie's death." Imposing accountability for the other 160 victims' deaths, then, was its own reward.

After the defense requested a change of venue from Oklahoma City on the grounds that media coverage of the bombing and Nichols's federal trial made a fair trial impossible, the state trial was transferred 120 miles away to the small town of McAlester, where it began in late March 2004.[28] Nichols's state trial never created the fervor in McAlester that his federal trial did in Denver; the media reported that local residents showed "indifference" to the proceedings, with "plentiful" parking by the courthouse and "no lines of spectators waiting for seats"; on the opening day of Nichols's defense, for instance, "the courtroom was nearly empty except for a cluster of reporters and a few victims' family members."[29] "It was just really kind of a rerun. It was just a different setting, but [the] same story," Janet Beck emphasized.

There were key differences between the federal and state trials; in Nichols's federal trial, the jury had been able to consider lesser offenses than first-degree murder like involuntary manslaughter, but in his state trial Judge Taylor did not feel that the evidence warranted a jury instruction on lesser charges. In addition, while Tigar had attempted to "put the government on trial" in the federal case, such strategies were likely not as effective on the state level after lead prosecutor Sandra Elliot told jurors that government errors were harmless, "the result of investigators dealing with massive amounts of evidence under difficult circumstances."[30] Nichols's defense heavily emphasized his alleged conversion to Christianity, introducing witnesses who testified that he had "worn out four Bibles through prayer and research, and that he wrote an 83-page letter to a prayer partner in Michigan while trying to make a point about Christian faith."[31]

As in previous trials, victim impact witnesses' testimony was edited at the last minute to conform to defense objections. Diane Leonard, who worked with the victim witness unit on Nichols's state trial to help "them understand what our people might need," recalled that the victim impact testimony in that proceeding was "horrid, horrid, horrid":

> The day impact testimony started they [the defense] were allowed to object to what the victims were going to say. You know they had to submit their testimony ahead of time in the state trial . . . and they ripped those to shreds. . . . the attorneys came out to tell their witnesses, ok, you can't say this, you can't say that . . . so one witness said, "I'm not going to testify. They've taken all my testimony away." People were crying. I had to rewrite testimony for some of those people. They were so upset and crying they couldn't read their testimony because it was so marked out. . . . that should not be allowed to happen. It was too much.

According to Leonard, that experience negated all the physical and emotional effort required to prepare impact testimony: "It's so horribly difficult to write that testimony. . . . And then to be just to the moment almost where you are to go on the stand and you're mentally preparing for it, . . . to have it trashed like that. It's just wrong, very wrong."

On May 26, 2004, the jury convicted Nichols of 161 counts of first-degree murder after deliberating for only four hours. Then, just like the jury in Nichols's federal trial, they deadlocked on Nichols's sentence after deliberating for 19.5 hours, forcing Judge Taylor to impose life imprisonment. After learning of the jury deadlock, prosecutor Wes Lane asserted that the state trial still had accomplished two crucially important objectives: "They have now had their day in court. Terry Nichols for the first time now is a convicted mass murderer, a term and title he's never had before and a responsibility he's always had."[32]

Both the prosecution and the defense had theories as to why jury deliberations had reached an impasse. Defense attorney Creekmore Wallace asserted that "the case might have been won in jury selection" and attributed the jury's failure to impose a death sentence to "the religious people on the panel."[33] Lane, on the other hand, gave an "educated guess" that there were "sympathy issues" on the part of the jurors who could convict Nichols of murder but not sentence him to death. "There has to be an emotional tie there," he said. "Otherwise, how do you explain a mass murderer not getting the death penalty? Surely someone got their heart strings swamped."[34]

On August 9, 2004, Nichols was sentenced to life without the possibility of parole on the Oklahoma state murder charges, which was devastating to many. Peggy Broxterman recalled:

> I thought sure being in Oklahoma where we'd lost so many people, you know, I thought sure he would get the death penalty because the evidence is there. . . . I was sitting on the second row, the lawyers came in and they kind of shook their head no, which meant he didn't get the death penalty. So when the judge came in and said, "I'm going to announce the verdict and if anyone doesn't want to be here when it's read, please leave now." And I got up and left. I was the only one to leave the courtroom. But I didn't want to hear them say life in prison, you know.

Broxterman could not understand why the jury deadlocked: "One of the things the jurors said was, 'He was not there.' Can you imagine you and I plotting a murder of somebody and we're both in and I pulled the trigger and I get the death penalty and you don't? It's just that stupid. . . . You're just as guilty as I am. We both plotted it." "I was devastated by the outcome. . . .

And of course it took about a month to recover from the devastation of the way it ended up," Diane Leonard recalled. Others, while angry, were more emotionally detached. "Well it was shocking because, I mean, it was so obvious . . . someone else gets convicted of something lesser than that and gets a death penalty," recalled Priscilla Salyers. However, she did not dwell on the verdict: "But I have to go back to the fact that it doesn't matter to me. He is gonna have to meet his maker one day. . . . [I just] walk away and, you know, life goes on." Similarly, Robin Brown noted, "To me, it's over. I mean, there's nothing else you can do, once the trials happen and the decisions are made, you're stuck."

A few participants approved of the trial's outcome. Ernestine Hill Clark was "very happy"; she was "content that he will never get out of jail and feel like we'll eventually get the whole truth."

Family members and survivors too sought explanations for the verdict, for if the outcome of Nichols's federal trial seemed extraordinary, it was unthinkable that an Oklahoma state trial, so close to the building that Nichols had conspired to destroy, would produce a similar sentence, albeit with the satisfaction of 160 murder convictions. Participants did not fault the prosecution; Peggy Broxterman emphasized that "the prosecutors were marvelous . . . they were clear, they were precise, they brought in all the evidence . . . it couldn't have been any better." While some found the verdict inexplicable, others felt that they knew where to lay the blame: the jury. Tom Hall noted, "I think I was disappointed in the jurors too and I was just trying to, I was just mystified trying to think what they didn't see." Broxterman felt that the jurors were distracted from the evidence by irrelevant details: "You don't take a case like this to a bunch of little, small-town people because first place they're all after church and they're all after God and they're all after religion and 'Oh my goodness, Terry found God and that meant a lot,' and, come on!" Cameron Crawford opined that jurors might have been opposed to the death penalty: "I wish I could think of some way to better qualify jurors. . . . And these people want—I mean, come on, they want to be on these panels. I mean this was a famous trial. And especially if they have an agenda against the death penalty, you know, it just takes one to say no, and of course these people want to get on these juries."

Finally, a few participants noted that Nichols's state trial not been run quite as professionally as his federal trial. Diane Leonard said, "It was a farce. It was so different than federal court." "That judge did not have control like

Judge Matsch did," she added, "He did not know how to handle a high-profile case in my judgment. He did not make them deliberate."

Other participants again laid some of the responsibility for Nichols's sentence upon institutional procedures. Survivor Charlie Younger, who commented on the difficulty of getting all jurors to determine that a defendant's crime merited the death penalty, questioned why Nichols merited an attorney at public expense when other defendants did not. Once again, the deciding factor in Nichols's state trial was very likely his lawyer's skill; as Younger stated, he "was obviously a very good lawyer and he, he went over backward to try to get this guy life in prison and managed it."

Notwithstanding its unexpected outcome, some participants felt Nichols's state trial did have an effect upon his toxic presence. For most, Nichols's presence had already diminished significantly by the time of his state trial, although proceedings temporarily intensified it. "Just the fact that it was in the forefront again, it was almost like reliving everything," recalled Vicki Hamm. But once the state trial clinched Nichols's fate of life in prison, his presence again diminished; as Paul Howell recalled, "That cleared my mind right there, and that was the end of it on him." A few participants insisted that involuntary ties to Nichols remained more enduring simply because Nichols will never be executed. Stan Mayer emphasized, "As long as he's alive, in a way there's a connection."

The 2004 McAllister trial did not mark the end of Nichols's media visibility; he has since made headlines regarding his efforts to obtain a diet rich in fiber. In March 2009, Nichols filed a *pro se* federal lawsuit, arguing that "God created mankind to consume unrefined whole foods that work in a synergistic way to keep one's body (i.e. God's holy temple) in good health to ward off various diseases," and complained of "chronic constipation, bleeding, hemorrhoids, along with pain and suffering."[35] Nichols has also purportedly engaged in three hunger strikes. On August 12, 2010, U.S. District Judge Christine Arguello dismissed his case.[36]

This new media visibility enhanced the sense of his presence for several participants, irritating those who would rather not hear anything more about him. Family member Peggy Broxterman, for one, declared, "I don't care if he gets fiber or not. And I don't want to hear about it." Weighing Nichols's dietary complaints against the gravity of his crimes, participants felt frustrated that such a small concern as dietary fiber should generate so much attention. For Diane Leonard, the insignificance of Nichols's concerns threatened to trivialize others' horrific experiences. Leonard had no doubt as to who has suffered more; survivors "still have glass coming out of them, and he's complaining about fiber."

Susan Urbach found this latest news more amusing than threatening. "I'm laughing because it is sort of funny and it's very sad in a sense in that, you know, his life is so regulated that that's his hell," she remarked Urbach. "His punishment is that the important thing to him is having fiber in his diet." Faith Moore resented the fact that she needed to hear about him at all: "Take a Metamucil, whatever! . . . Just sit there and do your time and be quiet. . . . to me it was just an attention-getter. Hey, look at me, I'm still here, I'm still here! Yeah, we know you're still there."

Nichols's state and federal trials both illustrate law's reconstructive limits, confirming that its efficacy as a site of memory work is contingent upon and constrained by a trial's outcome and victims' perceptions of justice break-downs. Nichols's federal trial was marked by incongruity between what for most family members and survivors was the desired conviction and sentence (first-degree murder and death) and those actually handed down (a con-spiracy conviction and life without parole). While his state trial produced the desired 160 first-degree murder convictions, it, too, did not result in a death sentence. Family members and survivors believed that in both cases "doing justice" was marred by systemic issues, in particular juror problems. Since the trials' results and procedures essentially impugned legal integrity and cultural authority, it came as no surprise that many found these trials less salient and significant than McVeigh's trial.

Fortier's Fate

On May 27, 1998, Michael Fortier was sentenced to 12 years in prison. How-ever, his sentencing proceeding had a very different effect upon family mem-bers and survivors than did those of McVeigh and Nichols. Fortier read a letter of apology during his sentencing hearing, providing a point where participants could thankfully part ways with him. As survivor Diane Dooley explained, "He became less of an intrusion after he apologized in court. . . . For me, it became final at that point."

But for many others, Fortier's toxic presence continued to generate anger. Cameron Crawford stated that he actually felt more anger toward Fortier than toward Nichols: "I think a little more anger because it was so simple for him to stop it. Just one phone call, he could have stopped this." Several participants felt that Fortier's sentence was too light. Ray Washburn wished Fortier had "either got life or death," and Richard Williams asserted, "The fact that he got 12 years . . . I don't think that's right. I think he should have suffered more for his involvement."

Others were initially bothered by Fortier's sentence but either gradually began to accept it or eventually were persuaded that it was appropriate. "At the time, when they said, 12 years, I'm like, 'What!'" recalled Doris Jones. "But then, it wasn't so overwhelming, . . . the feeling was not long-lasting like the others were." Paul Howell recalled, "It did [bother me] at first. . . . But then, after listening to the trials and find[ing] out what he was involved in, I think the 12 years probably was a good time for him." "I know it messed up his life a little bit," noted Howell, "but he also messed up a whole bunch of other lives, so he needed to suffer a little bit, but not as much as the other two." Fortier's cooperation assuaged a bit of participants' ire over his 12-year sentence. Diane Leonard viewed it as the price to pay for convicting McVeigh and Nichols: "You don't think it's fair, but you realize the reason it has to be the way it was. So, even though it doesn't seem like enough of a penalty, it's one that you're able to accept when you know that his testimony was very important in getting the other two."

Most participants felt that Fortier's presence eventually waned because he effectively disappeared from legal proceedings and from the media. For Richard Williams, "Once the trials were over and I knew that he was in prison, I don't think there was any realistic intrusion at all." Diane Leonard emphasized, "We never hear about him anymore. . . . So he's not intruding now at all." Susan Urbach still felt tied to Fortier "because he'll be getting out," but she acknowledged that this tie was not necessarily negative: "Maybe he can get his life together and again, you look at that remorse, repentance kind of thing and there is the possibility for him of a redemptive type of action."

Fortier was released from prison on January 20, 2006, after serving 10.5 years of his 12-year sentence. Charlie Younger remembers details of this moment—the last that anyone heard of him: "They moved him out of Oklahoma real quiet one morning. Everybody knew he was getting out. They wouldn't tell us when and where he was headed because they knew he might be a target for somebody, but I knew he did not go back to Kingman and we were told he was changing his name legally." Participants doubted that this undercover life would be easy. As Janet Beck observed, "He's probably just as bad off out of prison as he was in prison. I mean, if anybody finds out where he's at. . . . I would hate to live knowing that the government was watching every move I made."

Ultimately, regardless of the extent of a perpetrator's involvement and the length or severity of his sentence, some participants anticipated that they would experience the perpetrators' presences, especially from Nichols and Fortier, for their lifetimes. Faith Moore commented, "It's something I don't dwell on, I try not to, but it's always there. . . . Just like the bombing is always there. . . . with Nichols and Fortier they're still alive, . . . your life is always still tied to them." Survivor Richard Williams stated that there will always be "triggers" that renew offenders' presences: "It's almost easier sometimes if [the offenders] are gone to cope with it because you can always say, 'What if?' than it is if they're there and you can't find out information. . . . If you see that snippet, it's gonna grab you. . . . I think that's always gonna be a trigger."

Unexpected Friends: The McVeigh Jury Visits Oklahoma City

The conclusions of McVeigh's and Nichols's trials were key to participants' memory work, yet not even McVeigh's trial answered all of the victims' questions. Indeed, it generated more—how the jury had deliberated, what impressions jurors had formed of the defendants, and how jurors' personal lives had been affected by the trial.

Almost immediately after the jurors sentenced McVeigh to death, juror Vera Chubb publicly stated that she wished she could visit the site of the bombing.[37] Family members and survivors who belonged to the habeas group were very interested in bringing the McVeigh jurors to Oklahoma City, but, after conferring with legal officials, they elected to defer the visit until after Nichols's trial. It was readily apparent that both bombing victims and jurors were eagerly anticipating the visit. In a letter to the jurors outlining early plans, a habeas group member wrote, "I understand that there was a desire to touch us as we came on and off the witness stand. Believe me, the feeling was mutual. We have become very practiced huggers over the last few years . . . and we look forward to the time that we can see you, talk with you, touch you and hug you."[38] Group members wished to keep news of the jurors' visit quiet so as not to attract undue attention; accordingly, they told jurors, "We know you don't want a media event, and neither do we. This is a personal deal."

Lead members of the federal prosecution team opposed the idea from its inception. One individual was concerned that the jurors' visit was an "idea developed with good intentions . . . but without consideration of all of the possible adverse consequences, the greatest of which was the possible, albeit false, perception that the jury had developed an emotional alignment with the victims despite the court's repeated instruction." Other concerns ranged from whether others could perceive the visit as a reward to what tax consequences the visit could have for jurors.

Members of the habeas group were not won over by these attempts to dissuade them from bringing the McVeigh jurors to Oklahoma City but agreed to postpone the jurors' visit until after the Nichols trial. On June 19, 1998, 10 of the 12 jurors and 6 alternates, with spouses or other support persons in tow, traveled to Oklahoma City for a weekend visit sponsored by the Oklahoma City Bombing Death Penalty Appeals Reform Committee to thank them for their service. Diane Leonard and Charlie Younger flew up to Denver to meet the jurors and escort them back to Oklahoma City. "We felt that might give them a little more of a comfort level to know a couple of our folks before they got to Oklahoma City," Leonard explained.

After their arrival, the jurors were taken to the state capitol building, where they planted a Colorado blue spruce in memory of the bombing victims.[39] On Friday evening, the jurors attended a private cookout at one of the habeas group members' homes. On Saturday, jurors paid a ceremonial visit to the site of the bombing. Near the Survivor Tree, an elm that had weathered the blast, politicians and community members thanked the jurors for their service. Governor Frank Keating informed jurors "You will always be members of our family"[40] and remarked, "As a result of your willingness to listen to the facts and apply the law with an open mind, [you] have restored our faith and America's faith in the criminal justice system."[41] Oklahoma attorney general Drew Edmondson also praised jurors for "performing their civic duty 'so admirably.'"[42] Diane Leonard spoke of the fellowship between family members, survivors, and jurors: "We have learned— the list of victims is almost endless . . . and it includes you, the jurors."[43] Jury foreman James Osgood earned a standing ovation when he praised family members' and survivors' dignity and courage.[44] Because the Oklahoma City National Memorial and Museum structure had not yet been built, the jurors privately viewed an exhibit housed in a garage underneath the bombing site and placed roses on the empty lot where the Murrah Building once stood.[45] Finally, they were escorted along the chain-link fence surrounding the site that served as a makeshift memorial to which visitors had affixed stuffed animals, notes, photographs, flowers, and crosses.[46]

Visiting the bombing site affected jurors viscerally. Many described it as overwhelming, fear-inducing, and awe-inspiring. Juror Jim Candelaria said, "When I see the destruction, it scares me."[47] Juror Tanya Stedman "felt physically sick" because of "all the victims" and was amazed that more had not died.[48] Despite its difficulty, jurors believed that the site visit was healing.

Stedman described it as "very emotional but very rewarding in a sense that we really wanted to come full circle and actually physically stand on the site that we judged on. It felt really good to me."[49]

On Saturday evening, the jurors were feted at a dinner at the Cowboy Hall of Fame with 500 rescue workers, family members, survivors, and city officials. After the meal, the jury was seated on the stage, and following a performance of the song "Unexpected Friends," Charlie Younger presented the jury with the 10 most pressing questions solicited from family members and survivors prior to the dinner.

Questions spanned topics from jurors' experiences at trial to how the experience had affected them personally, and included what jurors thought of McVeigh's unemotional countenance during trial, what evidence convinced them that he was guilty, what part of the case jurors thought should have been handled differently (if any), how jurors were affected by sentencing testimony, how important and credible jurors felt Fortier's testimony was, and whether jurors had formed any opinions of Nichols's guilt or whether others were involved. Other questions addressed the trial's effects on personal lives and matters entirely outside McVeigh's federal trial. Family members and survivors wanted to know whether any members of the jury had been against the death penalty, how serving as a juror in McVeigh's trial had affected them and their families, how they had been treated by the media, what advice they would give to future jurors, why they wanted to come to Oklahoma to visit with family members and survivors, how visiting the bombing site had affected the perceptions of the bombing that they formed at trial, and even whether jurors approved of a state trial for McVeigh and Nichols. As family member Diane Leonard summarized:

> Of course we wanted to know what was the thing that helped them make their decision. . . . And what did they think about different parts of the trial. We just wanted to know who they were, these people who had sat through all of this and fought this battle for us. . . . We wanted to get to know them. We felt a personal connection to people we had not even met. And we wanted to express our gratitude for the sacrifices they made for taking the time to sit on this jury.

The jurors' visit to Oklahoma City enabled events to come full circle for both family members and survivors and the jurors themselves. Through this visit, connections were formed, stories were exchanged, and relationships were founded. Bombing victims had long yearned to meet the McVeigh jurors, from whom they had to keep their distance during McVeigh's trial. The desire to make these unique connections was forged in the crucible of the trial experience; not only had many family members and survivors sat through the trial day in and day out as the jurors had, but victim impact witnesses had shared intimate revelations on the stand. One unidentified witness explained, "We opened our hearts to these people. We told them things that you just don't tell most people about yourselves."[50] Diane Leonard recalled, "Meeting this jury was a larger piece of that puzzle than I ever realized until they arrived. We shared our deepest feelings with them on the stand."[51]

When asked to describe the bond between family members and jurors, family member Diane Leonard explained it in terms of a war metaphor; together, the two groups had soldiered through the trial:

> There was a bond there before we really even met each other because— I think it's a kind of bond that is kind of similar to soldiers who serve together. This trial was our war, you know? And they served in one part of the war, we were another part of the war, but we were all in that same war. And anytime people fight battles together, there's a connection. . . . For many people, you just meet and it's a very surface, superficial meeting . . . but after that event, I don't know if it's where your mind and heart are. Your mind is so ripped open that . . . you meet people on a different level. . . . And when we met these jurors, it was a connection like, I don't know, we just felt like we knew them. Even though we didn't hear them speak in the courtroom.

However this bond formed, it was enduring. As Leonard related, "When they left, all of us [were] left with a feeling of some additional questions [that] had been answered, but much more than that, we left with friendships that have lasted. I mean, I still send Christmas cards to most of the jurors. It was a deep connection."

Jurors also longed to commune with family members and survivors. Some stated "that they found it particularly frustrating to listen to the weeks of sorrowful victim testimony without being allowed to comfort those who were in so much pain."[52] Vera Chubb emphasized, "I needed to hear these people, I needed to touch them. I needed to hug them."[53] For juror Michael Leeper, this desire was a natural outgrowth of surmounting the institutional distance of the courtroom, now that it was proper to do so: "We had spent so much time with so many of these people, but just a few feet away from them. Had never been able to talk to them, ask them any questions, just reach out and touch them. And this was—this was the thing that we'd all wanted very much to do."[54] Similarly, juror Karen Munoz said, "It's formed a link for me now. It's one thing to see it in the courtroom, hearing testimony, not being able to reach out to the witnesses and say I really want to hold you."[55] Jurors could finally convey to family members and survivors what they had long wished to tell these individuals that they had only seen in the gallery and on the witness stand. As juror Martha Hite said, "All though the trial, . . . I wanted to tell the people of Oklahoma how terribly sorry I am. And so now I can."[56]

Both sides spoke of these newly formed connections in terms of family ties. As one bombing victim stated, "I thank them. My heart goes out to them. I know that it must be very difficult for them emotionally, and just want them to know that we love them, and we're a part of this extended family that reaches out and says, love you, we're there for you. It's important."[57] References to family relationships abounded in media coverage of the jurors' visit. News reports stated that jurors felt as if they had found a "second home,"[58] and that "several jurors said they feel like they have extended family members."[59]

Because the lived experiences of McVeigh's trial—attending, listening, testifying, rendering a verdict, and determining a punishment—were arduous tasks, both bombing victims and jurors wanted to offer support and love to one another. But because legal tenets disfavored or outright proscribed interpersonal contact between victims and jurors, these individuals had to take the initiative to make these connections. The jurors' visit injected a heretofore absent but much-needed dose of human feeling into a terribly traumatic ordeal that jurors and testifying victims had attempted to "strip of emotion."

Both groups wished to assure the other that they felt McVeigh's trial had had the best possible outcome. Dan McKinney explained: "[We wanted them] to know that for us that we felt so much that the right decision was made by them and that justice was served. And we wanted them to understand and feel that feeling in case they may have had some remorse or something and just felt bad about it."[60] Jurors, in their turn, also wanted to provide support to family members and survivors. Juror Martha Hite believed that her healing process had been hindered by a feeling that things were largely unfinished, even after McVeigh's trial was concluded: "I feel that I had to come to fully understand what has happened here, so I can move on knowing that they are going to be okay."[61] They characterized this as the capstone of McVeigh's trial. According to juror Michael Leeper, while they had felt "very, very comfortable" with their verdict and sentence, the visit "actually helped us in the fact that it put people [in]to the whole experience. And that's what we needed. We needed more of the sense of people."[62]

Opening themselves to emotion was a different and difficult experience for jurors who had to muzzle these feelings at trial. Jury foreman Jim Osgood stated, "We had to divorce ourselves from the emotion of this. It was our duty to do that as we deliberated and as we contemplated the facts and testimony of the case. And this is the first time we were able to feel it all."[63] These emotions confirmed that jurors had made the right decision in convicting McVeigh and sentencing him to death. Juror Marlene Wychale related that "part of it is closure—[the] right decision was made."[64]

"We Have Every Right": Criticisms of the Jurors' Visit

This visit was not uncontroversial; it "alarmed" lawyers and legal scholars, who were concerned that it could give the appearance of rewarding jurors for verdicts.[65] Attorneys from the McVeigh and Nichols defense teams as well as members of the prosecution deemed the visit improper. Steven Jones publicly stated that it was inappropriate[66] and an "emotional catharsis":[67] "Justice has to be based on facts and evidence. It must be blind to agony and it must be blind to sympathy. And in this case, it wasn't."[68] Michael Tigar termed it "outrageous," noting, "It amounts to a gift, and giving someone a gift on account of their public service is improper at best. . . . The Nichols jury did their job too, . . . but you don't see them receiving any special treatment."[69]

In the face of criticism, family members and survivors defended the visit "as a much-needed vehicle for closure for those who wished to thank the people responsible for putting the perpetrator away, as well as for jurors who wanted to put a place and faces on the testimony they heard 600 miles away in Denver."[70] Charlie Younger asserted, "No way is this a reward. . . . It's a gift from Oklahomans who needed to meet them." "We just wanted to show the jury, McVeigh's jury, that we really appreciated how they went about it. And what they did," Beverly Rankin emphasized.

Jurors also reacted indignantly to Jones's insinuations. Several emphasized that at the time of the visit they were no longer empaneled jurors but "private citizens," with comments such as "We're exercising our rights as private citizens, not as jurors, to witness this event."[71] Juror Tanya Stedman claimed, "We have every right to be here."[72] Others, such as foreman Jim Osgood, took umbrage at the notion that he and his fellow panelists had relied upon emotion in convicting or sentencing McVeigh: "We focused purely on the facts, purely on the testimony, purely on the evidence presented to us for some eight weeks."[73] Osgood explicitly countered Jones's remarks by affirming, "We remain committed to our deliberations, our focus on the facts, the testimony. Our objective process we used during our deliberations. No way did we use emotion to arrive at our verdict."[74] Vera Chubb intimated that Jones had no idea what the jurors had gone through during the trial, remarking, "I think if Mr. Jones had maybe been in our shoes, he would see the reason we're here also."

Coming Full Circle

As the McVeigh jurors' visit to Oklahoma City illustrates, culturally traumatic events produced unprecedented trials, which in turn engendered unique relationships. For family members and survivors, the jurors' visit was the perfect conclusion to the trial experience. McVeigh's trial may have marked the beginning of the end of legal proceedings, but it represented a new beginning for bombing victims and for jurors. The two groups felt as if they had worked together to accomplish the mutual goal of "doing justice," respected one another, and were grateful for each other's contribution. Victims recognized that jurors had been through a tremendously harrowing eight weeks and welcomed them into the circle of those who had been intimately affected by the bombing. Meeting face-to-face, both groups could share thoughts, answer each other's questions, and trade stories.[75]

Nichols's trials and the McVeigh jurors' visit to Oklahoma City together illustrate that much memory work must take place outside of the courtroom and demonstrate how important human bonds are to reconstructive efforts. Once memorials have been built and legislation passed, once trials have concluded and all the news coverage has been published or aired, it is these human bonds that persist. Institutions bring people into proximity with one another and yet hold them apart; news coverage and courtroom proceedings can both wake a nascent awareness of the need for interpersonal bonds and create opportunities to fulfill them, even as they generate and enforce physical and emotional distances. The eventual conclusion of institutional involvement in culturally traumatic events frees these individuals—family members, survivors, jurors, attorneys, and journalists—and even researchers who come along in ensuing years—to celebrate the inherent potential of interpersonal relations.

But even after the McVeigh jurors' visit to Oklahoma City, family members and survivors still did not enjoy the full fruits of this freedom. One more territory yet remained to be conquered in the reconstructive war that victims had fought in order to reclaim crucial psychological, emotional, and social terrains from McVeigh's toxic presence: his execution.

9

The Storm before the Calm

Awaiting McVeigh's Execution

Over the years since the bombing, family members and survivors had been forced to negotiate involuntary, unwelcome, and toxic ties to the perpetrators and had found McVeigh particularly troublesome because of his defiance and conspicuousness. Thus, as his execution approached, most felt that it would be a means of ending McVeigh's visibility or even his pernicious hold over their lives and emotions. Some victims dared to hope that his execution would facilitate more dramatic therapeutic evolutions such as that from victim to survivor. That grim event would indisputably have significant institutional consequences. It marked not only the moment when the criminal justice system would demand accountability, but also the culmination and conclusion of legal proceedings. It would surely engender one last flurry of media coverage, after which McVeigh would be forever silenced.

Confronted with the choice of whether or not they wished to view McVeigh's execution, family members and survivors took the time to carefully consider their attitudes toward McVeigh and his punishment up to that point. Their decisions were based on a host of complex factors—how their opinions on the death penalty had evolved, whether they felt a duty or responsibility to witness McVeigh's execution, whether they had forgiven him, whether they would have been willing to meet with him prior to his execution, and what behaviors they wished to see from McVeigh immediately before he was executed.

Not Vengeance but Justice: The Struggle for the Closed-Circuit Broadcast of McVeigh's Execution

It was not at all certain until a few months before McVeigh's execution that more than eight victim witnesses—the number of live execution witnesses permitted under federal regulations—would be able to attend. In January

2001, family members and survivors were asked to indicate whether they would be willing to attend the execution live in Terre Haute. These eight seats would be assigned by lottery, with no more than one person from the same family being selected. A letter from the U.S. Attorney's Office for the Western District of Oklahoma to family members and survivors informed them that the lottery was structured according to the same categories of victims used in allocating trial seats, with seven seats reserved for victims' family members, two seats reserved for survivors with physical injuries, and one seat reserved for other survivors; victims who suffered only property damage were not included. Selected individuals could only transfer the "right" to attend to others in their immediate family who were also listed in the database. If these persons changed their minds about attending, officials would select an alternate of the same victim category.

As the execution date drew near, numerous Oklahoma City bombing survivors and victims' families, including many participants in this study, sought to persuade Attorney General John Ashcroft to arrange for a closed-circuit broadcast of the execution from Terre Haute to Oklahoma City. They framed the struggle to televise McVeigh's execution in terms of their need to witness "justice," arguing that everyone who was affected by the bombing had a right to choose for themselves whether or not to watch.

Ashcroft visited Oklahoma City on April 10, 2001, and met with 100 survivors and victims' families who were united in their belief that seeing the execution was important. During his visit, Ashcroft toured the Oklahoma City National Memorial and Museum and heard stories from family members and survivors. Doris Jones described one of these accounts: "One girl expressed how her mother had been one of the last pulled out of the building and wasn't pulled out until after the building was imploded and the torment she had gone through. . . . this was something she just had a desperate need to do and that it wasn't vengeance. It was justice." Another story came from a young boy "who [had lost a parent]. . . . he was amazing. And he begged. He said, I couldn't attend any of the trials. . . . I think he was like 12 or 13 at this meeting. [He asked Ashcroft] will you bring the age [to witness the execution] down. Well, that didn't happen. He didn't get to, but the plea he made was amazing." Essentially, family members and survivors pleaded for an opportunity for memory work, not for vengeance. As Jones noted, "I think . . . the message overall that he heard [was] that it was seeing through the judicial process. It was not that we are so vengeful and ghoulish and had so much hatred. What he saw was pain, not hatred."

Two days later, on April 12, 2001, Ashcroft acceded to families' and survivors' requests to televise McVeigh's execution via closed-circuit broadcast. Announcing the new arrangements, Ashcroft confirmed the meetings with families and survivors had catalyzed his decision: "My time with these brave survivors changed me. What was taken from them can never be replaced nor fully restored. Their lives were shattered, and I hope that we can help to meet their need to close this chapter in their lives."[1] Ashcroft framed his decision to permit the broadcast in terms of resolution and closure for bombing victims. Accordingly, he reasoned, since the "Oklahoma City survivors may be the largest group of crime victims in our history," the Department of Justice "must make special provisions" "in accordance with our responsibilities to carry out justice."[2] To those ends, a reserved area was set aside at Terre Haute to accommodate victims who were not selected through the lottery system but still wished to travel to Terre Haute at their own expense. All victims who were not selected to attend the execution in Terre Haute and who were 18 years of age or older were permitted to witness the execution via closed-circuit transmission.

"An Eye for an Eye"? Participants' Opinion on the Death Penalty

Ideally, for memory work to be successful, traumatic crimes merit punishments of an appropriate severity. Certainly participants had different conceptions of what McVeigh's sentence should be, with some family members and survivors advocating life imprisonment without parole. But most family members and survivors wanted McVeigh to be executed, citing several reasons: taxpayer dollars would be used to keep him alive, he would constantly aggravate bombing victims, no other "John Doe" conspirators were involved (or McVeigh would never divulge such details even if they existed), and, most important, capital punishment was the morally deserved and efficacious punishment.

Whether a family member or survivor was for, against, or ambivalent toward the death penalty corresponded to what sentence they felt McVeigh deserved, which in turn reflected their satisfaction with the criminal justice system's involvement—how effectively they believed legal proceedings structured, shared, and ended the perpetrators' involvement. Notably, however, even if participants felt the "right" verdict was given, and the "right" sentence was handed down, the manner in which the sentence was imposed also influenced memory work. Death penalty proponents believed that effective executions were timely executions.

Participants' overall support for the death penalty declined slightly after the bombing. Fifteen participants reported no change in death penalty opinion or in opinion strength, 10 reported that their current opinion had grown stronger, one participant changed from anti- to pro–death penalty, three changed from pro- to anti–death penalty, three struggled with their anti–death penalty stance following the bombing but ultimately retained it, and four formed an opinion for the first time. Participants were most likely to form an opinion on the death penalty after the bombing. "I really, really didn't have an opinion [beforehand]," Marsha Kight acknowledged. "I was, like, how can you even make decisions about how you feel about something if you haven't experienced it firsthand?" Kight's opinion wavered for a time; she remarked in a media interview that during McVeigh's trial she "would like to have a big stick and be allowed to go into where he was in prison, and take the stick and rake it up and down his cell and say, 'You will never forget me.'"

Participants listed many reasons for supporting the death penalty. For Charlie Younger, it was a safety issue: "We cannot allow 'em to be released in a society and brutalize, and continue to kill and murder, that's just insane." Many said that certain perpetrators "deserved" the death penalty or that it was the proper "response" to murder; Ray Washburn remarked, "You commit a crime, you deserve what you get. . . . if you killed somebody, why don't the person that killed them, why don't they die?" Religion also played an important role; Robin Brown explained, "The Bible says, if you take a life you give your life." Murderers presumably knew what the punishment for murder was before they killed; in Janet Beck's words, "They made that choice, they knew what the law was." In a related argument, the death penalty was "on the books" and so should be applied. Lane Wharton recalled telling the Oklahoma governor and lieutenant governor, "Well, if it's not appropriate in this case where he killed 168 people, when would it ever be appropriate?" "The laws of our land state that if you do this, then this is the penalty, and I strongly believe that should be enforced," emphasized Diane Leonard. Support for the death penalty reaffirmed most participants' opinion that it was the ultimate response to the most heinous crimes.

But those who opposed the death penalty emphasized absence—of murdered victims, of civilized standards, of closure, and of accountability. They also were mindful of surfeit—an abundance of suffering, and of the extraordinary cost of executing offenders. Germaine Johnston observed, "I don't think that killing a person is going to bring back anybody else. . . . it just doesn't solve any problems." Jordan Holt and Diane Dooley saw the death penalty as rather barbaric; Dooley said that McVeigh had "done such a terrible thing, and yet we were going through as a civilized society and inflicting that same stuff on others that . . . were affected" such as McVeigh's family. Morgan Scott lamented diminished accountability for executed offenders because death was "really too easy," and so "it would have been better if he'd served life in prison and thought about his crimes." Marsha Kight believed that capital punishment may have to remain "on the books" for plea agreements, but she strongly believed that life in prison was more severe. A few opposed capital punishment because of Christian beliefs. For Jordan Holt, "whether I like it or not, McVeigh, like Hitler, is a child of God. . . . and even though I would never in my life find room for forgiveness I still knew in my mind that . . . I had no right in ending that life." Finally, opponents stressed the extraordinary financial costs of capital punishment. It "cost[s] more in this country in legal expenses and other expenses to execute a United States citizen of course than it costs to keep them in prison for life," said Dr. Paul Heath. Opposition to execution, therefore, was related to participants' expectations that execution would fail to achieve certain outcomes for victims and would harm the offender's family, the process of accountability, government coffers, and the national image.

Regardless of their stance on the death penalty, almost all participants indicted the current criminal justice system. Angela Richerson was upset by sentencing inconsistencies: "It angers me that people who kill one person can get the death penalty but people who kill five or six get off with the life sentence for the same state, you know, and it—I think it should be straight if, you know, if you kill somebody that means it's an eye for an eye." Stan Mayer lambasted the current system for being too slow and said that new policies should be created in certain "heinous" cases to effect death immediately after conviction: "I think that there are extreme situations and I don't know how they can legally be defined. . . . those people should be executed, on the spot, no waiting, no delay." Lane Wharton regretted that too many murderers escape the noose:

> Here in Oklahoma back when it was a territory . . . we had a hanging judge Parker. . . . And I had always heard this saying that the crime decreased in the Oklahoma territory when hanging Judge Parker [was] here, not because of the severity of the punishment, but because of the surety of it. . . . But our system seems like it's gotten to where there's so many loopholes and there's so many ways they can get around being punished, they think they can get away with anything.

Finally, Susan Urbach observed that accountability was lost in the adversarial games-playing and politics of criminal litigation, and even hindered the pursuit of justice: "Everyone pleads not guilty even if they have a video camera that actually shows them in great detail doing the crime" because "the defense is over here trying to play games of all sorts to try to get the person off or whatever" and lawyers for the defense and the state "may be trying to build a career." Death penalty opposition was itself a critique of the criminal justice system, where participants faulted it for being uncivilized, ineffective, or imposing further suffering.

Participants' stance on the death penalty played a key role in structuring their expectations of legal proceedings as well as their desired outcomes, guiding individual participants to choose certain venues over others for accomplishing memory work. Although family members and survivors had little choice but to rely on the criminal justice system to achieve accountability, they maintained a critical distance from it and even worried that its shortcomings would imperil its mission.

"I Wanted to Deal with Reality": Witnessing the Execution as a Duty or Responsibility

Like their desire to attend the trial, participants' desire to witness the execution was linked to the role that they expected this experience to play in memory work, implicating the perceived link between execution and closure. Those who wanted to witness felt that they were taking an active, participatory role in events, instead of allowing another opportunity to pass them by. Some were torn about whether or not to attend. Robin Brown, whose children were at that time very young, wanted to witness but believed that she needed to be cautious in case the experience changed her:

> I didn't know how it would have a long-range effect on me, but with having little people and knowing that I was going to have to come home and continue life as it was, I just was like, without knowing what kind of effect that would have on me, I was just like, maybe not a good idea at this point in time in my life. Now, if it was now, my kids are older and stuff, I probably would have put my name in.

But other participants decoupled execution witnessing from memory work; they either felt that witnessing the execution would not restore murdered loved ones to life or they were no longer focused on vengeance against McVeigh.

Those who chose to witness often sought a sense of completion (in the sense of terminating legal proceedings, as distinct from closure) or did so to bear witness to justice. A "duty" to one's self constituted a legitimate justification for watching McVeigh die, a way to banish what Doris Jones termed a "ghoulish" taint. But fulfilling a duty to others was also an adequate reason. Ron Brown characterized witnessing the execution as a duty that he and other live witnesses owed to their significant others: "I think we were there to do a job. A job for our loved ones." Many also sensed that attending the execution meant being a part of something much bigger than themselves. "Being able to be a part of, I hate to say history, . . . but it is part of the United States' history, this dramatic thing that he did and the bombing, being a part of watching the person that was mainly responsible," Brown observed. "I just felt that was what I could give back to my father-in-law, for being there." Similarly, Paul Howell described the decision to witness as a decision to "pick up the stick," and he also started doing media interviews at the same time.

Most participants did not feel a duty or responsibility to view the execution. Some, such as Faith Moore, felt witnessing was useless because it could not alleviate suffering or alter the past: "I didn't feel like that was going to make my pain or my hurt . . . or that of my girls any less. It wasn't going to change what had happened." Many, such as Richard Williams, had already "moved on" and did not feel that execution witnessing would assist them in bearing witness or completing memory work. A few felt that witnessing would be somehow distasteful; Ernestine Hill Clark, for one, thought it would be gruesome, explaining: "I knew I couldn't stomach it. I have read about executions." Others mentioned a host of additional reasons, including wanting to be with family, opposition to the death penalty, and a sense that others had a greater need or desire to witness.

Finally, several participants who attended the execution cited a need to "see justice done" or witness the conclusion of legal proceedings. Jamie Blansett remarked, "The execution was something I needed to do for myself. . . . I believed he needed to be punished because he knew those babies were in that day care." Diane Leonard witnessed for reasons of completion, to see the process through, to know exactly what happened, and because she had worked to have the execution broadcast via closed-circuit television. She commented: "It was a difficult thing for me to do because it's not, watching someone die is not something I just thought I really wanted to do, but I felt I'd fought so hard for that. I had been through the trials. . . . I had watched

that man and I needed to complete the process. I needed to see it through."
She also described witnessing the execution as a form of "self-preservation":
"I didn't want to guess about what [my husband] Don looked like, and I
didn't want to guess about what the execution was like. I wanted to deal with
reality."

For the majority who supported McVeigh's death sentence, his execution
was the "answer" to the bombing, and witnessing the execution was a way
to respond to McVeigh, an affirmative act in which they not only bore witness to justice but used their presence to protest his temerity in committing
the bombing and inflicting additional wounds through his offensive media
appearances. Although unable to attend the execution due to treatment for
bombing injuries, Stan Mayer couched it in dialogic terms: "The execution
was a response to what he did to us, and so I would like to have witnessed it."

Like his federal trial, McVeigh's execution provided opportunities for
further memory work, yet the impending execution necessitated that family members and survivors come to terms with more than just their opinion
on the death penalty and whether or not they wanted to witness McVeigh's
execution. They also had to grapple with a host of other questions, such as
whether they had forgiven him, wished to meet with him, and wanted to
hear him apologize. Participants' answers to these queries revealed whether
and how McVeigh's toxic presence continued to pervade their lives—how
much of an emotional distance they had been able to put between themselves and McVeigh, and the degree to which McVeigh, his activities, or his
death would affect memory work.

"I Am Going On with My Life": Forgiving McVeigh

One crucial question in negotiating McVeigh's toxic presence was whether
family members or survivors should, or could, forgive him. Like closure,
forgiveness is a complex term, engendering more questions than answers.
What is forgiveness—is it an act, a state, or a recursive, cyclical process? To
what extent is it interactive, responsive to the actions of a wrongdoer? Can
one forgive solely on one's own initiative, or does one forgive in response to
an apology? Most important for participants, how can one forgive not only
in the absence of a perpetrator's apology, but in the apparent absence of his
remorse? Can one ever fully forgive certain acts? Forgiveness involved emotional labor; family members and survivors did not feel rage toward McVeigh
one day and then wake up the next entirely free of anger and hatred. And it
required dedication and vigilance; certain injuries and judgments were likely

to linger, cropping up from time to time like weeds in victims' emotional gardens. Forgiveness could assuage, but it could not erase.[3]

The majority of victims found that it was indeed possible to forgive on one's own initiative, even without a remorseful wrongdoer; indeed, for many it was essential to forgive in order to redirect energies and remove an offender from routine thoughts. But other victims appeared to rub along just fine without forgiveness, having found alternative ways of divorcing themselves from McVeigh. For most, forgiveness signified a crucial step forward in memory work which meant that McVeigh was no longer a constant negative focus, a magnet to which an individual's negative emotions were instantaneously and involuntarily attracted.

Some participants felt that McVeigh's extreme culpability eradicated the possibility of forgiveness. Richard Williams could not forgive McVeigh because he had chosen to harm innocents: "I've never forgiven them for what they've done to change our lives forever and to take those away from us that were important to us. Because they had a choice. It's not like a natural disaster." Three participants said that the children's deaths in the day care center perhaps barred forgiveness; Diane Dooley believed that she did not have the ability to forgive McVeigh for what he did to *others*, particularly in terms of the murdered children: "I've forgiven him for . . . my injuries and what I was put through in a way. But I'm not sure I can ever . . . forgive him for the people . . . especially since I've got a child of my own, but the people who lost children that day. I mean that I can't reconcile really." Several participants said that they were under no obligation to forgive McVeigh because some external "trigger" of forgiveness was missing. Tom Hall and Cameron Crawford both remarked that forgiveness was a religious concept, and that they were under no obligation to forgive because they did not espouse religious beliefs. Still others emphasized that they did not have to forgive McVeigh because he never asked to be forgiven.

Participants who did forgive McVeigh often did so for their own benefit. Bud Welch explained, "It was all about me. . . . I was the one that got relief from all this pain. Totally. And it wasn't about McVeigh. He received nothing for me actually being able to feel the forgiveness." Susan Urbach described how forgiveness was healing: "I have so much energy, and you have to choose how you use your energy, and to hate is a real energy drainer." Priscilla Salyers spoke of forgiveness as "being able to pick up with your life [or] go on and let somebody control your life because you are so angry." For Robin Brown, to forgive was to remove McVeigh from her life; otherwise, "he's going to entrench himself."

A few forgave McVeigh out of pity. Ernestine Hill Clark, who pitied McVeigh and his father after reading about Timothy's childhood, said: "I began to feel toward McVeigh that here was a child where something had gone horribly, horribly wrong, and then as I felt toward his father that here was a father of a son that he was about to lose and how would I feel about that."

Interestingly, participants had differing conceptions of the relationship between forgiveness and hatred. Some who had forgiven McVeigh remarked that not to hate is to forgive, while others who had not forgiven McVeigh asserted that it was possible to not hate and yet not forgive. All, however, repudiated hatred. Susan Urbach regarded it as a "killer disease," and Vicki Hamm had to "let go" of these emotions, since "if I carried that hatred around, I would stay mad. And it was hard carrying that with me." But Diane Leonard let go of hatred and moved on without forgiving: "I haven't forgiven McVeigh. I haven't forgiven Nichols. But I don't think about them much anymore. I really don't. I don't focus on them. I don't have enormous hatred. . . . So I think you can be ok without forgiving."

Forgiveness decisions were also influenced by participants' Christian beliefs emphasizing mercy and reconciliation. Many found forgiveness to be a problematic Christian ideal; while some received guidance from the Christian imperative to forgive, others were deeply troubled by their inability to forgive McVeigh. Dot Hill explained, "That's part of the walk, is forgiveness. . . . it's required by God and that if there's a chance that . . . not forgiving someone would keep me from going to heaven then I'm going to forgive someone 'cause I'm going to heaven." But others acknowledged a tension between Christian beliefs and an inability or unwillingness to forgive. Jordan Holt remarked, "I don't care if that is one of the callings of Christianity or any religion to forgive someone. I'm not going to." Similarly, Beverly Rankin noted, "That's the Christian thing to do but I don't . . . I honestly don't think I could say that." Doris Jones found that the need to forgive evolved over time. After having not forgiven McVeigh for years because he never asked and because she believed it was for God to forgive, she later felt like she should make the attempt, explaining: "At church, I'm having this guilt inside. . . . And I know I should, religiously I should forgive him."

Many religious participants were troubled by the idea that McVeigh could spend eternity in heaven if he asked for and received divine forgiveness. As Doris Jones emphasized, that would mean McVeigh was in "the same place [my child] is. And I can't . . . ugh." Heaven was a soothing, palliative concept; the idea of deceased loved ones at "home" with their Lord was a cherished

one in participant interviews, and the insertion of McVeigh seemed traitor-
ous to the victims' memory. Some Christian participants diminished the discomfort that came from picturing McVeigh in heaven with the victims by
placing the burden to forgive upon McVeigh and God; McVeigh first had to
ask for forgiveness, and then it was up to God to provide it.

Participants' individual decisions about forgiveness all signaled that
negotiating an involuntary relationship to McVeigh was a necessary process in memory work. While forgiveness often enabled participants to terminate McVeigh's control over their lives and gain emotional distance from
him, others were able to accomplish these same objectives without this step.
Therefore, determinations as to how best to live with and end McVeigh's
toxic presence—key goals of memory work—were highly individualized.

"You Failed, Buddy": Willingness to Meet with McVeigh

Another critical aspect of negotiating McVeigh's unwelcome presence was
the desire to extract something from him that could only be obtained by
meeting him face-to-face, free of institutional intermediaries and constraints. Significantly, four participants actually tried to meet with McVeigh
but were rebuffed. Marsha Kight initially contacted Warden Harley Lappin at
Terre Haute asking for victim-offender mediation with McVeigh; when her
request was denied, she wrote to McVeigh but received no reply. Though Bud
Welch attempted unsuccessfully to meet with McVeigh, he was eventually
able to meet with McVeigh's father, Bill.

Participants wanted to meet with McVeigh to find out why he had committed the bombing, to see him in person and/or interact with him outside of the courtroom, to learn something from being in his presence, and
to confirm whether or not he had actually been in the Murrah Building
before April 19, 1995. They longed to breach the physical and interpersonal
distances between themselves and McVeigh, to converse with him in language free of legal jargon about subjects that might be irrelevant to determinations of guilt or innocence, to see him not only as an offender but as
a man, and to hear him describe his motivations and actions in his words
and not in those of his attorneys. Participants especially wanted to meet
with McVeigh to find out "why" he had bombed the Murrah Building—a
question at the heart of his federal trial, and one that many evidently felt
had not been fully answered.

Some also wanted to hear McVeigh apologize and express remorse; Dot
Hill remarked, "I'd like him to have truly, honest[ly] expressed to me his

remorse. His understanding that he misunderstood." But while memory may be idealistic, it is not blind to the likelihood that certain forms of reconciliation will not come to pass; participants acknowledged McVeigh's "soldier" mentality would have made apology unlikely. As Vicki Hamm noted, "Well, I would have asked him if he was sorry, although I don't think he was. I think he viewed himself as a warrior."

Participants also wished to tell McVeigh how the bombing had changed their lives. Confronting McVeigh with specific, personal tales of death, survival, and recovery would satisfy two reconstructive needs: bridging the gap between the impersonal act of terrorism and its terrifyingly personal effects, and telling McVeigh that he had failed to accomplish his mission. Bud Welch wanted to tell McVeigh of the impact of the loss of his daughter Julie to "break him a little bit," and Susan Urbach wanted to tell McVeigh that he "failed": "I think he wanted the revolution to rise up and all of that and, you know, you failed, buddy, you failed."

Many family members and survivors would have welcomed the opportunity to engage McVeigh outside of the courtroom, suggesting that the criminal justice system's constraints upon the victim-offender relationship inhibited memory work. Resisting the mediated access to McVeigh, Doris Jones wanted to break through the communicative barrier of the trial and "not have to go through a lawyer or go through a whatever, just to say, why did you do that?" Others simply desired real, interpersonal interaction with McVeigh outside the courtroom, believing that being in McVeigh's presence or initiating an interpersonal encounter with him might have allowed them to "reach" him.

Other participants regarded McVeigh himself as a form of bombing evidence that could yield personal insight. Ernestine Hill Clark wondered what she may have "picked up on" from being in McVeigh's presence: "I'm an intuitive person. I'm not psychic, but I can pick up in a rough way people's energy, and it would have been interesting to just be in his presence and ask him some questions and let him answer and see what I might or might not pick up on." Similarly, Paul Howell wanted to gauge McVeigh's capacity for deceit:

I wanted to look him in the eyes because . . . I know how to deal with people and I can tell [a] lot of times when people are lying to me. And so I wanted to see if he would lie or whether he would tell me the truth about why and so forth. . . . I think maybe right before his death, maybe if I could have got in there, maybe I could have found out something.

Finally, a few who believed they had seen McVeigh in the Murrah Federal Building or Journal Record Building prior to the bombing wanted confirmation that he had actually been there. This was an important part of formulating a personal chronology of the bombing, reassuring participants that they had not imagined these encounters. Dr. Paul Heath recalled meeting with McVeigh in the Veterans Affairs office the Thursday before the bombing, and wondered:

> Was there anything said on Thursday before the bombing when he was in my office that changed his mind one way or the other? My head knows nothing was going to change his mind, because the bomb materials were already bought by Terry Nichols. They were already stored. He was on his way up to build the bomb. Nothing that I said caused him to bomb the building. . . . [But] I'm the one who talked to him, I'd kinda like to know how he experienced that. Because I really tried to find a job for him. And he smiled, and he was just as happy as he could be.

Participants also wanted to meet with McVeigh to tell him that he was forgiven, to ask him if he would change anything if he could go back in time, and to find out who else was involved.

But in speculating about what it would have been like to meet with McVeigh, participants returned again and again to the obstacle of McVeigh's stoic demeanor. Ernestine Hill Clark qualified her remarks about what she would ask McVeigh with the statement "I mean if he would open up—he probably wouldn't have. I think he was a very guarded person by the time he did and very much crazed against the government." McVeigh's demeanor even persuaded those unsure about their willingness to meet him that such a meeting would be unproductive. As Dot Hill noted, "I don't think it would have done any good. You know, I don't know what I would have derived from it. Because just from what I saw, just from what I saw of him on television, and I'm not sure I would have ever gotten any real answers from him."

Those family members and survivors who did not want to meet McVeigh viewed his defiance as an intentional insult and felt that he would not be particularly forthcoming. They instead chose other avenues of memory work that did not involve a face-to-face meeting, for McVeigh never willingly made himself available to bombing victims as a tool for or site of memory work.[4]

Explanations and Apologies: Important Pre-execution Behavior

Participants wanted McVeigh to make certain gestures prior to his death, satisfying their need to weave him into a coherent and compelling personal narrative of the bombing. If interpreted as sincere, a final expression of remorse from McVeigh could have worked narrative wonders. Like a carrot on a stick, the execution extended the promise of a satisfying outcome—a remorseful McVeigh would have accepted the need for accountability, rather than having accountability forced upon him. Without any remorseful gestures, participants would have no choice but to derive a sense of accountability entirely from a forcefully imposed death sentence. To these ends, participants wanted McVeigh to tell them "what in his demented mind he was thinking," to tell the "truth" or the "real story," to show remorse, to "accept Jesus as his Lord and Savior" or "make his peace with God," to "admit guilt," or to make a statement for the victims' sake.

The gestures and statements that participants most hoped McVeigh would make prior to his execution tracked the questions they would have asked him in a face-to-face meeting; the execution was the last forum in which these queries could be answered, and because they had not been effectively answered up until that point, they remained open points of inquiry. Nor is it surprising that family members and survivors were slightly more hopeful that McVeigh would make efforts at explanation or reconciliation in his last moments; the penal tradition of providing a condemned offender a chance to impart "last words" is centuries old, and gallows speeches used to be prime opportunities for offenders to express regret for sinful moral failings and hunger for salvation. One's last actions before dying are presumed to be one's most honest, forthcoming, and forthright gestures; hence the legal evidentiary tenet known as the "dying declaration," which redeems from the pits of hearsay the last words of a dying man giving the identity of his killer. Nonetheless, participants did not have much confidence that their desires for reconciliation would be fulfilled and so were prepared for a witnessing experience that was cathartic for reasons other than remorseful last words.

A Need for "Peace and Quiet": Reactions to McVeigh's Media Visibility

As McVeigh's execution grew nearer, participants' sense of his toxic presence increased as he became more and more visible in the news media, hindering their memory work. Prior to his execution, it seemed that this man was everywhere. As Richard Williams explained, you "got to the point where you didn't want to read something about him on a daily basis. . . . I doubt very seriously there was a week, honestly a week went by [prior to the execution] that there wasn't something there."

Whether or not they supported the execution, the vast majority of participants hoped that it would at least diminish or terminate McVeigh's toxic presence, silencing him and removing him from the airwaves. Peggy Broxterman affirmed that "that was the most important thing of this whole thing, was the fact that he was put to death, no one would have to listen to him anymore. There would be no, 'He's in jail,' or 'He's meeting with this one,' or, 'How's he feeling?' Nothing. He's gone." "I was so tired of hearing that his lawyer had met with him and then, you know, he's going to write this book," Doris Jones remarked. "I was just like, you know, stop! Stop him, stop. So, yeah, I would have liked to have had him out of my life."

This media coverage wore on victims' nerves, perhaps antagonizing them more than at any other point in the four years since McVeigh's trial. Though Marsha Kight opposed McVeigh's execution, she became so frustrated that she remarked tongue in cheek in one media interview, "I'm about ready to change my mind [about his execution]. I'm tired of hearing about him." "It's just that he was using the press all the time," Kight recalled, "and, of course, I was responding to it, I was involved, and it got to be pretty wearing."

But victims were not the only ones who were tired of hearing from McVeigh; Attorney General John Ashcroft pleaded with journalists to tear down McVeigh's public platform on April 12, 2001, when he announced the closed-circuit execution broadcast:

I am aware that several media outlets have requested access to interview inmate McVeigh. As an American who cares about our culture, I want to restrict a mass murderer's access to the public podium. . . . I do not want anyone to be able to purchase access to the podium of America with the blood of 168 innocent victims. . . . If the news media conducts an interview with Timothy McVeigh, I would ask them for self-restraint. Please do not help him inject more poison into our culture; he has caused enough senseless damage already. We are already being sued to provide more publicity for this execution. I would ask that the news media not become Timothy McVeigh's co-conspirators in his assault on America's public safety and upon America itself.[5]

Political cartoon by Steve Sack printed in the *Minneapolis Star-Tribune* on April 15, 2001, reflects Attorney General John Ashcroft's efforts to muffle McVeigh before his execution. Reprinted with permission from Steve Sack.

These governmental attempts to muffle McVeigh were captured in humorous political cartoons such as the following one, in which Uncle Sam himself is grateful for the silence:

But these efforts to dim the spotlight on McVeigh were ultimately unsuccessful; the juggernaut of the impending execution was now in full motion, ensuring McVeigh's constant news presence. The publication of his authorized biography, *An American Terrorist*, a few months prior to his execution further aggravated the situation.

Assessing family members' and survivors' orientations to Timothy McVeigh while he was awaiting execution allows us to evaluate how institutional constraints affected the victim-offender relationship. While these limitations enhanced the legitimacy of legal proceedings and thus helped produce the accountability critical to memory work, they were also too narrow. The guilt/innocence inquiry was merely the threshold inquiry for most participants, who needed to know "Why?" Legal proceedings either avoided the most crucial questions or provided inadequate responses. Thus, although the criminal justice system successfully held McVeigh accountable through a conviction and death sentence, it did not fully satisfy family members' and survivors' reconstructive needs. These individuals were thereby left on their own to cope with McVeigh's defiant response to the horrors he had unleashed, to reconcile themselves to the unbridgeable gap between an impersonal act of terrorism and the terrifyingly personal scale of loss with which they had to cope in its aftermath, and to continue with memory work despite crucial questions that remained unanswered.

10

The Weight of an Impossible World

McVeigh Confronts His Public Image

I will get to the point of why I am writing you Tim. You know
you will be put to death, even though, in your mind, you did
what you thought was for the good of this country. . . . Why
in God's name don't you let the world know what you are all
about. . . . Why don't you bare your soul and at least try to make
people understand. After you're gone it will be too late. Oh yeah,
you are a perfectionist and you will not admit that you "lost it."
Well perfectionists are the people that lose it most often.

—Letter from Michael Fortier's mother
to Timothy McVeigh, June 19, 1999[1]

In the years preceding his execution, not only was McVeigh a toxic
presence in bombing victims' lives; they were also a devastating presence in
his. Immediately after his arrest, victims had criticized McVeigh's unemotional and defiant persona; later, they protested the utter implausibility of
his insistence that the Oklahoma City bombing was a military attack, with
victims' deaths constituting "collateral damage." News media broadcast and
built upon these remarks, forming them into a formidable public representation of McVeigh that was malicious, even monstrous. McVeigh responded to
this treatment with a slew of media interviews and an authorized biography.

Over the four years from June 13, 1997, when McVeigh was sentenced to
death, until June 11, 2001, when he was executed, McVeigh's public visibility escalated as appeals commenced, terminated, and recommenced, as he
granted media interviews, and as his looming execution spurred one final
marathon of intense media interest. During this period, it became increasingly evident that McVeigh lived in a very different world from family members and survivors. For McVeigh, the Murrah Building teemed with enemy
noncombatants, and he, a patriotic warrior, would lead the attack that

would vindicate the government's deadly actions at Waco, Ruby Ridge, and elsewhere.

But family members, survivors, and both the American and international publics lived in an entirely different universe, one in which the Murrah Building was a place where ordinary Americans far removed from controversial events such as Waco came to earn a living just like any other employees. The story of how McVeigh attempted to reconcile these two worlds—and, indeed, that he even believed it was possible to do so—is a grave lesson in what can (and must) get lost in translation, as well as what can happen when the news media attempt to play translator between a mass murderer, his victims, and the public.

What follows is not a detailed exposition of McVeigh's message for its own sake but a narrative of how victims were as much a presence in McVeigh's life as he was in theirs. If, as William Randolph Hearst once said, "you can crush a man with journalism," McVeigh learned this lesson firsthand. As McVeigh planned and carried out the Oklahoma City bombing, he purported to adopt the mind-set of a soldier carrying out a military mission. His victims and the nation, however, saw something entirely different: a fanatic with a cause, a mad bomber, a terrorist attempting to start a revolution, a mass murderer who took life callously and indiscriminately. McVeigh quickly learned that not all media coverage was good coverage, and he was apparently surprised by the ubiquity and hostility of media commentary. Journalists upturned his soapbox, discredited him, drowned him out, and damned him to hell. McVeigh felt that such coverage was not only unfair and inaccurate, but imperiled his Oklahoma City bombing "mission" by negating or overwhelming his ideological explanations for it. He was incensed when the American public paid attention to him only to further deride him, not to understand him or commend his actions.

But with his lawyers' help, McVeigh was determined to show the public a friendlier face. Above all, McVeigh wanted to be taken seriously, but a man made into a monster was likely to be seen as bestial, not rational. As a man who craved control, McVeigh was frustrated by media coverage awash in victims' laments and felt it was imperative that he salvage his mission and redeem his message before dying. What began as a statement of defiance became damage control. From his perp walk until his execution, McVeigh was engaged in dialogue not only with his victims (particularly a handful with high media visibility) but also with the image of himself that the victims and others had helped to create.

Although we may never be able to identify exactly why McVeigh bombed the Murrah Building, and although we certainly do not want to and cannot excuse his decision to do so, we must nonetheless examine the two-way, reciprocal relationships that emerged after the bombing between McVeigh and journalists and bombing victims. These relationships created contested dialogues that irrevocably bound McVeigh to both those who were attempting to drown him out and those trying to keep him on the surface of public consciousness. McVeigh's attempts at reputation management and his feelings toward victims are as integral to the story of the Oklahoma City bombing as the way in which victims experienced his toxic presence as mediated, aggravated, and ameliorated by the mass media and criminal justice system. This portrait of McVeigh is compiled from several sources: author interviews with journalists who had met McVeigh at least once in person and exchanged multiple letters with him; an interview with his former defense attorney whom he regarded as a friend and ally; McVeigh's letters to journalists (many of which are now held in the Oklahoma City National Museum Archives); and interviews and letters that *Buffalo News* reporters Lou Michel and Dan Herbeck conducted and exchanged with McVeigh in the course of authoring his authorized biography, entitled *American Terrorist: Timothy McVeigh and the Oklahoma City Bombing* (now deposited in the American Terrorist Collection in the Friedsam Memorial Library, St. Bonaventure University).

A Terrifying Tour of Duty

What victims saw as a heinous instance of mass murder, McVeigh regarded as a military mission. He clearly saw himself as a soldier[2] and analogized his reasons for the bombing to other U.S. military actions abroad.[3] To McVeigh, the government had never resolved Waco and Ruby Ridge, necessitating that he "go on the offensive."[4] This stoic soldier mind-set allegedly accounted for his lack of remorse:

> It's a military act.... That's the way I handle taking a human life.... It's like breaking the neck of the chicken. Look at the atom bomb at Hiroshima, 70,000 people were wiped off the map. To this day, the pilot of that plane says it was a dirty job, but he had to do it.

For McVeigh, then, the bombing was an act of war, and those who worked in the Murrah Building were "eligible combatants, whether they're on the front lines or not," and thus fair targets as members of the "support structure."[5]

But family members, survivors, rescue workers, residents of Oklahoma, and the American public did not and could not see the Oklahoma City bombing in such martial terms. They could understand McVeigh's righteous indignation over Waco and Ruby Ridge, but his decision to bomb the Murrah Building was riotous; being angry at the government was far different from taking innocent lives in retribution.

Pressed to Meet the Press: McVeigh's Relationships with Journalists

Defense attorney Stephen Jones first set McVeigh on the path of reputation management when, before his federal trial, Jones arranged for reporters from local and national news organizations to meet with his client for off-the-record interviews in a "beauty contest" to select who would get the first "on-the-record" interview. Journalist were permitted to converse with McVeigh for only a short period of time, were prohibited from recording the interview or taking any photographs, and were told that topics such as Waco and the bombing were off-limits.

Reporters Phil Bacharach of the *Oklahoma Gazette* and Terri Watkins of KOCO-TV in Oklahoma were among those invited to Jones's "beauty contest"; McVeigh met with Watkins in December 1995 and with Bacharach in 1996. The point of these meetings, in Watkins's words, was not to discuss the bombing but to "try to convince him that we were the right person to do the interview" because McVeigh sought exposure and image reform on a national scale. Indeed, McVeigh chose David Hackworth to conduct his first interview. Hackworth, a highly decorated former army colonel who had authored a book, *About Face*, concerning his experiences in the Korean and Vietnam Wars, had caught McVeigh's interest by approaching him "soldier-to-soldier" with his interview request.[6]

Upon meeting McVeigh, journalists were startled to find that he did not match their preconceived expectations of what the Oklahoma City bombing suspect would be like. "It's cliché to say that you expect pure evil and he just came off as something entirely different than that, but it was just absolutely true," Bacharach observed, describing McVeigh as "friendly, very laid back, gregarious, had a good sense of humor." Watkins also had a similar impression: "He was polite, he was cordial, he was all those things." "There was certainly a very monstrous side to him, but it was very compartmentalized," recalled Bacharach, adding, "he just did not convey that side much in the written word, and certainly not in person."

Following that initial interview, many of the journalists who met McVeigh continued to write him letters, enclosing news stories, magazines, books, or other items they thought might attract his interest and prompt a reply letter. McVeigh responded to several of these letters. McVeigh and journalists both gained from these correspondences. McVeigh implored reporters to send him news of the bombing. He was willing to give things in return and intended his letters to influence media coverage. He once informed Bacharach, "Feel free to lift story ideas off of me as you wish. I would never hold it against you if you were 'inspired' by one of my 'off-the-record' letters. . . . That's what communication between people is all about—inspiring others to think."[7] But he also sent reporters private letters, noting in the upper right-hand corner that these missives were "not for reprint." Journalists knew that McVeigh was not chatting them up just to be friendly; they knew that he wanted a public megaphone. For Terri Watkins, the issue of manipulation "was a two-way street. He had points that he wanted to make and he knew I needed stories. . . . He was trying to manipulate his image and manipulate the public, not so much me. I was the vehicle."

An Oklahoma City National Memorial and Museum exhibit features letters that McVeigh exchanged with Nolan Clay, a reporter for the *Daily Oklahoman.* Image courtesy of the Oklahoma City National Memorial and Museum Archives.

For their part, reporters who corresponded with McVeigh frequently felt uncomfortable over the tensions between their professional activities and personal emotions. Bacharach, for example, admitted to feeling "very torn"; he had been at the Murrah Building approximately a half hour after the blast and became "reasonably close" to many family members and survivors over the years, yet he "spent years trying to develop some sort of rapport with McVeigh because I was a reporter and I wanted to do a lengthy interview with him." Corresponding with McVeigh could prompt journalists to feel "guilty by association." In another instance, the first time Bacharach was in the Denver courtroom, he was seated in the gallery between two family members when McVeigh walked in with his attorneys and acknowledged him with a nod of his head. Bacharach recalled, "I just felt horrible. It was embarrassing, and I just felt kind of gross. . . . at any rate, the last thing I wanted to do was to get chummy nods of the head from a mass murderer."

One way journalists sought to ease these conflict-of-interest tensions was to be very open with victims about the contents of McVeigh's letters prior to the publication of any news stories; reporter Terri Watkins, for example, shared her letters from McVeigh with members of the habeas group:

> We realized very quickly that any communication with McVeigh, or even knowledge that I communicated with McVeigh, would not necessarily go over well with the victims' families. So we did something we had never done before and have never done since. That was, call that group in and meet with them and show them the letter that we were going to do a story on. They had no input into the story, they had no control over the story and they could not say do or don't do it. But we didn't want to surprise them. So, the letter was passed around, it was read, it was discussed, and then the story would air.

This was not standard journalistic practice. "It wasn't done for appreciation. It was done out of courtesy," Watkins emphasized. "The rules [of coverage] don't apply because somebody threw them out the window when a building blew up," she noted. Watkins found that victims were affected by these missives: "Anger's probably the best word for it. And frustration with it, the things he said and did. . . . I was a bit surprised, they were not angry with me. . . . They were fascinated by the handwriting, they were fascinated by what he said."

Over the four years between his conviction and his execution, McVeigh used journalists, particularly his biographers Lou Michel and Dan Herbeck, to cultivate and publicize a more favorable image of himself, his actions, and his ideologies. In his missives, particularly those to Michel, McVeigh attempted to showcase his thoughts and motivations so that others could appreciate the complexity of his intellect: "I'm trying to show you that my opinions . . . are not just 'jumping to unsupported conclusions,' but my beliefs/opinions are formed over years of diligent observation, and are <u>educated</u> conclusions."[8] On another occasion, he bragged of his ability to read and recall information: "One thing that separates me from the '5-minute attention span' masses is that I <u>remember</u> what I've read in the past—I have it all stored away and available for reference and cross-reference at any time."[9] As if to further this image of a serious, thoughtful Timothy McVeigh, he told Michel that he wanted to include a photo of himself in a "'thinker'-type prison pose (fingers on head, furrowed brow)" in the biography.[10]

McVeigh was also very self-conscious about his communications and often reminded journalists that he was forsaking eloquence for efficiency. McVeigh was concerned about what would happen to his correspondence after his execution, confiding to Michel, "I hate to think what the likes of [another reporter] would do. . . . I didn't exactly pick up a dictionary or consult punctuation rules when I'm writing an informal personal letter such as this."[11] Bacharach found McVeigh's self-concern and self-scrutiny interesting: "I was struck that he would care that people might pick apart his writing ability. . . . someone who kills 168 people . . . he's concerned they're going to make fun of his punctuation."

McVeigh's care over his image extended to his physical appearance. Before his perp walk, he requested a new pair of pants after he discovered that his had a hole. He worried over acne before Michel's first interview visit and the taping of his *Sixty Minutes* interview.[12] And he ruminated over what photograph would be appropriate for the front of the biography, recommending "anything but that bright-red, dorky-looking prison jumpsuit I only wear to visits! Shit, I'd even take the Perry 'Face of Terror' over those!"[13]

"V" for "Victim"

Over time, McVeigh came to feel that bombing victims hindered his media efforts at rehabilitation management. He consistently objected to the exceptionality of what he callously termed the "woe-is-me" crowd, objecting that their victimization was the same as that experienced by innocents harmed by U.S. attacks on foreign soil: "These people, the victims, seem to elevate themselves as something special. They say that no one should have to go through this post-traumatic grief that their whole city is going through. At the same time, we're doing it to other nations all the time."[14] He was frustrated by the depth and visibility of victims' grief, and he complained that victims were perpetually wallowing in their misery:

> I had no hesitation to look right at them and listen to their story, but I'd like to say to them, I've heard your story many times before. The specific details may be unique, but the truth is you're not the first mother to lose a kid, you're not the first grandparent to lose a granddaughter or a grandson. I'll use the phrase, and it sounds cold, but I'm sorry I'm going to use it because it's the truth: get over it.

McVeigh was also irritated by and derisive of family members' and survivors' advocacy efforts. He intimated that victims had imperiled legal authority by repeatedly petitioning Congress, "upset[ting] years of fundamental federal court doctrine."[15] Claiming victims were blocking his communicative efforts, McVeigh warned Michel that he would likely "see a backlash from the victims, families, etc. about the prospect of me 'profiting off of this disaster' (or some equal crap)," and that "some victims may try to thwart the publication [of my biography]."[16] He also cautioned Michel to not give in to pressure "if the victims 'demand' that you donate the profits."[17] Elsewhere, he coldly opined, "These DOK [*Daily Oklahoman*] victims get mad if anyone makes money besides themselves."[18]

Yet, McVeigh also purported to be aware of what most victims had experienced. He acknowledged their hatred of him and even agreed that it was justified. He emphasized, "I'm not out to personally insult the majority of victims; my motivations are not to continue to hurt them."[19] McVeigh believed that victims would not hate him quite so much if they only knew he did not mean to attack them personally: "To this day, I do not have a personal beef with the majority of victims. (So all this "attitude," (expressed by victims now) that I take pleasure in attacking them, as some personal vendetta, would not be so pronounced (by them), if it had been better explained to them.)"[20]

There was a fundamental misunderstanding between bombing victims and McVeigh: family members and survivors could not understand his lack of remorse, and McVeigh was equally puzzled by their inability to do so. In an early interview with Michel, McVeigh disclosed that he had received a letter from Kathy Wilburn, whose two grandsons he had murdered in the bombing. McVeigh appeared to be frustrated not by her anger but by her inability to understand why he did not show emotion for the murdered bombing victims:

> People, I don't know if they can't understand or won't understand, but when you see a picture of a pilot climbing out of his plane, coming back from a bombing mission, is he crying? If a cop shoots a perp, does he come home and cry? . . . In these fields of fire rescue and law enforcement, you learn to suppress, to block out emotion. . . . People grow accustomed to it. You ever see a person from a Third World country encounter a disaster? It's like, OK, let's pick our shit up and move somewhere else. You don't see this weeping.[21]

McVeigh also objected when victims deemed his logic faulty or made comments that he felt were insulting, or when he felt that media coverage betrayed a pro-victim bias. One news article from the Canadian Press quoted family member Jim Denny, whose two children were injured in the bombing, as saying that he did not understand McVeigh's comparison between the Oklahoma City bombing and the Gulf War. Enclosing the article in a letter to Michel, McVeigh noted in the margin, "I won't be too harsh on JD, b/c I know emotion clouds reason and logic . . . and I know what his kids went thru (and are still going thru), but what world is <u>this</u> guy living in?!?"[22] Another Associated Press article headlined "Many Want to See McVeigh Execution" highlighted the remarks of family member Constance Favorite, who jokingly gave advice for how to accommodate all the victim witnesses: "Hold it in the middle of an Oklahoma field." Ignoring the obvious double standard in his remarks, McVeigh penned in the margin, "Stm't of general barbarity of Americans."[23]

McVeigh's overall attitude toward the majority of the bombing victims was inconsistent. At times, he derided, even mocked, their thoughts and feelings, yet on other occasions he claimed to feel "empathy" for them. McVeigh was clearly aware of how his behaviors impacted family members and survivors, noticing that when he "laugh[ed] at pretrial. It bothered victims." He confirmed that his attitude at trial was at times defiant:

> My attitude was, and is, *carpe diem*, seize the day, enjoy every day. I'm not going to go into that courtroom, curl into a fetal ball and cry, just because the victims wanted me to do that. I've already accepted my death, victims, you're getting what you want, I'm getting what I want. . . . The victims

won't be happy with my death. They think it's going to bring closure, but it won't.[24]

In one stunningly offensive remark, he analogized the Murrah Building employees to functionaries on the Death Star, the Galactic Empire's space station and weapon made famous in the *Star Wars* movies:

> The federal government is an army of people. They're like storm troopers in Star Wars. Although they may be individually innocent, they're part of the whole. . . . In the storm troopers analogy, they blow up the entire Death Star. In different scenes, you'd see different women sitting at consoles in the Death Star, or you'd see storm troopers running around, not shooting at anybody. Guess what, they all got blown up in the Death Star, and the audience was happy. As a whole, the Death Star represented the whole empire. Death Star, Murrah Building, they're all working for the same cause.[25]

Yet, shortly after that, he claimed that empathizing with Iraqis against whom he had fought in Desert Storm "allowed me to have empathy for these current victims."[26] In another contradictory statement, McVeigh related, "I tell you now, I took no pleasure in what I did. At the same time, I am regretful that there was some collateral damage, not knowing there would be customers in the offices of some of those agencies, like Social Security."[27] Family members and survivors understandably found this heartless use of "collateral damage" incomprehensible, callous, and offensive.[28]

Journalists who met and corresponded with McVeigh believed him when he said he did not intend to inflict further, postbombing wounds upon the majority of victims. Terri Watkins felt that, although McVeigh knew how his behavior affected the victims, he did not care, and was too selfish to go out of his way to further wound them:

> He wanted all the attention on him and what he had done and what he was trying to accomplish. He didn't want the attention on the victims. . . . I think sometimes [the victims] knew it [that they were irritating him], and they poked him with a hot stick. . . . Their efforts were never geared at poking McVeigh. They were always geared at trying to find a vehicle to help themselves and other victims of crimes. . . . If it poked at McVeigh, it was a side benefit and they enjoyed it. If it prevented him from getting something he wanted, all the better. But that's the goal. It was to make the

victims more important than the person who committed the crime. . . . I mean, we all know who Bundy was, but do we know who he killed?

McVeigh openly declared his hostility toward and desire to combat a select few highly visible "spokes-victims," whom he termed "venomous," and referenced them by name. In a letter to Michel, he ranted,

> There are a few who have so pissed me off (a certain level of animosity, indeed hatred, is understandable, and I accept that as something they have a right to, so I will not lash back at the majority) but those few who have "crossed that line"—those are the few (not the majority) who I defend against with verbal attacks of my own. (The "Woe-is-me" crowd, for example, didn't refer to the whole group; just the small group who seize the spotlight.) Most of my purely caustic or sarcastic remarks have been delivered with these people in mind; not intended as an attack on the collective community. In this spirit, I absolutely reserve my right to give back to these few what they give me—bitter, acidic comments—with no apologies made for my counter-attacks (I just wish it could somehow be understood that it's not a collective attack on the whole, b/c, as I said, I have no personal gripe with the majority of these people.) (While they may not understand this, it's nonetheless truth.) While they can all, to a certain level, get understandably personal in their attacks on me and I'll let it go; those few that cross that line, I will get personal back to.[29]

A "Monster's Ball": Raging against the Media Machine

McVeigh believed that high-profile victims directly contributed to his media demonization, and this profoundly upset and frustrated him. His strongest motivation for agreeing to media interviews and an authorized biography was to counter those images. In medieval England, jailers would fete condemned prisoners—termed "monsters"—on the eve of their execution at farewell feasts that became known as "monster's balls." As his execution approached, McVeigh became something of a media belle at his own monster's ball, courted by everyone from top-flight reporters such as Ed Bradley to well-respected regional reporters such as Lou Michel.

McVeigh believed that his demonization began with his perp walk. As he told Ed Bradley on *Sixty Minutes*, "When I was marched out of the Perry County courthouse in the orange jumpsuit, that was the beginning of a propaganda campaign."[30] Nor was McVeigh reticent about discussing his efforts to combat this "propaganda campaign":

> MCVEIGH: Maybe one of the benefits of me talking to you today is that you'll see that maybe not everything is true that you've heard about me.
> BRADLEY: For example, what's not true?
> MCVEIGH: Well, am I—am I pure evil? Am I the face of terror, sitting here in front of you, or am I able to talk to you man to man?
> BRADLEY: Most people in this country think you are the face of evil, don't they?
> MCVEIGH: They do. But sitting down here now—and let me make clear I'm not sitting here trying to influence you, and I'm not putting on a game face. I'm not conning anybody. I'm just being me. And maybe people will listen, as opposed to not listening at a trial.[31]

McVeigh particularly resented labels that portrayed him as a loner, unemotional or monstrous, which he felt were applied to him and not to deserving others. He would point out, for example, that American rock musician Bob Seger "understood the call of the road" but was "not also called a 'loner' and/or a 'drifter'—It's all about spin, isn't it?"[32] He also observed that the media deemed his facial expressions at trial "stone-faced" or "emotionless" while it described others as "sitting impassively."[33]

To McVeigh, an authorized biography was the best and most comprehensive forum in which to confront and destroy such labels. To these ends, he "auditioned" numerous journalists for the role of biographer. Lou Michel's ties to McVeigh's hometown ultimately won him the coveted position of, as McVeigh once dubbed him, the "McVeigh historian."[34] Michel, in turn, brought aboard a senior colleague, journalist Dan Herbeck.

"I want to address every 'demonization' stereotype that's ever been offered—from 'survivalist' to 'dishwasher,'" McVeigh wrote to Lou Michel early on in their working relationship.[35] To project the right image—that of a sane, intelligent, calm, rational, responsible, and principled soldier on an unpopular but necessary mission—he discussed his personality, recounted nearly every aspect of the bombing and its aftermath, took credit for nearly every part, emphasized the deliberate manner in which he carried out his plans, argued that everything had turned out just as he had intended, and asserted that he had won whether or not he was executed.

McVeigh knew that, in order for his ideological messages to be credible, it was most important to convey that he was not mentally ill. Early on,

McVeigh disclosed to Michel the results of his psychological examinations in prison: "I was seen repeatedly by 3 defense 'shrinks' (two psycho, 1 psychia.) pre-trial. I got along great with 2; the 3rd grew frustrated b/c his job was to formulate a possible 'mental defect' mitigation—and he couldn't find any basis for such. None of these 3 professionals, when everything was explained, found anything wrong with me."[36] He vehemently denied that he was a socio-path, pointing to his "'sensitive' (yet private) side," and contended that "if I am 'sociopathic,' still, I am only a reflection of the average American."[37]

As if to offer the ultimate proof that he was rational and sane, McVeigh described his experiences in late 1992 with what he referred to as "delayed PTSD."[38] Although he termed PTSD "a misnomer," he remarked that "as long as I was busy with something, it didn't seem to affect me. . . . However, whenever life became boring, I would start to 'slip' (feel upset at everything, super-restless, etc.)."[39] He attributed that condition to his Gulf War service and characterized it as isolating: "Now that you've seen the extremes, expe-rienced the ultimate highs, lows and realities—well, who gives a shit about conversation about the weather. . . . The daily grind, all of a sudden, has got-ten much more intolerable. . . . you separate yourself from these encounters, and thus from the people, to escape these conversations."[40] Yet, McVeigh was resentful that the media appeared to credit rescue workers' PTSD accounts but not his own, complaining, "What's funny is how these articles [about vic-tims and rescue workers] are all sympathy, with experts weighing in, etc.— but how no such consideration was given me or my life. . . . the way I look at it, either hand out the sympathy equally, or hand out none at all!"[41]

McVeigh also wanted to establish that he both had the capacity to feel emotion and was a soldier at heart. He claimed to feel sympathy for other groups, most often the Iraqis against whom he had fought in the Gulf War, animals, and the Branch Davidians at Waco—particularly the children. But when it came to emotional displays, McVeigh acknowledged his reticence, telling Ed Bradley, "I was raised in an environment where men don't cry. You hold it back." To underscore his masculinity, he bragged of his ability to "take on" those who challenged him and his intimidating presence. McVeigh even referred to his haircut as hygienic, efficient—and intimidating: "If you project the military aura, people aren't going to fuck with you. In fact, that's one of the reasons I kept my flat-top haircut throughout the trial. It's like wearing the Kevlar suit, it intimidates others, it automatically gives you the advantage."

In describing the bombing conspiracy itself, McVeigh was profoundly angered by insinuations that he was not its mastermind. He claimed to have chosen not only the target but also the timing. Infuriated about Nichols's state trial, McVeigh railed, "It was <u>my choice</u> and <u>my control</u> to hit the bldg. when full."[42] He actually went so far as to declare that he did not need anyone else: "Show me where I needed anyone else—financing? Logistics? Specialized tech. skills? Brain-power? Strategy? Or, the old fashioned 'means, motive, opportunity' test? . . . Show me where I needed a dark and mysterious 'Mr. X'!!"[43] He repeatedly emphasized that he was calm and collected, even after the bomb detonated, that he "<u>never lost composure</u>," was "never hyped-up, always in control," and even walked "calmly" to his getaway car.[44]

McVeigh was not so calm, however, when he discussed the Murrah Building's America's Kids day care center in unbelievably insensitive terms:

> It really pissed me off, the prosecution presented that it [the day care center] was easily visible. Mike Fortier and I were in front of the building, that glass was black, just a sheen. You couldn't see kids in there. . . . I recognized beforehand that someone might be walking down the road with their kid, or bringing their kid to work. However, if it was known there was an entire day care center there, it might have given me cause to switch targets, and that might have made the difference. That's a large amount of collateral damage. That issue really irked me.[45]

He told Michel, "You know I would've ruled out Murrah if I knew there was a daycare center."[46] But McVeigh still could never bring himself to publicly express remorse for the children's deaths; when pressed by Ed Bradley, he said only, "I thought it was—it was terrible that there were children in the building."[47]

Another key part of McVeigh's reputation management scheme was to establish that everything had been orchestrated with a single purpose in mind. He insisted that his arrest by Oklahoma state trooper Charlie Hanger was part of a master plan in which he intended to be caught and to lead the media on a scavenger hunt of clues. Arrest merely fit McVeigh's strategy of "suicide by cop, the deluxe package."[48] He felt capture would heighten his media exposure, "sort of like setting yourself up for sacrifice, in a way." He even insisted that his facial expression during his perp walk was chosen to cultivate a specific public impression:

> There were steps leading down from the courthouse, and I had to concentrate on where those steps were going to be without dipping my head down

and looking down because people would take dipping my head down as a sign of defeat or something. . . . It was hard to pick out individual things because they're all yelling at once, right? But I do distinctly remember one I heard, "Look over here, motherf*****, baby killer, look me in the face." My immediate thought was, I'm not gonna give you the pleasure of looking over there.[49]

Defiance also characterized McVeigh's attitude toward his trial and execution. At some points, he claimed that he intended to exploit legal proceedings for publicity, using his trial as a "propaganda game" to create "polarization";[50] at others, he asserted that he sought to uphold "principles" such as fighting "corruption, perversion, and lies."[51] He also asserted that he sought a public execution for reasons of "principle." In a letter to journalist Nolan Clay of the *Daily Oklahoman*, McVeigh raised questions of "equal access"[52] and urged officials to "hold a *true* 'public' execution—allow a public broadcast."[53] He invited Michel and Herbeck to witness his execution for "principled" reasons, including as a "deterrent to abuse" and to "document [the] process for historical purposes."[54] McVeigh denied that he was an "egomaniac" or that he would engage in theatrics in his final moments: "It's not b/c I'm staging some big, dramatic final stmt (like Mel Gibson in Braveheart: "Freedom!")— (although, I thought about it!). It's enough simply to show the process. (Let others grandstand.)."[55] But despite these "principles," McVeigh was eager to use his execution to maximize publicity opportunities, vowing that if there was "video feed,"

> I'm going to throw it back in their face, I'm going to demand they televise it nationally. I'm going to say if you fuckers want to make a spectacle of it, I'm going to point out exactly what you're doing, . . . they're going to be watching a large screen TV in a friggin auditorium. . . . I'm going to make the whole nation watch, or try to.[56]

And he could not resist a few grandiose parting statements; at one point, he proposed that Michel arrange a book signing of *American Terrorist* at a local Terre Haute bookstore on May 14 and 15, his original execution date.[57] He also advised Michel to prepare for the execution "as if you were about to go into battle (and don't take that advice lightly), but I would also urge that you not look upon my death as something to grieve over," ending the letter with a rather cavalier "I'll see you at the show."[58]

The capstone of McVeigh's reputation management strategy was to claim the laurels of victor and not vanquished; casting his prosecution as persecution, he asserted that he had put the government, victims, and other critics in a "no win situation."[59] McVeigh claimed that he could not lose no matter his trial's outcome; if he remained alive, he had thwarted those who wanted him dead, and if he was executed, then his trial had exposed the government as corrupt: "The beauty of it is, they lose even if I don't get the death penalty. Because that means they lose in court."[60] McVeigh claimed to be using "the system" against itself "to further my own personal and revolutionary goals! So, I don't 'blame' the system—I take full responsibility for my own actions—I instead simply used the system to my own maximum advantage!"[61] He also continued to compare "body counts": "The final tally has been, in the crudest terms, 168 to 1. If you had it on a scoreboard. Of course there's been suicides, and psychological impact on many federal employees. So I sit here content that there is no way they can beat me by executing me."[62]

The Publication of American Terrorist

McVeigh believed his biography would form the basis for his legacy. *American Terrorist: Timothy McVeigh and the Oklahoma City Bombing* was published in April 2001, just two months before his execution. In writing the book, Michel and Herbeck interviewed McVeigh's family members, former acquaintances, and, most important, McVeigh himself (for more than 75 hours). *American Terrorist* purported to give the "first complete, candid, no-holds-barred account of his story—an account given with no compensation or right of approval, that includes his long-awaited confession."

What did McVeigh himself think of his authorized biography? In letters to Michel, he seemed to waver between approval and frustration. In a letter sent to Michel shortly after the book's release, he expressed exasperation that the book lacked specifics after he had spent so much time delivering detailed accounts to his biographers: "While it is accurate . . . it is also frustrating. We spent <u>hours</u> nitpicking the tiniest of details of different stories/experiences from my life; <u>hours</u> clarifying 'why' etc., and mostly, the book <u>generalizes</u>."[63] His frustration reached its apex on April 19, 2001, when, ostensibly angered after viewing a *Primetime* interview featuring Michel, McVeigh wrote him a long letter addressing the costs of leaving out more detailed information on his lack of sympathy for bombing victims, complaining, "Now do you see why I was so disappointed all that stuff got cut out?—it's core [underlined in triplicate] to my perspective!"[64] In later missives, however, McVeigh conveyed his approval of the book and indicated he was happy it was a success.

McVeigh's authorized biography angered many in Oklahoma City, who said they first learned that the book would focus almost entirely on McVeigh after the authors were interviewed by Diane Sawyer on ABC's *Prime Time Thursday* and *Newsweek* published a brief excerpt on its website.[65] As one news article covering the controversy asserted, Herbeck and Michel were subsequently "denounced by some for exploiting tragedy, for being too willing to accept McVeigh's version of events and for providing McVeigh with a national platform from which to advance his claim to political martyrdom," as well as "trying to profit from 'blood money.'"[66] The authors, in their turn, replied that they had taken "months of unpaid leave and spent thousands of hours away from our families" and had written the book "for historical purposes," terming it "the equivalent of sitting down with Lee Harvey Oswald or John Wilkes Booth and hearing their stories."[67]

Family members, survivors, and citizens involved with the Oklahoma City National Memorial were enraged by the book. Several blamed the authors for telling them that they were writing a book on the memorial, not on McVeigh. In comments to the press, Bob Johnson, the first chairman of the memorial task force and then a member of the Oklahoma City National Memorial Trust, emphasized that "there is no affiliation between the Memorial and the authors or publisher of this book" because the "Memorial has not endorsed, approved or sponsored this book." Johnson also stressed that the book was antithetical to the memorial's purpose:

> Our mission is to remember the 168 innocent people who were killed by McVeigh and Nichols, to remember the hundreds of survivors who were subjected to the horror of the attack, and to educate regarding the seriousness of violence as a means of effecting government change. Any book dealing with the life and philosophy of Timothy McVeigh is not consistent with our mission.[68]

The back cover of the book featured a photograph of the memorial at nighttime, with illuminated chairs representing the murdered victims foregrounding one of the Gates of Time. Richard Williams recalled that this image created controversy over "what they could or could not use about the memorial in and on the cover of their book." In a letter concerning the book's publication sent to the Oklahoma City National Memorial board and staff, executive director Kari Watkins wrote:

The authors/publishers have NO authority whatsoever, to use the Memorial's name and we will NOT take any money from this book. We did not and will not endorse or authorize the use of our name or photograph, which we believe in this case, implies sponsorship or endorsement. Because this is a National Memorial, we cannot stop people from taking pictures of this memorial. We will, however, make every attempt to stop people from using this Memorial to market their goods.[69]

The authors attempted to assuage angered individuals by contributing an unspecified portion of their royalties to the Oklahoma City National Memorial but were "rebuffed."[70]

Susan Urbach recalled that the book raised hackles among bombing victims: "People were almost upset if you were going to read it or buy it. 'Don't support that guy!' or whatever." Williams deemed the book "very informative" but was adamant that "that was not what we had been told was going to be the primary focus of the book." And there was no doubt that it could make for difficult reading. "I bought it intending to read it, and I couldn't get through it," Diane Dooley recalled. Family members and survivors were particularly enraged by McVeigh's claim that he had not known that the America's Kids day care center was on the second floor of the Murrah Building. Some, however, appreciated the book's insights. Survivor Vicki Hamm remarked, "That book helped me tremendously." "How better to know about the person McVeigh [was] than words from his own mouth," she commented, noting that the biographical information "made me feel like I knew him." After reading the book, Susan Urbach was left with the overwhelming impression that "the prosecution got a ton right."

"We've Had a Good Run, Lou"

But in the end, no one could tell McVeigh's story as completely as he had hoped. Michel and Herbeck could not allow McVeigh to use his authorized biography to establish an ideological platform without damaging or outright destroying their professional credibility. In light of his extensive media experience, McVeigh should have known that any mainstream author with whom he worked would have to filter his statements through an interpretive screen, inevitably leaving out some information he deemed essential.

McVeigh amicably parted ways with Lou Michel a few weeks before his execution. In a letter dated May 23, 2001, he terminated his professional relationship with Michel on the grounds that Michel was using the material from their correspondence for newspaper articles, and not for a revised edition of the book. Notably, this split came only after McVeigh felt he had lost "control" over what was happening to his missives:

I am aware that much of the material we covered in the past did not make the book. . . . I am also aware that much of what you ask for now will not likely make future prints of the book, and likewise, you are asking now for purposes of running articles in your employer's paper. The permanence of a <u>book</u> as a future reference piece was the core of our mutual cooperation. Newspaper articles, on the other hand, are "a dime a dozen," and I'm really not interested in continuing to give <u>The Buffalo News</u> exclusive after exclusive. B/c I cannot control what you give the paper from my letters (intended primarily as material for [the] book), I think we need to pretty much end our relationship. As for material for future <u>updates</u> to the book . . . you can just as easily summarize from news stories as you can summate from my letters. We've had a good run; mutually fair. Let us break it off now, cleanly, and while on good terms. Not one for long, drawn out, emotional fare, I will simply re-state: We've had a good run, Lou. Peace. Tim

McVeigh had hoped that his authorized biography would serve as his legacy, that it would put right most of what he felt had gone wrong with his public image. But in clarifying McVeigh's intentions and perspectives, the book also highlighted mistakes and illuminated character flaws. It explained much but did not justify anything. More than anything else, it revealed how McVeigh's bellicose ideology, even accepted on its own terms, was flawed and incomplete. McVeigh described himself first and foremost as a soldier. According to philosopher Nancy Sherman, who has interviewed soldiers preparing for, in the midst of, and returning home from war, soldiering is adopted as an identity—people "become" soldiers for life.[71] Military culture has and continues to emphasize stoic ideals, and traditional military training schools soldiers to detach from emotions that could make them vulnerable, teaching them to develop a "bulletproof mind" so that combat experiences do not affect them "at the core."[72] Eventually, however, wars end and soldiers return home with a new challenge: "to hold on to one's humanity, especially as one kills."[73]

But McVeigh's adoption of stoicism was not reasonable, and so he failed this moral challenge. McVeigh was stoic past the point of self-sufficiency and battle readiness, to the extreme of "radical, emotional independence from others."[74] He certainly held himself apart from others, especially as his execution drew near. According to Michel, he did not even hug his father and his sister good-bye when they came to visit him for the last time. Part of the human capacity for reason is knowing when to be stoic and when to leave stoic ideals behind, yet McVeigh lacked this ability.

From bombing to execution, McVeigh was trapped in a Catch-22 situation stemming from the conflict between civilian emotional norms and military stoicism. He considered himself a soldier at war and believed that to be emotional in war was to be vulnerable, yet at the same time he was aware that his apparent lack of emotion fueled criticism and negative media coverage. In order to refute "demonizing" labels and render his ideology and mission credible, McVeigh had to establish that his decision to bomb the Murrah Building was somehow a rational militaristic strategy. But to be seen as rational, he first had to express sorrow for the devastation wrought by the Murrah Building bomb, which he felt no true soldier could do. Rational credibility required emotional display, but this would have destroyed martial credibility; to gain credibility on one ground, McVeigh had to surrender it on another. Therefore, McVeigh's inability to express sorrow for the Murrah Building victims imperiled his mission. Ultimately, McVeigh was unable to prove that he could take off his uniform, step out of his militant mind-set, and adjust to civilian norms, that he knew when and when not to kill, marking him a terrorist and not a soldier.

11

Done to Death

*The Execution and the End of the
Victim-Offender Relationship*

Dear Mr. McVeigh:

The purpose of this letter is to inform you that a date has been
set for the implementation of your death sentence, pursuant to
the Judgment and Order issued on August 14, 1997, by Chief
U.S. District Judge Richard P. Matsch of the United States District Court for the District of Colorado. . . . the Director of the
Federal Bureau of Prisons has set May 16, 2001 as the date for
your execution by lethal injection.

Soon, I will come to your housing unit to personally discuss
with you many of the details surrounding the execution. At that
time, I will be available to answer any questions you may have
regarding the execution procedures.

Sincerely,

Harley G. Lappin, Warden[1]

Timothy McVeigh was executed in the early morning hours of June
12, 2001, necessitating that family members and survivors who would witness his death live begin the long journey from Oklahoma City and elsewhere to Terre Haute, Indiana, the day before. Every witness who embarked
on this momentous trip—whether they were to witness the execution live
or remotely, or were just planning to stand outside the prison—found that
it had its bizarre moments. Live witness Paul Howell literally packed his
suitcase while two journalists filmed his activities. The morning that he
was to leave, Howell stepped outside of his home to retrieve his newspaper
and found about "20 different TV stations" camped outside, all hungry for

updates and images. Howell refused media requests to repeatedly pack and unpack his suitcase so that station after station could obtain this prized footage, prompting journalists to arrive at a compromise—one crew would film the footage and distribute it to all in attendance. Leaving the media circus behind, Howell drove to the FAA Center to rendezvous with other live witnesses en route to boarding a private plane bound for Indiana.

Live witness Cameron Crawford took the train to Terre Haute. Riding the rails south, Crawford was profoundly grateful he was able to witness McVeigh's execution live. He recalled:

> I think that was the most important thing to me. I could have viewed it at the FAA Center if I had to and I mean, what are you going to do; if that's what happened, that's what happened. But it was just complete relief when I found out I was one of the 10 selected. Because I mean I can't . . . there aren't enough words to describe how important it was for me to do that. Oh, wow. It's just—I still can't believe it. . . . Oh, God, I don't even know if I can put that into words. . . . Physically being there.

Other live witnesses arrived on commercial aircraft; Ron Brown caught a flight from Florida, and Peggy Broxterman and her husband flew in from Nevada, shadowed by a newspaper reporter from her hometown. U.S. Marshals met the Broxtermans and Brown at Indianapolis International Airport and drove them down to Terre Haute.

When the private plane carrying live witnesses from Oklahoma City reached Terre Haute, it landed at a military complex and taxied into a hangar, where passengers disembarked. A short while later, a decoy convoy of vans with darkened windows departed from the hangar in order to distract the news media; witnesses were then loaded into other vans and driven in the opposite direction. Live witnesses ended their journeys at a modest, nondescript hotel on the rural outskirts of Terre Haute.

Family member and anti–death penalty advocate Bud Welch also planned to travel to Terre Haute for McVeigh's execution—only to stand on the outside of the prison, not to witness from inside the death house. Before traveling to Terre Haute, Welch had attended a murder victims' families conference at Boston College, where international press stalked him hoping to get interviews. Media organizations even paid for Welch's airfare to Indianapolis as well as accommodations in Terre Haute for him and two companions.

The night before the execution, live witnesses and their support persons attended a reception and dinner with Bureau of Prisons personnel from the Terre Haute Federal Correctional Complex where McVeigh had been housed. Clergy and mental health professionals were also in attendance. Over dinner, prison officials briefed witnesses on what would take place the following morning. Ron Brown described the dinner as a "soothing time," and Peggy Broxterman and Cameron Crawford termed the mood as upbeat. "Everyone was up. . . . a lot of laughter and talk and everything like that. I mean it wasn't somber," recalled Broxterman.

The 10 live witnesses assembled at approximately 5:00 the next morning. As they were being transported into the prison complex in a van with blacked-out windows, witnesses could see the tall grandstands that the major news networks had erected for the occasion. People stood on the side of the road waving signs. For Brown, that was when "reality hit that this is really going to happen." Witnesses were taken to the prison chapel, where they socialized, ate breakfast, were briefed a second time, and waited for the summons to the death house. Counselors stood by in case witnesses became distressed, a step that Broxterman described as unnecessary: "Not one person that went to that execution needed any kind of counseling. I mean, we were there because we wanted to be there."

Almost 700 miles away from Terre Haute in Oklahoma City, remote witnesses, too, had awakened early—many recalled getting up at 3:00 a.m. They had to meet at the National Guard headquarters at 4:00 a.m. to be checked in and bused to the FAA Center, where the execution would be broadcast. When Doris Jones's son-in-law told her on the morning of the execution that he was not going to go, she replied that she would still attend: "I have to do this. That's the least I can do is follow it through. I fought a long, long battle to not face, to not see it to the end." When witnesses entered the FAA Center, they saw a large, blank screen at the front of a large room; they helped themselves to breakfast foods and other refreshments and stood around and visited with one another while they were waiting for the execution to begin. As in Terre Haute, mental health professionals and clergy members were on site to assist remote witnesses as needed.

Back in Terre Haute, when all preparations had been completed and the moment of McVeigh's execution was nigh, the witnesses once again embarked in the van for the brief trip to the death house. Here, the van pulled up between a makeshift wall and the building so as to preserve witnesses' privacy. Witnesses were escorted into the viewing room, where they saw a curtained window with one-way glass on the wall adjacent to the execution chamber. All of the witnesses remained standing; Brown recalled standing on a chair in the back to see over others' heads. A couple of uniformed prison guards lingered behind in the viewing room with the witnesses.

Bud Welch had risen at the crack of dawn on June 11, 2001, and was outside the prison by 6:00 a.m. at the request of media organizations who wanted to interview him live on early morning broadcasts such as *The Today Show* and *Good Morning America*. That day was one long parade of media interviews. "I just went from, you might say, one platform to another," Welch recalled. The prison grounds teemed with thousands of demonstrators and reporters. According to Welch, the anti–death penalty protesters far outnumbered pro–death penalty demonstrators: "We had about 2,000 people that came out and demonstrated against his execution, had about 15 or 20 that came and supported it. And they had their typical ugly signs . . . one of them had a sign that said, 'Kill 'em all, let God sort them out.'"

Meanwhile, at the FAA Center in Oklahoma City, the time for socializing with one another was over. Officials asked witnesses to be seated. To the surprise and delight of the remote witnesses, U.S. Attorney General John Ashcroft was present at the FAA Center and spoke briefly with them before the execution, explaining that he would be unable to witness the execution with them because he had to be in a different area so that he could stop proceedings if necessary. Officials then informed witnesses that when the broadcast began, they would see the curtains part in the viewing room, that McVeigh would already be strapped onto the execution table with the IVs inserted, and that it would be over very quickly. A brief delay ensued while officials corrected some problems with the closed-circuit feed. A few moments later, the remote feed clicked on.

According to Doris Jones, remote witnesses saw the curtains open in the other viewing rooms, where they could see "a little movement." Then the image changed from a long camera shot to one looking down upon McVeigh from a point directly over the execution table, and witnesses suddenly found themselves face-to-face with a close-up of his face, from his collarbone to the top of his head. Many found this shocking, because witnesses had not been warned ahead of time what McVeigh's image would actually look like.

When the curtain between the viewing room and the death chamber slid open, and the closed-circuit broadcast began, McVeigh was lying on an execution table draped with a white sheet. "But it was very cold, a cold feeling when the curtain went back because everything just looked so sterile in that room, and I can remember that the sheets . . . looked like they had been just pressed," Ron Brown recalled. Two men were in the lethal injection chamber with McVeigh: prison warden Harley Lappin and U.S. Marshal Frank Anderson. Live witnesses could see a large camera mounted on the ceiling directly over the execution table. Victim witnesses watched as McVeigh raised his head to look into each of these adjacent witnessing rooms, nodding to his witnesses and to reporters, and then staring blankly in their direction before lying back down. Theirs was the only adjacent room other than the executioner's compartment just behind McVeigh's head designed to obstruct his view. Had the one-way glass not obscured McVeigh's view, he would have seen two photographs of murdered victims staring at him along with the 10 live victim witnesses.

Thereafter, the execution proceeded as planned. Warden Harry Lappin, his arms crossed, asked McVeigh if he had any last words. There ensued a 20-second pause; McVeigh had no oral final statement to deliver but instead had chosen to write his final words, and prison officials had distributed photocopies of William Ernest Henley's poem "Invictus" to reporters in media packets. Lappin then recited the charges against McVeigh and asked Marshal Anderson if they could proceed. Anderson picked up a red phone in the chamber, spoke to a Justice Department official for final authorization, and received the necessary confirmation. According to a media witness, 10 minutes after the cur-

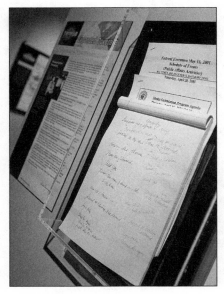

An Oklahoma City National Memorial and Museum exhibit features the media packet given to journalists prior to McVeigh's execution, as well as the yellow tablet on which reporter Linda Cavanaugh took notes as she witnessed the execution live in Terre Haute. Image courtesy of the Oklahoma City National Memorial and Museum Archives.

tain had parted, a guard confirmed that the first drug in the lethal injection cocktail, sodium thiopental, had rendered McVeigh unconscious. McVeigh's last voluntary movements appeared to be two hard swallows and a blink. With the administration of the second drug, the muscle relaxant pancuronium bromide, he grew very pale, his stare became glassy, and his lips became white. By the time that the third drug, potassium chloride, was administered to stop his heart, McVeigh appeared jaundiced, and his eyes, still open, were slightly rolled back. McVeigh was pronounced dead at 7:14 a.m.[2] Shortly after the execution, President George W. Bush made a public statement, remarking, "Today, every living person who was hurt by the evil done in Oklahoma City can rest in the knowledge that there has been a reckoning."[3]

Back in Oklahoma City, after the closed-circuit execution was over, many remote witnesses departed immediately for media interviews, for the Oklahoma City National Memorial, for other gatherings, or simply for home. As they were leaving, witnesses recalled that a church group distributed little white bears as symbols of peace.

In Terre Haute, after McVeigh was pronounced dead and the curtains again closed, live witnesses were escorted out of the viewing room and back

Media platforms erected on the western edge of the Oklahoma City National Memorial and Museum grounds on June 11, 2001, the morning of McVeigh's execution. The outdoor memorial is to the left of the platforms. Image courtesy of the Oklahoma City National Memorial and Museum Archives.

The grounds of the Oklahoma City National Memorial and Museum on the morning of McVeigh's execution. White tents covering media platforms are visible in the distance.

into the van and were driven back to the prison chapel. Broxterman all but skipped out of the viewing room: "[Another witness] and I walked out of that execution and we sang, 'Ding, dong, McVeigh is dead, da, da, da.' We sang because we were happy that McVeigh was dead and we didn't give a damn who cared." Another live witness, Sue Ashford, later stated in a media interview that she "clapped and said, 'Oh, yeah! He's finally dead!'"[4]

Victim witnesses who had agreed to give media interviews were driven in golf carts with armed escorts to news media platforms. Media officials were only permitted to speak to witnesses when they were deposited at certain media stations. After an interview with one media outlet had concluded, officials would call ahead to the next station to let people there know that a witness was on the way. Journalists interviewed witnesses for approximately three hours. After they were done, witnesses returned to the prison chapel, exchanged good-byes, and departed for home.

Although he had been on the outside of the prison, Welch, too, had endured a grueling day. He had kept up a punishing schedule of media interviews; morning shows bled into afternoon broadcasts, which in turn blurred into evening programming. All in all, the press kept Welch occupied on the prison grounds for 17 hours, until 10:00 p.m. He did not leave Terre Haute to return home to Oklahoma City until Wednesday. It was, as Welch termed it, "a hell of a week."

Several family members and survivors chose not to attend McVeigh's execution. Janet Beck and Beverly Rankin gathered with many others at their church for a breakfast and prayer service; they wanted to be together but not to watch McVeigh die. Marsha Kight, who was living in Washington, D.C., sat by a stream in a park and wrote a poem, with reporters from *People* magazine hovering at a distance. Her poem addressed McVeigh's impending execution; Kight ruminated on what was in his mind, what he would say to his father and mother, and whether he thought all of that had, in the end, been worth it.

Richard Williams had taken leave from work in order to spend the day at the Oklahoma City National Memorial and Museum awaiting the news of McVeigh's death. Local and national news media had inundated the memorial as they had Terre Haute; tall media scaffolds erected for the occasion towered over the outdoor memorial. Williams had several interviews scheduled at the memorial that morning; on *Good Morning America*, he told Charley Gibson that he "needed to be down at the memorial with my fellow survivors and family members who were not attending the closed-circuit feed or at the execution itself." When McVeigh was actually pronounced dead, Williams was in the conference room with others. Immediately afterward, he was approached by executive director Kari

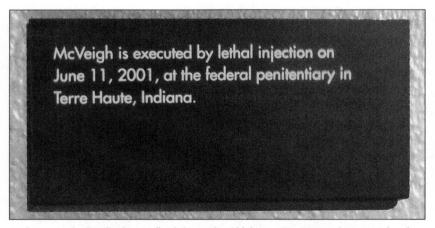

McVeigh is executed by lethal injection on June 11, 2001, at the federal penitentiary in Terre Haute, Indiana.

A plaque on the "Wall of Justice" exhibit in the Oklahoma City National Memorial and Museum announces McVeigh's execution. Image courtesy of the Oklahoma City National Memorial and Museum Archives.

Watkins, who asked him if he would be willing to go into the museum and exchange a plaque on the "Wall of Justice" exhibit announcing that McVeigh had been sentenced to death for one stating that he had been executed. Beneath the glare of media lights, Williams hung the new plaque, integrating McVeigh's execution into the museum's official chronology of the bombing narrative.

For years, the healing, voluntary relationships that family members and survivors had formed with one another had paralleled other destructive, involuntary relationships that chained them to the perpetrators. But on the morning of McVeigh's execution, these two relationships intersected at long last. As family members and survivors congregated to await the closed-circuit broadcast or waited in the Terre Haute prison chapel to be transported to the death house, they tapped the strong interpersonal bonds they had forged with one another to sustain them through whatever the day would bring—including a final confrontation with McVeigh.

Prior to his execution, McVeigh was still a poisonous presence in the lives of most victims' family members and survivors. He could manipulate or unsettle them at will with callous media commentary, his stoic demeanor, or his defiance, arrogance, and "in-your-face" visibility. For years, McVeigh's toxic presence had dampened, interrupted, and delayed memory work, that reconstructive labor that brought them ever closer to a "new normal" or narrative resolution. Each time they glimpsed the perp walk footage of McVeigh exiting the Perry courthouse, saw a new media interview, or came across a reference to his authorized biography, it rubbed salt into wounds that had become increasingly raw.

Those who chose to witness the execution would confront McVeigh again in his final moments. This confrontation, however, would occur on very different terms. McVeigh was no longer a man presumed innocent but a condemned offender strapped to an execution table to die. And witnesses to that death had endured a tremendous tragedy and were adamant that they were going to not only survive but *live*. As a result of the execution, family members and survivors expected to finally exorcise McVeigh's presence. In addition, McVeigh's execution would largely terminate institutional involvement in and mediation of participants' memory work: it marked the end of legal proceedings, the point beyond which there was little reason for the media to cover McVeigh in death as they had in life. With McVeigh removed as a reconstructive roadblock, and with legal proceedings against him finally at an end, memory work could resume or reach new stages.

The Execution as Modern Spectacle and Site of Memory Work

Due to technological innovation, McVeigh's execution was the most widely witnessed execution in American since the mid-twentieth century, when public executions had become private affairs inside prison walls. Both Michel Foucault and Pieter Spierenburg have discussed at length the symbolic spectacle of medieval public executions and the collective lessons that the populace took away from them:

> Public torture and execution must be spectacular, it must be seen by all almost as its triumph. The very excess of the violence employed is one of the elements of its glory: the fact that the guilty man should moan and cry out under the blows is not a shameful side-effect, it is the very ceremonial of justice being expressed in all its force.[5]

The public execution was simultaneously a reminder of the sovereign power over life and death and a morality play with religious implications; condemned prisoners delivered impassioned "gallows speeches" in which they lamented their sins and pleaded for salvation.[6] The ideal criminal was a Christian penitent figure who was convinced that his punishment was righteous and was determined to endure it to save his soul. To die unreconciled to authorities, fellow men, and God was to meet death as a beast, a mere animal.[7]

But in the nineteenth century, the execution moved out of public view with the invention of the prison. The state dissected death by execution into silent and rehearsed routine processes.[8] Today's executions appear at first to have little in common with their forebears. Now, up to 10 witnesses gather in a death house inside the prison walls, if at all. Violence is no longer a celebrated part of the execution ritual; indeed, the execution protocol is designed to minimize the sensation and visibility of pain through anesthetics and paralytics. Executions are publicized primarily in the news media, which dutifully record last moments, last meals, last words, and last remarks of victims' family members and state officials.[9]

Nowadays, a new type of witness—the victim's family member—has come to occupy a seat in the witnessing room. These witnesses fulfill a very different role than media and official execution witnesses. Official witnesses to executions represent the state and ensure an execution is carried out; journalists confirm that the state is not executing in a wanton or cruel fashion and report the execution's orderly completion to the public. Victim witnesses, however, do not represent the state or the public at large, but instead embody the most localized and private of interests.[10] Victim witnessing augurs a change in the conception of justice that at first sounds rather pedestrian: that crimes are committed not only against the state but also against victims.

It was always a given that McVeigh's execution would be a spectacle, albeit one very different from its early modern counterpart—a "once-in-a-lifetime" event ineffectually costumed as "business as usual." McVeigh's execution was not only an event that victims' family members and survivors experienced in common; it was also an interaction between McVeigh and witnesses, a "communicative event," in which someone engages in making meaning by drawing on culturally embedded interactive norms. The term "communication" is more likely to engender images of two people in conversation than a prisoner being put to death by lethal injection. But as a state-instituted ritual, punishment is a social act with communicative dimensions, and capital punishment is its most extreme form. Criminal law's efficacy presumes communication, institutional expressions that some acts are illegal and that those who commit crimes will be punished. Punishment in general, and capital punishment in particular, are part of a dialogue, a framework of action and reaction. Like other interactions, an execution is a negotiated exchange of meaning that takes place in a social context seething with factors that may facilitate or hinder human interaction. Thus, McVeigh's execution was an event with expressive as well as social consequences.

McVeigh's gaze and silence both played significant roles in framing the execution as an event steeped in meaning and rich in sense-making potential—in essence, as communicative. Witnesses perceived that McVeigh's gaze held communicative import, in particular confirming their prior impressions that he was defiant and remorseless. Similarly, different forms of silence played crucial roles in ripening the execution into a productive site for memory work: witnesses' silence, McVeigh's silence, and the execution as a means of silencing McVeigh.

McVeigh's Gaze

Prisoners condemned to die can invite or open an interaction with spectators either by looking into the witness rooms or by addressing witnesses through "last words." Often, the condemned does make some effort to communicate but rarely makes the gestures that witnesses say they most desire. During his execution, McVeigh's gaze established his visual awareness of witnesses. Live witnesses Paul Howell and Cameron Crawford recalled that when the curtain was opened, McVeigh lifted his head and slowly stared into the adjoining witness rooms, in which his own witnesses, media witnesses, official witnesses, and bombing victims waited.[11] He then lay back down and stared up at the ceiling, into the closed-circuit camera.

Execution witnesses are often intensely interested in watching the offender's face throughout the procedure, to the point that corrective measures may have to be taken when logistics such as the location of the execution table or the defendant's girth make this impossible.[12] Prison personnel have altered table height or slant to allow victim witnesses positioned at the feet of an obese inmate to see over his midsection to his face. Witnesses in the Terre Haute death chamber only had seconds in which they could possibly make eye contact with McVeigh. Cameron Crawford recalled that McVeigh raised his head in an effort to look at victim witnesses: "I never expected him to look at us. And then . . . it was like drum roll. His head turns to his right. He rolls over and he looks at all of us. Or at our window. Four, maybe five seconds and then turns his head back."

Most closed-circuit witnesses felt that the placement of the camera directly over the execution table in Terre Haute was ideal because it allowed them to study McVeigh's facial expressions at length. After the camera clicked on, McVeigh's image appeared suddenly, and witnesses were "shocked" or "jarred" by the unexpected sight. Priscilla Salyers recalled, "I visualized you [were] going to see like him across the room on the bed and he [would be] strapped down and everything, [but] when the curtains opened his face was right there, big, huge, I mean the camera was like right on his face. . . . Yeah, like shoulders up, that shocked me."

But this shock did not prevent most closed-circuit witnesses from unhesitatingly endorsing this camera placement, since they wanted to see McVeigh's face for a variety of reasons. Ray Washburn's spouse affirmed, "I'm glad I saw him that close up and everything 'cause that way I knew from his eyes and his expression what he was feeling." Priscilla Salyers credited her ability to see McVeigh's face with enabling spiritual forgiveness: "I think the face thing is what really brought it to reality with me. . . . it was a face-to-face thing and I think that's probably what drew me in to what I needed to go through."

Other witnesses would have preferred to see more details. Jamie Blansett wanted to see all of McVeigh's body despite being somewhat wary of doing so, and Dot Hill would have liked to see additional preparations for the execution as well as a more expansive view that included all of McVeigh's body along with the corrections staff and other people in the witness rooms. She thought it odd that they could not see more: "I mean honestly this was a protected room . . . we knew each other. So what's wrong with us seeing who's there? . . . I would just like for it to have been like we were there in that room, rather than just watching from the chest up. . . . We didn't even get to see the injection go in, we didn't get to see the needle in his arm." Hill was interested in seeing these procedures not for the satisfaction of seeing McVeigh in pain but because they were parts of the execution and thus potentially tasks that witnesses should be able to view. Some states do permit witnesses to view early procedures such as IV insertion; Ohio, for instance, broadcasts images of these preparations via closed-circuit feed to a television mounted in the witness room. At times, this visibility has unforeseen results; on September 15, 2009, Ohio's attempts to execute Romell Broom by lethal injection failed after the execution team tried for at least three hours to insert an IV while witnesses watched via closed-circuit television. Ohio governor Ted Strickland ultimately granted Broom a temporary reprieve at the prison warden's request.

McVeigh's gaze gave rise to an intense perception among closed-circuit witnesses that he was aware that his death was being witnessed and that he wanted to create a certain impression. Not only did live and closed-circuit witnesses feel that McVeigh was aware of them, but they perceived that he was actually and purposefully *looking at* all witnesses, even remote ones. McVeigh's gaze led witnesses to believe that he might interact with them in some further way. Larry Whicher said that McVeigh "actually lifted his head and looked directly into the camera and it was as if he was looking directly at us." To Whicher, McVeigh's stare was "a totally expressionless, blank stare— and his eyes were unblinking, they appeared to me to be coal black and he didn't need to make a statement. I truly believe that his eyes were telling me he had a look of defiance and that if he could he'd do it all again."[13]

McVeigh's stare was so intense that numerous closed-circuit witnesses described his gaze as unmediated, despite the closed-circuit feed. Priscilla Salyers said that "it was almost like he was just staring at each person. . . . It's almost like it was a face-to-face contact with him." Doris Jones perceived that McVeigh was not only aware of witnesses' presence but that his gaze seemed to penetrate through the camera to reach them: "As he stared at the camera, knowing that we were watching, . . . he was just staring right through you. I mean absolutely everyone said the same thing. It looked like he was looking right at you."

In the closed-circuit image, McVeigh was reclining on his back so that his gaze was directed upward to the ceiling as a matter of course, and so it is unclear whether his upturned gaze into the camera (and through its lens to the witnesses in Oklahoma City) was targeted at the ceiling, the remote witnesses, both, or neither. Thus, though live witnesses had a more immediate encounter with McVeigh through their close physical proximity to his body, closed-circuit witnesses actually experienced a more intimate connection with McVeigh through his gaze and felt its full force. Remote witnesses indisputably imposed meaning upon that gaze. As Larry Whicher said in a media interview immediately following the execution: "I think that stare in the camera is something that will stay with me. . . . It won't haunt me, but I think it will be a memory that will stay with me and make me think there are others like that in the world."[14]

"I'm Going to Stare at You Until You Look Me in the Eye": Gazing Norms

Witnesses interpreted McVeigh's gaze as confrontational or defiant, particularly combined with his silence at the warden's request for "last words."[15] Because of its apparent hostility, the implications of McVeigh's communicative gaze for the formation of individual and collective memory are closely tied to social norms and interpretations of gazing. For sighted people, gaze is an important social behavior.[16] Above all else, it conveys visual attention,[17] expresses emotion, allows one to monitor others' actions, regulates interaction, and directs relationships.[18] Eye contact also signals the level of intimacy between two interactants; the greater the eye contact, the closer the relationship between them.[19] According to sociologist Erving Goffman, gaze is rule-governed; "people are expected to gaze in certain ways, and it is disturbing to others if they gaze in a different manner."[20] Mutual gaze, then, indicates attention and interactional potential.[21]

However, the execution was by no means an "ordinary" space, where normal rules and conventions of interaction and gaze applied. It was a liminal space, involving many changes of status—living to dead, sentence pronounced versus sentence carried out—that invoked a ritualistic context. The rules for witnessing an execution are simple in form: gaze is expected and encouraged, as it is for theatrical audiences who are expected to await the spectacle and fix their gazes upon the stage when the curtain goes up. The rules for the condemned, however, are much more temporal and tenuous. The lethal injection protocol lacks the restrictions on gaze inherent in other forms of execution—the hood for hanging, the blindfold for death by firing squad, the face mask for electrocution—that are foisted upon the condemned not only to restrict his gaze but also to protect witnesses from being horrified by his unsightly visage. The only restriction that a prisoner executed by lethal injection faces is the execution table that restrains him prone on his back;

his head movements are unrestricted, leaving him free to gaze into witness rooms surrounding the death chamber.

McVeigh's gaze prompted witnesses to feel that he was both conscious of and paid careful attention to their presence. Gauging from comments by the closed-circuit witnesses, McVeigh's staring was likely more marked for them than for live witnesses, since it was prolonged, and therefore interpreted as unexpected behavior or a breach of social norms.[22] An attentive gaze may indicate that an interaction is starting or is likely to start, serving as a summons to pay attention because the gazer is paying attention.[23] This awareness is not always positive or pleasant; a gaze can divide even as it unites, as in an openly hostile stare that objectifies its target.[24] As French philosopher Maurice Merleau-Ponty observed, people can be "stripped of existence" or "transformed into an object" by "being looked at by someone who dares not strike up any relationship."[25] Finally, a gaze may signify an attempt to establish dominance, threat, anger, aggression, or challenge.[26] The interpretation of another's gaze is therefore heavily dependent on social context and on personal perception.[27]

The fact that executions are usually framed as adversarial encounters between inmates and victim witnesses partially explains why witnesses interpreted McVeigh's gaze as confrontational or defiant. Witness responses suggest that they could have perceived McVeigh's gaze as one of two particularly aggressive gazes, a "stare-down" or a "hate stare." A stare-down is a "dominance encounter" in which one party holds another's gaze, a contest in which each attempts to outstress the other, ending only when one party looks away.[28] Jessie Sternburg wanted to stare down McVeigh at his trial in Denver: "I just stared at him, I said I'm gonna stare at you until you look me in the eye and he did. And I said . . . you're going to look away before I do." Both gazes are especially antagonistic and deliberately breach the nonstaring accord between strangers that Erving Goffman termed "civil inattention"; they are "insulting partly because [they] impl[y] the person stared at doesn't really count as a person at all."[29] McVeigh's remarks to his biographers suggest that he hoped to objectify the targets of his gaze in defiance of social norms, asserting his "right" to dominate and intimidate them.

"You Can Whip Me If You Want To": McVeigh's Communicative Gaze

McVeigh had different gazes for each type of witness. According to live witness Paul Howell, McVeigh had a "different kind of, thank [you]–type smile" for his witnesses and a "kind of like, okay guys, it's going to happen type situation" for media witnesses. These contrasted with his behaviors toward victim witnesses, where he "glared into the room, you know, trying to figure out who was who, who was in there and where we were standing at." Ron Brown, however, reported that "he had that cocky look. . . . he struck me as being—I guess, in control. He wanted to still be in control. And not talking and not saying anything, I guess in his head he probably thought he was still in control."

What is immediately obvious is that McVeigh's gaze did have communicative dimensions for remote witnesses, so much so that one journalist was prompted to refer to McVeigh's gaze as "a look they will long remember, the long hard stare into the camera" composed of a "blankness" and an "unblinking gaze."[30] Closed-circuit witnesses certainly perceived that McVeigh was attempting to send a message. Witnesses described his expression as confrontational ("staring" into the camera) and "stern" or "defiant" ("I've seen it a lot in my grandchildren. You know that kind of defiance of 'you can whip me if you want to but it's not hurting'"). They also characterized it as overtly malicious, terming it a "go to hell" or "eat shit and die" expression, one that "just spit on us all some more" and was "evil" ("It was almost like the devil was inside him, looking at us").[31] For Diane Leonard, McVeigh's expression was "very, very defiant until the last instant" until his facial expression relaxed upon his death. Witnesses also remarked that McVeigh's face registered pride or arrogance, that he flouted a "triumphant" or "fuck you all, I won" look, one that said, "I did the right thing and I'm not sorry" or "I'm willing to die for my idea."

Ironically, other witnesses described his expression as registering absence, explaining that it was blank ("nothing"), unremorseful ("no remorse"), uncaring ("didn't give a flip," "didn't care"), and free of suffering ("you're not hurting me," "no sign of discomfort," "showed no pain"). Still other closed-circuit witnesses asserted in media interviews or statements that McVeigh exhibited signs of fear. Survivor Calvin Moser said, "To me, he had the look of, 'I'm not in control of this. As much as I've criticized the government, the government has me.'"[32] Family member Oneta Johnson noted, "He looked up and stared at us, but I saw his jaw quiver."[33]

Several execution witnesses, unprompted by the interviewer, remarked on the similarities between McVeigh's gaze during the execution and his gaze in previous television images. Remote witness Diane Leonard noted, "He didn't just look. He had that same look in his eyes when they arrested him. Do you remember him coming out of the courthouse and that stern look on his face?

That's the look he had. . . . Like defiant. I did it. I did the right thing and I'm not sorry." Remote witness Jamie Blansett remarked, "Very cold. He was the whole time. Any time you ever saw him on TV." When asked to describe McVeigh's gaze, live witness Cameron Crawford replied:

I'd say leaning toward more like a glare like, you know, boy—I can't give him credit for anything. You know, the guy . . . has never had much of a look in his eye. Even when I listen to like that *60 Minutes* interview, I saw that not too long ago. . . . and I have wondered since then, why did he even look at us? Was he trying to give us something? I don't know."

McVeigh's defiant expression had a range of effects upon victims, from angering them to disappointing them to hurting them further or, in one case, enabling forgiveness. Many felt that it made McVeigh's toxic presence even more poisonous. "What I was hoping for, and I'm sure most of us were, we could see some kind of, maybe, 'I'm sorry,'" asserted live witness Paul Howell. "You know, something like that. We didn't get anything from his face."[34] Similarly, remote witness Jamie Blansett mentioned, "He died like he didn't care, and I cried because of that, because he did not care," and Ray Washburn observed, "He got the final word. . . . I thought I would feel something more satisfying."[35] Finally, Jay Sawyer, a nonparticipant closed-circuit witness whose mother was murdered in the bombing, remarked in a media interview, "Without saying anything he got the final word, absolutely. His teeth were clenched, just like when he was first arrested. His teeth were clenched, his lips were pursed, and just a blank stare. It was the same today."[36]

But according to Priscilla Salyers, confronting McVeigh face-to-face is what enabled her to have an intensely spiritual experience in which she forgave him:

I am still not looking at him, and he kind of raised up, and I think was glaring into the camera, and all of sudden it's like, you know because I have this faith. . . . all of sudden he came to me. . . . I started to think of him as Timothy McVeigh, the soul, and not Timothy McVeigh, the man, and I started praying for him that this is his last chance, this is his last breath, and I prayed for him and it just like overtook me. . . . I was able to let it go, I guess to me that was the true forgiveness, not "Oh yeah, Timothy, you could be my best buddy"–type forgiveness. So it's forgiveness in different stages. . . . To me this was a true forgiveness, letting it go.

But Dot Hill believed that McVeigh's presence actually began when she witnessed his execution, when she prayed that he would "with his last breath receive Jesus as his Lord and Savior so he could go to heaven":

> I wanted to see him pay, which meant he needed to die. And the whole time I'm sitting there [at the execution] I'm praying for him, . . . I'm praying that he seeks God's forgiveness and even while I'm praying that I'm thinking I wish I had never had this happen. I wish this had never happened, and I wish I'd never known him. I wish I'd never had to be praying for him.

In contrast, live witnesses did not sense that McVeigh was attempting to communicate with them. Paul Howell noted that McVeigh "glared" into the victim witness room, but he did not interpret anything significant in McVeigh's expression other than confusion: "We didn't get anything from his face."[37] Similarly, other than characterizing his look as being akin to a "glare," Cameron Crawford did not know whether McVeigh was "trying to give us [live witnesses] something." Live witnesses might have wished for more interaction; nonparticipant Anthony Scott confessed in a media interview, "I wish that there might have been eye to eye contact, but he couldn't see us."[38] Paul Howell's disappointment was also evident: "I was hoping to look at this man, but it didn't work, guys. So we went with what we felt like going in."[39] This communicative ambiguity may have made it difficult for live witnesses to categorize McVeigh's emotional state at the moment of his execution. Howell observed, "I mean, he's not a monster, guys. I mean, not when you're looking at him in the face. I mean, he's just a regular human being. But, you know, there's no facial expressions on him whatsoever so there was no way of knowing just exactly what he is and how he is."

Witnesses, whether live or closed-circuit, wanted to respond in turn to McVeigh's gaze. Dot Hill said that she wanted McVeigh to be able to see her, "just so that he could see that I'm not a monster. That we are not monsters, we're just people too. And all we did was go to work that day. That's it." Similarly, Doris Jones remarked, "I would like for him to look at my face and know the pain that I knew he's caused. And to see my daughter and to know that you killed my daughter and her baby." Paul Howell wanted to express defiance: "I wanted to see him when he was in the chair, like that, and I wanted him to see me. Because I wanted him to know that no matter what he did or didn't do, we were going to survive this thing and we would be better afterward." Similarly, Anthony Scott recalled, "I wanted him to see me, to somehow let him know that you didn't break the spirit that you thought you were going to break."

If McVeigh had been able to see into the victim witness room, he would have actually glimpsed 12 witnesses—10 living, breathing individuals and 2 photographs of murdered victims. A few family members brought in small photographs of their murdered loved ones. Cameron Crawford brought a photograph of his murdered sibling, and Peggy Broxterman an image of her murdered son. After entering the witnessing room in Terre Haute, both witnesses stood in the front row and placed their images up to the glass. As Crawford recalled:

> I was again lucky enough, I got in the front row and [another live witness] and I had both had a picture. . . . She had her [son's] picture, and we put them right up to the window. Not that he could see it. It was more symbolic, and we had to do it very discreetly because we had guards behind us. But, yeah, stuck a picture up there so [my sibling] could watch it happen.

Although witnesses expected the execution to be a moment of resolution and thus memory work, McVeigh's gaze did nothing to fulfill that expectation. With the exception of Priscilla Salyers, who was able to forgive McVeigh, witnesses did not gain the "satisfaction" from McVeigh's gaze that they could have if he had not appeared so defiant or nonplussed by the prospect of impending death. Instead, witnesses felt as if McVeigh were once again challenging them, although some were able to mitigate that sensation by realizing that they would walk out of the encounter alive whereas McVeigh would not. The intimacy of closed-circuit technology merely confirmed witnesses' earlier impressions of McVeigh. If witnesses found the execution to be "fulfilling" or "satisfying," it had to be for some other reason than his gaze, such as its status as the final legal proceeding, the moment when McVeigh was held accountable. Ultimately, witnesses who were unsettled by McVeigh's gaze returned to these same overarching concerns to explain why they felt relief after McVeigh was executed.

Dimensions of Silence in the McVeigh Execution

Like gaze, silence played a profound role in McVeigh's execution. Silence has a multitude of meanings; it can convey power or control, weakness and submission, knowledge or ignorance, affection or dislike, reverence or disgust, attention or distraction.[40] Silence is not merely a counter to speech, an absence bereft of verbal presence; this impoverished perspective conceptualizes man as a machine that chatters while functioning properly and is silent only when it breaks down.[41] Instead, silence, like speech, can accomplish numerous communicative tasks, including apology, refusal, complaint, and inquiry.[42] But for silence to be communicative, others must invest it with meaning, and this occurs within human interaction. To place silence and speech on the same communicative spectrum is not to equate one with the other; while words can initiate interaction, silence cannot.[43] When silence is meaningful, it may fulfill several social functions: a linkage function of connecting or disconnecting two or more people, an affective function of restoration or injury, a revelation function of disclosure or concealment, a judgmental function of approval or disapproval, and an activating function of thought or idleness.[44] The McVeigh execution highlighted three primary dimensions of silence: that of the witnesses, that of McVeigh himself, and that of the execution as imposing silence upon McVeigh.

"Almost Like a Family Reunion": Witnesses' Silence

At the FAA Center in Oklahoma City, family members and survivors engaged in intermittent conversation before the execution. Several witnesses spoke of this time as something of a reunion or social gathering. Dot Hill recalled that juice and fruit were available in the kitchen in the back part of the viewing room, and that "it was almost like just a little social gathering before a meeting." Similarly, Priscilla Salyers commented, "It had been a long while since a lot of us had been together, and we all were there for one purpose. . . . we were able to talk and laugh and share things that have gone on with our families because I mean we're like a whole community. . . . it's almost like a family reunion."

The social dimensions of collectively witnessing the execution were especially apparent for live witnesses, many of whom traveled to Terra Haute together, and all of whom dined together the evening before and the morning of the execution. Cameron Crawford, who already knew many of the other live witnesses, explained: "You only have 10 people, that I knew about half of us was really weird. So we had a nice sense of camaraderie right off the bat." He and the others shared a similar attitude toward the execution; they very much wanted to be there, and so poked fun at the many counselors and other professionals present at dinner the evening before the execution:

They were . . . I'm exaggerating, maybe 20. But I mean preachers, psychologists, psychiatrists, therapists. . . . it's sort of like they're just waiting for all of us to crack up or something. . . . we were in a pretty good mood given you-know-what. Maybe we hadn't thought about what we're getting ready to do, the gravity of it. . . . I think the people I was close to there kind of felt the same way. Like God, just get out. Anyway, we made a joke of it.

Crawford recalled that witnesses' "good mood" persisted through the execution itself: "I think there was one person and this was not even until we were in the [witness] room that one person seemed you know to be very solemn about it. . . . we were just kind of, I don't want to say joking and certainly not laughing, but it was not a somber experience in that room." Peggy Broxterman recalled, "When they first pulled the curtain and McVeigh was lying there, I said, 'You son of a bitch!' And someone in back of me went, 'Right on.'" "It was a happy, elated occasion. I was thrilled," she affirmed. Live witness and nonparticipant Sue Ashford later remarked, "It was very exciting for me because I've waited for this for so long. I didn't want him to breathe our air anymore."[45]

The atmosphere in the witnessing room in Oklahoma City was very different than the jocular atmosphere in Terre Haute. Despite the food and fellowship, an air of nervous anticipation was palpable in the FAA Center. Ray Washburn's spouse said that closed-circuit witnesses were "milling around," "really restless," and "on edge" before the execution began because "their anticipation was kinda getting to them." Priscilla Salyers remarked that different witnesses awaited the execution in differing frames of mind: "There were some that were just somber like me. . . . I remember [I heard] one woman go, 'This is a great day for an execution.' I mean, you had every feeling in there." Diane Leonard recalled, "It appeared to me that everybody I talked to was pretty nervous. One girl just passed out. She just was too overwhelmed. She stayed, though. She got better."

During the remote broadcast, witnesses were "very quiet," and participants did not remember any audible crying. Ray Washburn's spouse was allowed to describe to her husband what was going on, even though "everybody else was cautioned to be quiet, be orderly. . . . they didn't want any outbursts, they didn't want any kind of clapping or yelling or loud crying or anything like that." Priscilla Salyers was surprised by this silence: "I was amazed, when he actually died. . . . I really expected some people to, to have an outburst, clap or something." In Terra Haute, however, there was some talking in the execution chamber as some of the witnesses who had brought photographs made comments. Cameron Crawford recalled that one witness said, "'Hey, you son of a bitch, over here, look at this picture.' You know, yelling at him."

Thus, in McVeigh's execution, silence was situation-specific. While the experience of the closed-circuit witnesses was structured through silence, for live witnesses, the converse was true. It at first seemed surprising that live witnesses reported a noisier environment in Terre Haute than closed-circuit witnesses back in Oklahoma City; one might expect prison strictures would impose silence upon live witnesses, and that the greater the distance from the execution, the looser the controls might become. An explanation may be found, however, by focusing not on actual physical distance (how far removed witnesses were from McVeigh) but on communicative distance (whether the target of witness' communications was within range). This renders it more likely that closed-circuit witnesses in Oklahoma City had little reason to break silence because McVeigh, their communicative target, was literally remote, appearing through a mediated image. It was the live witnesses—separated from McVeigh by only a wall—who stood in closest proximity to him.[46]

Accordingly, live witnesses were much more likely than remote witnesses to attempt to communicate with or at McVeigh during the execution. Thus, while remote witnesses experienced McVeigh's gaze more intensely than did live witnesses, live witnesses' physical and therefore communicative proximity to McVeigh was far greater than that of remote witnesses. This prompted some live witnesses to take advantage of their proximity in order to verbally challenge or lambast McVeigh, suggesting that live witnessing may prompt the active release of more aggression than does remote witnessing. While remote witnesses were able to visually confront McVeigh, live witnesses enjoyed greater physical proximity to him, allowing them to assume an "active" role in the execution and providing a different confrontational opportunity.

"No Apology Was in That Man": Witness Perceptions of McVeigh's Silence

The Bureau of Prisons execution protocol manual provides an opportunity for the warden to invite the "condemned" to utter any "reasonably brief" last words that will then be "transcribed by a BOP staff member and provided to the media."[47] The condemned only has a very brief time to respond, and to refuse this invitation to give "last words" is to remain silent forever, barring a last-minute reprieve. But McVeigh did not make any final statement, remorseful or otherwise, opting instead to have a handwritten copy of William Ernest Henley's poem "Invictus" photocopied and distributed to media representatives.

Some execution witnesses wanted McVeigh to say something instead of remaining silent, but others were fearful that he would use the opportunity to inflict further injury. Witnesses' hopes for a remorseful statement were dimmed by their perceptions that it was not in McVeigh's nature to apologize; while they desired an apology, they either did not expect one or would not have believed McVeigh if he had apologized. As Ray Washburn remarked, "I think it'd have been important if he'd apologized, but I don't think he'd meant it. . . . no apology was really in that man as far as I could tell." Only one witness, Dot Hill, said that she was angered by McVeigh's silence, but she also was not surprised that McVeigh chose to remain silent in view of his military training. Some witnesses were thankful that McVeigh was silent, in view of the harmful statements he could have made, and grateful that he did not make "death sounds."

In communicative interactions, the refusal to speak can be troubling and potentially toxic, conveying animosity, disregard, distraction, or even stupidity.[48] In hostile situations colored by anger and violence, where silence appears the antithesis of noisy rage, silence can be a weapon, and giving someone "the silent treatment" may actually inflict the most wounding cuts.[49] When delivered in response to an offer or invitation, silence can communicate disengagement or disregard.[50] Here, silence embodies rejection—of the offer, and potentially of the offeror as well. Doris Jones perceived McVeigh's silence during his execution as an explicit rebuff: "He'd just been so defiant the whole time, and that I'm willing to die for my idea, my cause. I mean, he felt like he was a martyr . . . he was doing the same thing that I was doing. He talked the talk. He's going to go all the way through." In the point-counterpoint pattern of the warden's proffer and McVeigh's refusal to speak, witnesses interpreted McVeigh's silence as his response. They were not interested in McVeigh's actual reasons for remaining silent. Rather, they assumed they already knew them, and these assumptions allowed them to interpret his silence as pregnant with defiance.

McVeigh's silence confirmed witnesses' prior impressions that he was a defiant and remorseless offender. It therefore did not disturb the narrative frameworks they had built concerning McVeigh's identity as a perpetrator or his relationship to the Oklahoma City bombing. If anything, McVeigh's silence was a blessing in light of the fact that he could have taken that final opportunity to further irritate witnesses in some way. Such a gesture would undoubtedly have been far more unsettling than his expected silence. Thus, although it was not ideal, McVeigh's silence did not unduly jeopardize witnesses' memory work.

"He's Gone": McVeigh's Death as Imposing Silence

Although many characteristics of an "ideal" execution, such as an apology, were not present, McVeigh's execution was ultimately successful because it effected a silence in which victims' families and survivors could find therapeutic respite and peace. The execution permanently silenced McVeigh; a living Timothy McVeigh had been simultaneously a reminder of his potential to "jab" at victims, of the bombing, and of injustice. As Richard Williams asserted, "You know, after someone is executed you are completely finished with every battle you have to fight in that arena. No more McVeigh battles to fight. Don't have to worry about what's gonna come out in the newspaper that he said to some reporter somewhere." Susan Urbach recalled, "I was so glad . . . the day of the execution and after that when those media, those blocks of media trucks left the memorial. . . . I knew from that moment on, we would never have the same amount of coverage. It wasn't the same kind of news story ever again. And I was grateful for that."

Participants characterized the postexecution silence very differently depending on whether they were for or against the death penalty. Those opposing the death penalty spoke of relief from recurrent *media* activity—not from McVeigh himself—and felt that McVeigh's media visibility declined drastically after his death. Diane Dooley recalled that "it went on for a little while, but . . . there was a finality to it after he was executed," and Jordan Holt said, "I just wanted the media to quit talking about it [the execution]. . . . I just wanted as much return to normalcy as I could have." But Holt noted that, while diminished coverage was an improvement, it would also have "died down" if McVeigh had been sentenced to life imprisonment. Urbach specifically attributed a sense of relief following the execution to media coverage instead of McVeigh's presence:

> It's not so much that he is or isn't alive, it's that his—here we go again, access to media. See he had access to media, and you know maybe that's another thing, maybe that's another type of punishment that needs to be given is nonaccess to media because if he wouldn't have been writing peo-

ple and calling people and giving interviews and making pronouncements and so on, you know, it'd be a lot easier to live with him being in prison for the rest of his life.

But for participants who supported the death penalty, relief stemmed from the termination of McVeigh's life, not the cessation of media coverage. These individuals placed the blame on McVeigh; it was as if the media were just doing their job, fulfilling their expected (albeit unfortunate) social function by broadcasting news of and statements from McVeigh. Charlie Younger said, "When those people are executed and you know they're *gone*, there is a change for the people that were victims of that crime. It's gotta be better. It was for me." Describing her relief after the execution, Jessie Sternburg observed, "It's still death, but yeah, there was that relief. We don't have to hear his crap anymore. He can't hurt us. He's gone. He got what he deserved. . . . You know he can't write no books anymore, he can't grant no interviews." She could only forgive McVeigh "when his mouth was shut."

Most death penalty proponents connected their relief to McVeigh's inability to intentionally or incidentally harm others through his visibility. Their remarks illustrated that they took McVeigh's communications personally. Jamie Blansett explained, "I don't have to listen to his mouth ever again, ever. . . . That's what I wanted. You know, I wanted someone to silence him because all he did was hurt people still and he got his kicks out of it. . . . even in prison he still had freedom of speech." Paul Howell remarked, "And him [McVeigh] and I had a disagreement or conversation going on between the two of us most of the time. . . . I wanted to go because I wanted to see this man shut up and leave us alone." For Howell, McVeigh's willingness to use the media to aggravate family members and survivors was one reason he felt McVeigh needed to be executed:

McVeigh, even though he knew that he was getting the death sentence, he was defiant all the way up to the point where it actually happened, okay? He would speak out to the media. He would tell the families to grow up, it's collateral damage that we killed your kids, you know. And everything that he did was doing nothing but hurting the family members here in Oklahoma. So the only way for us to have any kind of peace was to execute this man. Now on Nichols, Nichols is a little different because since he's been tried and convicted, you don't hear about him. And so even though he was 90 percent involved . . . I can live with him being in prison for the rest of his life, for the simple reason that he is not defiant and he's not going out and getting on the news and so forth and trying to hurt the family members.

Similarly, Doris Jones, a family member and closed-circuit witness, explicitly referred to the execution as effectively silencing McVeigh:

Seeing it through and to know that he really was silenced. That he really is dead. I saw him die. It can't be any of this—we saw President Kennedy on a yacht or we saw . . . you know, Elvis Presley working at Burger King or whatever, you know. I mean, you hear all this crap. And, I mean, I know I saw him die, and I know he is silenced. And that is what I wanted. I wanted him to be silenced, and I saw him being silenced.

Participants agreed that the execution at once muzzled the media and stifled McVeigh. Numerous participants described this feeling as "relief," implying that the execution had therapeutic consequences. But upon first consideration, it is unclear exactly what family members and survivors meant by this term. Like other ambiguous concepts such as closure and forgiveness, relief is an illusorily simple concept. To obtain greater clarity, it is imperative to further interrogate this sensation—how it was experienced, and what reconstructive accomplishments it facilitated.

Often, participants experienced relief as a physiological sensation. As Cameron Crawford described:

Witnessing his execution was so cathartic for me. . . . the minute he was dead . . . the weight lifted off your shoulders. Peace. I mean, I felt a real peace. Within myself. And again because I'm not carrying him in my head. He's gone. He's out of my head now. And that's more room for [my murdered sibling]. To think I have to share room with that son of a bitch with such a nice guy like my [sibling]. That sucks.

Similarly, Paul Howell said the execution had a definite physical impact: "And so after the execution was over with, it was just like a 10-pound pack had come off my back. And so it was just a big relief. I knew from that point on we could all start healing good." McVeigh's death enabled Dot Hill to "put him to rest," restoring her physical and psychological autonomy. As she explained:

I'm not sure it was until after he was dead that I began to kind of let him go . . . from having any control in my thoughts. Not to say that I don't think of the bombing every day and him as a result of that, but not to the level of controlling my emotions. . . . I don't think he intentionally did [anything affirmative to control my thoughts], it was just knowing that he was alive.

Some felt that the execution unshackled them from McVeigh. Doris Jones felt liberated: "He was there until the execution. I mean, yeah, I totally felt bound to him. . . . and then the execution kind of set me free." Stan Mayer also felt released from McVeigh's presence: "It was a wonderful thing in terms of . . . he has not hurt me or continued his terror since the day he died." McVeigh's death also made his presence easier for participants to compartmentalize. Diane Leonard described the execution as "the closing of a chapter": "If you're in the midst of that chapter, you're dealing with it day in and day out and that went on for several years. . . . I knew that once that execution was behind us, that chapter on Tim McVeigh was closed."

Relief was also tied to the fact that legal proceedings were over, and accountability had finally been obtained. Many described the extraction of accountability as a transaction, frequently referring to McVeigh's need to "pay for" his crimes. Until the execution, McVeigh "had not finished the process of paying for his crime yet," in Dot Hill's words. Faith Moore emphasized, "To me, the execution is him paying his debt for his crime." She felt that Nichols and Fortier had not yet paid their debts: "They'll never be held accountable until the day they die and stand before God and have to give an account for what they've done." Vicki Hamm derived "a sense of justice" from the fact that "the person I felt was responsible had paid a price for what he did." Participants needed to make sure that McVeigh's accounting was complete. As Hamm explained:

I was bound to him because I had to follow this through and find out what happened, and in that way I was tied to him until the end of it. And the end of it was his execution. . . . that gave me a sense of peace, and it's like I didn't have to focus on him so much anymore because that part was over.

But not everyone experienced emotions as overwhelming as ebullience or even as palpable as relief. Sometimes, participants were conscious of a much quieter sense of finality. Survivor Richard Williams explained the impact of the execution as not a sense of relief but "a moving on to the next phase of my life and my career": "It's another part of that process that we had to go through to get to where we are now. . . . It just wasn't for me on that particular day the most important thing in my life."

Furthermore, not all participants obtained respite from McVeigh's presence; a few still felt him in their lives, either at certain times or more frequently. "In a way he's still there. I mean, it's not like just because physically he's not here that he's still not part of my whole life experience," Diane Dooley clarified. "There are times I feel like he's an intrusion. When I can't do things with my hand, like buttoning my little girl's buttons. . . . yeah, I'm still mad at him at times. So he's still an intrusion, but it's not front and center, 24 hours a day." Richard Williams also insisted that McVeigh's presence had not vanished completely, stressing, "When he was executed he was still there. . . . what happened was still there and the story of him was still there and the information was still there. . . . You can't close that out just because he was executed." Bud Welch lamented an absence of relief from execution, noting, "Even people that are not anti–death penalty that have gone through, for example, Tim McVeigh's execution. . . . They are still angry, still [have] not dealt with it, even though they delivered the body to them."

The execution was especially troubling to anti–death penalty participants who felt that, if anything, it strengthened McVeigh's presence. Ernestine Hill Clark became aware of McVeigh's presence only at the trigger moment of his execution and felt that event affected her physical well-being: "I did feel sick, I mean, just sick at heart for several weeks after the execution. . . . I just felt the finality of that and the fact that now we would never get to interview him in his 60s or 70s, that the mystery would go on." To cope, Clark had to distance herself from everything having to do with the execution:

> When I was around too many people that were rejoicing over the fact that he was going to be killed or actually rejoicing on the day he was killed, I had to go into isolation, because it just, it just hurt my soul. As much as I hated what he did and in the beginning hated him, I could not stand the fact that these people were rejoicing at his execution, and I had to get away. . . . And in Oklahoma, that put me, I mean, I was in a minority so small I wasn't even sure I could find somebody else who agreed with me. That was very difficult.

Those family members and survivors who felt relief experienced these physical sensations and psychological consequences for varying lengths of time after the execution. As the moments immediately following his death became first hours and then days and weeks, as witnesses returned home and resumed their routines, as the media disassembled their platforms and departed Oklahoma City and Terre Haute (all but forsaking these locales for New York City exactly three months later on September 11, 2001), and after coverage of McVeigh and his final moments slowed from a torrent to a trickle and then ceased, most family members and survivors realized that McVeigh's toxic presence had either greatly diminished or dissolved. No longer did they have to live in McVeigh's shadow. The execution had certainly not erased what McVeigh had done, but it was much harder for a dead man to exert control over the living.

A Very Easy Death: Witness Objections to McVeigh's Passing

Many witnesses were angered by the ease of McVeigh's passing, which seemed manifestly inequitable when compared with the terrible deaths of their loved ones, colleagues, and friends murdered in the Murrah Building as well as the years of physiological and psychological agony endured by bombing survivors. In other words, although McVeigh was dead, it was not fair that he had apparently escaped comparable suffering. But how did participants form expectations about McVeigh's execution? And, more important, if, as many witnesses claimed, they knew what execution by lethal injection entailed prior to witnessing McVeigh's death, why were they disappointed when McVeigh did not suffer?

Dead Man Watching: Learning about Executions in a Culture of Life

Witnesses' expectations of what McVeigh's execution would be like were more likely to be influenced by media depictions than actual life experiences. Movies such as *Dead Man Walking* and *The Green Mile* helped participants to visualize what different types of executions—lethal injections and electrocutions—might look like. Released in January 1996, *Dead Man Walking* was based on the experiences of anti–death penalty advocate Sister Helen Prejean. Many believed it supported the death penalty, or even that it galvanized the victims' rights movement. As Cameron Crawford stated:

Oddly enough, the thing that kind of puts me over to maybe the ultimate penalty is death is *Dead Man Walking*. . . . [Actress] Susan Sarandon and [director] Tim Robbins are both, you know, the most liberal people in Hollywood. They're making this movie trying to turn people against the death penalty. . . . I think it was a turning point for victims. It was a big shift at that time. Not just our case, but I think just thinking all around about victims' rights. Really started that. That was a time when we started to see a good shift in our favor.

A few participants specifically mentioned that *Dead Man Walking* had educated them about execution procedures. Tom Hall recalled, "It was probably a year or two years before the execution, a friend of mine rented this movie, *Dead Man Walking*, . . . and said you need to watch this show, . . . so that was kinda one story, but I think I pretty well understood it." The execution scene from *Dead Man Walking* actually helped to persuade Crawford that execution was the most appropriate—and perhaps satisfying—punishment for McVeigh:

He's walking [to the chamber] and one thing he said, "They're not taking my shoes off. I'm dying in these shoes." He has slippers and a diaper on. It's like . . . ok. Now I can see Tim McVeigh in a diaper scared shitless. You know walking down this hallway, you know what, maybe that one moment of fear . . . maybe that is worse than spending 70 years in a cage. I don't know.

Other participants learned about executions through other television dramas or broadcast news. Angela Richerson commented, "We have seen something about how they do it . . . some of the TV programs, it's like euthanasia of a dog or animal, and it's a lot easier than . . . the way a lot of the people they kill die." The purported ease of execution by lethal injection prompted many to form opinions about this method prior to McVeigh's execution; Jessie Sternburg observed that "the execution process was entirely too kind. That's what I thought. This isn't punishment. You know, if I take my dog and have him put to sleep tomorrow, they are not going to pump him full of Benadryl to make him comfortable. They're just going to kill him." The fact that Oklahoma frequently executed inmates meant that residents were routinely exposed to such stories through the news. Dr. Paul Heath noted, "Mostly I got that from the media, . . . having the death penalty in Oklahoma, you heard a little bit about it on many occasions in terms of injections and how it was done and how they died, those kinds of things. So I was fairly familiar with it." Therefore, the stage was set for witnesses to interpret McVeigh's death by comparing it to other dramatic and educational representations of executions.

It is not surprising that most family members and survivors derived much of their information about death and executions from television programming and news media rather than from life experience. In the United States, we tend to keep our dead at a safe distance; funeral homes and hospitals sequester death and render it a matter for medical and mortuary experts.[51] Death itself is in "bad taste," unclean and unhealthy.[52] As any good forensic television drama reveals, dead bodies are invested with noxious gases, leaking fluids, and other unpalatable, impure, and unhealthy substances. On one level, a corpse is pollution, unwanted and decaying debris to be buried as quickly as possible, even after it is embalmed.[53] Yet religious salvation may accompany and sanctify what is unclean; the metamorphosis of the dying body into the corpse enables a rebirth, a mystic infusion of the divine into the decaying.[54] Thus, a dying body is a site of great physical, cultural, and potentially spiritual tension between the clean and the unclean, between the earthly and the divine, between the profane and the sacred.

But just because death is now more invisible does not mean that dead bodies are culturally insignificant. How we approach dead bodies is always tied to our particular cultural vantage point. Death prompts a concern with bodily boundaries;[55] it is a transition between states of being or, more properly, between being and nonbeing. Physical or social spaces where dying or dead bodies come in contact with living and healthy bodies are uncomfortable because they represent human vulnerabilities.[56]

Nevertheless, bodies remain important mourning objects. In the West, there is a cultural myth that mourners need a body to grieve; the body supposedly makes a loss "real," and grieving may be impeded by its absence.[57] Thus, funerals are sometimes held for mourners despite the absence of any tangible remains to bury.[58] Hence, our cultural definition of death includes something other than the cessation of breath; mechanical means or bodily processes alone do not determine when life departs. Our visual awareness of another's death is the capstone to the dying process, rendering death something that must first be seen, then pronounced, before it becomes official. This principle is deeply troubling in the aftermath of tragedies such as the Oklahoma City bombing or the attacks of 9/11, when it may not be possible to locate remains, denying survivors not only "the physical arrangements of mourning . . . but also the psychic capacity to absorb and feel these deaths."[59]

As execution witnesses discovered, the act of witnessing another person die illuminates an inherent experiential and epistemological distance between the living and the dying. Witnesses to death cannot apprehend the physical experience of dying; it is alien and therefore unnatural.[60] To communicate the dying experience, we must translate it from the private into the public and back again,[61] often through visual mediums such as sculpture, film, and photography. Such representations help to stabilize death, restoring order and balance and safely distancing viewers from death's immediacy.[62] These objects confront viewers with reflexive awareness of death's inevitability.[63]

The importance of sight and the visible body as a trigger for mourning and memory work has several implications for McVeigh's execution. Like the televised portrayals of executions that educated many family member and survivors about lethal injection, the visual experience of McVeigh's execution was mediated by architecture and photography. For both live and closed-circuit witnesses, McVeigh's death occurred at a distance, framed in one instance by a viewing window that did not permit interaction between the prisoner and victim witnesses, and facilitated in the other by closed-circuit broadcast and overhead camera placement. This made the execution the last in a long series of mediated images that had injected McVeigh into participants' lives. It was nothing new for mechanical portals to offer a window into his soul. From first to last, McVeigh's toxic presence had been intertwined with and engendered by electronic representations; it was commenced or cultivated by perp walk footage, nurtured by trial broadcasts, and quashed or concluded by execution images. Ironically, these mediated images brought families and survivors extraordinarily close to McVeigh at the same time as they created an irreconcilable distance between them. The closer they got to McVeigh, the farther away most wanted to be.

Witnesses alleged that McVeigh's execution was in several senses transformative and therapeutic. It enabled a sense of relief, a respite from McVeigh's presence, and a sense of peace. How was the act of witnessing the execution linked to these sensations? Did the sight of a man slipping into sleep and then passing away help or hinder memory work? What, if anything, did the sight of McVeigh's death communicate to witnesses?

"The Easy Way Out": The Execution as Image

Visual depictions of death both are part of and also affect death's cultural interpretation. Death images are not merely visual representations of life's end. They also acquire a variety of other meanings. Some are peaceful, heroic, or otherwise redemptive; others are violent, demeaning, and disturbing. A peaceful death typically does not involve pain or suffering and may consist of an elderly individual lying serenely in his bed at home surrounded by mourning friends and family. Such a death is a profound contrast to murder, the shocking, violent, sudden ripping away of a life. The more painful and prolonged the experience of death, the more terrible that death becomes; that is why torture is an aggravating factor, increasing a defendant's odds of receiving a death sentence. Such terrible deaths merit special consequences. Whereas mourning and funereal ceremony seem appropriate to commemorate a peaceful, heroic, or redemptive death, murder requires something more—inquiry, accountability, punishment. These deaths are abnormal occurrences that must be taken apart, studied, and understood in order to create a "record" of the fatal circumstances and to prevent similar episodes from occurring in the future.

Photographic conventions reflect our responses to these diverse types of deaths, as illustrated by a comparison between McVeigh's execution and mourning and forensic photography. Mourning photographs are thought to aid grieving, resolving the troubling contradiction between keeping the deceased's memory alive and accepting the finality of loss.[64] One convention of Victorian mourning photography was the "last sleep," which conveyed that death was gentle and painless and did not disfigure.[65] Subjects were most often posed seated in a chair or lying abed, and not in a coffin.[66] Sometimes the deceased's eyes were opened or painted as being open after the photograph was taken.[67] Today, photographs of stillborn babies taken shortly after delivery portray the infant dressed and swaddled in blankets, very much like a living newborn.

But not all postmortem photographs are cherished by loving families; in forensic photographs of crime scenes, the deceased's identity is almost incidental. Forensic photographers are primarily concerned not with preserving the dignity of the deceased but with portraying the manner of his death. These "official" images of violent death are especially shocking and troublesome because they render visible what lies beneath the skin, what is meant to remain hidden.[68] Taken after horrific wrongdoing, these photographs represent inquiries into the unnatural, summoning viewers to create an investigatory narrative.[69] But crime scene photographs also symbolize the assertion of control and allow officials to interrogate the murdered body so as to reconstruct a biography of death. The murdered body arguably retains more agency than bodies that meet a natural end, raising new questions instead of putting old ones to rest.[70]

Images of McVeigh's execution exhibited characteristics of both private memorial photography and forensic images. Like memorial photography, they offered acknowledgment of death and the potential for peace and served as a confirmation of his death that could aid survivors in coming to terms with loss. This explains why participants believed that witnessing McVeigh's execution was in some sense therapeutic. Both types of images provided survivors with a tangible representation so that they did not have to rely on imagination. Lethal injection is considered the most serene, "humane" execution method, one that induces a sleep, invoking the Victorian photographic theme of "eternal slumber." Thus, the execution conveyed awareness of an ending, offering therapeutic confirmation to those hungry for legal finality.

At the same time, McVeigh's death was effected with the same meticulous, clinical precision that a forensic photographer would employ in photographing a crime scene. Like forensic pictures, images of McVeigh's execution obtained significance not through a commemoration of his life—thereby validating and valuing him as a subject and human being—but through the communication and confirmation of his death. But that death was an untimely end, outside of the natural life cycle. Witnesses interrogated McVeigh's body by viewing his execution. Although taking another's life is the ultimate act of violence, McVeigh's death appeared to be so rapid and peaceful that witnesses did not perceive the lethal injection to be a violent act. Though unnaturally induced, it resembled a peaceful, rapid, and painless passing. Accordingly, a number of execution witnesses felt that this peaceful death was a manifest injustice; various reactions included statements that McVeigh should have been electrocuted, hanged, or mutilated. Because live and remote witnesses perceived McVeigh's death to be a "response" to the 168 murders and countless instances of suffering McVeigh had dealt to innocents, they contrasted his manner of death with victims' terrible deaths and survivors' years of physical and mental suffering and recuperation.

There was much sentiment among witnesses that lethal injection was too "easy" of a death for McVeigh. Doris Jones emphasized, "I think he should be hanged, you know, and in . . . public . . . because injection was too easy. Even the electric chair execution to me, was too easy. But of course that's been outlawed and that didn't happen of course. . . . I wanted something severe." Witnesses were angered that McVeigh passed peacefully as if he were going to sleep, without any evidence of pain upon his countenance. Ray Washburn's spouse remarked, "He pissed me off 'cause he didn't show anything. I wanted him to do a little sufferin'. It upset me because he didn't." Dot Hill also wanted McVeigh's death to be more violent: "I don't think it was gruesome enough. I think it should have been more painful. I think it should have been the electric chair at the minimum. . . . He just went to sleep. That's the easy way out." Jamie Blansett wished McVeigh's death would have been more akin to the deaths of his victims: "To be honest with you I wanted them to blow him up. I wanted him to be hurt. I think he was actually afraid 'cause it was the unknown, but I wanted him to be mutilated like my friends were."

Some witnesses found it unsettling that McVeigh's eyes remained open even after he was pronounced dead, creating the impression that he was still alive. Surprisingly, only live witness Paul Howell commented on this unsettling development, although he recalled that it also disturbed others. Howell described the fact that McVeigh died with his eyes open as "jarring" and said that it "bothered" him:

> And I really didn't realize how bad it was until I got back to Oklahoma City. And I talked to some of the people out at the FAA Center, that was up at the FAA Center. And they told me that was the last thing, they had seen him staring completely at them. And it really bothered the heck out of a lot of people. . . . Even if they had to delay it for a second or two for somebody to walk in and close his eyes. That is something that I don't think anybody ought to see.

Howell recalled that this unnerving development prompted witnesses to question whether or not McVeigh was in fact dead: "A lot of people thought, 'Well is he dead, is he not?' And they didn't realize he was even dead until they turned off the TV. . . . I was concerned, not so much for me but for the people there in Oklahoma City because they're the ones who've seen it and we didn't."

Witnesses were also disconcerted by the fact that McVeigh took only moments to die and juxtaposed this brief interim to the years of suffering caused by the bombing. Jamie Blansett remarked, "I was [angry] 'cause I thought, you know, this hasn't taken any time to kill him and you know it took hours to get some people out, some people didn't come out alive. You know, I have friends that are still getting glass out of their body." She compared the brevity of the execution to the length and complexity of attendance preparations and to a restroom visit she made shortly before the execution began: "My [support person] goes, 'We got up at 3 o'clock in the morning to come down here for this?' 'Cause I just thought it'd take a long time. . . . It took me longer to get out of the restroom than it took for him to die." She approved of McVeigh's death sentence and was glad she decided to attend the execution, but was disappointed it seemed so banal: "To me it was a letdown because it didn't last long enough. I wanted him to suffer. I wanted him to hurt, you know. . . . people that were hurt had to walk, to endure the pain." Live witnesses also exhibited anger at the speed of his death; Sue Ashford said in an interview immediately following the execution, "He didn't suffer at all. . . . The man just went to sleep or, as I said, the monster did. I think they should have done the same thing to him as he did in Oklahoma."[71] Thus, participants' remarks illustrated their belief that an offender's death should closely resemble the death(s) of his victim(s) in terms of suffering and duration.

An "Ideal" Execution

Institutions such as the criminal justice system and the mass media frequently hold executions out as points of resolution or "closure" for victims' families, proceedings that enable them to feel relief after years of waiting in sentencing limbo. It is not surprising, then, that the concept of a "hallmark execution" could turn upon the reconciliation of the condemned to his crime and of the victim's family to the condemned. Analyzing postexecution media interviews with murder victims' families, legal scholars Samuel Gross and Daniel Matheson identified elements of a "hallmark execution." In this "ideal" execution, the condemned looks directly at the victim's family members and apologizes honestly, the victim's family accepts the apology and forgives the offender, and the killer achieves peace and is reconciled to God before being put to death.[72] Notably, the prisoner's visible suffering is not mentioned; presumably, if the victim's family is reconciled to him, there is no need for relatives to obtain satisfaction from his suffering.

McVeigh's execution exhibited none of these qualities; instead, his gaze unsettled witnesses and, in conjunction with his silence, confirmed their prior impressions that he was a defiant and remorseless offender. Yet, victim witnesses characterized the execution as satisfying in that it enabled them to reconnect once more with one another and silenced both McVeigh and the news media. McVeigh's execution, then, ultimately succeeded as an "ideal" execution because it was open to all who had provided notice that they wanted to view it. This suggests that whether or not any execution is "ideal" actually depends on the circumstances of the crime as well as the offender's behavior prior to execution.

McVeigh's execution was also successful in that it was expeditiously carried out, almost four years to the day since his death sentence. Only then did participants feel the dust could settle, silence descend, and narrative frameworks of memory solidify. While McVeigh's defiant gestures may have unsettled victim witnesses and a refusal to deliver apologetic last words might have saddened them, neither behavior was particularly surprising at this late stage. Similarly, the fact that his death appeared peaceful in complete contrast to his victims' murders did not shock witnesses already angered by a perceived systemic imbalance between defendants' rights and victims' marginalization. The surety of McVeigh's death—and the diminishment or termination of the victim-offender relationship—was thus the most crucial factor for victim witnesses, and McVeigh's execution accomplished this objective.

In light of this conclusion, let us reconsider McVeigh's final handwritten statement, the words that he intended to be his parting shot. The quatrains of William Ernest Henley's poem "Invictus" resound with defiance and stoic resolve:

> Out of the night that covers me,
> Black as the Pit from pole to pole,
> I thank whatever gods may be
> For my unconquerable soul.
>
> In the fell clutch of circumstance
> I have not winced nor cried aloud.
> Under the bludgeonings of chance
> My head is bloody, but unbowed.
>
> Beyond this place of wrath and tears
> Looms but the Horror of the shade,
> And yet the menace of the years
> Finds, and shall find, me unafraid.
>
> It matters not how strait the gate,
> How charged with punishments the scroll.
> I am the master of my fate:
> I am the captain of my soul.[73]

Departing the live and remote execution viewing sites, witnesses could literally and figuratively leave McVeigh behind in the lethal injection chamber. Although McVeigh surely meant these verses as one last sardonic salute to the world, they more accurately described the freedom that awaited family members and survivors. Execution witnesses were profoundly conscious of the fact that they had survived both the bombing and McVeigh as they stepped, "bloody, but unbowed," into an auspicious June morning. At last, McVeigh's control over their emotions, their news, and their world was over. Now his legacy lay in their hands. And they were determined to ensure that, in the words of Robin Brown, "he's going down in history as a cold-blooded killer, but not as a voice for change."

Conclusion

McVeigh Memorialized

Nine years after his execution, we are left worrying that Timothy McVeigh's voice from the grave echoes amid a new rising tide of American anti-government extremism. On this date which holds great meaning for the anti-government movement, the McVeigh tapes are a "can't turn away, riveting" reminder.

—Rachel Maddow, "The McVeigh Tapes,"
MSNBC April 19, 2010

It is clear now, more than 15 years after the Oklahoma City bombing and 10 years after McVeigh's execution, that although memories of McVeigh and his coconspirators have faded, their presences have not been altogether banished. Attention has now shifted from the duties of prosecution and execution to the difficult task of incorporation—how best to acknowledge and explain the role that McVeigh, Nichols, and Fortier played in the bombing without giving them further credit or airtime. This task has challenged family members, survivors, and Oklahoma City National Memorial and Museum personnel to negotiate the perpetrators' presences in new and different ways. McVeigh, most of all, is a critical part of the Oklahoma City bombing story, a narrative now told and retold through so many different media: news media, the memorial, even high school textbooks. McVeigh's legacy has been consigned to history, and to the hands of those who will write it.

After June 11, 2001, media coverage of McVeigh gradually ceased, particularly after the events of September 11, 2001, put Oklahoma City forever in the shade three months to the day after McVeigh died. The terrorist attacks abruptly tore the news media's focus away from Oklahoma City, which perversely had positive effects for many family members and survivors. According to Tom Hall, declining media coverage about McVeigh and the bombing led to an increase in well-being for many bombing victims, particularly those who could not leave the media until the media left them:

> The instant 9/11 happened up in New York, that took the whole spotlight off of us tremendously. . . . it's sad to say, but it did the people here more good than anything when that happened. The fact that it got the spotlight off of them and it quit pulling off the scab there for a week, so to speak. . . . And a lot of people here had gotten themselves wrapped up in the attention that the news media brought with them. It kind of consumed some people, and when that went away, I saw some of those people get better.

Paradoxically, over time McVeigh has become a more visible actor in narratives of the Oklahoma City bombing, which in the past had shied away from focusing upon the perpetrators in favor of victims, family members, survivors, and rescue workers. It took a decade and a half for McVeigh's most in-depth media interview to be broadcast, long past the time when Oklahoma City—and America—believed that they had heard the last of him. But at 9:00 p.m. on April 19, 2010, the bombing's 15th anniversary, viewers who tuned in to MSNBC for a special edition of the *Rachel Maddow Show* entitled "The McVeigh Tapes: Confessions of an American Terrorist" heard McVeigh describe how he had planned and carried out this terroristic act. McVeigh's voice, captured on interview tapes belonging to his biographers Lou Michel and Dan Herbeck, at last described the conspiracy, the bombing, and its aftermath, albeit at a strange and arguably inappropriate time.

To create the documentary, MSNBC first licensed the tapes from Michel and Herbeck and then digitized an avatar resembling McVeigh to re-create Michel's interviews and depict the events leading up to and following the blast. A press release touting the documentary boasted that "viewers will hear Timothy McVeigh's chilling confession in his own words for the first time."[1] The release also purported to give victims the last word, emphasizing that "survivors and family members of the bombing victims are given a voice in the film, bravely stepping forward to offer the final word on the true impact and meaning of McVeigh's brutal attack."[2]

Personnel at the Oklahoma City National Memorial reported that an MSNBC film crew visited the site in December 2009, requesting that wreaths decorating the survivor chairs be removed so as not to date their footage, that they be given complete access to all sites including the archives, and that all licensing be arranged. In addition, they only wanted to show the outside of the National Memorial and did not want to reference it in their broadcast.

After asking the film crew to leave—the first time she had done so in her tenure at the memorial—executive director Kari Watkins composed an e-mail to victims' families and survivors, informing them that

> in my gut opinion, they only wanted faces and photographs to be the b-roll as we call it in TV news to cover the audio track of Timothy McVeigh and I could NOT get a comfort level with this. . . . I couldn't sleep suspecting all they wanted [was] all the pictures from this place, but had no interest in telling the story about what the Memorial & Museum stands for and what we do every day. . . . I regret this, because we could probably all learn something from these tapes, but I was not successful in convincing them [that] tell[ing] the story of this Institution (Memorial & Museum) was as important as the public hearing McVeigh's voice.[3]

In an e-mail sent on December 15, 2009, to the Memorial's Conscience Committee, operations director Joanne Riley, who had been involved with the Oklahoma City National Memorial and Museum from its earliest days, related, "They are soliciting family members, survivors, and rescue workers to include their voices in some sort of format to be included with the interviews they allegedly have of McVeigh." "If you want to be interviewed, of course, it is totally your decision," Riley affirmed. "It is your story." She emphasized, however, that "this is NOT a Memorial project. We will not allow our story to be told in the voice of McVeigh or without any editorial control."

Riley's e-mail likely had a profound effect on family members' and survivors' willingness to be interviewed for the documentary; thereafter, many individuals who had signed up to be interviewed canceled. Survivor Richard Williams no doubt spoke for many when he applauded Watkins's actions in an e-mail reply: "I personally would want to hear what McVeigh has to say. I have for 15 years now but not at the expense of the integrity of the family members, survivors, rescue workers, and those from the community that have helped guide us these past years."[4]

For his part, documentary producer and writer Toby Oppenheimer seemed surprised by these negative reactions, and in an online question-and-answer session attributed family members' and survivors' unwillingness to be interviewed to a purported reluctance to recall and discuss the bombing:

> Visiting Oklahoma City for the purposes of this film was very difficult. I was quite astounded by what a raw nerve the bombing still is 15 years later

among the citizens of the city. It was very tough finding survivors of the tragedy who were interested in speaking with us, as they understandably didn't want to revisit the painful memories associated with the tragedy. Some survivors who did agree to sit down for interviews often called back a day later to politely back out. We were eventually very fortunate to have a handful of extremely open, articulate survivors and family members come forward to share their feelings about the tragedy. Their involvement was crucial to making this film as powerful and effective as it is.[5]

The broadcast was potentially upsetting in other ways as well. Joanne Riley remarked, "I'm the one that works with the families and survivors and rescue workers, and I was pretty upset over the whole tape thing because I remember one family member saying the only thing that's really accomplished for me is if we do not have to hear from him anymore." The *Maddow Show* broadcast came as something of a surprise because it brought her into a new and uncomfortable intimacy with McVeigh: "I had never even heard a recording of his voice before until I saw that, and it just kind of freaked me out. I watched a little bit, and I thought, you know, I can't, I cannot watch this." Riley criticized the broadcast for cherry-picking family members and survivors whom she considered unrepresentative: "If I was to go out and pick a representation of the people, the family members, survivors, or rescue workers here in Oklahoma City, those would not have been the people I would have picked. Okay? Absolutely, hands down, not. And I know them. I know all of them." Riley believed that her involvement with the memorial had fundamentally changed her ability to read or view material on McVeigh: "Because I deal with the other side, I deal with the effect of this, and I can't listen to the why of it like this, I just can't." In the past, she had tried to read *An American Terrorist* but "never could finish it."

McVeigh will remain newsworthy for decades to come, and media representations of him and his actions as well as the other perpetrators will continue to inform and influence future generations. But in and of itself, such media coverage is too intermittent and perhaps too brief, superficial, and at times sensational to be regarded as the "last word" on McVeigh. Indeed, as I hope this book has demonstrated, there are likely no "last words" on McVeigh, given the fluidity of memory work. Because memory is in continual flux, perhaps the most and possibly only appropriate institution to shepherd the legacy of the bombing is the Oklahoma City National Memorial and Museum.

The museum has always been a symbol of hope, healing, and reconstruction. For Priscilla Salyers, "I am proud of it because it's like, look what we do with our pain and our anger, we could have done so much destruction. And we learned to listen to each other, to compromise, and I said—it's not just the physical memorial, but it was a healing process." Volunteer family members and survivors have found these experiences very therapeutic. For Vicki Hamm, volunteering at the memorial provided an outlet to talk about the effect of the bombing on the Oklahoma City community:

> I'd get down there [to the memorial] and I would have breath of energy or, you know, a sudden increase in energy. I felt like if I go in there, I felt like a new person. And I talked to people. That's where I went to talk more about it. I didn't tell my experience. I told the story of the Murrah Building and the people that worked in there. The life that was once there on the inside.

Volunteering in the memorial archives has allowed Janet Beck to literally contrast the days immediately after the bombing with what life is like now: "We're going through pictures and stuff. Things that, you know, back then were traumatic to us. When we go back to look now, we think about the good times that were associated with that and things instead of looking at the tragedy, or the bad stuff." Similarly, Ernestine Hill Clark described the memorial both as a truth-telling mechanism and as a site that was symbolic of the culture of Oklahoma City:

> The memorial was so important to me. I wanted to be sure that the truth was told and by that time we were already hearing people that would come up and claim what all had happened that day and they would give facts that I knew weren't true. . . . but I also wanted people coming from other places who had been so wonderful to us. I wanted them to experience a warm welcome and to feel the warmth of the good part of Oklahoma City even while they were visiting the memorial, so that was important to me. I felt like I needed to pay back.

At first, McVeigh and everything he stood for seem intuitively at odds with a primary mission of the Oklahoma City National Memorial—remembering those changed forever by McVeigh's murderous acts. At the same time, McVeigh is indisputably a part of the bombing narrative; without him, April 19, 1995, would most likely have remained the way it began—an ordinary day, a day like any other. One of the most difficult tasks that memorial personnel faced was learning how to incorporate McVeigh and his coconspirators into the bombing's narrative—whether and how to portray the perpetrators, their actions, and their histories. Though McVeigh might have sought to be "the master of [his] fate" and the "captain of [his] soul" while he was alive, memorial staff and advisers are now a primary architect of his legacy and can erect a structure that is more flexible, more permanent, and more visible than any biographical or media accounts.

But including McVeigh in museum exhibits carries profound risks. To purposefully incorporate McVeigh's "perp walk" footage or other photographs of him, Nichols, or Fortier into such displays is to invoke their toxic presences within a sacred space. How is it possible to acknowledge that such perpetrator images are relevant and even essential to understanding traumatic events, to walk the thin line between rendering perpetrators invisible and offensively pervasive in memorial spaces?

The Oklahoma City National Memorial is not the first to have confronted this difficult question. In the United States Holocaust Museum, the design team worked to enforce moral distinctions between perpetrators and victims by "mut[ing] the allure" of Nazi symbols and perpetrators' presence. Quotations from Adolf Hitler were silk-screened onto the walls instead of appearing in the raised letters used for quotations by the likes of Holocaust survivor Elie Wiesel, and the incendiary presence of a large Nazi flag was quashed by placing it behind a scaffold encrusted with photographs.[6] There was also the question of how to display photographs of high-ranking Nazi officials amid concerns that "showing the faces high up, as portraits, might seem to memorialize these mass murderers."[7] Although the museum had collected perpetrator-related artifacts and photographs, design efforts to marginalize perpetrators were so successful that early versions of museum exhibits "almost fell into the trap of showing Jews and others as victims of an invisible evil."[8] After walking through the permanent exhibition, the director of Jerusalem's Yad Vashem Historical Museum "was bothered that 'the Nazis appeared as a superhuman force that just took over,' as if . . . there was this metaphysical evil that mysteriously killed the Jews."[9] By the time the museum opened, however, "perpetrators were very much in evidence throughout, in text, photographs, and artifacts."[10]

The design team at the Oklahoma City National Memorial and Museum had to negotiate similar challenges. When the facility opened in April 2000, only a few photographs of McVeigh and Nichols were present. In determining how best to fit the perpetrators into the exhibits, Richard Williams noted, "We decided . . . we would simply tell what the evidence had told us in order of the events as they happened." But those who wrote the exhibit narrative chose to treat information about the investigation and the perpetrators differently than information about the rescue efforts; about victims' families, survivors, and rescue workers; and about the bombing's personal, social, and political impact. In addition, the memorial committee consciously decided not to include much about McVeigh in the memorial in order to avoid giving voice to his views.[11]

Part of the reason for these exclusions was the fact that only four years had elapsed since the bombing. The museum's operations director, Joanne Riley, emphasized that "at that time, we still were dealing with trials and dealing with a lot of things, and they felt like that we should minimally talk about the perpetrators. And that was pretty well the consensus across the board." The perpetrators, and even processes of accountability, were not to be a prominent focus within museum exhibits. "We realized that the justice process and all that was a part of the story, but we did not want that to be the emphasis of the story," Riley recalled. "The emphasis of the story we wanted [was on] the people who were most personally affected, the families who lost someone, the survivors, the rescue workers, the people from the community, we wanted this to be their story."

In those early days, some family members, survivors, and even visitors had strong reactions to including the perpetrators in the museum at all. "It was too soon," noted Riley. Balancing the competing needs of these populations was a challenge. Thus, those involved grappled with the decision of how best to represent McVeigh and his coconspirators. Janet Beck recalled:

And there was a lot of discussion on how important, how prominent should he be in the museum. . . . your head says, he has to be represented, if it wasn't for him it wouldn't have happened, but your heart says, we don't want anything to do with him, we don't want anything out there, we don't want anybody influenced by him. . . . one of the fears is that somebody would come through and see him and idolize him and say, well look what, you know, he's got this whole museum built around him because of what he did, and that's definitely not what we wanted.

Exhibition design necessitated compromise; decisions were made to include information about and images of the perpetrators, but in a manner that defused to the greatest extent possible their potential to wound, sensationalize, or publicize. One such compromise, according to Riley, concerned how to include McVeigh's picture in the museum. "When we have the 'Wall of Justice,' . . . we have the Pat Lopez [courtroom] drawings," Riley remarked, "we decided that the only images we would handle of McVeigh being in here would be . . . a sketch when we first opened. . . . Because we did not want his image out there."

Another way in which to minimize the perpetrators' presences was to structure visitors' physical progression through the museum story line so the perpetrators were in a sense avoidable. The story of holding the offenders accountable—the investigation into the bombing, the suspects' arrests, and legal proceedings—is told in a narrative separate from the "main" exhibit trail that constitutes the visitor's direct path through the museum. "One of the things we decided early on was that, even though it would be in sequence in the museum as it happened, it would be considered the 'dark side' and would not be in or on the direct path of the visitor," Richard Williams recalled. This lessened the chances that visitors would be unwittingly confronted with this uncomfortable material; as Williams stressed, one had to make an effort to encounter it by "mak[ing] a side trip into an exhibit area to learn of the investigation, trials, execution, et cetera." The "dark side" includes not only the perpetrators but also the story of how they came to be held accountable. "You notice that the design of the museum intentionally puts the investigation in a side area, so there's like a fast track through the museum," Riley related, "but when we first opened, if I was a family member and I did not want to go in there and deal with that, I did not have to. That was the intent."

Addressing the evocative term "dark side," Richard Williams explained that these "were the exact words our committee used when describing how to tell the story without making it the focus of the museum experience." This strategy proved to be successful; Williams observed that "it was . . . without doubt the right thing to do to tell that part of the history/story. . . . Some thought we shouldn't tell it, some thought we should have given more to it. I think we did it right for the right reasons, and it has worked well."

At first, the exhibit that most centrally concerned the defendants was the two-panel installation known as the "Wall of Justice" that includes chronological time lines of the prosecutions along with sketches from the trials and blowups of three newspaper articles: a *Rocky Mountain News* article from June 2, 1997, announcing a guilty verdict in the McVeigh case; a *Daily Oklahoman* article from December 24, 1997, describing a guilty verdict in Nichols's federal trial, and another *Daily Oklahoman* article dated May 27, 2004, announcing a conviction in Nichols's state trial.

Segments of the "Wall of Justice," an Oklahoma City National Memorial and Museum display chronicling the prosecutions of Timothy McVeigh and Terry Nichols. Images courtesy of the Oklahoma City National Memorial and Museum Archives.

There is no mention of McVeigh's execution with the exception of a non-descript four-by-eight-inch bronze plaque that was installed within an hour of his death stating, "McVeigh is executed by lethal injection on June 11, 2001, at the federal penitentiary in Terre Haute, Indiana."[12] The plaque, which hangs next to the *Rocky Mountain News* article detailing McVeigh's conviction, replaced one stating that McVeigh's execution had been postponed from May 16 to June 11. Richard Williams, who helped to hang the new plaque on the day of McVeigh's execution, remarked to the media on that occasion that "this is a part of the evolution of the museum," describing the execution as "a very significant change in the timeline."[13]

Though it introduces subject matter that can be uncomfortable or downright difficult, the "dark side" of the bombing story must be told. As Riley noted, the mission statement "says that all who come here know the impact of violence." "There was a reason that line stayed in there," she added. "You're . . . coming here to take in what the memorial can give you. The peace, comfort, hope, and serenity. But that one line is very important. All who come here know the impact of violence, and you can't really take in that one sentence without knowing what happened, how it happened."

From the earliest days, Riley recalled, there were some "family members, survivors . . . who said, 'We don't want this museum to be too comfortable. We don't want it to be something you just kind of look through and go, oh, that makes me feel better.'" The museum was not to be all about feel-good symbols such as teddy bears, but also about the hard work that reconstruction—of lives and crimes—demanded. The museum's dedication to exploring the impact of violence goes much deeper than mere words, as Riley discovered the first time that the exhibit design was presented to family members and survivors:

> We're in the middle of the museum designer just laying this out, [saying] . . . you're gonna walk through here, you're gonna see this, . . . people were crying and the psychologist [from Project Heartland] jumps up in the middle of it and he goes, "Okay, we're going to stop right now." And I'm thinking, oh my gosh, we're shut down. But what he wanted to do, he told everybody to . . . stop, take a deep breath, you're gonna get through this. Because people were starting to sob, you know, it was starting to come out. So, I don't think they want people to come through here and walk away just all warm and fuzzy and, okay, I feel better about this. They want people to walk away moved, changed, and with kind of a challenge of this happened, now what can we do?

This emotional experience underscored just how imperative it was to carefully incorporate the "dark side" into the exhibit story line. This aspect of the bombing chronology necessarily illustrates the impact of violence in a profoundly different way than the serene architecture of the parklike outdoor memorial. According to Riley:

> You can't equate thinking about the impact of violence and terrorism with, I'm just going to go through life, and I saw this really nice place and it had a nice reflecting pool, and I can sit and meditate and then take it all in and everything and walk away and think, well that was a great experience, that was pleasant, that was wonderful. You've got to come away feeling like, okay, this is what violence does. And I think you can go out and sit in the outdoor site, and you can look at those 168 chairs and everything, and that's powerful and that does say the same thing. But when you come in the museum you are experiencing this story.

Over the years, as the museum has grown and its exhibits have expanded, the "dark side" has extended more and more into the light. By now, Riley remarked, "We have kind of blurred the lines of that design." The rear axle housing from the Ryder truck was the first piece of the bombing vehicle that the memorial received; Riley characterized this as "a crucial piece, it was *the* piece." Together with other Ryder truck artifacts—metal, aluminum, a piece of rubber tire—the rear axle was added to the permanent collection a few months after the verdict in Nichols's state trial. These items fit seamlessly into preexisting exhibits on details of the investigation.

Reflecting on the growth of the museum collections, Riley described the process of gradual acceptance, narrative expansion, and museum growth as natural. "I even said whenever we first opened the museum that there's things that we cannot really talk about now that we would be able to talk about 10 years from now, 20 years from now," she said, "because as time goes on, you learn to be able to put those things in perspective and you realize how important it is that the story be told deeper and so we can prevent something like that happening again." Moving forward, she observed, "It's time to start looking at, delving more into explaining to the visitor a little more of what we can see is of 'why.'" The question of "why" the bombing took place does not necessarily include information about McVeigh's personal history but instead implicates the broader social origins of McVeigh's motivations:

We don't want to know that Timothy McVeigh was born in [New York], . . . we don't want to be telling that story. To me, if we start going any direction . . . we need to delve into why would someone do something like this? What kind of hate, what kind of thing causes someone to reach the point where they just coldly and callously go in and kill 168 innocent people?

Because McVeigh never testified, Riley noted, "that's kind of hard to keep that in the context of the judicial process, the investigation and everything."

Riley was frank that the museum's current permanent displays do not go into much depth on the origins of the bombers' motivations: "We don't talk about Ruby Ridge, we don't talk about Waco, we don't talk about the militia concept." She noted that many visitors find it hard to understand why there is no information about other violent incidents and organizations such as abortion clinic bombings and the Ku Klux Klan even when museum officials tell them that, back in 1995, these were not considered acts of terrorism or terrorists. Thus, the question of "why" such violence occurs may ultimately inform future exhibits: "The visitor asks that every single day. Well, why? Why did he do this? Why Oklahoma City? . . . Maybe we need to just get our feet wet and do a special exhibit." Helping visitors to draw such connections between incidents of violence is certainly within the memorial's mission. The bombing story contains many such educational lessons, including spotlighting militia groups. As Janet Beck observed, "We thought all the bad stuff's in Montana or Michigan or somewhere, not right here, and it was a shock to find out . . . you just kind of go along with blinders on and pretend like it doesn't exist, when it does exist and it exists in your backyard."

Riley was adamant that, even as the museum's collection expands and evolves into new areas of the bombing story, one thing will not change: "One thing we have decided, that we have put in writing, and I will always be the champion of this, is that the perpetrators' stor[ies] will never, never, ever be told in this memorial without also telling the stories of the family members and survivors and rescue workers." And there are ways in which exhibits can detail the impact of the perpetrators' heinous actions without explicitly focusing on their lives. In a sense, everything in the museum bears upon the perpetrators, because the bombing would otherwise never have happened. Videos in the museum's permanent exhibit discuss the bombing's impact upon Perry, Oklahoma, where McVeigh was held after he was first arrested, and upon Herington, Kansas, where Nichols lived for a brief time before he turned himself in. "People don't think about how far [the impact of the bombing spreads]," emphasized Riley. "That's the reason I think that video was so important, that it wasn't just about Oklahoma City, . . . [it] had this ripple effect."

And so time moves on, and memory follows. As they have for more than 15 years, visitors still leave things on the chain-link fence that adjoins the outside memorial, which continued to surprise Beverly Rankin: "It's just amazing that people are still so concerned and it's not—they haven't forgotten—and as long as the memorial is there doing its job they won't forget."

Even if they retain only a minimal presence in such commemorative forums, images of the perpetrators help to fulfill our need to somehow embody the "evil" responsible for a traumatic event. They complete the visual field of the bombing's aftermath, filling in an agentic gap that would otherwise become a black hole, devouring viewers' emotional and psychological resources that should be allocated to victims and rescuers. The manner in which the memorial can and should represent McVeigh is necessarily different than the modes in which he has been represented within media coverage. Charged with satisfying entirely different commercial and informational priorities, the news media were always creatures whose primary appetites were dictated by market forces. These priorities obliged reporters to portray McVeigh as a larger-than-life figure, a spectacle; as seen on TV, McVeigh was largely an evil presence, one to be feared and despised. This is not to deny that many of these representations engaged victims' families and survivors as well as a broader national audience in crucial activities such as interrogating McVeigh's behaviors, debating who he was and what had motivated his actions.

In contrast, the memorial task force endeavored to remember and represent murdered victims as well as living survivors and rescue workers, and focused on making these memorial constructions as full and robust as possible. This goal centered around creating and ensuring an altogether different sort of presence, one that was hallowed, sacred, and heroic. Initially, the memorial design team attempted to respect this presence and preserve its sanctity by rendering the perpetrators as much of an absence as possible. Perpetrators' presences in this sacred space was not only unwelcome but also perceived as counterproductive to the task of memorializing the bombing victims and survivors. Over the years, however, officials have gradually come to realize that, although perpetrators' presences will always be intrusive, their visibility in the exhibit story line points to an important and irreplaceable part of the story and is yet another way of holding them accountable. These offensive presences remain relatively weak, however; the strongest voices are still those of victims, their family members, and survivors, which emphasize tragedy and turmoil but also rebirth and rebuilding through remembrance.

It is also poignant that the memorial—conceived of, designed, and staffed by those who have the most reason to wish to forget McVeigh—is leading the charge to help, indeed compel, others to learn about and remember the terrible lessons of his crimes. On July 1, 2010, Oklahoma House Bill 2750, requiring that Oklahoma students be taught about the Oklahoma City bombing, became law. According to the text of the bill, "A study of the bombing and its aftermath can help students learn the impact of violence, the senselessness of using violence to solve problems or effect government change, and the importance of personal responsibility."[14] Interestingly, legislators viewed this matter as so pressing that HB 2750 declared an "emergency," which had the effect of pronouncing the curricular revision "necessary for the preservation of the public peace, health and safety."[15] The Oklahoma City National Memorial and Museum will make curricular materials available to public schools across the state.[16]

Such measures have helped to alleviate family members' and survivors' concerns that the powerful impact of the lessons to be learned from the

Oklahoma City bombing may fade with time. "I always tried to make sure the focal point of an interview was [my sibling] so he would be remembered by people who hadn't even known him. I was so afraid of people forgetting about him. Funny, now I fear people forgetting the entire bombing," related Cameron Crawford. Susan Urbach proposed that it may at some point be advisable and appropriate for the memorial staff to collect oral history from family members and survivors to keep their stories alive:

> I do foresee a time, say 20 or 30 years down the line, where from a historical and documentary perspective it may be time to visit some of us before we die, and get one last historical chronicling. I see something like that coming from the memorial itself, which would be okay.

Now, 15 years after the bombing, it seems that the time is now ripe for more inclusive forms of remembrance, ones that incorporate the perpetrators without excusing their ideologies and actions. Notwithstanding their continued dislike of media coverage of the perpetrators, the tensions inherent in family members' and survivors' involuntary relationships with Nichols and Fortier have relaxed a bit to the point that some have grown more curious about these men. Two factors have contributed to this inquisitiveness: media coverage about the perpetrators has drastically declined, and the passage of time has enabled participants to gain more distance from this difficult subject.

Sometimes participants' curiosity assumes the form of a reluctant interest, accompanying a perceived need to keep tabs on Nichols. Charlie Younger acknowledged, "We need to be cognizant of the fact that that act happened and it potentially could happen again, so we can't relax our guard." Ernestine Hill Clark recalled reading an entire article about Nichols within the last year, and believes that she has evolved as a media consumer from a very vulnerable individual intimately connected to this subject into an inquisitive media user who is more detached from the stories: "It's from a little bit more distance and it's more out of curiosity as in what's going on with him now, rather than becoming emotionally involved." Family member Cameron Crawford said that he wanted to be "kept abreast of any Nichols information that's important to know. Don't want to hear, but I need to."

Participants were also more likely to be actually curious, rather than cautious, about Fortier's whereabouts following his release. Many confessed to harboring continued interest in Fortier. "There have been times when I've wondered what happened to him and his [wife]," noted survivor Ernestine

Hill Clark. "I'm still curious about Fortier. I know that sounds silly. . . . I would love to know at whatever age he is now, what his thoughts are on all of that." Family member Cameron Crawford also admitted, "I would love to hear about him. I'd love to hear where he's living. I would love to know what he thinks. . . . how is he, you know, what kind of house does he live in or does he have a job? I'm not going to go after him, I don't want to see him. . . . just human curiosity." Diane Dooley admitted that she would like to know what impact these events have had upon Fortier: "You sort of hope that . . . that was a wake-up call for him. . . . Did he come out of prison and learn something and turn his life around and have some purpose?" But Richard Williams believed that it would be extremely dangerous for Fortier if participants' curiosity was ever satisfied: "I think there are others out there besides family members, survivors, and rescuers that would like to talk with him or have a talk with him. . . . I think there are others out there who would probably make sure that he didn't talk to anybody again."

Thomas Mann once said, "A man's dying is more the survivors' affair than his own." We must remember McVeigh, but on our own terms, not his. Thus, in the media, in the memorial, and in school textbooks, McVeigh, Nichols, and Fortier will forever be remembered as perpetrators, never as children or decorated soldiers, fathers, or brothers. They will be remembered not as extraordinary terrorists but as ordinary men who committed an act of exceptional wickedness. Heroism will be reserved for murdered victims and their relatives and for survivors, first responders, rescue workers, and others whose lives over the years have become intertwined with the Murrah Building and also with McVeigh. Yet, at the same time as we remember these individuals and commemorate their roles, we must also remember McVeigh out of respect for those he sought to destroy. Even if it were possible to put him out of sight and out of mind, such invisibility would increase the chances that another American—another McVeigh—would one day commit a similar atrocity. Memory is a prayer for vigilance, a way in which we endeavor to keep our world safe for those we love, and those they will come to love.

Yet, at the same time, we must remember that the narrative of McVeigh and Oklahoma City is a difficult story, and that difficult stories have difficult endings. We would like to think that acts of remembrance, such as memorials and historical narratives, lead to greater vigilance in our ability to prevent atrocity, and thus serve as restraints. This goal is commensurate with civic enlightenment and is considered integral to civic empowerment. But "never again" is a fairy tale. Recognizing that we are "changed forever" is the beginning, not the end, of prevention efforts. Acts of remembrance are our defenses against the anxieties generated by McVeigh and the bombing, our fears that we will remember them incompletely, inaccurately, or inadequately—or, worse, that we will cease to remember at all, or that remembrance will be fruitless in inhibiting violence.

But when we have in our midst someone like McVeigh, considered by most to be a "moral monster" who not only conceives an invidious worldview but has the conceit to act upon it, another challenge must take precedence: Can we do anything to stop him? And if we fail at this task, then what can we do after the terrible fact other than build memorials and hope that our acts of remembrance are sufficient? We must be careful lest acts of remembrance relax our continual vigilance or lead to a reluctance or refusal to confront actual depths of suffering, careful lest we closet our fears in a positive, naive hope in an unblighted future. The myth of closure is a warning that we must not wall ourselves within false comfort, using as building blocks sacred narratives of remembrance that honor our pasts but do little to protect our futures.

Appendix: Methodology

In designing this project, I had two primary goals: to prioritize the quality and reflexive depth of data, and to enroll as participants those individuals who were most emotionally invested in the execution. Qualitative methods have been widely used in the fields of anthropology, communication, and sociology, particularly to conduct exploratory research on emergent topics. One particular qualitative methodology that has received particular attention is grounded theory, which facilitates the development of explanatory theories through the conduct of research, instead of research that tests a preconceived hypothesis. Grounded theory also emphasizes the role of data such as participants' voices in constructing theory. The current study utilized open-ended questions as an interviewing tool to assess the bombing's impact on each participant, the effects of their membership in postbombing support groups, their reactions to McVeigh's trial and execution, and their pre- and post-execution expectations and perceptions.

Participant Recruitment

The 33 participants included in this study were survivors of the Oklahoma City bombing or victims' family members. A total of 36 participants were interviewed; however, 3 were not included because they were rescue workers, and not victims or survivors who were present at the moment of the bombing. To reach this population, I first contacted the Oklahoma Department of Health, which put me in touch with Dr. Betty Pfefferbaum, a psychiatrist and attorney specializing in child trauma who had conducted years of research with this population and published many studies on the effects of the bombing on the health of city residents. Dr. Pfefferbaum expressed interest in serving as my clinician on this project and placed me in contact with Dr. Paul Heath, a survivor of the bombing and the secretary and treasurer of a community service organization known as the Murrah Federal Building Survivor's Association. Dr. Heath agreed to send letters requesting interviews to organization members. To maintain confidentiality, I forwarded the introductory letters, envelopes, and postage to Dr. Heath, who addressed and mailed the letters. The interview request letters described the project, mentioned Dr. Heath's mediating role to assure recipients that their identities were protected, and informed recipients that they could either telephone Dr. Pfefferbaum's secretary or e-mail me to schedule interviews.

Out of approximately 235 letters mailed, I received approximately 12 requests for interviews. Thereafter, I switched to the alternate participant recruitment method of snowball sampling—asking participants who had completed interviews if they knew of anyone else who would consent to being interviewed. These participants then placed me in contact with other potential interviewees. Toward the end of my research project, I made special efforts to contact live witnesses to McVeigh's execution. Thus, a total of 33 participants were enrolled in the study in three stages. First, members of the Murrah Building Survivor's Association who responded to the interview request letters were included in the study. Second, interviews were conducted with others recommended as potential participants by those who had already completed interviews. Finally, witnesses who viewed the execution live at Terre Haute, Indiana, were recruited. All participants were over 18 years of age (participants' ages ranged from mid-30s to early 70s) and thus were able to legally consent to participation, and all initial interviews were completed between 2004 and 2006.

Interviewing Methods and Procedures

Two prior studies had used short survey instruments to ascertain the psychiatric effects of witnessing an execution on journalists and to identify college students' attitudes toward execution witnessing. In my original research, I wanted to focus not on psychiatric symptoms but on the social and communicative dimensions of capital trials and executions, and so believed that a survey instrument would too narrowly constrain my data. Conducting intensive interviews with open-ended questions allowed me to conversationally guide participants through the task of describe how the bombing, trials, and McVeigh's execution impacted their lives while granting participants complete freedom of response (unlike a survey instrument with a limited range of responses) and enabled me to retain the flexibility to ask follow-up questions. Of course, that flexibility came with a price; the intensive in-person interviews were more costly than surveys and necessitated transcription and more time-consuming data analysis. However, since I was conducting exploratory research, I placed a high priority on the quality and depth of interview information versus the quantity of participants. In addition, participants would have found a survey instrument that covered the same subject matter as my intensive interview questionnaire to be excessively lengthy and fatiguing.

Because no interview instrument existed, I created my own. Questions concerning the impact of the Oklahoma City bombing, group membership, and attendance at capital trials straightforwardly asked participants to recall the day of the bombing and the weeks following. With respect to the McVeigh execution and its impact on participants' lives, I wrote specific questions after researching the execution and watching online media interviews with victims' families and survivor witnesses. Prior to interviewing participants, I refined the questions as a result of input from other academics and the two institutional review boards that reviewed my protocol and interview instrument.

Interviews with all participants took place in the spirit of narrative inquiry, which "aspires to an ideal of participation and involvement" and "dissolves traditional boundaries between researchers and subjects."[1] I was aware that my own experiences with parental loss would influence this project and soon found that my father's death in a car accident caused by a truck driver's negligence as well as an ensuing wrongful death lawsuit gave me insight into coping with sudden loss and the impact of legal proceedings on accountability, finality, and healing. Thus, when participants inquired into my reasons for conducting research on this subject matter, I described the early life experiences in which my inquiry was rooted. I always acknowledged, however, that my own experiences were very different from and incomparable to the Oklahoma City bombing, and I did not discuss them further unless participants asked me more about them. My willingness to share my own life experiences with participants, together with my genuine enthusiasm for this inquiry, gained me a measure of trust and confidence that I otherwise doubt I would have been able to achieve with participants, many of whom had been interviewed many times by media sources.

I conducted the interviews at any site in Oklahoma City that was comfortable for the participant. While most interviews took place in participants' homes, two interviews took place in a private room at the Oklahoma Health Sciences Center in downtown Oklahoma City, and two took place in a downtown hotel room. All participants were asked for permission to tape the interview, and all consented. Prior to each interview, I read through an informed consent form and Health Information Privacy Act form with each participant, who then signed these forms and received copies for his or her records. I then turned the tape recorder on, and the interview commenced.

Three interviews with participants who lived in Texas, Minnesota, and Georgia were conducted electronically over a land line telephone. In these cases, two copies of the consent forms were mailed to participants beforehand together with a stamped envelope addressed to myself, and the interview was not scheduled until I had received a completed packet in the mail. After an interview appointment was scheduled, I called each participant at home, discussed the consent form at that time, ascertained if he or she had any questions, obtained permission to record the interview, and commenced the interview.

Recontact Interviews

After I had obtained a publication contract with NYU Press in 2009, I set out to reinterview as many of the original participants as I could find and eventually succeeded in reinterviewing 21 of the original 27 participants. I was unable to reach the remaining 6, who had either moved on without leaving a forwarding address or chosen not to respond to the mailed interview request. Although their initial informed consent documents gave me permission to reproduce their comments in future publications, I chose to refer to them only by aliases so as to protect their identities. I also conducted six new interviews at this time. All of the recontact interviews and additional full-length interviews were conducted by telephone. Because I had identified themes such as the victim-offender relationship and the importance of the news media in participants' recovery—issues about which I had not asked in my original interview—the recontact interviews focused most heavily on these issues.

Throughout this project, no participant was financially compensated for participating in the intensive interview. To offer an incentive for interview participation, each respondent was informed of the lack of research on this subject matter and the altruistic benefits of participation. I did promise to give copies of this book to all participants. All costs for this study were paid for by means of my personal funds, a research grant through the Annenberg School at the University of Pennsylvania, and a grant from Indiana University.

Notes

NOTES TO PREFACE

1. James Young describes "collected memory" as "the many discrete memories that are gathered into common memorial spaces and assigned common meaning." James Young, *The Texture of Memory: Holocaust Memorials and Meaning* (New Haven: Yale University Press 1993), xi.

2. Andrew Freinkel, Cheryl Koopman, and David Spiegel, "Dissociative Symptoms in Media Eyewitnesses of an Execution," *American Journal of Psychiatry* 151 (1994): 9; Marla L. Domino and Marcus T. Boccaccini, "Doubting Thomas: Should Family Members of Victims Watch Executions?" *Law and Psychology Review* 24 (2000): 51.

NOTES TO CHAPTER 1

1. "Dennis Tito Discusses His Space Odyssey," interview by Larry King, *Larry King Live*, CNN, May 15, 2001, http://transcripts.cnn.com/TRANSCRIPTS/0105/15/lkl.00.html.

2. Maria Hinojosa, "Exhibit of Lynching Photos Is a Harsh Display of Hatred," CNN photograph, January 18, 2000, http://archives.cnn.com/2000/US/01/18/lynching.photography/.

3. Barbie Zelizer has noted that other types of photographs, such as images of ruined buildings, also implicate people who face death or are dying: "Buried under the mounds of earth caused by landslides, lost in the waters of typhoons or shipwrecks, disintegrated by the force of a terrorist's bomb, the victims of presumed death rely on the public to imagine their demise. . . . Although people may know they are being shown a smashed building, the depiction becomes significant in light of what it implies, not in terms of what it shows." Barbie Zelizer, *About to Die: How News Images Move the Public* (New York: Oxford University Press, 2010), 69.

4. Stephanie Marlin-Curiel, "Re-collecting the Collective: Mediatised Memory and the South African Truth and Reconciliation Commission," in *The Image and the Witness: Trauma, Memory, and Visual Culture*, ed. Frances Guerin and Roger Hallas (London: Wallflower Press, 2007), 69–81, 77.

5. Frances Guerin and Roger Hallas, eds., "Introduction," in *The Image and the Witness: Trauma, Memory, and Visual Culture* (London: Wallflower Press, 2007), 9 (citing Hans Belting, "Introduction," in *Likeness and Presence: A History of the Image Before the Era of Art*, trans. Edmund Jephcott [Chicago: University of Chicago Press, 1994], 11).

6. Guerin and Hallas, "Introduction," 5.

7. Zelizer, *About to Die*, 53. This semantic burgeoning illustrates how, as Zelizer explains, news photographs such as perp walk footage "function through a qualification

of reason—a combination of contingency, the imagination, and emotions—that settles not at the image's original point of display but over time by different people putting it to multiple uses in new contexts." Ibid.

8. Nick Bryant, "Pain Remains for McVeigh Victims," BBC, June 11, 2001, http://news.bbc.co.uk/2/hi/americas/1383171.stm.

9. Peter Hartley, *Interpersonal Communication*, 2d ed. (New York: Routledge, 1999), 20–24.

10. Attempts to define exactly what interactions constitute interpersonal communication are fraught with peril. Mark Knapp et al., "Background and Current Trends in the Study of Interpersonal Communication," in *Handbook of Interpersonal Communication*, 3d ed., ed. Mark L. Knapp and John A. Daly (London: Sage, 2002), 9. Communication scholars disagree on the "number of communicators involved, the physical proximity of the communicators, the nature of the interaction units used to explain an encounter, and the degree of formality and structure attending the interactants' relationship." Ibid. Perhaps all it is possible to agree on is that interpersonal communication involves "at least two communicators; intentionally orienting toward each other; as both subject and object; whose actions embody each other's perspectives both toward self and toward other." Arthur P. Bochner, "Interpersonal Communication," in *International Encyclopedia of Communications*, ed. Eric Barnouw et al. (New York: Oxford University Press, 1989), 336. Cappella emphasizes the ability to influence another as the focus of interpersonal communication analysis. Joseph N. Cappella, "Interpersonal Communication: Definitions and Fundamental Questions," in *Handbook of Communication Science*, ed. Charles R. Berger and Steven H. Chaffee (London: Sage, 1987), 228. Despite this lack of consensus, however, certain definitional practices are more common than others. For instance, it is most common to limit the number of participants in an interpersonal encounter to two, and another assumption involves limiting such interactions to face-to-face exchanges involving close physical proximity. Knapp et al., "Background and Current Trends in the Study of Interpersonal Communication," 9.

11. Donald Horton and R. Richard Wohl, "Mass Communication and Para-Social Interaction: Observation on Intimacy at a Distance," *Psychiatry* 19 (August 1956): 3; reprinted in *Inter/Media: Interpersonal Communication in a Media World*, 2d ed., ed. Gary Gumpert and Robert Cathcart (New York: Oxford University Press, 1979), 188–211.

12. Ibid., 188–91, 195.

13. Ibid.

14. Analyzing the para-social relationships that viewers of television news form with newscasters, Levy notes, "Even though this affective tie is completely the subjective invention of the audience, para-socially interactive viewers believe it is genuine and they interpret the behavior of the news personae as reciprocating this 'real' bond." Mark Levy, "Watching TV News as Para-Social Interaction," in *Inter/Media: Interpersonal Communication in a Media World*, 2d ed., ed. Gary Gumpert and Robert Cathcart (New York: Oxford University Press, 1979), 185.

15. Sam Handlin, "Profile of a Mass Murderer: Who Is Timothy McVeigh?" Court TV, 2001, http://www.courttv.com/news/mcveigh_special/profile_ctv.html (copy on file with author).

16. "McVeigh Shows No Remorse at Execution," Court TV, http://www.courttv.com/news/mcveigh_special/0612_noremorse_ap.html (copy on file with author).

17. Judee K. Burgoon and Gregory D. Hoobler, "Nonverbal Signals," in *Handbook of Interpersonal Communication*, 3d ed., ed. Mark L. Knapp and John A. Daly (London: Sage, 2002), 262.

18. Susan F. Sharp, *Hidden Victims: The Effects of the Death Penalty on Families of the Accused* (Piscataway, NJ: Rutgers University Press, 2005), 1.

19. Ibid., 36. See generally Elizabeth Beck, Sarah Britto, and Arlene Andrews, *In the Shadow of Death: Restorative Justice and Death Row Families* (New York: Oxford University Press, 2007); Elizabeth Beck et al., "Seeking Sanctuary: Interviews with Family Members of Capital Defendants," *Cornell Law Review* 88 (2003): 382–418.

NOTES TO CHAPTER 3

1. Susan Greene, "McVeigh Execution: Closure or Fallacy? Some Seek Catharsis, But Others Fear He'll Have a Platform for Hate," *Denver Post*, May 10, 2001, A01.

2. Doug Swanson, "Family Members, Survivors Who Witness Execution Are Seeking 'Closure,'" *Dallas Morning News*, June 11, 2001, 9.

3. Douglas Turner, "Bush Hopes McVeigh Execution 'Brings Closure' to Family of Victims," *Buffalo News*, May 4, 2001, A12; Bill Hemmer et al., "McVeigh's Execution Brings Closure," *CNN Live Event/Special*, CNN, June 11, 2001, http://transcripts.cnn.com/TRANSCRIPTS/0106/11/se.10.html.

4. Greene, "McVeigh Execution."

5. Kevin Fagan, "Oklahoma City Bombing; Timothy McVeigh Execution; Families Will Find Closure Elusive; Seeing McVeigh Die May Have a Cost, Psychologists Say," *San Francisco Chronicle*, June 10, 2001, A1.

6. Mike Tolson, "Execution of Timothy McVeigh; Relatives of Victims Get Closure But Not Comfort," *Houston Chronicle*, June 12, 2001, A11.

7. See, e.g., Swanson, "Family Members, Survivors Who Witness Execution Are Seeking 'Closure.'"

8. Franklin Zimring, *The Contradictions of American Capital Punishment* (New York: Oxford University Press, 2003), 48.

9. Ibid.

10. Martha Minow, "Surviving Victim Talk," *UCLA Law Review* 40 (1993): 1411, 1415.

11. Alyson M. Cole, *The Cult of True Victimhood* (Stanford, CA: Stanford University Press, 2007), 35.

12. Hans Boutellier, *Crime and Morality: The Significance of Criminal Justice in Post-Modern Culture* (New York: Springer, 2000), 45–46.

13. *Payne v. Tennessee*, 501 U.S. 808 (1991).

14. See, e.g., Susan Bandes, "Victims, 'Closure,' and the Sociology of Emotion," *Law and Contemporary Problems* 72 (2009): 1–26.

15. *Payne v. Tennessee*, 501 U.S. 808, 825 (1991).

16. Ibid., 832.

17. Ibid., 834.

18. See Jody Lyneé Madeira, "Why Rebottle the Genie? Capitalizing on Closure in Death Penalty Proceedings," *Indiana Law Journal* 85 (2010): 1477.

19. Cole, *Cult of True Victimhood*, 137.

20. See Vik Kanwar, "Capital Punishment as Closure: The Limits of Victim-Centered Jurisprudence," *New York University Review of Law and Social Change* 27 (2002): 216 (stating that "the cultural production of a feeling of closure for the secondary victims has become, at least implicitly, an independent justification for the retention and enforcement of the death penalty in the United States," and that closure itself has "become the central trope of the growing victim-centered jurisprudence"); Susan Bandes, "When Victims Seek Closure: Forgiveness, Vengeance, and the Role of Government," *Fordham Urban Law Journal* 27 (2000): 1599, 1605 (2000) ("Governor Jeb Bush of Florida, for example, in his current campaign to truncate the death penalty appeals process in that state, has 'emphasized the suffering of victims' families and complained that inmates spend about fourteen years on death row before they are executed'"); Bandes, "Victims, 'Closure,' and the Sociology of Emotion," 28–29.

21. Richard K. Sherwin, *When Law Goes Pop: The Vanishing Line between Law and Popular Culture* (Chicago: University of Chicago Press, 2000), 166.

22. Samuel R. Gross and Daniel J. Matheson, "What They Say at the End: Capital Victims' Families and the Press," *Cornell Law Review* 88 (2003): 486, 489; Jody Lyneé Madeira, "A Constructed Peace: Narratives of Suture in the News Media," *Canadian Journal of Law and Society* 19, no. 2 (2004): 93–94.

23. See, e.g., Wayne A. Logan, "Through the Past Darkly: A Survey of the Uses and Abuses of Victim Impact Evidence in Capital Trials," *Arizona Law Review* 41 (1999): 143; Bandes, "When Victims Seek Closure," 1606; Bandes, "Victims, 'Closure,' and the Sociology of Emotion," 4; Wayne A. Logan, "Confronting Terror: Victims' Rights in an Age of Terror," *Georgetown Law Journal* 96 (2008): 721.

24. Several scholars have noted the need for a more comprehensive definition of closure. See, e.g., Marilyn Peterson Armour and Mark S. Umbreit, "The Ultimate Penal Sanction and 'Closure' for Survivors of Homicide Victims," *Marquette Law Review* 91(2007): 381, 398; Bandes, "When Victims Seek Closure," 1602; Peter Hodgkinson, "Capital Punishment: Meeting the Needs of the Families of the Homicide Victim and the Condemned," in *Capital Punishment: Strategies for Abolition*, ed. Peter Hodgkinson and William A. Schabas (Cambridge: Cambridge University Press, 2004) 332, 353–54; Margaret Vandiver, "The Death Penalty and the Families of Victims: An Overview of Research Issues," in *Wounds That Do Not Bind: Victim-Based Perspectives on the Death Penalty*, ed. James R. Acker and David R. Karp (Durham, NC: Carolina Academic Press, 2006), 235. Other scholars have attempted to define closure, and question whether it is possible. Paul Rock, *After Homicide: Practical and Political Responses to Bereavement* (Oxford: Oxford University Press, 1998), 58–59; Vik Kanwar, "Capital Punishment as 'Closure,'" 215–16; Peter Loge, "The Process of Healing and the Trial as Product: Incompatibility, Courts, and Murder Victim Family Members," in *Wounds That Do Not Bind: Victim-Based Perspectives on the Death Penalty*, ed. James R. Acker and David R. Karp (Durham, NC: Carolina Academic Press, 2006), 411, 412 n.5.

25. Charlie Younger remarked: "I don't like the word closure because, people have a tendency to suggest that people should get over it, period and there's a time frame they give 'em that's a grace period then it should all be gone it just don't happen. It all depends on the individual and how they deal with things, and for most people, nobody's ever totally over it they get better. That's all I know. And it's not over for any of us."

26. Stan Mayer noted: "Almost immediately people would say, 'You're ok now, aren't you?' Why? Why do people do that constantly, you know, from, from like the day after onward, you're ok now, aren't you? Things will be better, you know, things are better now, right? And they'll look at you . . . it's like a demand to hear—and what counselors and, and victims all said—was you need to be able to say, fine, things are fine."

27. Barbie Zelizer, *Covering the Body: The Kennedy Assassination, the Media, and the Shaping of Collective Memory* (Chicago: University of Chicago Press, 1992), 34 (citing Claude Lévi-Strauss, *The Savage Mind* [Chicago: University of Chicago Press, 1966], 259).

28. Jeffrey Alexander, "Cultural Trauma and Collective Identity," in *The Meanings of Social Life: A Cultural Sociology*, ed. Jeffrey Alexander (Oxford: Oxford University Press, 2003), 85.

29. Piotr Sztompka, "The Trauma of Social Change: A Case of Postcommunist Societies," in *Cultural Trauma and Identity*, ed. Jeffrey C. Alexander et al. (Berkeley: University of California Press, 2004), 161.

30. Ibid., 162.

31. Alexander, "Cultural Trauma and Collective Identity," 85.

32. Ibid.

33. Ibid., 93.

34. Kenneth Thompson, *Moral Panics* (New York: Taylor and Francis, 1998), 20–24.

35. Ibid., 102.

36. Nancy K. Miller and Jason Tougaw, eds., "Introduction: Extremities," in *Extremities: Trauma, Testimony, and Community* (Chicago: University of Illinois Press, 2002), 1.

37. Ibid.

38. Frank Weed, *Certainty of Justice: Reform in the Crime Victim Movement* (Piscataway, NJ: Transaction, 1995), 51.

39. Miller and Tougaw, "Introduction," 2.

40. Jennifer L. Dunn, *Judging Victims: Why We Stigmatize Survivors, and How They Reclaim Respect* (Boulder, CO: Lynne Rienner, 2010), 4.

41. Cole, *Cult of True Victimhood*, 34.

42. Ibid., 138.

43. Ibid.

44. Wendy Kaminer, *I'm Dysfunctional, You're Dysfunctional: The Recovery Movement and Other Self-Help Fashions* (New York: Vintage 1992), 40–41.

45. Erika Doss, *Memorial Mania* (Chicago: University of Chicago Press, 2010), 156.

46. Joseph D. Amato, *Victims and Values: A History and a Theory of Suffering* (New York: Praeger, 1990), 212.

47. The connections between memory and trauma are well documented; studies of memory have long been concerned with trauma's effects on collective sense-making and remembrance. In *Mourning and Melancholia*, Freud conceptualized mourning as a reconstructive process in which the remembered love object is recognized as lost and distinctive from the self. Sigmund Freud, "Mourning and Melancholia," in *The Freud Reader*, ed. Peter Gay (New York: Norton, 1989), 587. Mourning would be analogous to a process of "working through" a memory conflict. Dominick LaCapra, *History and Memory after Auschwitz* (Ithaca: Cornell University Press, 1998), 184.

48. Alexander, *Meanings of Social Life*, 3.

49. Ibid.

50. Elizabeth Hallam and Jenny Hockey, *Death, Memory and Material Culture* (Oxford: Berg, 2001), 2–3.

51. Daniel Reisberg and Paula Hertel, *Memory and Emotion* (New York: Oxford University Press, 2004), 11.

52. Bernard Rimé, Susanna Corsini, and Gwénola Herbette, "Emotion, Verbal Expression, and the Social Sharing of Emotion," in *The Verbal Communication of Emotions: Interdisciplinary Perspectives*, ed. Susan R. Fussell (Florence, KY: Psychology Press, 2002), 285, 205.

53. Sally Planalp, *Communicating Emotion: Social, Moral, and Cultural Processes* (Cambridge: Cambridge University Press, 1999), 183.

54. Peter Brooks, "Narrativity of the Law," *Law and Literature* 14 (2002): 1, 18.

55. As defined by Labov and Fanshel, narrative analysis relies on order and structure and is "one means of representing past experience by a sequence of ordered sentences that present the temporal sequence of those events by that order." William Labov and David Fanshel, *Therapeutic Discourse: Psychotherapy as Conversation* (New York: Academic Press, 1977), 106.

56. Madeira, "Constructed Peace," 93–94.

57. Charlotte Linde, *Life Stories: The Creation of Coherence* (New York: Oxford University Press, 1993), 127–28.

58. Paul Connerton, *How Societies Remember* (New York: Cambridge University Press, 1989), 17.

59. Marilyn Armour, "Meaning Making in the Aftermath of Homicide," *Death Studies* 27 (2003): 520 (stating that "people who have experienced traumatic loss . . . assimilate the loss by constructing a coherent self-narrative that preserves a sense of continuity about who they have been and are now").

60. Planalp, *Communicating Emotion*, 111.

61. Roger C. Schank, *Tell Me a Story: A New Look at Real and Artificial Memory* (New York: Simon and Schuster, 1990), 44 (we tell stories to describe ourselves not only so others can understand who we are but also so we can understand ourselves).

62. Madeira, "Constructed Peace," 95.

63. Joseph L. Hoffman, "Revenge or Mercy? Some Thoughts about Survivor Opinion Evidence in Death Penalty Cases," *Cornell Law Review* 88 (2002): 538 (noting that "one clearly common, and potentially debilitating, aspect of victimization is the severe and ongoing loss of control that many victims experience").

64. Stephanos Bibas, "Harmonizing Substantive-Criminal-Law Values and Criminal Procedure: The Case of Alford and Nolo Contendere Pleas," *Cornell Law Review* 88 (2003): 1361, 1410.

65. Rock, *After Homicide*, 53.

66. Dana Cloud, *Control and Consolation in American Culture and Politics: Rhetoric of Therapy* (Tuscaloosa: University of Alabama Press, 1998), 88.

67. Doss, *Memorial Mania*, 78.

68. Carrie A. Rentschler, "Witnessing: US Citizenship and the Vicarious Experience of Suffering," *Media, Culture and Society* 26 (2004): 297.

69. See generally Jody Lyneé Madeira, "When It's So Hard to Relate: Can Legal Systems Mitigate the Trauma of Victim-Offender Relationships?" *Houston Law Review* 46 (2009): 401.

70. See Stephanos Bibas and Richard A. Bierschbach, "Integrating Remorse and Apology into Criminal Procedure," *Yale Law Journal* 114 (2004): 85, 136.

71. See generally Madeira, "When It's So Hard to Relate."

NOTES TO CHAPTER 4

1. K. Chase Stovall-McClough and Marylene Cloitre, "Traumatic Reactions to Terrorism: The Individual and Collective Experience," in *Psychological Effects of Catastrophic Disasters: Group Approaches to Treatment*, ed. Leon A. Schein et al. (Binghamton, NY: Haworth Press, 2006), 133. See also Sidney Cobb, "Social Support as a Moderator of Life Stress," *Psychosomatic Medicine* 38 (1976): 300–314; S. Cohen and G. McKay, "Interpersonal Relationships as Buffers of the Impact of Psychological Stress on Health," in *Handbook of Psychology and Health*, ed. Andrew Baum, Jerome E. Singer, and Shelley E. Taylor (Mahwah, NJ: Erlbaum, 1984), 253–67; Charles J. Holahan and Rudolf H. Moos, "Social Support and Psychological Distress: A Longitudinal Analysis," *Journal of Abnormal Psychology* 90 (1981): 365–70; Fran H. Norris and Stanley A. Murrell, "Social Support, Life Events, and Stress as Modifiers of Adjustment to Bereavement by Older Adults," *Psychology and Aging* 5 (1990): 429–36.

2. Stovall-McClough and Cloitre, "Traumatic Reactions to Terrorism," 134. See also Norris and Murrell, "Social Support, Life Events, and Stress as Modifiers of Adjustment to Bereavement by Older Adults," 133; Chris R. Brewin, Bernice Andrews, and John D. Valentine, "Meta-analysis of Risk Factors for Posttraumatic Stress Disorder in Trauma-Exposed Adults," *Journal of Consulting and Clinical Psychology* 68 (2000): 748–66; Zahava Solomon, Mario Mikulincer, and Ehud Avitzur, "Coping, Locus of Control, Social Support, and Combat-Related Posttraumatic Stress Disorder: A Prospective Study," *Journal of Personality and Social Psychology* 55 (1988): 279–85; Phoebe Tucker et al., "Predictors of Posttraumatic Stress Symptoms in Oklahoma City: Exposure, Social Support, Peritraumatic Response," *Journal of Behavioral Health Services and Research* 27 (2000): 406–16; Carol S. North et al., "Psychiatric Disorders among Survivors of the Oklahoma City Bombing," *Journal of the American Medical Association* 282 (1999): 759.

3. M. Katherine Shear et al, "The Syndrome of Traumatic Grief and Its Treatment," in *Psychological Effects of Catastrophic Disasters: Group Approaches to Treatment*, ed. Leon A. Schein et al. (Binghamton, NY: Haworth Press, 2006), 288–333.

4. Ibid.

5. Megan O'Rourke, "Good Grief: Is There a Better Way to Be Bereaved?" *New Yorker*, February 1, 2010, http://www.newyorker.com/arts/critics/atlarge/2010/02/01/100201crat_atlarge_orourke.

6. See Lula M. Redmond, *Surviving: When Someone You Love Was Murdered: A Professional's Guide to Group Grief Therapy for Families and Friends of Murder Victims* (Clearwater, FL: Psychological Consultation and Educational Services, 1989).

7. See Therese A. Rando, *Treatment of Complicated Mourning* (Champaign, IL: Research Press, 1993).

8. See Morton Bard, "A Retrospective Study of Homicide Survivor Adaptation," final report, Grant No. R01 MH31685, National Institutes of Mental Health, Rockville, Maryland (1982).

9. Paul Rock, *After Homicide: Practical and Political Responses to Bereavement* (Oxford: Oxford University Press, 1998). xiii, xix.

10. Ibid., 40.

11. Ibid., xix.

12. Ibid., 39–43, 53.

13. Melissa S. Wattenberg et al., "Present-Centered Supportive Group Therapy for Trauma Survivors," in *Psychological Effects of Catastrophic Disasters: Group Approaches to Treatment*, ed. Leon A. Schein et al. (Binghamton, NY: Haworth Press, 2006), 568–69.

14. Rock, *After Homicide*, 95.

15. Ibid., 101–4, 97.

16. Ibid., 101–2.

17. Ibid., 47.

18. Ibid., 49

19. Ibid., 50.

20. Edward T. Linenthal, *The Unfinished Bombing: Oklahoma City in American Memory* (New York: Oxford University Press, 2001), 176–81.

21. Oklahoma City Memorial Foundation, Memorial Mission Statement, http://www.oklahomacitynationalmemorial.org/secondary.php?section=10&catid=195.

22. See "Symbolism," Oklahoma City National Memorial and Museum, accessed April 25, 2007, http://www.oklahomacitynationalmemorial.org/secondary.php?section=2&catid=30. Two "Gates of Time" serve as entrances to the outdoor memorial and symbolize time standing still during the moments of the explosion. In between the Gates of Time is a reflecting pool where Fifth Street ran between the Murrah Building and the Journal Record Building; this mirrors visitors, who are forever changed by their visit. In the footprint of the Murrah Building are 168 empty chairs standing in nine rows to symbolize the nine floors of the building. The left foundation wall from the Murrah Building still stands on the left side of the footprint; here one may see the Survivor Wall, listing more than 800 bombing survivors. On a circular promontory situated on the sloped lawn rising to the Journal Record Building stands the Survivor Tree, an American elm that survived the blast. A path toward the entrance to the Journal Record Building leads through the Rescuers' Orchard, a gallery of trees bearing fruit and flowers. Outside the memorial itself is the Children's Area, paved with tiles created in 1995 by children around the nation. Finally, a 200-foot section of "the Fence" remains on the western side of the outdoor memorial, where visitors can leave notes, stuffed animals, and wreaths as in the days immediately after the bombing.

23. See Oklahoma City National Memorial and Museum, http://www.oklahomacitynationalmemorial.org.

24. These "chapters" are described on the website as progressing from a background on terrorism and history of the site to an audio recording of the blast, the confusing and chaotic aftermath of the first moments after the bombing, survivor experiences in the first hours after the explosion, the early beginnings of the law enforcement investigation into the blast, the world reaction, the processes of rescue and recovery, the process of waiting for death notifications, a gallery of honor for deceased victims, funerals and mourning, criminal prosecutions and sentencing, and remembrance and rebuilding.

25. Linenthal, *Unfinished Bombing*, 106.

26. Comprehensive Terrorism Prevention Act Bill No. S. 735, 104th Cong., s7481 (1995).

27. Ibid.

28. Ibid., s7482.

29. Rock, *After Homicide*, 29.

30. D. Rob Davies, Gary M. Burlingame, and Christopher M. Layne, "Integrating Small-Group Process Principles into Trauma-Focused Group Psychotherapy: What Should a Group Trauma Therapist Know?" in *Psychological Effects of Catastrophic Disasters: Group Approaches to Treatment*, ed. Leon A. Schein et al. (Binghamton, NY: Haworth Press, 2006): 401. See also Jacob D. Lindy and John P. Wilson, "Respecting the Trauma Membrane: Above All, Do No Harm," in *Treating Psychological Trauma and PTSD*, ed. John P. Wilson and Matthew J. Friedman (New York: Guilford Press, 2001).

31. Paul Connerton, *How Societies Remember* (New York: Cambridge University Press, 1989), 21.

32. Ibid.

33. Ibid.

34. Daniel S. Weiss, "Psychodynamic Group Treatment," in *Psychological Effects of Catastrophic Disasters: Group Approaches to Treatment*, eds. Leon A. Schein et al. (Binghamton, NY: Haworth Press, 2006), 794. See also Constance Milbrath et al., "Sequential Consequences of Therapists' Interventions," *Journal of Psychotherapy Practice and Research* 8 (1999): 40–54; Charles H. Stinson, Constance Milbrath, and Mardi J. Horowitz, "Dysfluency and Topic Orientation in Bereaved Individuals: Bridging Individual and Group Studies," *Journal of Consulting and Clinical Psychology* 63 (1995): 37–45.

NOTES TO CHAPTER 5

1. Lou Michel and Dan Herbeck, *American Terrorist: Timothy McVeigh and the Oklahoma City Bombing* (New York: Harper, 2001), 169.

2. See Edward T. Linenthal, *The Unfinished Bombing: Oklahoma City in American Memory* (New York: Oxford University Press, 2001), 101.

3. See, e.g., "Oklahoma City Bomb Survivors Face Psychological Traumas," CNN, April 19, 1995; Connie Chung and Dr. Bob Arnot, "People Hospitalized and Traumatized by Oklahoma City Bombing Left to Deal with Injuries and Tragic Memories," *Evening News*, CBS, April 21, 1995; "Coping with Trauma," *Daily Oklahoman*, April 20, 1995, 12; "Helping Kids Deal with Bombing," *Daily Oklahoman*, April 21, 1995, 9; Randy Lee Loftis, "The Kindness of Strangers; Volunteers Help Search Teams Survive Trauma," *Dallas Morning News*, April 30, 1995, 1A; Cristine Russell, "How to Cope with Psychological Wounds, Whether from National Disaster or Personal Trauma," *Washington Post*, May 2, 1995, Z05; Susan Hightower, "Business Focuses on Healing," *Austin American-Statesman*, May 5, 1995, D3; Bernice McShane, "Emotional Wounds Need Healing," *Daily Oklahoman*, May 7, 1995, 4; Rebecca Howland, "Demolition May Fail to End Trauma," *Dallas Morning News*, May 24, 1995, 22A; Patsy Phillips and Barbara Graham, "Survival Mode: When the Trauma Is Over, a Return to Normal Is Vital," *Dallas Morning News*, December 10, 1995, 6J.

4. Allen Meek, *Trauma and Media: Theories, Histories and Images* (New York: Routledge, 2010), 6.

5. Ibid., 16.

6. Todd Gitlin, *The Whole World Is Watching* (Berkeley: University of California Press, 1980), 5, 52.

7. Meek, *Trauma and Media*, 173

8. Barbie Zelizer, *Covering the Body: The Kennedy Assassination, the Media, and the Shaping of Collective Memory* (Chicago: University of Chicago Press, 1992), 34.

9. Michael Schudson, "The Politics of Narrative Form: The Emergence of News Conventions in Print and Television," *Daedalus* 3, no. 4 (1982): 98; Robert Darnton, "Writing News and Telling Stories," *Daedalus* 104, no. 2 (1975): 264; Gitlin, *The Whole World Is Watching*, 4.

10. Gitlin, *The Whole World Is Watching*, 7.

11. Schudson, "Politics of Narrative Form," 98–99.

12. Ronald N. Jacobs, *Race, Media, and the Crisis of Civil Society: From Watts to Rodney King* (New York: Cambridge University Press, 2000), 8; Jeffrey Alexander and Philip Smith, "Discourse of American Civil Society," *Theory and Society* 22 (1993): 156.

13. Ibid.

14. Gitlin, *The Whole World Is Watching*, 4.

15. Harvey Molotch and Marilyn Lester, "News as Purposive Behavior: On the Strategic Use of Routine Events, Accidents, and Scandals," *American Sociological Review* 39 (1974): 108.

16. Frank Weed, *Certainty of Justice: Reform in the Crime Victim Movement* (Piscataway, NJ: Transaction, 1995), 36.

17. Hans Boutellier, *Crime and Morality: The Significance of Criminal Justice in Postmodern Culture* (Norwell, MA: Kluwer Academic Publishers, 2000), 50; Weed, *Certainty of Justice*, 39–40.

18. Jennifer L. Dunn, *Judging Victims: Why We Stigmatize Survivors, and How They Reclaim Respect* (Boulder, CO: Lynn Rienner, 2010), 12–13.

19. Erika Doss, *Memorial Mania* (Chicago: University of Chicago Press, 2010), 78.

20. Ibid.

21. Ibid., 79.

22. Weed, *Certainty of Justice*, 90.

23. Usually, audience members do not question or contest news conventions, and so they not only stabilize news but also perpetuate their own utility. The increased consolidation of media organizations into corporate conglomerates in recent years has only enhanced this process, resulting in more clichés, less diversity, more focus on the financial bottom line, less local news, more sensationalistic blood and gore, and greater polarization along "conservative" or "liberal" perspectives on the social order.

24. McVeigh's mother did indeed appear to have a complicated reaction to her son's involvement in the bombing. Although Mickey issued a statement immediately after McVeigh's arrest expressing "deep sympathy for the victims and their families," in 1997 she wrote an open letter to the public that was quite hostile. In this missive, she stated that McVeigh was not guilty and warned others to leave her family alone: "For your information, no one in my family, including my son, is a threat to anyone, even ourselves. . . . It is the FBI, the ATF and the media that need to be investigated and

followed—not my son nor family." "McVeighs in the Spotlight," *Denver Post*, June 12, 1997. The day after that letter was published in the *Orlando Sentinel*, Mickey was reportedly confined to a Florida mental hospital after suffering a psychotic episode. Ibid. In a 1999 media interview, Mickey pleaded for the world to move on and acknowledged her inability to come to terms with McVeigh's involvement. Associated Press, "McVeigh's Mother Speaks Out," *Topeka Capital-Journal*, December 3, 1999.

25. Gordon Witkin and Karen Roebuck, "Terrorist or Family Man? Terry Nichols Goes on Trial for the Oklahoma City Bombing," *U.S. News and World Report*, September 28, 1997.

26. Scott Parks and Victoria Lowe, "McVeigh Fits Pattern of Notorious Killers, Expert Says Ex-agent Sees a 'Dangerous' Profile Emerge in Bomb Suspect's History," *Dallas Morning News*, July 9, 1995, 1A.

27. Nichols's offspring were also mentioned by Michael Tigar in closing arguments on January 5, 1998.

28. Pete Slover, "Wife Says Terry Nichols Had No Role in Bombing, She Describes Suspect a 'Gentle Person,' 'Victim' But Expresses Wish for Divorce," *Dallas Morning News*, June 27, 1995, 1A.

29. George Rodriguez and Susan Feeney, "Neighbors Describe Pair's Anti-government Feelings," *Dallas Morning News*, April 22, 1995, 1A.

30. Gregg Jones, "Bombing Allegations Baffle Terry Nichols' In-laws in Philippines, but Wife's Family Raised Questions about Child's Death; Attorney Labels Suspicions 'Baseless,'" *Dallas Morning News*, May 27, 1995, 1A.

31. Lois Romano, "Nichols Defense Rests Its Case after Jury Hears More from Wife," *Washington Post*, December 12, 1997, A02.

32. Witkin and Roebuck, "Terrorist or Family Man?"

33. Ibid.

34. Sandy Shore, "Testimony Ends in Nichols Case," *Milwaukee Journal Sentinel*, January 3, 1998, 6A.

35. Stephen Power, "Army Pal Called Unlike McVeigh: Bombing Case Figure Seen as 'Happy-Go-Lucky,'" *Dallas Morning News*, May 29, 1995, 1A.

36. Ibid.

37. Lois Romano, "Nichols's Attorney Depicts Fortier as 'Thieving' Liar; Witness Undergoes Withering Cross-Examination," *Washington Post*, November 14, 1997, A03.

38. Lee Hancock, "Ex-McVeigh Friend Reaches Plea Agreement, Testifies before Grand Jury," *Dallas Morning News*, August 9, 1995, 14B.

39. David Willman, "Oklahoma City Bomb Blew Fortier onto Razor's Edge," *Los Angeles Times*, June 4, 1995, http://articles.latimes.com/1995-06-04/news/mn-13490_1_oklahoma-city.

40. Ibid.

41. Tom Kenworthy, "McVeigh Attorney Skewers Government Witness as Lying Drug User," *Washington Post*, May 1, 1997, A17.

42. Ibid.

43. Ibid.

44. Ibid.

45. Ibid.

46. Ibid.

47. *United States v. McVeigh and Nichols*, Pre-trial Transcript, "Hearing on Motions," 96-CR-68-M (D. Colo., October 4, 1996).

48. Ibid.

49. Ibid.

50. Ibid.

51. Ibid.

52. Ibid.

NOTES TO CHAPTER 6

1. Lawrence Douglas, *The Memory of Judgment: Making Law and History in the Trials of the Holocaust* (New Haven: Yale University Press, 2001), 1.

2. Paul Gerwitz, "Victims and Voyeurs: Two Narrative Problems at the Criminal Trial," in *Law's Stories: Narrative and Rhetoric in the Law*, ed. Peter Brooks and Paul Gerwitz (New Haven: Yale University Press, 1996), 151.

3. Another's death nullifies memory formation, but it does not terminate memorial debts; the living are still enmeshed in webs of obligation and representation. William James Booth, *Communities of Memory: On Witness, Identity, and Justice* (Ithaca: Cornell University Press, 2006), 98.

4. *Lujan v. Defenders of Wildlife*, 112 S. Ct. 2130, 2136 (1992).

5. David Luban, "Difference Made Legal: The Court and Dr. King," *Michigan Law Review* 87 (1989): 2152.

6. Booth, *Communities of Memory*, 115.

7. Ibid.

8. Barbie Zelizer, *Covering the Body: The Kennedy Assassination, the Media, and the Shaping of Collective Memory* (Chicago: University of Chicago Press, 1992), 2.

9. Maurice Halbwachs, *The Collective Memory* (Chicago: University of Chicago Press, 1982), 140.

10. Ibid., 58.

11. Mark Osiel, *Mass Atrocity, Collective Memory, and the Law* (Piscataway, NJ: Transaction, 1999), 76.

12. Victor Turner, *From Ritual to Theatre* (Baltimore: PAJ Publications, 1982), 75, 93.

13. Osiel, Mass Atrocity, 18.

14. Ibid., 72.

15. Halbwachs, *Collective Memory*, 140.

16. Stephen L. Winter, "The Cognitive Dimension of the Agony between Legal Power and Narrative Meaning," *Michigan Law Review* 87 (1989): 2230, 2270.

17. Ibid.

18. Kim Lane Scheppele, "Foreword: Telling Stories," *Michigan Law Review* 87 (1989): 2073, 2079.

19. Osiel, *Mass Atrocity*, 31.

20. Booth, *Communities of Memory*, xi. Sociologist Émile Durkheim posited that trials, verdicts, sentences, and punishment all embody the "conscience collective"; imposing punishment expresses and reinforces communal norms and values. David Garland, *Punishment and Modern Society* (Chicago: University of Chicago Press, 1990), 67, 57. Legal scholar Robert Cover has opined that law in its entirety is best expressed not

simply as a body of rules and doctrines but as a redemptive narrative of social struggle or as a normative universe whose inhabitants share "interpretive commitments." Winter, "The Cognitive Dimension of the Agony between Legal Power and Narrative Meaning," 2270; Robert Cover, "The Supreme Court, 1982 Term—Foreword: Nomos and Narrative," *Harvard Law Review* 97 (1983): 4–5, 7. From this perspective, laws are not only social demands upon us but also expressive signs in a communicative system "enabl[ing] us to submit, rejoice, struggle, pervert, mock, disgrace, humiliate, or dignify." Ibid., 8.

21. Gerwitz, "Victims and Voyeurs," 138.

22. Ibid., 137.

23. 42 U.S.C. § 10606(b)(4).

24. Booth, *Communities of Memory*, 98.

25. Ibid., 112.

26. Ibid., 116.

27. Ibid., 123.

28. Ibid., 121.

29. Ibid., 126.

30. Ibid., 130.

31. Ibid.

32. Ibid., 132

33. *United States v. McVeigh*, "Official Trial Transcript, Examination of Kay Ice, Peggy Broxterman, Jeannine Gist, Sharon Coyne, Andy Sullivan, Todd McCarthy, Ruth Hightower, Sue Mallonee, Susan Urbach and Katherine Youngblood," 96-CR-68 (D. Colo. June 5, 1997).

34. Ibid.

35. Carrie A. Rentschler, "Witnessing: US Citizenship and the Vicarious Experience of Suffering," *Media, Culture and Society* 26 (2004): 297.

36. Bruce A. Arrigo and Christopher R. Williams, "Victim Vices, Victim Voices, and Impact Statements: On the Place of Emotion and the Role of Restorative Justice in Capital Sentencing," *Crime and Delinquency* 49 (2003): 603.

37. Jody Lyneé Madeira, "A Constructed Peace: Narratives of Suture in the News Media," *Canadian Journal of Law and Society* 19 (2004): 93, 114–17.

38. Joseph L. Hoffman, "Revenge or Mercy? Some Thoughts about Survivor Opinion Evidence in Death Penalty Cases," *Cornell Law Review* 88 (2002): 530, 538.

NOTES TO CHAPTER 7

1. President William Jefferson Clinton, "Remarks by the President at Announcement of Victims' Rights Constitutional Amendment," *Online Newshour*, PBS, June 25, 1996, http://www.pbs.org/newshour/bb/law/june96/victim_announcement_6-25.html.

2. Lawrence H. Tribe, opposite letter to the editor, "McVeigh's Victims Had a Right to Speak," *New York Times*, June 9, 1997, A25.

3. *United States v. Nichols*, "Terry Lynn Nichols' Motion in Limine Concerning Victim Identification Testimony," 96-CR-68-M (D. Colo. October 24, 1997) (quoting Statement of the Court in Questioning of Juror No. 948, Tr. 3595).

4. *United States v. McVeigh*, "Official Trial Transcript, Examination of Mathilda Westberry, David Florence, Teresa Brown, Sharon Medearis, Susan Walton, Eric

Thompson, Dora Reyes, Pamela Whicher, Kathleen Treanor, Laura Kennedy, Cheryl Elliott, Todd McCarthy and Susan Urbach," 96-CR-68 (D. Colo. June 4, 1997).

5. See Terry Maroney, "Law and Emotion: A Proposed Taxonomy of an Emerging Field," *Law and Human Behavior* 30, no. 2 (2006): 132.

6. *Saffle v. Parks*, 494 U.S. 484, 491 (1990); *California v. Brown*, 479 U.S. 538, 545 (1987).

7. See Arlie Russell Hochschild, *The Managed Heart* (Berkeley: University of California Press, 1983), 30.

8. Paul Gerwitz, "Victims and Voyeurs: Two Narrative Problems at the Criminal Trial," in *Law's Stories: Narrative and Rhetoric in the Law*, ed. Peter Brooks and Paul Gerwitz (New Haven: Yale University Press, 1996), 145.

9. Ibid., 144. This rejection of emotion has often been publicly criticized. See David Brooks, "The Empathy Issue," *New York Times*, May 28, 2009, A25.

10. Hochschild, *Managed Heart*, 30.

11. President William Jefferson Clinton, "Remarks at Announcement of the Victims' Rights Constitutional Amendment."

12. Hochschild, *Managed Heart*, 30.

13. *United States v. McVeigh*, 918 F. Sup. 1467, 1471 (W.D. Okl. 1996).

14. Ibid.

15. Ibid., 1472.

16. Ibid.

17. Ibid.

18. *United States v. Skilling*, "Transcript of Oral Argument," 8–9 (U.S. March 1, 2010), http://www.supremecourt.gov/oral_arguments/argument_transcripts/08-1394.pdf.

19. Mark Johnson, "Congress Rewriting Laws to Support Victims' Rights," *Richmond Times Dispatch*, April 30, 1997, A-8.

20. Arnold Hamilton, "Extended Gallery: Oklahoma Bomb Survivors to View Telecast of Trial," *Dallas Morning News*, March 23, 1997, 47A.

21. *United States v. McVeigh and Nichols*, "Motion and Brief in Support of Closed-Circuit Televising of Trial Proceedings to Oklahoma City," 96-CR-68-M (D. Colo. May 1, 1996).

22. *United States v. McVeigh and Nichols*, "Response of Timothy McVeigh to Government's Motion for Closed-Circuit Televising of Trial Proceedings under Section 235 of the Anti-Terrorism Statute and Request for Oral Argument," 96-CR-68-M (D. Colo. June 3, 1996).

23. Ibid.

24. Ibid.

25. Ibid.

26. Ibid.

27. Ibid.

28. Ibid.

29. Johnson, "Congress Rewriting Laws to Support Victims' Rights," A8.

30. Ibid.

31. Ibid. These regulations included "no talking, no food, no demonstrative behavior and no newspaper reading," and no reentry for those leaving the courtroom outside of break periods. Brian Ford, "OC Site to Be Extension of Courtroom in Denver," *Tulsa*

World, March 30, 1997, A5; G. Robert Hillman, "Telecast Draws Few Spectators," *Denver Post*, April 1, 1997, A1.

32. Ford, "OC Site to Be Extension of Courtroom in Denver."

33. *United States v. McVeigh*, "Pre-trial Transcript Hearing on Motions," 96-CR-68-M (D. Colo. October 4, 1996).

34. Ibid.

35. Ibid.

36. This is borne out in an exchange between Judge Matsch and prosecuting attorney Vicki Behenna in which Behenna sought to persuade the judge not to exclude victim witnesses. Ibid.

37. Ibid.

38. Ibid.

39. Ibid.

40. Ibid.

41. *United States v. McVeigh and Nichols*, "Memorandum of Marsha and H. Tom Kight, Paul A. Heath, Jean Bell, Maureen Bloomer, Marvin Buckner, Martin and Margie Cash, Jannie Coverdale, Chris and Sandra Cregan, Dawn and Jodie DeArmon, Dorris and Ernest Delman, Leslie and Mike Downey, Cecil Elliot, Donna Hawthorne, Paul Howell, Sharon Littlejohn, Diane Leonard, Cathy and C. Neil McCaskell, Amy Petty, Roy Sells, Terri Shaw, Patricia and Enterice Smiley, Steve Smith, Tina Tomlin, Richard and Kim Tomlin, Judy Walker, Paul Willetta, and the National Organization for Victim Assistance Urging the Court to Reconsider Exclusion of Victim Impact Witnesses," 96-CR-68-M (D. Colo. October 4, 1996).

42. Robert E. Boczkiewicz, "Bombing Defendant Uses Victims' Words to Oppose Admission," *Daily Oklahoma*, November 13, 1996, 9.

43. Ibid.

44. Dan Rather, "Terry Nichols, Defendant in Oklahoma City Bombing Case, Tries to Polish His Image as His Trial Grows Closer," *Evening News*, CBS, January 24, 1997.

45. Ibid.

46. *United States v. McVeigh*, 106 F.3d 325 (10th Cir. 1997).

47. Cong. Rec. H1048 (March 18, 1997).

48. Cong. Rec. H1050 (March 18, 1997).

49. Cong. Rec. S2507 (March 19, 1997).

50. Cong. Rec. S2508 (March 19, 1997).

51. Cong. Rec. 1050 (March 18, 1997).

52. Cong. Rec. 1051 (March 18, 1997). See also the remarks of Representative Bill Delahunt. Cong. Rec. 1052 (March 18, 1997).

53. *United States v. McVeigh*, "Hearings on Motions (Victims Rights Clarification, Motion for Voir Dire of Jury, Motion for Recess, Motion in Limine, Motion for Voir Dire of Witnesses)," 96-CR-68 (D. Colo. June 3, 1997).

54. *United States v. McVeigh*, "Defense Closing Arguments," 96-CR-68 (D. Colo. May 29, 1997).

55. Ibid.

56. Ibid.

57. Jo Thomas, "The Oklahoma City Bombing: The Trial Judge Warns Both Sides against 'Lynching,'" *New York Times*, June 4, 1997, A1.

58. Michael Fleeman, "Judge Acts to Prevent 'Lynching,'" *Herald Sun (NC)*, June 4, 1997, A1; Thomas, "Oklahoma City Bombing," A1.

59. Fleeman, "Judge Acts to Prevent 'Lynching.'"

60. Ibid.

61. Jillian Lloyd, "How Emotion Plays Out in U.S. Courtrooms," *Christian Science Monitor*, November 7, 1997, 1.

62. Mark Osiel, *Mass Atrocity, Collective Memory, and the Law* (Piscataway, NJ: Transaction, 1997), 80.

63. Ibid., 82.

64. The Israeli Supreme Court purported to adhere to such modesty in the trial of former Nazi soldier Adolf Eichmann. See *Attorney General of Israel v. Eichmann*, 36 I.L.R. 5, 18–19 (Isr. Dist. Ct. 1961).

65. Osiel, *Mass Atrocity*, 216.

66. Ibid., 242.

67. Ibid., 136.

68. Selma Leydesdorff, "A Shattered Silence: The Life Stories of Survivors of the Jewish Proletariat of Amsterdam," in *Memory and Totalitarianism*, ed. Luisa Passerini (Piscataway, NJ: Transaction, 1992), 145, 147–48.

69. Ibid., 104.

70. Ibid., 164.

71. Ibid., 80.

72. Even trials of great historical moment, such as the Nuremberg trials, seemed in the words of one journalist to be "insufferably tedious." See ibid., 91.

73. Ibid., 210.

74. Lawrence Douglas, *The Memory of Judgment: Making Law and History in the Trials of the Holocaust* (New Haven: Yale University Press, 2001), 3.

75. Gerwitz, "Victims and Voyeurs," 145. According to legal scholar Paul Gerwitz, "bounding" emotion places a limit on certain "emotional exchanges" that are "excessively inflammatory" or "based on . . . prejudice," and must be subject to "reasoned examination"; after victim impact evidence is given, for instance, prosecution and defense lawyers should be allowed to make arguments to the jury prompting them to "think about their emotional responses and test them through thought, and vice versa." Ibid., 146.

76. Ibid., 157–58.

NOTES TO CHAPTER 8

1. Valerie Richardson, "Emotion Subdued at Trial of Nichols," *Washington Times*, November 10, 1997, A3.

2. Jo Thomas, "At Second Bombing Trial, Stories Are Terse, but Still Powerful," *New York Times*, November 5, 1997, A10.

3. Ibid.

4. Judith Crosson, "U.S.: Oklahoma Bomb Trial Jury Told to Rein in Emotions," *AAP News Feed*, January 1, 1998.

5. Richardson, "Emotion Subdued at Trial of Nichols," A3.

6. Ibid.

7. Ibid.

8. Ibid.

9. Ibid.

10. Ibid.

11. Peter G. Chronis, "Jury Makeup Was Key, Indecision Seen as Victory for Defense," *Denver Post*, January 12, 1998, B1.

12. Lois Romano and Tom Kenworthy, "Nichols Spared Death Penalty," *Washington Post*, January 8, 1998, A01.

13. Ibid.

14. Ibid.

15. Ibid.

16. Lynn Bartels, "Exoneration for Nichols Came Near; Bomb Trial Jury Voted; 10–2 to Acquit at First," *Rocky Mountain News*, June 1, 1998, A1.

17. Ibid.

18. Ibid.

19. Ibid.

20. Ibid.

21. Ibid.

22. Ibid.

23. Associated Press, "Nichols Should Suffer the Same Fate as . . . McVeigh," *St. Louis Post-Dispatch*, January 8, 1998, A4.

24. "Oklahoma to Try Terry Nichols on Murder and Bomb Charges," *New York Times*, March 30 1999, http://www.nytimes.com/1999/03/30/us/oklahoma-to-try-terry-nichols-on-murder-and-bomb-charges.html. In a preliminary hearing, District Judge Allen McCall initially permitted the government to upgrade a manslaughter charge to murder for the unborn son of Carrie Lenz, Doris Jones's daughter, since the fetus was 24 weeks or older; District Judge Steven Taylor, however, later ruled that this was impermissible because Nichols had not been given enough notice of the additional count. Barbara Hoberock, "Court Denies Second Fetus Murder Charge," *Tulsa World*, November 22, 2003, A15.

25. Ibid.

26. Ibid.

27. Kevin Johnson, "Oklahomans' Feelings Are Mixed on Nichols' Trial," *USA Today*, May 10, 2004, 3A.

28. Times Wire Reports, "Judge OKs Change of Venue in Nichols Trial," *Los Angeles Times*, September 8, 2003, http://articles.latimes.com/2003/sep/08/nation/na-briefs8.5.

29. Johnson, "Oklahomans' Feelings Are Mixed on Nichols' Trial," 3A.

30. Barbara Hoberock, "Analysis: Venue Raises Questions," *Tulsa World*, May 30, 2004, A13.

31. AP, "Religious Conversion May Have Saved Nichols," *FoxNews.com*, June 13, 2004, http://www.foxnews.com/story/0,2933,122527,00.html.

32. Barbara Hoberock and Rod Walton, "Hung Jury Means Life Sentence for Nichols," *Tulsa World*, June 12, 2004, A1.

33. Ibid.

34. Ibid.

35. Terry Nichols federal filing, http://www.thesmokinggun.com/file/terry-nicholss-gut-wrenching-pain.

36. *Terry Nichols v. Federal Bureau of Prisons*, Civil Action No. 09-cv-00558-CMA-CBS (D. Colo. August 12, 2010), http://online.wsj.com/public/resources/documents/081210nicholsorder.pdf.

37. "McVeigh Trial Jurors Visit Oklahoma City," *St. Petersburg Times*, June 20, 1998, 4A.

38. "Introductory Letter to Jurors" (June 26, 1997) (on file with Oklahoma City National Memorial Archives).

39. Lois Romano, "Year after Guilty Verdict, Jurors Visit Bomb Site," *Washington Post*, June 21, 1998, A01.

40. Broadcast transcript, KOTV Channel 6 (June 20, 1998) (on file with Oklahoma City National Memorial Archives).

41. Rochelle Hines, "Jurors Weep at Site of Carnage," *Daily Telegraph (Australia)*, June 22, 1998, 25.

42. Romano, "Year after Guilty Verdict, Jurors Visit Bomb Site."

43. Broadcast transcript, KOTV Channel 6 (June 20, 1998) (on file with Oklahoma City National Memorial Archives).

44. Romano, "Year after Guilty Verdict, Jurors Visit Bomb Site."

45. Ibid.

46. Ibid.

47. Broadcast transcript, KOTV Channel 6 (June 20, 1998) (on file with Oklahoma City National Memorial Archives).

48. Broadcast transcript, KTUL Channel 8 (June 20, 1998) (on file with Oklahoma City National Memorial Archives).

49. *Good Morning America*, ABC, June 22, 1998.

50. Broadcast transcript, KTUL Channel 8 (June 20, 1998) (on file with Oklahoma City National Memorial Archives).

51. *Good Morning America*, ABC, rebroadcast on KOCO, June 22, 1998.

52. Romano, "Year after Guilty Verdict, Jurors Visit Bomb Site."

53. Ibid.

54. *Today Show*, NBC, June 22, 1998.

55. Broadcast transcript, KTUL Channel 8 (June 20, 1998) (on file with Oklahoma City National Memorial Archives).

56. Roger O'Neil, *Today Show*, NBC, June 21, 1998.

57. *Today Show*, NBC, June 20, 1998.

58. Broadcast transcript, KFOR (June 22, 1998) (on file with Oklahoma City National Memorial Archives).

59. Broadcast transcript, KOTV Channel 6 (June 22, 1998) (on file with Oklahoma City National Memorial Archives).

60. *Good Morning America*, ABC, June 22, 1998.

61. Romano, "Year after Guilty Verdict, Jurors Visit Bomb Site."

62. *Today Show*, NBC, June 22, 1998.

63. Broadcast transcript, KTUL Channel 8 (June 20, 1998) (on file with Oklahoma City National Memorial Archives).

64. Broadcast transcript, KOTV Channel 6 (June 20, 1998) (on file with Oklahoma City National Memorial Archives).

65. Romano, "Year after Guilty Verdict, Jurors Visit Bomb Site."

66. Ibid.

67. Hines, "Jurors Weep at Site of Carnage," 25.

68. *Today Show*, NBC, June 20, 1998.

69. Romano, "Year after Guilty Verdict, Jurors Visit Bomb Site."

70. Ibid.

71. *The World Today*, CNN, June 20, 1998.

72. Broadcast transcript, KOTV Channel 6 (June 20, 1998) (on file with Oklahoma City National Memorial Archives).

73. Ibid.

74. Broadcast transcript, KWTV (June 20, 1998) (on file with Oklahoma City National Memorial Archives).

75. Nor was the McVeigh jurors' visit to Oklahoma City the only such trip. In 1999, many members of the habeas group and their spouses traveled to Denver to visit once more with jurors, who arranged a tour bus trip to various Colorado destinations. Judge Gaspar Perricone, who presided over the remote courtroom, also returned a few years later to visit family members and survivors in Oklahoma City, many of whom in turn visited him in Colorado.

NOTES TO CHAPTER 9

1. "Attorney General John Ashcroft, "Statement Regarding the Execution of Timothy McVeigh," press release, Department of Justice (April 12, 2001), http://www.usdoj.gov/opa/pr2001/April/169ag.htm.

2. Ibid.

3. Nick Smith, *I Was Wrong: The Meanings of Apologies* (New York: Cambridge University Press, 2008), 132–33.

4. This explains why, in existing victim-offender mediation programs implemented in several states, both victims' family members *and* the offender have to voluntarily consent to such a meeting. Otherwise, finding themselves opposite a defiant or outright hostile offender could detrimentally affect family members' memory work.

5. Ashcroft, "Statement Regarding the Execution of Timothy McVeigh."

NOTES TO CHAPTER 10

1. Letter from Michael Fortier's mother to Timothy McVeigh (June 19, 1999) (on file with the American Terrorist Collection, Friedsam Memorial Library Archives, St. Bonaventure University).

2. Letter to Lou Michel from Timothy McVeigh (April 16, 1999) (on file with the American Terrorist Collection, Friedsam Memorial Library Archives, St. Bonaventure University).

3. Ibid.

4. Letter to Lou Michel from Timothy McVeigh (April 24, 2001) (on file with the American Terrorist Collection, Friedsam Memorial Library Archives, St. Bonaventure University).

5. Transcript of Lou Michel interview with Timothy McVeigh, p. 21 (on file with the American Terrorist Collection, Friedsam Memorial Library Archives, St. Bonaventure University).

6. Lou Michel and Dan Herbeck, *American Terrorist: Timothy McVeigh and the Oklahoma Bombing* (New York: Harper, 2001), 290–91.

7. Letter to Phil Bacharach from Timothy McVeigh (April 2, 1998) (provided by Phil Bacharach).

8. Letter to Lou Michel from Timothy McVeigh (May 12, 1998) (on file with the American Terrorist Collection, Friedsam Memorial Library Archives, St. Bonaventure University).

9. Letter to Lou Michel from Timothy McVeigh (June 1, 1999) (on file with the American Terrorist Collection, Friedsam Memorial Library Archives, St. Bonaventure University).

10. Letter to Lou Michel from Timothy McVeigh (May 29, 1998) (on file with the American Terrorist Collection, Friedsam Memorial Library Archives, St. Bonaventure University).

11. Letter to Phil Bacharach from Timothy McVeigh (January 22, 1999) (provided by Phil Bacharach).

12. Letter to Lou Michel from Timothy McVeigh (April 16, 1998) (on file with the American Terrorist Collection, Friedsam Memorial Library Archives, St. Bonaventure University); letter to Lou Michel from Timothy McVeigh (February 18, 2000) (on file with the American Terrorist Collection, Friedsam Memorial Library Archives, St. Bonaventure University).

13. Letter to Lou Michel from Timothy McVeigh (February 12, 2000) (on file with the American Terrorist Collection, Friedsam Memorial Library Archives, St. Bonaventure University).

14. Transcript of Lou Michel interview with Timothy McVeigh, p. 9 (on file with the American Terrorist Collection, Friedsam Memorial Library Archives, St. Bonaventure University).

15. Letter to Lou Michel from Timothy McVeigh (May 12, 1998) (on file with the American Terrorist Collection, Friedsam Memorial Library Archives, St. Bonaventure University).

16. Letter to Lou Michel from Timothy McVeigh (April 12, 1998) (on file with the American Terrorist Collection, Friedsam Memorial Library Archives, St. Bonaventure University); letter to Lou Michel from Timothy McVeigh (April 13, 1998) (on file with the American Terrorist Collection, Friedsam Memorial Library Archives, St. Bonaventure University).

17. Letter to Lou Michel from Timothy McVeigh (April 13, 1998) (on file with the American Terrorist Collection, Friedsam Memorial Library Archives, St. Bonaventure University).

18. Letter to Lou Michel from Timothy McVeigh (January 27, 2000) (on file with the American Terrorist Collection, Friedsam Memorial Library Archives, St. Bonaventure University).

19. Letter to Lou Michel from Timothy McVeigh (May 12, 2001) (on file with the American Terrorist Collection, Friedsam Memorial Library Archives, St. Bonaventure University).

20. Letter to Lou Michel from Timothy McVeigh (April 19, 2001) (on file with the American Terrorist Collection, Friedsam Memorial Library Archives, St. Bonaventure University).

21. Transcript of Lou Michel interview with Timothy McVeigh, pp. 8–9 (on file with the American Terrorist Collection, Friedsam Memorial Library Archives, St. Bonaventure University).

22. Letter to Lou Michel from Timothy McVeigh (March 25, 2000) (on file with the American Terrorist Collection, Friedsam Memorial Library Archives, St. Bonaventure University).

23. Letter to Lou Michel from Timothy McVeigh (March 6, 2001) (on file with the American Terrorist Collection, Friedsam Memorial Library Archives, St. Bonaventure University).

24. Transcript of Lou Michel interview with Timothy McVeigh, p. 32 (on file with the American Terrorist Collection, Friedsam Memorial Library Archives, St. Bonaventure University).

25. Ibid., 21.

26. Ibid., 49.

27. Ibid, 32.

28. McVeigh actually used this term incorrectly; "collateral damage" refers to harm to an unintended target, intimating that McVeigh did not intend civilians to die in the bombing. But he intentionally detonated the truck bomb outside the Murrah Building at 9:00 a.m. when employees were beginning their workday, not in the dead of night when the building would be empty. Indeed, government employees were arguably McVeigh's targets as much as the Murrah Building itself.

29. Letter to Lou Michel from Timothy McVeigh (April 19, 2001) (on file with the American Terrorist Collection, Friedsam Memorial Library Archives, St. Bonaventure University).

30. Interview, *60 Minutes*, CBS, June 2000.

31. Ibid.

32. Letter to Phil Bacharach from Timothy McVeigh (April 11, 1998) (provided by Phil Bacharach).

33. Letter to Terri Watkins from Timothy McVeigh (March 26, 1998) (on file with Oklahoma City National Memorial Archives).

34. Letter to Lou Michel from Timothy McVeigh (December 12, 2000) (on file with the American Terrorist Collection, Friedsam Memorial Library Archives, St. Bonaventure University).

35. Letter to Lou Michel from Timothy McVeigh (April 12, 2000) (on file with the American Terrorist Collection, Friedsam Memorial Library Archives, St. Bonaventure University).

36. Letter to Lou Michel from Timothy McVeigh (April 21, 2000) (on file with the American Terrorist Collection, Friedsam Memorial Library Archives, St. Bonaventure University).

37. Letter to Lou Michel from Timothy McVeigh (February 19, 2001) (on file with the American Terrorist Collection, Friedsam Memorial Library Archives, St. Bonaventure University).

38. Letter to Lou Michel from Timothy McVeigh (June 1, 1999) (on file with the American Terrorist Collection, Friedsam Memorial Library Archives, St. Bonaventure University).

39. Ibid.

40. Ibid.

41. Ibid.

42. Ibid.

43. Letter to Lou Michel from Timothy McVeigh (June 3, 2000) (on file with the American Terrorist Collection, Friedsam Memorial Library Archives, St. Bonaventure University).

44. Letter to Lou Michel from Timothy McVeigh (April 10, 2001) (on file with the American Terrorist Collection, Friedsam Memorial Library Archives, St. Bonaventure University); transcript of Lou Michel interview with Timothy McVeigh, p. 29 (on file with the American Terrorist Collection, Friedsam Memorial Library Archives, St. Bonaventure University).

45. Transcript of Lou Michel interview with Timothy McVeigh, p. 16 (on file with the American Terrorist Collection, Friedsam Memorial Library Archives, St. Bonaventure University).

46. Ibid., 42.

47. Interview, *60 Minutes*, CBS.

48. Letter to Lou Michel from Timothy McVeigh (June 26, 1999) (on file with the American Terrorist Collection, Friedsam Memorial Library Archives, St. Bonaventure University).

49. "McVeigh Tapes," *Rachel Maddow Show*, MSNBC, April 19, 2010.

50. Transcript of Lou Michel interview with Timothy McVeigh, p. 26 (on file with the American Terrorist Collection, Friedsam Memorial Library Archives, St. Bonaventure University).

51. Letter to Lou Michel from Timothy McVeigh (April 19, 2001) (on file with the American Terrorist Collection, Friedsam Memorial Library Archives, St. Bonaventure University).

52. Letter to Nolan Clay from Timothy McVeigh (February 1, 2001) (on file with Oklahoma City National Memorial Archives).

53. Ibid.

54. Letter to Lou Michel from Timothy McVeigh (October 13, 2001) (on file with the American Terrorist Collection, Friedsam Memorial Library Archives, St. Bonaventure University).

55. Ibid.

56. Transcript of Lou Michel interview with Timothy McVeigh, p. 58 (on file with the American Terrorist Collection, Friedsam Memorial Library Archives, St. Bonaventure University).

57. Letter to Lou Michel from Timothy McVeigh (January 26, 2001) (on file with the American Terrorist Collection, Friedsam Memorial Library Archives, St. Bonaventure University).

58. Letter to Lou Michel from Timothy McVeigh (November 17, 2000) (on file with the American Terrorist Collection, Friedsam Memorial Library Archives, St. Bonaventure University).

59. Transcript of Lou Michel interview with Timothy McVeigh, p. 24 (on file with the American Terrorist Collection, Friedsam Memorial Library Archives, St. Bonaventure University).

60. Ibid.

61. Letter to Lou Michel from Timothy McVeigh (June 1, 1999) (on file with the American Terrorist Collection, Friedsam Memorial Library Archives, St. Bonaventure University).

62. Transcript of Lou Michel interview with Timothy McVeigh, p. 47 (on file with the American Terrorist Collection, Friedsam Memorial Library Archives, St. Bonaventure University).

63. Letter to Lou Michel from Timothy McVeigh (April 5, 2001) (on file with the American Terrorist Collection, Friedsam Memorial Library Archives, St. Bonaventure University).

64. Letter to Lou Michel from Timothy McVeigh (April 19, 2001) (on file with the American Terrorist Collection, Friedsam Memorial Library Archives, St. Bonaventure University).

65. Tom Morganthau, Andrew Miller, and Flynn McRoberts, "Outcry over a Killer's Story," April 9, 2001, http://www.msnbc.com/news/552989.asp.

66. Ibid.

67. Ibid.

68. "Bob Johnson's Comments to the Press—March 28, 2001" (March 29, 2001) (on file with Oklahoma City National Memorial Archives).

69. Kari Watkins, confidential memo to board and staff re: media regarding "American Terrorist" book release, Thursday March 29, 2001 (on file with Oklahoma City National Memorial Archives).

70. Ibid.

71. Nancy Sherman, *The Untold War: Inside the Hearts, Minds, and Souls of Our Soldiers* (New York: Norton, 2010), 4.

72. Ibid., 30.

73. Nancy Sherman, *Stoic Warriors: The Ancient Philosophy behind the Military Mind* (New York: Oxford University Press, 2005), 121.

74. Ibid., 164.

NOTES TO CHAPTER 11

1. Letter to Timothy McVeigh from Warden Harley G. Lappin (January 16, 2001) (on file with the American Terrorist Collection, Friedsam Memorial Library Archives, St. Bonaventure University).

2. Kevin Johnson, "Witnesses See the End Come Quickly, Quietly," *USA Today*, June 12, 2001, http://www.usatoday.com/news/nation/june01/2001-06-12-mcveigh-witness.htm.

3. "Remarks by President Bush on McVeigh Execution," press release, White House, http://www.whitehouse.gov/news/releases/2001/06/20010611.html.

4. "Timothy McVeigh Executed," *Larry King Live*, CNN, June 11, 2001, http://www-cgi.cnn.com/TRANSCRIPTS/0106/11/lkl.00.html.

5. Michel Foucault, *Discipline and Punish: The Birth of the Prison*, trans. Alan Sheridan (New York: Random House, 1979), 34.

6. Pieter Spierenburg, *The Spectacle of Suffering* (New York: Cambridge University Press, 1984), 43, 54.

7. Ibid., 55, 60–61.

8. Anthony Giddens, *Modernity and Self-Identity* (Stanford, CA: Stanford University Press, 1991), 162.

9. Legally, the execution image has been characterized as having a disruptive and disturbing potential, motivating the state and courts to place boundaries upon such images. The criminal justice system carefully controls access to executions, lest others, particularly journalists, photograph or film the execution, violating the dual rubrics of privacy and safety; 28 C.F.R. § 26.4(f) prohibits photographic, audio, and visual recording devices at federal executions. In cases addressing the media's right to film an execution, judges have disagreed on the import of the execution image, variously finding that it has no special quality and that it is "qualitatively different from a mere verbal report about an execution." *Garrett v. Estelle*, 556 F.2d 1274, 1278 (C.A. Tex. 1977); *Halquist v. Department of Corrections*, 732 P.2d 1065, 1067 (Wash. 1989). In addition, they have found that filming and/or televising an execution would breach participating staff and officials' privacy, security in the chamber, and the inmate's "residual right to privacy"; would introduce novel questions such as where the camera would be placed; and they have posited a "suicidal cameraman theory," designed to protect attendees from "heavy objects of any sort" such as cameras that, if thrown in the witness room, might strike "the [gas] chamber." *KQED v. Vasquez*, 1991 U.S. Dist. LEXIS 21163 at **8 (June 7, 1991). In one case, the judge upheld a ban on cameras in the execution chamber to prevent inmates from being "dehumanized" and to preserve the solemnity of execution. *Entertainment Network v. Lappin*, 134 F. Supp. 2d 1002, 1018 (S.D. Ind. 2001).

10. Admitting victim witnesses into executions is a fairly recent development, with many states first allowing victims' families to witness in the early to mid-1990s (a handful of states still do not allow this). States such as Oklahoma may have passed legislation allowing family members to witness after state legislators, themselves survivors of homicide, wanted to attend the execution of the responsible offenders. Other states commit the determination of whether victims should be allowed to witness not to legislation but to the prison warden's prerogative. This information comes from recorded interviews with capital victim witness advocates in Oklahoma, Missouri, North Carolina, South Carolina, Virginia, Ohio, Georgia, Alabama, and Florida.

11. Paul Howell said: "Once they opened up the curtains, and he looked at his lawyers, gave them kind of a nod. Then he turned his head to the media, looked at them for a few seconds, nodded to them and turned to us and looked at us, and it was only a couple of two or three seconds. I guess he realized then that he could not see us. And so once that happened and he turned back around and stared right straight at the ceiling."

12. In an interview with one state official, the official described an execution at a prison where the victim viewing room was positioned at the foot of the execution table, which was positioned horizontally. During the execution of an obese offender, victims complained that they were not able to see past the offender's girth to his face. Afterwards, the head of the execution table was positioned at a sloping angle to allow witnesses to see the offender's face at all times.

13. Transcript, "Judge Denies Stay of Execution for McVeigh, Appeal Expected, CNN Breaking News, June 6, 2001, http://transcripts.cnn.com/TRANSCRIPTS/0106/06/bn.03.html.

14. Terry Horne, "Viewers Struck by Look in McVeigh's Eyes," *Indianapolis Star*, June 12, 2001, http://www2.indystar.com/library/factfiles/crime/national/1995/oklahoma_city_bombing/stories/2001_0612b.html.

15. Michael Argyle and Mark Cook, *Gaze and Mutual Gaze* (New York: Cambridge University Press, 1976), 74.

16. Ibid., ix.

17. Ibid., 84.

18. Adam Kendon, "Some Functions of Gaze Direction in Social Interaction," *Acta Psychologica* 26 (1967): 1–47.

19. See Michael Argyle, *Bodily Communication*, 2d ed. (Madison, CT: International Universities Press, 1988).

20. Ibid., 112 (citing Erving Goffman, *Behavior in Public Places* [New York: Free Press, 1963]).

21. Ibid., 112, 114.

22. According to Kendon, 11 out of 20 subjects in an experimental interview situation spontaneously commented on variations in an interviewer's gaze pattern when it deviated from normal, whereas none mentioned the gaze when the interviewer's gaze patterns remained normal. Argyle and Cook, *Gaze and Mutual Gaze*, 83.

23. Ibid., 85.

24. Ibid.

25. Ibid.

26. See Henry Thomas Moore and Adam Raymond Gilliland, "The Measurement of Aggressiveness," *Journal of Experimental Social Psychology* 7 (1921): 623–26; Stephen Thayer, "The Effect of Interpersonal Looking Duration in Dominance Judgments," *Journal of Social Psychology* 79 (1969): 285–86; Ralph V. Exline, Steve L. Ellyson, and Barbara Long, "Visual Behavior as an Aspect of Power Role Relationships," in *Nonverbal Communication of Aggression*, ed. Patricia Pliner, Lester Krames, and Thomas Alloway (New York: Plenum Press, 1975), 21–52; Phoebe Ellsworth, "Direct Gaze as a Social Stimulus: The Example of Aggression," in *Nonverbal Communication of Aggression*, ed. Patricia Pliner, Lester Krames, and Thomas Alloway (New York: Plenum Press, 1975), 53–75; Phoebe Ellsworth and Ellen J. Langer, "Staring and Approach: An Interpretation of the Stare as a Nonspecific Activator," *Journal of Personality and Social Psychology* 33 (1976): 117–22; Elliot Liebow, *Talley's Corner*, (Lanham, MD: Rowman and Littlefield, 1967); Donald Karl Fromme and Donna Clegg Beam, "Dominance and Sex Differences in Nonverbal Responses to Differential Eye Contact," *Journal of Research in Personality* 8 (1974): 76–87. Allan Mazur et al., "Physiological Aspects of Communication via Mutual Gaze," *American Journal of Sociology* 86 (1980): 63, 64; Brenda J. Smith, Fonda Sanford, and Morton Goldman, "Norm Violations, Sex, and the 'Blank Stare,'" *Journal of Social Psychology* 103 (1977): 49–55. Scientific studies have concluded that participants' level of comfort with staring was a "strong predictor" of dominance in subsequent interactions, with participants who reported being more comfortable with the stare taking a dominant role in subsequent conversation and decision-making tasks. Mazur et al., "Physiological Aspects of Communication via Mutual Gaze," 70.

27. Ibid.

28. Ibid., 52.

29. Argyle and Cook, *Gaze and Mutual Gaze*, 74.

30. Horne, "Viewers Struck by Look in McVeigh's Eyes."

31. Ibid.

32. Ibid.

33. Ibid.

34. "McVeigh Shows No Remorse at Execution," Court TV, http://www.courttv.com/news/mcveigh_special/0612_noremorse_ap.html.

35. Nick Bryant, "Pain Remains for McVeigh Victims," BBC, June 11, 2001, http://news.bbc.co.uk/2/hi/americas/1383171.stm.

36. Ibid.

37. "Family Members Witness [sic] to McVeigh Execution Recount Their Experience," live event, CNN, transcript, June 11, 2001, http://transcripts.cnn.com/TRANSCRIPTS/0106/11/se.08.html.

38. Ibid.

39. Ibid.

40. Adam Jaworski, *The Power of Silence: Social and Pragmatic Perspectives* (Newberry, CA: Sage, 1993), 38, 69.

41. Ibid., 46 (quoting Ron Scollon, "The Machine Stops: Silence in the Metaphor of Malfunction," in *Perspectives on Silence*, ed. Deborah Tannen and Muriel Saville-Troike [Norwood, NJ: Ablex, 1985], 21–30).

42. Wlodzimierz Sobkowiak, "Silence and Markedness Theory," in *Silence: Interdisciplinary Perspectives*, ed. Adam Jaworski (Berlin: Walter de Gruyter, 1997), 46.

43. Ibid., 77.

44. Ibid., 67.

45. "Timothy McVeigh Executed," *Larry King Live*, CNN, June 11, 2001, http://www-cgi.cnn.com/TRANSCRIPTS/0106/11/lkl.00.html.

46. This change in focus was provoked by a conversation I had with a colleague concerning the college graduation of his daughter. Graduation day temperatures soared to 90 degrees, and there was limited shade for attendees, prompting college officials to open a remote witnessing location featuring a big screen in the campus chapel. Attendees in the chapel, including my colleague, could see everything of note—individual graduates receiving degrees, the enthusiastic cheering of live spectators. However, when remote witnesses' loved ones received their degrees, the remote witnesses did not cheer or clap; a "sheepish few" clapped, but did so halfheartedly and stopped their clapping very soon. There seemed to be little communicative purpose without a receiver present, particularly in view of the code of silent witnessing that was imposed. This may also be the case with the differences in communicative activity in the closed-circuit location in Oklahoma City and the witness room in Terra Haute. I am indebted to William J. Bowers for providing this insight.

47. Bureau of Prisons Execution Protocol, 2001, http://www.thesmokinggun.com/archive/bopprotocol24.html.

48. Jaworski, *Power of Silence*, 25.

49. Ibid., 49.

50. Ibid., 52 (quoting Deborah Tannen, "Silence: Anything But," in *Perspectives on Silence*, ed. Deborah Tannen and Muriel Saville-Troike [Norwood, NJ: Ablex, 1985], 97).

51. Giddens, *Modernity and Self-Identity*, 161.

52. Ibid., 162.

53. Ibid., 27.

54. Ibid.

55. Ibid., 162.

56. Mary Douglas, *Purity and Danger: An Analysis of the Concepts of Pollution and Taboo* (London: Routledge and Kegan Paul, 1966), 121.

57. Ibid., 68 (quoting J. W. Worden, *Grief Counseling and Grief Therapy* [London: Routledge, 1991]), 61.

58. "In the absence of its primary focus—the prepared corpse—ritual time and space can be used to make more tangible that for which there is no material evidence." Ibid.

59. Robert Jay Lifton, "The Concept of the Survivor," in *Survivors, Victims, and Perpetrators: Essays on the Nazi Holocaust*, ed. Joel E. Dimsdale (New York: Hemisphere, 1980), 124.

60. Elizabeth Bronfen, *Over Her Dead Body: Death, Femininity, and the Aesthetic* (Manchester, England: Manchester University Press, 1992), 45.

61. Ibid.

62. Ibid., 24.

63. Ibid., 25.

64. Ibid., 174 (quoting Emanuel Lewis, "Mourning by the Family after a Stillbirth or Neonatal Death," *Archives of Disease in Childhood* 54 [1979]: 303–6).

65. Ibid., 64.

66. Ibid., 72.

67. Ibid.

68. Katherine Dunn, "Introduction," in *Death Scenes: A Homicide Detective's Scrapbook*, ed. Sean Tejaratchi (Los Angeles: Feral House, 1996), 17, 11.

69. Elizabeth Hallam, Jenny Hockey, and Glennys Howarth, *Beyond the Body: Death and Social Identity* (New York: Routledge, 1999), 92, 98.

70. Ibid., 99.

71. "McVeigh Shows No Remorse at Execution," Court TV, http://www.courttv.com/news/mcveigh_special/0612_noremorse_ap.html.

72. Samuel R. Gross and Daniel J. Matheson, "What They Say at the End: Capital Victims' Families and the Press," *Cornell Law Review* 88 (2003): 486.

73. "Final Written Statement of Timothy McVeigh" (June 11, 2001) (on file with Oklahoma City National Memorial Archives). See also William Ernest Henley, "Invictus," in *The Columbia Anthology of British Poetry*, ed. Carl Woodring and James S. Shapiro (New York: Columbia University Press, 1995), 685.

NOTES TO CONCLUSION

1. "The McVeigh Tapes: Confessions of an American Terrorist," *Rachel Maddow Show*, MSNBC, April 19, 2011, http://www.msnbc.msn.com/id/36135258/.

2. Ibid.

3. Kari Watkins, e-mail message to victims and survivors, "Update on MSNBC Production," December 15, 2009.

4. Richard Williams, reply e-mail to Kari Watkins, "Update on MSNBC Production," December 15, 2009.

5. "'The McVeigh Tapes': Inside the Documentary," MSNBC, http://www.msnbc.msn.com/id/36634501/ns/msnbc_tv-documentaries.

6. Edward T. Linenthal, *Preserving Memory: The Struggle to Create America's Holocaust Museum* (New York: Columbia University Press, 1995), 200.

7. Ibid., 203.

8. Ibid., 201.

9. Ibid.

10. Ibid., 204.

11. Peter Jennings and Todd Brewster, *In Search of America* (New York: Hyperion, 2002).

12. "New Plaque at Bombing Memorial after McVeigh's Death," http://www.courttv.com/news/mcveigh_special/0612_plaque_ap.html.

13. Ibid.

14. Oklahoma House Bill 2570 §1(A), enacted into law as Oklahoma Statutes §70-11-103.6i, "State Board of Education—Adoption of Oklahoma City Bombing to Curriculum" (2010).

15. Ibid.

16. Ibid.

NOTE TO APPENDIX

1. Arthur P. Bochner, "Perspectives on Inquiry III: The Moral of Stories," in *Handbook of Interpersonal Communication*, 3d ed., ed. Mark L. Knapp and John A. Daly (Thousand Oaks, CA: Sage, 2002), 77.

Index

Christianity, forgiveness for McVeigh and role of, 193

Chubb, Vera, 176, 179, 182

claims-making process, cultural trauma and, 46–48

Clark, Ernestine Hill: attempted face-to-face meetings with McVeigh, 195–196; on closure, 44; on emotional trauma, 67–68; on forgiving McVeigh, 193; on Fortier and Nichols, 34, 107, 110–111, 272–273; on McVeigh's media visibility, 28–29, 110–111; media consumption patterns of, 105–106; on Nichols state trial, 168–169, 172; Oklahoma City Bombing National Memorial and Museum and, 263; reaction to McVeigh's perp walk, 11; skepticism of media by, 103–104; on storytelling, 89–91; support group experiences of, 79, 83–84; on witnessing McVeigh's execution, 190; writing as coping mechanism for, 69

Clay, Nolan, 215

Clinton, William Jefferson, 75, 133, 138, 147–148

closed-circuit broadcasts: court prohibition of, 133, 136; gaze of McVeigh during execution and, 231–239; of McVeigh execution, 184–186, 224–258, 304n.46; of McVeigh trial, 58–59, 129, 135–136, 140–142

closure: absence of, for survivors and families of victims, 41–45; cluster concept of, 48–50; communicative behavior and collected memory and, xxiii–xxiv; contemporary cultural views of, xxii–xxiii; cultural status of victim and, 39–41; definitions of, 38–39, 282n.25, xix–xx; institutional sites of, 54–59; McVeigh jury visit to Oklahoma City and, 182–183; memory work and, xxiii–xxv; new opportunities for, 59–60; quest for, 45–48; reassessment of, 48–50; as reflexive process, 50–53; survivors' and families of victims' quest for, 38–60

coddling reactions, closure and, 53

collective memory work: closure and, 49–50; executions and, 240–249

communication process: closure and, 48–50; emotions and, 51–53; family members of victims and survivors' reactions to McVeigh and, 14–16, 280n.10; McVeigh's gaze at execution as, 235–239; silence of McVeigh's execution and, 242–249

communicative theory of closure, 48–50

community groups: memorial practices in wake of bombing and, 70–77; support role of, 65, 93–94

compartmentalization: closure and, 44–45; by McVeigh, 204–207; McVeigh's media visibility and, 29–31

Congress, victims rights legislation and role of, 147–149

Congressional Record, 76

"conscience collective," Durkheim's concept of, 290n.20

Constitution of the United States: legal standing requirements in, 119–120; victim impact testimony and, 39–40, 146–149

coping behaviors, closure and, 43–45, 48–50

counseling: execution of McVeigh and presence of, 222–223; importance for bombing survivors and family members of victims of, 29

Cover, Robert, 290n.20

coworkers, social networking with survivors by, 87

Coyne, Randy, 149

Crawford, Cameron: on agency and advocacy activities, 92; on death penalty, 249–250; death penalty appeals reform and, 27; execution of McVeigh and, 222–223, 240–241, 246, 250; on family and personal life of perpetrators, 113; on forgiving McVeigh, 192; on Fortier, 174, 273; gaze of McVeigh during execution and, 231–232, 237–239; on historical legacy of bombing, 271–272; on McVeigh's courtroom behavior, 152; on McVeigh's media visibility, 21, 24; on media coverage, 101; on Nichols courtroom behavior, 164; on Nichols state trial, 172; reaction to McVeigh's perp walk, 11–12; support group experience of, 63–64, 80, 88

Crime Victims' Bill of Rights, 146–149

criminal defendants, constitutional rights of, 39

criminal impact of offenders, 19–25

criminal justice system: closure in culture of, 40–41; defendants' narrative and, 122–130; efficacy of law and memory work in, 156–160; as institutional closure site, 54–59; mediation of victim-offender relationship by, 17–18

cultural norms: accountability and bearing witness and, 118–120; closure and victim's cultural status, 39–41; of gazing, 234–235; on legal efficacy and trial proceedings, 156–160; in media and criminal justice system, 56–59; sharing of personal information and, xxii; trauma and, 45–48; visual images of death and, 252–256

Dahmer, Jeffrey, 17

Daily Oklahoman newspaper, 215, 266

Davis, Clifford, 76

Dead Man Walking (film), 249–250

death. *See also* execution: author's experience with, xx–xxi; cultural norms concerning, 250–252; visual images of, 252–256

death penalty: appeals process, proposed reform of, 24, 27–28, 31, 63–64, 139; closure linked to, 39–41, 282n.20; culture of executions and, 249–250; execution of McVeigh and debate over, 224, 245–246; habeas group reform advocacy and, 73–76; jury deadlock in Nichols trial of, 165–167; survivors' and victims' families opinions concerning, 186–189

defendants in criminal trials: change of venue rulings and, 139–140; narrative of, 122–130

Denison, Bob, 74

Denny, Jim, 209

Deutchman, Niki, 163, 166

Dooley, Diane: on benefits of story telling, 89–90; biography of McVeigh and, 218; compartmentalization as closure tactic for, 44; execution of McVeigh and, 248; on forgiving McVeigh, 192; on Fortier, 35, 110, 174, 273; on grieving process, 67; on McVeigh's courtroom behavior, 153; on McVeigh's media visibility, 22, 24, 29–30, 32; on Nichols sentencing, 167; opinion on death penalty, 187–188; personal impressions of McVeigh, 5, 26; skepticism of media, 104–105; support network experiences of, 79; verdict in McVeigh trial and, 155; withdrawal from memorial activities by, 93

Durkheim, Emile, 290n.20

Edmondson, Drew, 147, 177

emotions: change of venue ruling and, 139–140; closed-circuit trial broadcast debate concerning, 140–143; closure and role of, 51–53; legal perspectives on, 136–139, 156–160, 294n.75; McVeigh jury visit to Oklahoma City and, 176–183; in media and criminal justice system, 56–59; policing affect in sentencing phase testimony and, 155–156; victims' emotional landscape, understanding of, 65–70; victims' impact testimony and, 135–136, 143–149

execution: closed-circuit broadcast of, 58–59, 184–186; closure through, 45; cultural norms and, 249–250; dimensions of silence in, 239–249; expectations and objections to, 249–256; habeas group reform proposals and, 75–76; "ideal" execution concept, 256–258; as image, 252–256; McVeigh's gaze during, 231–239; media coverage of, 198–200;

Howick, Karen, 140
human relationships, impact of Oklahoma City bombing in, 63–65
Hunt, Susan, 163
"hyper-catharsis," closure and, 40–41
hypervigilance, family members and survivors feelings of, 68

Ice, Kay, 74
Ice, Paul Douglas, 12
"ideal" of true victim, 47–48
identity management, media participation of family members and survivors and, 97–102
Imhofe, James, 74
information sharing, attendance at trial as means of, 127–130
institutional support networks, limitations of, for bombing victims family members and survivors, 28–29
internal process, closure as, 50–53
interpersonal communication, family members of victims and survivors' reactions to McVeigh as, 14–16, 280n.10
intervention, closure as, 50–53
interviewing methodology, 275–278
intimacy: family members of victims and survivors' perceptions of, with McVeigh, 14–16; offenders' forced intimacy with victim, 19–25
"Invictus" (Henley), 243, 257

Jackson, Michael, 6–7
Jennings, Peter, 5
Johnson, Norma Jean, 43
Johnson, Robert, 71, 217
Johnston, Germaine: on closure, 43; compartmentalization as closure tactic for, 33–34; on Fortier's media image, 107–108; on McVeigh's courtroom behavior, 152; on McVeigh's media visibility, 24, 26; on Nichols state trial, 168; opinion on death penalty, 187; on relations with coworkers, 87
Jones, Doris: on Ashcroft's visit to Oklahoma City, 185; attempted face-to-face

meetings with McVeigh, 195; attendance at McVeigh trial, 126; on benefits of story telling, 89–90; on closure, 43; execution of McVeigh and, 223–225, 246–247, 254; family tensions experienced by, 88; on forgiving McVeigh, 193–194; on Fortier sentencing, 175; gaze of McVeigh during execution and, 233, 238; on grieving behavior, 67; habeas group and, 74–75; on jury at Nichols trial, 163; on McVeigh's courtroom behavior, 152, 153; on McVeigh's media visibility, 21, 23, 30, 32–34, 198; media consumption patterns of, 105–106; on media coverage, 99, 101; on Nichols courtroom behavior, 164; on Nichols sentencing, 167; Nichols state trial and, 169, 295n.24; support group experiences of, 71–72, 86–87; on victim's testimony rights, 122; witnessing McVeigh's execution as, 190
Jones, Stephen, 107, 114–117, 154, 162, 204
journalists' relations with McVeigh, 204–207
Journal Record Building, Oklahoma City Bombing National Memorial and Museum in, 73, 123, 286n.22
jury issues: criticism of McVeigh jury visit, 181–183; deadlock in Nichols trial over death penalty, 165–167; McVeigh jury Oklahoma city visit, 176–182; in Nichols state trial, 171–174; at Nichols trial, 163
justice: attendance at trial seen as, 129–130; efficacy of law and memory work in trial proceedings as, 156–160; narrative packaging of, 55–59; victim impact testimony as, 122–130

Keating, Frank, 177
Kight, Marsha: advocacy efforts by, 77, 91; attempted face-to-face meetings with McVeigh, 194; attendance at McVeigh trial, 127; execution of McVeigh and, 228; on grieving process, 66–67, 69; on McVeigh's media visibility, 198; on media coverage, 102; on Nichols family

presence at trial, 165; opinion on death penalty, 187; support group experiences of, 85; victim impact testimony by, 125

Kubler-Ross, Elizabeth, 66

Labov, William, 284n.55
Lane, Wes, 168, 171
Lappin, Harley, 194, 221
Leahy, Patrick, 148
Leeper, Michael, 179–181
legal practice: emotion work and, 136–139; marginalization of victims in, 57–59; media coverage compared with, 114–117; memory work and closure in, 118–120, 156–160; story telling at trial and, 120–121
Lenz, Carrie Ann, 21, 86, 295n.24
Lenz, Michael James, 21
Leonard, Diane: on agency and advocacy activities, 92; attendance at McVeigh trial, 126, 129; on closure, 43; compartmentalization as coping tactic for, 31, 33; death penalty appeals reform and, 27, 92–93; execution of McVeigh and, 190–191, 241–242, 247; on forgiving McVeigh, 193; on Fortier sentencing, 175; gaze of McVeigh during execution and, 236–237; on grieving process, 68, 149–151; habeas group and, 74; impressions of Nichols, 108; McVeigh jury visit to Oklahoma City and, 176–179; on McVeigh's courtroom behavior, 153–154; McVeigh's media visibility and, 21–22, 107; on media coverage, 99–100; on Nichols state trial, 169–174; on Nichols trial, 163; support group experience of, 80; on verdict in McVeigh trial, 155; on victim's testimony rights, 122, 143, 146
Leonhard, Donald Ray, 21
Lippens, Nancy Cobb, 69
Los Angeles Times, 113
loss of control, family members and survivors feelings of, 67–70
Lucas, Frank, 147–148

Macy, Robert H., 167–168

Mann, Thomas, 273
Manson, Charles, 9
Maroney-Denison, 74
Matheson, Daniel, 256
Matsch, Robert (Judge): change of venue ruling by, 139–140; closed-circuit broadcast ruling by, 140–143; on emotional perspective at trial proceedings, 136–139, 158–160; jurors in Nichols trial and, 166–167; on media presence at trials, 99; Nichols sentencing decision by, 163; pre-trial rulings by, 115–116; ruling against families and survivors attendance at trial, 77; sentencing phase of trial and, 155–156; victim impact testimony ruling of, 120, 133–136, 143–149, 162
Mayer, Stan: on anger experienced by, 70; on closure, 42; death penalty appeals reform and, 27–28; execution of McVeigh and, 191, 247; on McVeigh's courtroom behavior, 152; on McVeigh's media visibility, 22–23, 32–35; on Nichols state trial, 173; opinion on death penalty, 188; skepticism of media by, 103–104; support group experiences of, 80–81
McCall, Allen, 295n.24
McCollum, Bill, 147–148
McKinney, Dan, 74, 180
McVeigh, Bill, 111–112, 194
McVeigh, Jennifer, 111
McVeigh, Mickey, 111, 288n.24
McVeigh, Timothy: arrest and perp walk of, 2–18; attempted face-to-face meetings with, 194–197; biography of, 217–220, 299n.28; closing arguments and guilty verdict in trial of, 154–155; combating toxic presence of, 19–25, 28–31; courtroom behavior of, 151–154, 196–19; execution of, 221–258, xxvi; family and personal life of, 110–114, 288n.24; family members' and survivors' personal impressions of, 5–7, 25–26; forgiveness of, 191–194; gaze of, during execution, 231–239;

McVeigh, Timothy (*continued*)
incorporation into Oklahoma City
National Memorial of, 264–274;
interviews and statements by, 15–16,
260–274; journalists' relations with,
204–207; legacy of, 259–274; legal narrative for, 114–117; media visibility of,
15–16, 21–28, 56–57, 95–96, 106–110, 184,
197–220; military mission perspective
of, 203–204; Nichols contrasted with,
31–34; perp walk of, 10–16, 211–215;
police mug shot of, 20; publication of
biography, 215–220; survivors' encounters with, 24–25, 194–197; tape-recorded
interviews with, 260–264; trial of, 77,
118–130, 133–136; victim impact testimony against, 146–149; view of families
and survivors, 207–211
media: change of venue ruling and impact
of, 139–140; closure vocabulary used
by, 38, 40–41, 118–120; consolidation
and polarized coverage by, 288n.23;
decline in coverage of bombing,
259–260; effects on survivors' and
victims' families of, 95–117; execution
of McVeigh and, 221–222, 227–258;
family members of victims and survivors' reaction to McVeigh and, 10–12,
279n.7; Fortier's low media coverage
and, 35–36; images of executions
in, 250–252, 302n.9; as institutional
closure site, 54–59; journalists' relationships with McVeigh, 204–207; jury
interviews with, 166–167; legal narratives and, 114–117; McVeigh's visibility
in, 15–16, 21–25, 56–57, 184, 197–220;
mediation of victim-offender relationship by, 16–18; memory work and,
96–97, 118–120; MSNBC documentary
and, 260–274; narratives of trauma
in, 46–48; national *vs.* local coverage,
103–104; Nichols trial coverage by, 163;
Nichols' visibility in, 107–109; para-
social interaction and, 14–16, 280n.14;
perpetrators' family and personal
lives in, 110–114; perpetrators' images

in, 106–110; perp walks imagery in,
7–10; silence of McVeigh's execution
and, 244–249; skepticism concerning, 102–105; survivors' and family
members' assessment of, 105–106; text
construction and para-social interaction in, 16; tuning out by bombing
survivors and victim's family members
of, 30–31
memorial practices in wake of bombing,
70–77
memory work: attendance at trial and,
129–130; closure as, 38, 49–50, xxiii–
xxv; criminal justice system and, 54–59;
efficacy of law and, 156–160; emotional
landscape of victims and, 65–70; executions as, 230–231, 239; impersonality
of events and, 150–151; McVeigh as
barrier to, 16–18; McVeigh jury visit to
Oklahoma City and, 176–183; media
depictions of, 54–59, 96–97, 118–120;
narrative analysis and, 52–53; reflexive
behavior and, 50–53; trauma and, 50,
283n.47; victim impact testimony as,
122–130, 135–136; witnessing McVeigh's
execution as, 189–191
Mendeloff, Scott, 154
Merleau-Ponty, Maurice, 235
Merrell, Frankie, 66, 77
Michel, Lou, 15–16, 203, 207–209, 212–220,
260
military career of McVeigh, 25–26,
207–213, 219
Moore, Faith: alienation from support
groups, 79; execution of McVeigh and,
190, 247; impressions of Fortier, 176; on
McVeigh's media visibility, 22, 25–26,
30; on Nichols' media image, 108; reaction to McVeigh's perp walk, 12
moral judgment: courts' reliance on, 57–59,
137–139; grieving and collapse of, 68;
perp walk images and, 8–10
Mourning and Melancholia (Freud), 66
MSNBC, documentary on bombing by,
260–264
Munoz, Karen, 180

narrative formation and analysis:
benefits of companionship from, 89–91;
defendant's narrative and, 122; mass
media and memory work and, 96–97;
memory work and, 51–53, 284n.55; in
trial proceedings, 120–121
national culture, closure in context of, 50
National Organization for Victim Assistance (NOVA), 77, 91
Neureiter, Reid, 145
Newsweek magazine, 217
Nichols, Christian, 112
Nichols, James, 111
Nichols, Josh, 112
Nichols, Marife, 112
Nichols, Nicole, 112
Nichols, Terry, 146–149, xxvi; conviction
of, 165–167; courtroom behavior of,
164; family members and personal life
of, 111–113; family's presence at trial
of, 165; jury at trial of, 163; legacy of,
259; legal *vs.* media narratives of, 117;
McVeigh's discussion of state trial
of, 214; media visibility of, 107–109,
117, 272; in Oklahoma City Bombing
Museum exhibits and, 264, 266, 270;
pro se lawsuit and hunger strikes by,
173–174; sentencing of, 158; state trial
of, 167–174, 295n.24; toxic presence
of, 21, 31–34; trial of, 77, 124, 129–130,
133–136, 161–174
Nickles, Don, 74
Nightmare on Elm Street (film), 15
Norick, Ronald, 71
normalcy, media bias towards, 97–102

Oklahoma City bombing: author's
experience with, xxi–xxii; timeline of,
xiii–xviii
Oklahoma City Bombing Death Penalty
Appeals Reform Committee, 177
Oklahoma City Bombing National
Memorial and Museum: Ashcroft's visit
to, 185; exhibit design and content at,
262–274; families and survivors role
in, 30–31, 72–73, 91; grieving process

and establishment of, 44, 70; incor-
poration of McVeigh into, 263–274;
McVeigh execution broadcast at, 226,
228, 304n.46; McVeigh's view of, 203,
217–218; MSNBC documentary and,
260–264; site for, 286n.22, 286n.24;
support networks and, 64; "Wall of
Justice" exhibit at, 228–229, 265–267
Oklahoma City Murrah Building Survivors
Association, 70, 76, 79–81, 86, 275–276
Oklahoma City Murrah Federal Building
Memorial Task Force, 70–73
Oklahoma City National Memorial Trust,
217
Oklahoma City Small Business Council, 9
Oklahoma House Bill 2750, 271
On Death and Dying (Kubler-Ross), 66
Oppenheimer, Toby, 261–264
Osgood, Jim, 181–182
Osiel, Mark, 157
Oswald, Lee Harvey, 6

packaging of narratives, impact on
memory work of, 54–59
para-social interaction, media images of
perp walks and, 14–16
participant recruitment, methodology for,
275–278
"patterned closure," media depictions of,
118–120
Payne v. Tennessee, 39–40, 134–135
Pelley, Scott, 114
People magazine, 228
perpetrators of criminal acts: criminal
and personal impact of, 19–25; media
coverage of family and personal lives
of, 110–114; museum exhibitions using,
264–274
perp walk: family members of victims and
survivors' reaction to, 10–16, 23–24;
McVeigh's discussion of, 214–215; media
coverage of McVeigh during, 2, 7–16,
211–212; as penal ritual, 6–7
Perricone, Gaspar, 143
personal impact of criminal offenders,
19–25

personality: offender's toxic presence and role of, 36–37; perp walk images as insight into, 11–12

Pfefferbaum, Betty, 275

photography, death and, 252–256

Picture of Dorian Gray, The (Wilde), 152

popular culture, closure in, 43–45

post-traumatic stress disorder: of bombing survivors and families of victims, 65–70; cultural trauma and, 47–48; McVeigh's experience with, 213

Prejean, Helen, 249

Prime Time (television program), 216–217

Prime Time Thursday (television program), 217

privacy, cultural trauma and, 47–48

prosthetic memory, support group interactions and, 86–87

public opinion, on closure and death penalty, 39–41

Rachel Maddow Show, 260–264

Rankin, Beverly: advocacy efforts of, 93; attendance at McVeigh trial, 127; execution of McVeigh and, 228; on forgiving McVeigh, 193; habeas group and, 74; on jury at Nichols trial, 163; McVeigh jury visit to Oklahoma City and, 181; on media impact, 106–107; on relationships in wake of bombing, 65

reflexivity: closure and, 50–53; of media and criminal justice system, 56–59

repetition, of perp walk images, 10

reputation, cultural norm of, in media and criminal justice system, 56–59

resolution process, of bombing victims family members and survivors, 28–29

Reyes, Michael, 74

Richerson, Angela, 43, 87, 127, 152–153, 188, 250

Rickel, Taylor, 42, 88–89

Riley, Joanne, 261–262, 265–269

Rocky Mountain News, 266–267

Ruby, Jack, 6

Ruby Ridge crisis, 107, 203

"rule of law," as narrative concept, 121

Ryan, Patrick, 156, 162

Sack, Steve, 199

Salyers, Priscilla: on benefits of story telling, 89; on closure, 42; execution of McVeigh and, 240–242; on forgiving McVeigh, 192; gaze of McVeigh during execution and, 232–233, 237; on McVeigh's visibility, 13; on Nichols state trial, 172; Oklahoma City Bombing National Memorial and Museum and, 263; support group experiences of, 80–81, 84–86; on tensions with family as survivor, 88

Sawyer, Diane, 217

Sawyer, Jay, 237

Scalia, Antonin (Justice), 40

Scott, Anthony, 238–239

Scott, Bobby, 148

Scott, Morgan, 87, 111, 188

Seger, Bob, 212

Seidl, Clint, 74

Seidl, Glen, 74, 76

Seidl, Kathy, 74, 76

sentencing proceedings: for Fortier, 174–176; in Nichols state trial, 171–174; in Nichols trial, 163, 166–167; policing affect of emotions in, 155–156

September 11 attacks, 10, 249–252, 259–260

Shepherd, Karan, 13

Sherman, Nancy, 219

Sherwin, Richard, 40–41

silence, executions and dimensions of, 239–249, 304n.46

Simpson, Nicole Brown, 142–143

Simpson, O. J., 142–143, 159

Sixty Minutes (television program), 207, 211–214

Skilling, Jeffrey, 140

Smith, Janice, 12–13

Smith, Jason, 74

social drama, trial as, 121, 157–160, 290n.20

social relations, impact on memory work of, 54–59

spectacle, execution as, 230–231

Spierenburg, Pieter, 230

spiritual organizations, importance of, 29
Star Wars (movie series), 210
Stedman, Tanya, 177–178, 181
Sternburg, Jessie, 83, 153, 164, 169, 235, 250
storytelling. *See also* narrative formation
and analysis: benefits of companionship, 89–91; differing experiences and
limitations of, 82; during grieving process, 80–82; mass media and memory
work and, 96–97; path to survivorhood
through, 47–48; in trial proceedings,
120–121
Strickland, Ted, 233
"suicidal cameraman theory," 302n.9
support networks: agency and advocacy
as outgrowth of, 91–94; for bombing
survivors and family members of
victims, 28–29; choices about participation in, 78–79; impact of, 63–64,
78–94; importance of companionship
in, 86–89; narrative benefits of, 89–91;
Oklahoma City Murrah Building
Survivors Association as example of,
76; overcoming differences through,
81–85; similar experiences of participants in, 79–81
Supreme Court of the United States,
perspective on emotions and rulings
of, 138–139
survivor guilt, experience in support
groups of, 83–85
survivorhood, cultural trauma and path
to, 47–48
survivors of Oklahoma City bombing:
absence of closure for, 41–45; attempted
personal encounters with McVeigh,
24–25, 194–196; attendance at McVeigh
trial, 126–130; biography of McVeigh
and, 217–220; closed-circuit trial broadcasts and, 140–143, 184–186; closure
defined by, 38–39, 282n.25; collective
memory work by, 49–50; emotional
landscape for, 65–70; execution of
McVeigh and, 221–258; exhibits at
Oklahoma City National memorial and,
264–274; expectations and objections to

McVeigh's execution by, 249–256; forgiveness of McVeigh, 191–194; Fortier's
visibility and, 21, 31, 34–36, 272–274;
gaze of McVeigh during execution and,
231–239; impersonality of events for,
149–151; interviews with, xxv–xxvi; jury
at Nichols trial and, 163; McVeigh jury
visit to Oklahoma City and, 176–183;
McVeigh's media visibility and, 28–29,
197–220; McVeigh's view of, 207–211;
media coverage and, 97–102; MSNBC
documentary and, 260–264; Nichols
family encounters with, 165; Nichols's
visibility and, 21, 31–34, 272–274; opinion
on death penalty of, 186–189; participation in support groups by, 78–79;
perp walk images and, 8–12; personal
impressions of McVeigh, 25–28; silence
of McVeigh's execution and, 240–249;
tensions with families of victims and,
82–85; victim impact testimony by,
122–130, 133–136, 143–149; as witnesses to
McVeigh's execution, 38–39
Survivor Tree, 177

Tarver, Edmund, 42–44
Taylor, Steven, 171, 295n.24
Terre Haute Correctional Complex, 223
"Threnody" (musical composition), 69
"Through a Glass Darkly" (Clark), 69
Tigar, Michael, 112, 161–163, 166–167, 181
time, closure and role of, 44–45
Time magazine, McVeigh's image on cover
of, 15–16
Today Show, The (television program), 224
trauma: closure and, 45–48; memory and,
50, 283n.47; narrative analysis of, 52–53
trauma membrane phenomenon, support
group tensions and, 83
trial proceedings of bombing suspects:
accountability and bearing witness in,
118–120; change of venue rulings in, 133,
136, 139–140, 169–170; closed-circuit
broadcasts of, 58–59; closing arguments
and guilty verdict in McVeigh trial,
154–155;

trial proceedings (*continued*)
efficacy of law and memory work in, 156–160; emotional perspectives and needs and, 136–139; families of victims and survivors attendance at, 77, 126–130; legal and media narratives of, 114–117; McVeigh's courtroom behavior during, 151–154; McVeigh trial, 77, 118–130, 133–136; Nichols courtroom behavior during, 164; Nichols family presence at Nichols trial, 165; Nichols state trial, 167–174, 295n.24; Nichols trial, 77, 124, 129–130, 133–136, 161–174; sentencing phase testimony and, 155–156; story telling in, 120–121; victims' impact testimony at, 124–130, 133–136
Turner, Victor, 121

United States Holocaust Museum, 264
United States v. Skilling, 140
United States v. Terry Nichols, 159–160
United States v. Timothy McVeigh, 118, 133–134, 159–160
Urbach, Susan: on agency and advocacy activities, 92; attempted face-to-face meetings with McVeigh, 195; biography of McVeigh and, 218; on closure, 42; death penalty appeals reform and, 27–28; execution of McVeigh and, 244; on forgiving McVeigh, 192–193; on Fortier sentencing, 175; on grieving process, 68–69; on historical legacy of bombing, 272; impressions of Fortier, 109; impressions of McVeigh, 9, 25, 107, 111; on McVeigh's courtroom behavior during, 151–152; on media coverage, 99–100; on Nichols family presence at trial, 165; on Nichols state trial, 168–169, 174; opinion on death penalty, 189; on support group participation, 79; victim impact testimony by, 125; writing as coping strategy for, 69

vengeance, closure and, 52–53, 59–60
verdicts, in media and criminal justice system, 56–59

victimhood: emotional landscape of, 65–70; "ideal" of true victim and, 47–48, 282n.26; passivity of, in media and criminal justice system, 57–59
victim impact testimony: as act of justice, 122–130; communicative theory of closure and, 49–50; emotions expressed through, 143–149; legal efficacy of, 158–160; Matsch's initial exclusion of, 133, 136; McVeigh trial proceedings and, 118–120; media and criminal justice system and, 55–59; in Nichols state trial, 170–171; at Nichols trial, 162; permission to states for, 39–40, 77, 134; sentencing phase of trial and, 155–156; witnesses' recollections of, 124–130
victim-offender mediation programs, 297n.4
victim-offender relationship: closure and, 39–41; collapse of moral order and, 68; execution and end of, 221–258; experiences with, 19–37; gaze of McVeigh during execution and, 231–239; importance of first impressions in roots of, 12–16; institutional mediation of, 16–18; involuntary bonds in, 12–16, 18; McVeigh's public image and, 201–220; McVeigh's view of, 207–211; media images of, 97–102; origins of, 5–18; para-social ties compared with, 14–16; perp walk images and, 8–12; personal and criminal impact of offenders and, 19–25; victim testimony and, 122–130
victim participation: in criminal justice system, 58–59, 118–120; media coverage of bombing and, 95–96
Victim Rights Clarification Act (VRCA), 147–149
Victims' Families/Survivors Liaison subcommittee, 71
Victims' Rights and Restitution Act, 122
Victims Rights Clarification Act of 1997, 70
victims' rights movement, 70–71, 122, 141–142, 249–252
violence, cultural trauma of, 46–48

About the Author

Jody Lyneé Madeira is an associate professor of law at the Indiana University Maurer School of Law in Bloomington, Indiana.